African Women in the Atlantic World

WESTERN AFRICA SERIES

The Economics of Ethnic Conflict:
The Case of Burkina Faso
Andreas Dafinger

Commercial Agriculture, the Slave Trade
& Slavery in Atlantic Africa
Edited by Robin Law, Suzanne Schwarz
& Silke Strickrodt

Afro-European Trade in the Atlantic World:
The Western Slave Coast c. 1550–c. 1885
Silke Strickrodt

The Politics of Peacemaking in Africa:
Non-State Actors' Role in the Liberian Civil War
Babatunde Tolu Afolabi

Sects & Social Disorder:
Muslim Identities & Conflict in Northern Nigeria
Edited by Abdul Raufu Mustapha

Creed & Grievance:
Muslim-Christian Relations & Conflict Resolution in Northern Nigeria
Edited by Abdul Raufu Mustapha & David Ehrhardt

The Politics of Work in a Post-Conflict State:
Youth, Labour & Violence in Sierra Leone
Luisa Enria

African Women in the Atlantic World:
Property, Vulnerability & Mobility, 1660–1880
Edited by Mariana P. Candido & Adam Jones

Overcoming Boko Haram:
Faith, Society & Islamic Radicalization in Northern Nigeria
Edited by Abdul Raufu Mustapha and Kate Meagher

African Women in the Atlantic World

PROPERTY, VULNERABILITY & MOBILITY, 1660–1880

Edited by Mariana P. Candido & Adam Jones

JAMES CURREY

In association with The Institute for Scholarship in the Liberal Arts,
College of Arts and Letters, University of Notre Dame

James Currey
is an imprint of
Boydell & Brewer Ltd
PO Box 9, Woodbridge
Suffolk IP12 3DF (GB)
www.jamescurrey.com
and of
Boydell & Brewer Inc.
668 Mt Hope Avenue
Rochester, NY 14620-2731 (US)
www.boydellandbrewer.com

Contributors © 2019

First published 2019
Paperback edition 2020

All rights reserved. No part of this book may be reproduced in any form, or by electronic or mechanical means, including information storage and retrieval systems, without permission in writing from the publishers, except by a reviewer who may quote brief passages in a review

British Library Cataloguing in Publication Data
A catalogue record for this book is available on request from the British Library

ISBN 978-1-84701-213-5 (James Currey cloth)
ISBN 978-1-84701-215-9 (James Currey Africa-only paperback)
ISBN 978–1–84701–264–7 (James Currey paperback)

The publisher has no responsibility for the continued existence or accuracy of URLs for external or third-party internet websites referred to in this book, and does not guarantee that any content on such websites is, or will remain, accurate or appropriate

Typeset in 11/13pt Bembo with Albertus MT display
by Avocet Typeset, Somerton, Somerset, TA11 6RT

Contents

Acknowledgements viii
List of Illustrations ix
Contributors xi

Introduction 1
MARIANA P. CANDIDO & ADAM JONES

Part One: Property

1
Adaptation in the Aftermath of Slavery
Women, Trade & Property in Sierra Leone, c. 1790–1812   19
SUZANNE SCHWARZ

2
Women, Land & Power in the Lower Gambia River Region   38
ASSAN SARR

3
Women & Food Production
Agriculture, Demography & Access to Land in Late Eighteenth-Century Catumbela   55
ESTEBAN A. SALAS

4
Women's Material World in Nineteenth-Century Benguela   70
MARIANA P. CANDIDO

Part Two: Vulnerability

5
Prostitution, Polyandry or Rape?
On the Ambiguity of European Sources for the West African Coast, 1660–1860   89
    ADAM JONES

6
Parrying Palavers
Coastal Akan Women & the Search for Security in the Eighteenth Century   109
    NATALIE EVERTS

7
To be Female & Free
Mapping Mobility & Emancipation in Lagos, Badagry & Abęokuta 1853–1865   131
    ADEMIDE ADELUSI-ADELUYI

8
Gendered Authority, Gendered Violence
Family, Household & Identity in the Life & Death of a Brazilian Freed Woman in Lagos   148
    KRISTIN MANN

Part Three: Mobility

9
From Child Slave to Madam Esperance
One Woman's Career in the Anglo-African World c. 1675–1707   171
    COLLEEN E. KRIGER

10
Writing the History of the Trans-African Woman in the Revolutionary French Atlantic   191
    LORELLE SEMLEY

11
Spouses & Commercial Partners
Immigrant Men & Locally Born Women in Luanda
1831–1859   217
    VANESSA S. OLIVEIRA

12
Women, Family & Daily Life in Senegal's Nineteenth-Century Atlantic Towns   233
    HILARY JONES

Bibliography   248
Index   279

Acknowledgements

This project was first conceived at a meeting of the African Studies Association of the United Kingdom, in which Silke Strickrodt played a major role in framing the topic and bringing the editors together. We deeply regret the circumstances that made her unable to participate in the final product. Her ideas have helped to shape this project from the outset, and we thank her for her friendship and intellectual contribution.

The chapters were assembled in a three-day workshop held at the O'Connell House/ Keought-Naughton Notre Dame Center in Dublin in March 2017. Robin Law, in particular, drew our attention to many ways in which the papers might be improved. The editors are also grateful to the Institute for Scholarship in the Liberal Arts, the Helen Kellogg Institute for International Studies and the Keough-Naughton Institute for Irish Studies at the University of Notre Dame for financial support in making the workshop and publication possible. The editors thank Matthew Sisk, GIS Librarian at the Hesburgh Libraries Center for Digital Scholarship, who prepared some of the maps included in this volume.

Finally, we acknowledge a debt to Jaqueline Mitchell at James Currey for her enthusiasm and guidance and to the anonymous reviewers for their comments.

Mariana P. Candido
Adam Jones

List of Illustrations

ILLUSTRATIONS

1	Female settlers in Freetown, 1805	30
2	Woman in Angola pounding grain with a mortar and pestle	59
3	Two women identified as baptised, Benguela, 1820s	80
4	Benguela woman with gold earrings, different types of necklaces and bracelets	83
5	Woman of the Gold Coast, identified as being of mixed race	112
6	Johanna Vitringa Coulon of Elmina with her daughter Mercy Hughes	116
7	A *signare* wearing an elaborate dress, gold earrings, necklaces and bracelets, Senegal, 1810s	202
8	View of Luanda, 1825	219
9	The *signare* Marianne Blanchot with her husband in Saint Louis, before 1866	241

MAPS AND PLANS

1	Western Africa	xiv
2	The Upper Guinea Coast, 1820	21
3	The Gambia River	40
4	West Central Africa, 1850	54
5	The Gold Coast from Issini to Alampi	108
6	The Colony of Lagos and neighbouring territories, 1888	133
7	Tracing Awa's and Alabọn's routes	134
8	Sketch of Abẹokuta, c. 1865	144
9	Royal African Company trading sphere on the Upper Guinea Coast, late seventeenth century	173
10	Plan of James Island	176
11	Anne Rossignol's travels	190
12	Mid-nineteenth-century Angola	216
13	Pre-colonial Senegambia	236
14	Saint Louis du Senegal, 1880	238

CHARTS

1	Agricultural producers of Catumbela	62
2	Access to land in Catumbela	65

TABLES

1	Inventories available at Tribunal da Província de Benguela	75
2	Marriage petitions (1831–1859)	227

Contributors

Ademide Adelusi-Adeluyi's research into the history of Lagos combines a set of interdisciplinary interests in African and urban studies, cartography and spatial humanities. She is an Assistant Professor of History at the University of California, Riverside, where she is working on a spatial history of mid-nineteenth-century Lagos and a cartographic database that maps Lagos history.

Mariana P. Candido is Associate Professor of History, University of Notre Dame. Her publications include *An African Slaving Port and the Atlantic World: Benguela and its Hinterland* (Cambridge University Press, 2013), *Fronteras de Esclavización: Esclavitud, Comercio e Identidad en Benguela, 1780–1850* (Colegio de Mexico Press, 2011), translated into Portuguese under the title *Fronteras da Escravidão* (Universidade Katyavala Bwila, 2018) and two co-edited books (Museu Nacional da Escravatura, 2017; Africa World Press, 2011).

Natalie Everts is an historian and publicist whose research focuses on intercultural contact situations in the early modern era and primary source materials on Asian and African indigenous societies in Dutch collections. In addition to various articles she is the editor of source publications including *Formosan Encounter: A Selection of Documents from Dutch Archival Sources, 1623–1668* (Shung Ye Museum of Formosan Aborigines, 1999). Her monograph on the Eurafrican community of Elmina is in preparation.

Adam Jones worked as a teacher in Sierra Leone, wrote his PhD in Birmingham and taught in Frankfurt am Main. From 1994 to 2016 he was Professor of African History and Culture at the University of Leipzig. He has published several critical editions of European sources for West African history, as well as a history of Africa before 1850 (in German).

Hilary Jones is Associate Professor of History at Florida International University. Author of *The Métis of Senegal: Urban Life and Politics in French West Africa* (Indiana University Press, 2013), she specialises in Africa's social and political history, comparative race and slavery, and French colonialism. Her research has appeared in the *Journal of African History* and *Slavery & Abolition* as well as in several edited collections and research works.

Colleen Kriger, Professor of History at the University of North Carolina at Greensboro, specialises in precolonial West and Central Africa. She focuses primarily on social and economic history, material culture and Euro-African Atlantic trade. Her recent book – *Making Money: Life, Death, and Early Modern Trade on Africa's Guinea Coast* (Ohio University Press, 2017) – is a social history of seventeenth-century trade on the Upper Guinea Coast.

Kristin Mann is an historian of Africa interested in slavery, the slave trade, abolition and emancipation; law and colonialism; marriage, gender and domesticity; the making of the African diaspora; and black Atlantic history and culture. Her current book project, *Transatlantic Lives: Slavery and Freedom in West Africa and Brazil*, reconstructs the lives of two groups of Yoruba speakers enslaved during the fall of the Oyo Empire.

Vanessa S. Oliveira obtained a PhD in History from York University, Toronto in 2016 and is currently a postdoc fellow at the University of Toronto. Her book, *Abolition, Gender and Slavery at Luanda, 1808–1867*, is forthcoming from University of Wisconsin Press. Oliveira has published articles in *History in Africa*, *Portuguese Studies Review*, and *African Economic History*, as well as chapters in edited volumes. She is the co-editor with Paul Lovejoy of *Slavery, Memory and Citizenship* (Africa World Press, 2016).

Esteban Alfaros Salas is a PhD candidate in African history at the University of Notre Dame. His dissertation examines social and economic transformations in the region of Benguela associated with the involvement of its societies in the Atlantic slave trade, including classifications, land use and food production. His research has been supported by the Luso-American Foundation, the Kellogg Institute, and the College of Arts and Letters' Advisory Council at Notre Dame.

Assan Sarr is an Associate Professor and Director of Graduate Studies in the Department of History at Ohio University. His research interests include peace and conflict in Africa, land tenure, agrarian change, oral history, slavery and Islam in West Africa's Senegambia region. He is the author of *Islam, Power and Dependency in the Gambia River Basin* (University of Rochester Press, 2016) and articles which have appeared in *African Economic History*, *African Studies Review*, *Journal of West African History* and *Mande Studies*, as well as several book chapters.

Suzanne Schwarz is Professor of History at the University of Worcester and Honorary Research Fellow at the Wilberforce Institute for the study of Slavery and Emancipation at the University of Hull. She is co-editor with Paul E. Lovejoy of *Slavery, Abolition and the Transition to Colonialism in Sierra Leone* (Africa World Press, 2015).

Lorelle Semley is Associate Professor of History at the College of the Holy Cross, Worcester, MA. She is the author of two books: *To Be Free and French: Citizenship in France's Atlantic Empire* (Cambridge University Press, 2017) and *Mother Is Gold, Father Is Glass: Gender and Colonialism in a Yoruba Town* (Indiana University Press, 2011). Her other publications include articles in *Law and History Review*, *Radical History Review* and *Gender & History*.

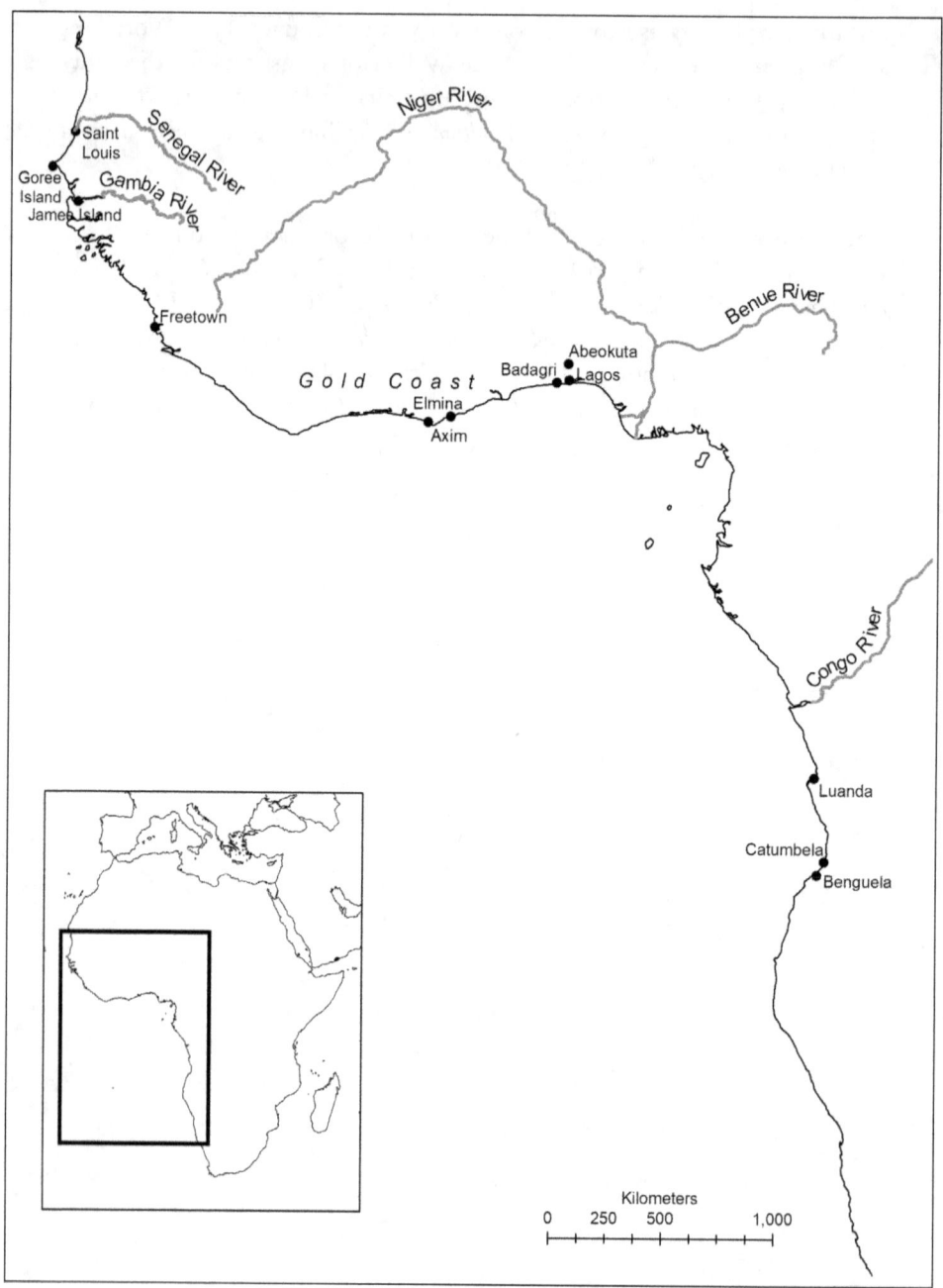

Map 1 Western Africa
(Source: Center for Digital Scholarship, University of Notre Dame, 2017)

Introduction

MARIANA P. CANDIDO & ADAM JONES

In recent decades the number of historical studies on African women has grown dramatically. Studies have revealed how colonialism has affected women's economic lives, household organisation, bodies and health. Attention has been paid to women's role in resistance to colonialism and liberation, education, and nation-building after independence.[1] Scholars have also examined women's role in conflict and civil war.[2] Yet despite the pioneering contribution of two early edited volumes, *Women in Africa* and *Women and Slavery in Africa*,[3] much remains to be done regarding African women's history before the formal imposition of colonial rule in the late nineteenth century. Women's participation in agriculture and production, religious beliefs and practices, as well as in political and social institutions before the twentieth century has received little attention.[4]

---

[1] For example, Claire C. Robertson, *Sharing the Same Bowl: A Socioeconomic History of Women and Class in Accra, Ghana* (Bloomington: Indiana University Press, 1984); Kathleen E. Sheldon, *Pounders of Grain: A History of Women, Work, and Politics in Mozambique* (Portsmouth, NH: Heinemann, 2002); Kathleen E. Sheldon, 'Markets and Gardens: Placing Women in the History of Urban Mozambique', *Canadian Journal of African Studies* 37, no. 2/3 (2003): 358–95; Rachel Jean-Baptiste, *Conjugal Rights: Marriage, Sexuality, and Urban Life in Colonial Libreville, Gabon* (Athens, OH: Ohio University Press, 2014); Jean Allman and Victoria B. Tashjian, *I Will Not Eat Stone: A Women's History of Colonial Asante* (Portsmouth, NH: Heinemann, 2000); Susan Geiger, Jean Marie Allman and Nakanyike Musisi, *Women in African Colonial Histories* (Bloomington: Indiana University Press, 2002).
[2] Among others, Iris Berger, *Threads of Solidarity: Women in South African Industry, 1900–1980* (London: James Currey, 1992); Egodi Uchendu, *Women and Conflict in the Nigerian Civil War* (Trenton, NJ: Africa World Press, 2007).
[3] Nancy J. Hafkin and Edna G. Bay, eds, *Women in Africa: Studies in Social and Economic Change* (Stanford, CA: Stanford University Press, 1976); Claire C. Robertson and Martin A. Klein, eds, *Women and Slavery in Africa* (Madison: University of Wisconsin Press, 1983).
[4] For the invisibility of African women in almost all volumes of the UNESCO *General History of Africa* see Paul Tiyambe Zeleza, 'Gender Biases in African Historiography', in *African Gender Studies: A Reader*, ed. Oyeronke Oyewumi (New York: Palgrave Macmillan, 2005), 209.

This book focuses upon the coastal regions of West and West Central Africa between the late seventeenth and late nineteenth centuries. In this period the region constituted what Mary Louis Pratt has termed a 'contact zone' – an intercultural space in which, as Wyatt MacGaffey has shown, communication between Africans and non-Africans was characterised by a 'working misunderstanding' and by 'dialogues of the deaf'.[5] This applied to gender as much as to other dimensions of social life. Building upon earlier research, we here analyse how women in Africa used the opportunities offered by the Atlantic commerce and relationships with European men to negotiate their social and economic positions. Interactions between African women and European men led to the emergence of a 'mixed' population, that tended to be socially identified as different, and labelled as *mulatto* or *métis*, terms that acquired pejorative connotations over time and are explored in subsequent chapters.

Four developments of primarily external origin – the emergence of the transatlantic slave trade, its gradual abolition, the expansion of what contemporaries called legitimate commerce and finally the partition of African societies among European powers – each in its turn provoked major turmoil. This book explores how African women experienced these changes, how gender roles were thereby socially constructed and transformed, the constraints that were imposed on women and the strategies they employed to overcome them.[6]

Most towns on Africa's Atlantic coast had a sizeable majority of women. In Cacheu on the Upper Guinea Coast, for example, there lived 514 women and 386 men in 1731. In nearby Ziguinchor there were 602 women and 475 men, while 775 women and 345 men lived in Geba.[7] Ouidah too had a predominantly female population.[8] In 1891 Accra had 7,917 men and 8,350 women living in the limits of the urban centre.[9]

---

[5] Mary Louise Pratt, *Imperial Eyes. Travel Writing and Transculturation* (London: Routledge 1992); Wyatt MacGaffey, 'Dialogues of the deaf. Europeans on the Atlantic coast of Africa', *Implicit Understandings*, ed. Stuart B. Schwartz (Cambridge: Cambridge University Press, 1994), 249–67.

[6] Studies that have considered these issues include Pamela Scully, *Liberating the Family? Gender and British Slave Emancipation in the Rural Western Cape, South Africa, 1823–1853* (Portsmouth, NH: Heinemann, 1997); Eugénia Rodrigues, *Portugueses e africanos nos Rios de Sena: Os prazos da coroa em Moçambique nos séculos XVII e XVIII* (Lisbon: Imprensa Nacional, 2014); Emily Lynn Osborn, *Our New Husbands Are Here: Households, Gender, and Politics in a West African State from the Slave Trade to Colonial Rule* (Athens: Ohio University Press, 2011); Rhiannon Stephens, *A History of African Motherhood* (New York: Cambridge University Press, 2014); Linda M. Heywood, *Njinga of Angola: Africa's Warrior Queen* (Cambridge, MA: Harvard University Press, 2017).

[7] Philip Havik, *Silences and Soundbites: The Gendered Dynamics of Trade and Brokerage in the Pre-colonial Guinea Bissau Region* (Munster: LIT, 2004), Table 2, 'Population Census 1731'.

[8] Robin Law, *Ouidah: The Social History of a West African Slaving 'Port' 1727–1892* (Athens: Ohio University Press 2004), 76.

[9] John Parker, *Making the Town: Ga State and Society in Early Colonial Accra* (Portsmouth, NH: Heinemann, 2000), 190, footnote 78.

In West Central Africa, Luanda had 5,647 women and 4,108 men, i.e. roughly 72 men per 100 women in 1781.[10] Benguela had 1,352 women and 892 men residing on its limits in 1797, or 66 men per 100 women.[11] A similar demographic imbalance was also present in East Africa in the early nineteenth century, for instance on Mozambique island and in Tete.[12] Thus, the various coastal centres constituted women's spaces, in which women were economic, political and intellectual actors. Where African women show up in historical records, they often do so making claims to rights and property, enjoying spatial and social mobility.

In African coastal and interior centres, women played important political or religious roles.[13] While elite women enjoyed economic and political benefits, many of those who lived in political and market centres were migrants or enslaved, lacking the protection and support of local networks. Free or enslaved, outsiders had to adjust to new societies and foster new relationships and patronage.[14] Religion, although not one of the major topics in this book, clearly helped to shape identities, as in the case of Muslim women of Lagos or the Christian *signares* (from the Portuguese *senhora*, signifying women of wealth and influence) of Senegal and the *donas* (wealthy African or mixed-race women) of Luanda and Benguela.

---

[10] José C. Curto and Raymond R. Gervais, 'The Population History of Luanda during the Late Atlantic Slave Trade, 1781–1844', *African Economic History*, no. 29 (2001): 1–59, 55.

[11] Arquivo Histórico Ultramarino (AHU), Angola, caixa 87, document 51, 'Mapa das Pessoas Livres e escravos, empregos, e os oficios que varios tem,' 1 January 1798. See Mariana P. Candido, *Fronteras de esclavización: esclavitud, comercio e identidad en Benguela, 1780–1850* (Mexico City: Colegio de Mexico Press, 2011), 76–9.

[12] Filipa Ribeiro da Silva, 'Counting People and Homes in Mozambique in the 1820s. Population Structures and Household Size and Composition', *African Economic History* 45, no. 1 (2017): 56–7. An exception was Freetown, where at the beginning of the nineteenth century men constituted the majority. Suzanne Schwarz, 'Adaptation in the Aftermath of Slavery: Women, Trade and Property in Sierra Leone, c. 1790–1812', unpublished paper.

[13] Iris Berger, 'Rebels or Status-Seekers? Women as Spirit Mediums in East Africa', *Women in Africa: Studies in Social and Economic Change*, ed. Nancy J. Hafkin and Edna G. Bay (Stanford, CA: Stanford University Press, 1976); John K. Thornton, *The Kongolese Saint Anthony: Dona Beatriz Kimpa Vita and the Antonian Movement, 1684–1706* (Cambridge: Cambridge University Press, 1998); Isabel de Castro Henriques, 'As outras africanas: As reais e as inventadas', *Oceanos*, no. 21 (1995): 53–63; Selma Pantoja, *Nzinga Mbandi mulher, guerra e escravidão* (Brasília: Thesaurus, 2000); Nwando Achebe, *The Female King of Colonial Nigeria: Ahebi Ugbabe* (Bloomington: Indiana University Press, 2011).

[14] For periods before 1700 see Neil Kodesh, *Beyond the Royal Gaze: Clanship and Public Healing in Buganda* (Charlottesville: University of Virginia Press, 2010), 90–2. For changes after 1700 see Paul E. Lovejoy, 'Concubinage and the Status of Women Slaves in Early Colonial Northern Nigeria', *The Journal of African History* 29, no. 2 (1988): 245–66; Nakanyike Musisi, 'The Environment, Gender, and the Development of Unequal Relations in Buganda: A Historical Perspective', *Canadian Woman Studies* 13, no. 3 (1993), 54–9; Ty M. Reese, 'Wives, Brokers, and Labourers: Women at Cape Coast, 1750–1807', *Women in Port: Gendering Communities, Economies, and Social Networks in Atlantic Port Cities, 1500–1800*, ed. Douglas Catterall and Jody Campbell (Leiden: Brill, 2012), 291–314; Rebecca Shumway, 'Castle Slaves of the Eighteenth-Century Gold Coast (Ghana)', *Slavery & Abolition* 35, no. 1 (2014): 84–98.

4 • *Introduction*

African populations tend to play only a peripheral role in studies on the Atlantic world,[15] although a few historians have demonstrated the active role of Africans in the creation and maintenance of that world.[16] Africa's major contribution to the Atlantic world in the period before the 1860s was of course the forced migration of roughly 12.5 million enslaved Africans to the Americas; yet movement was not exclusively one-directional, nor were its implications limited to the commercial and economic realm. The trade also fostered, and relied upon, social relations linking communities on the Atlantic rim, and it encouraged cultural and religious exchange.[17] Men and male youths constituted the majority of those persons shipped to the New World, which was presumably one reason for the gender imbalance near the coast discussed above.[18] Several chapters in this volume deal with the consequences of the export of slaves for the population that remained locally.

Studies of the history of women and gender relations in the Atlantic world are often written by non-Africanists with limited knowledge of African history.[19] There is little appreciation of the diversity of cultural, political and economic life on Africa's Atlantic coast, despite the publication of some important case studies.[20] Since the 1980s relatively little

---

[15] See, for example, Richard William Weisberger, Dennis P. Hupchick, and David L. Anderson, *Profiles of Revolutionaries in Atlantic History, 1700–1850* (New York: Columbia University Press, 2007); John Donoghue, *Fire under the Ashes: An Atlantic History of the English Revolution* (Chicago: The University of Chicago Press, 2013); Janet L. Polasky, *Revolutions without Borders: The Call to Liberty in the Atlantic World* (New Haven, CT: Yale University Press, 2015). For a good summary see Paul E. Lovejoy, *Jihād in West Africa during the Age of Revolutions* (Athens: Ohio University Press, 2016).

[16] John K. Thornton, *Africa and Africans in the Making of the Atlantic World, 1400–1800* (New York: Cambridge University Press, 1998); John K. Thornton, *A Cultural History of the Atlantic World, 1250–1820* (New York: Cambridge University Press, 2012); David Northrup, 'Vasco Da Gama and Africa: An Era of Mutual Discovery, 1497–1800', *Journal of World History* 9, no. 2 (1998): 189–211; Kristin Mann and Edna G. Bay, *Rethinking the African Diaspora: The Making of a Black Atlantic World in the Bight of Benin and Brazil* (London: Routledge, 2001); Jane Landers, *Atlantic Creoles in the Age of Revolutions* (Cambridge, MA: Harvard University Press 2010); David Wheat, *Atlantic Africa and the Spanish Caribbean, 1570–1640* (Chapel Hill: The University of North Carolina Press, 2016).

[17] Robin Law and Kristin Mann, 'West Africa in the Atlantic Community: The Case of the Slave Coast', *The William and Mary Quarterly* 56, no. 2, Third Series (1999): 307–34; Mann and Bay, *Rethinking the African Diaspora*; James H. Sweet, *Recreating Africa: Culture, Kinship, and Religion in the African-Portuguese World, 1441–1770* (Chapel Hill: The University of North Carolina Press, 2003); Robin Law, Suzanne Schwarz and Silke Strickrodt, eds, *Commercial Agriculture, the Slave Trade and Slavery in Atlantic Africa* (Woodbridge: James Currey, 2013).

[18] See Mariana P. Candido, 'Concubinage and Slavery in Benguela, c. 1750–1850', *Slavery in Africa and the Caribbean: A History of Enslavement and Identity Since the 18th Century*, ed. Olatunji Ojo and Nadine Hunt (London: I.B. Tauris, 2012), 65–84; Vanessa Oliveira, 'Trabalho escravo e ocupações urbanas em Luanda na segunda metade do século XIX', *Em torno de Angola: Narrativas, identidades e conexões atlânticas* (São Paulo: Intermeios, 2014), 265–67.

[19] A recent volume, for instance, mistakenly claims that West Africa 'had a long tradition of matriarchy': Catterall and Campbell, *Women in Port*, 4.

[20] For important studies that place African women at the centre of attention see Lorelle

comparative historical work has been done on women's roles in African societies, although a number of recent monographs on coastal communities pay attention to gender relations.[21] There are also several articles dealing with women entrepreneurs and the ways in which they facilitated cross-cultural trade through their position in indigenous kinship networks on the one hand and, on the other, their relationships with foreign traders. Most such studies cluster around the Upper Guinea Coast and the Gold Coast.[22] Communities that thrived on the trade also attracted groups and individuals from the interior of the continent. These included large numbers of enslaved Africans, of whom most were shipped off the coast but some – mainly women – remained in the coastal communities, usually as slaves or wives.

Since the 1980s much of the discussion on women in pre-twentieth-century Africa has focused on their power or lack of it. Political power tends to be associated with the ability to control material and spiritual sources. While women held formal political power in only a few cases, their agricultural production and commercial activities were vital to the survival of most communities, including their ability to attract migrants and refugees who could be incorporated into host societies as slaves or poor dependants. In Dahomey women exercised military power as guards and soldiers, as well as – in the royal household – as queen mothers and advisers, influencing power succession and palace life.[23] In Matamba and

(contd) Semley, *To Be Free and French: Citezenship in France's Atlantic Empire* (Cambridge: Cambridge University Press, 2017); Jane Landers, 'Founding Mothers: Female Rebels in Colonial New Granada and Spanish Florida', *The Journal of African American History* 98, no. 1 (2013), 7–23; David Wheat, 'Nharas and Morenas Horras: A Luso-African Model for the Social History of the Spanish Caribbean, c. 1570–1640', *Journal of Early Modern History* 14, no.1 (2010): 119–50.

[21] Studies that pay attention to African women include James F. Searing, *West African Slavery and Atlantic Commerce: The Senegal River Valley, 1700–1860*, 78 (Cambridge: Cambridge University Press, 1993); Sandra E. Greene, *Gender, Ethnicity, and Social Change on the Upper Slave Coast: A History of the Anlo-Ewe* (Portsmouth, NH: Heinemann, 1996); Kristin Mann, *Slavery and the Birth of an African City: Lagos, 1760–1900* (Bloomington: Indiana University Press, 2007); Pernille Ipsen, *Daughters of the Trade: Atlantic Slavers and Interracial Marriage on the Gold Coast* (Philadelphia: University of Pennsylvania Press, 2015); Carina E. Ray, *Crossing the Colour Line: Race, Sex, and the Contested Politics of Colonialism in Ghana* (Athens: Ohio University Press, 2015).

[22] Philip J. Havik, 'Women and Trade in the Guinea Bissau Region', *Studia* 52 (1994): 83–120; Philip J. Havik, 'Sóciais, intermediárias e empresárias: O gênero e a expansão colonial na Guiné', *O rosto feminino da expansão portuguesa*, vol. 2, 2 vols (Lisbon: Comissão para a Igualdade e para os Direitos das Mulheres, 1995), 87–90; Natalie Everts, 'A Motley Company: Differing Identities among Euro-Africans in Eighteenth-Century Elmina', *Brokers of Change: Atlantic Commerce and Cultures in Precolonial Western Africa*, ed. Toby Green (Oxford: Oxford University Press, 2012), 53–69; Reese, 'Wives, Brokers, and Labourers', 291–314; Pernille Ipsen, '"The Christened Mulatresses": Euro-African Families in a Slave-Trading Town', *The William and Mary Quarterly* 70, no. 2 (2013): 371–98

[23] Edna G. Bay, *Wives of the Leopard: Gender, Politics, and Culture in the Kingdom of Dahomey* (Charlottesville: University of Virginia Press, 1998); Edna G. Bay, 'Belief, Legitimacy and the Kpojito: An Institutional History of the "Queen Mother" in Precolonial Dahomey', *The Journal of African History* 36, no. 1 (1995): 1–27.

Ndongo, Queen Njinga controlled a large number of subjects and territories, engaging in the sale of captives into the transatlantic slave trade. In Kongo political power was exercised through the control of numerous dependants, including wives who could provide labour and 'produce' children.[24] Power was always contested and negotiated, and some women challenged patriarchy, presenting alternative visions of power through healing practices or as mediums in spirit possession; yet this could produce a backlash in the form of accusations of witchcraft, as in the case of Kimpa Vita of Kongo.[25]

In parts of Atlantic Africa, another form of power emerged with the advent of Europeans in the late fifteenth century. While it is widely assumed that colonialism started in Africa with the Berlin Conference (1884–1885), significant parts of the coast were already under some degree of European control by the mid-seventeenth century or even earlier. In Angola and Benguela, Saint Louis and on the Gold Coast we find colonial states or chartered companies imposing legislation, adopting bureaucratic practices and in some cases evicting the indigenous population long before the 'scramble for Africa'. Natalie Everts, Kristin Mann, Hilary Jones, Vanessa Oliveira and Ademide Adelusi-Adeluyi examine how European authorities affected women's position in society. The introduction of a new order of things and practices of governance, such as land registration, mapping, censuses, systems of taxation and official reports, changed the opportunities open to women in places as distant as Lagos, Luanda, Saint Louis, Freetown or the interior of Benguela. Women, like men, negotiated the European intrusion with different degrees of success.[26]

Another issue that has received attention in the past has been that of labour. Women who controlled the labour of enslaved and poor dependants constituted a challenge to patriarchal power, as Assan Sarr, Hilary

[24] Heywood, *Njinga of Angola*; Susan Herlin Broadhead, 'Slave Wives, Free Sisters: Bakongo Women and Slavery c. 1700–1850', *Women and Slavery in Africa*, ed. Claire C. Robertson and Martin A. Klein (Madison: University of Wisconsin Press, 1983), 160–81; Jan Vansina, *Paths in the Rainforests: Toward a History of Political Tradition in Equatorial Africa* (Madison: University of Wisconsin Press, 1990). For more on the accumulation of dependants see Joseph C. Miller, *Way of Death: Merchant Capitalism and the Angolan Slave Trade, 1730–1830* (Madison: University of Wisconsin Press, 1988); Suzanne Miers and Igor Kopytoff, eds, *Slavery in Africa: Historical and Anthropological Perspectives* (Madison: University of Wisconsin, 1977); Jane I. Guyer and Samuel M. Eno Belinga, 'Wealth in People as Wealth in Knowledge: Accumulation and Composition in Equatorial Africa', *The Journal of African History* 36, no.1 (1995), 91–120.

[25] Thornton, *Kongolese Saint Anthony*; David L. Schoenbrun, 'Gendered Histories between the Great Lakes: Varieties and Limits', *The International Journal of African Historical Studies* 29, no. 3 (1997): 461–92; Kodesh, *Beyond the Royal Gaze*, 19–20.

[26] See Ann Laura Stoler, 'Colonial Archives and the Arts of Governance', *Archival Science* 22, no. 2 (2002): 87–109; Peter Pels, 'The Anthropology of Colonialism: Culture, History, and the Emergence of Western Governmentality', *Annual Review of Anthropology* 26 (1997): 163–83; Jean Comaroff and John L. Comaroff, *Of Revelation and Revolution, Volume 1: Christianity, Colonialism, and Consciousness in South Africa* (Chicago, IL: The Chicago University Press, 1991); Jean-Baptiste, *Conjugal Rights*.

Jones and Esteban Salas show in this volume.²⁷ Contact with the Atlantic world affected labour practices and gender relations, especially in societies close to the coast. Women had to deal with the consequences of the demographic imbalance caused by the Atlantic slave trade. This could mean having to replace male labour lost to warfare, raids or the slave trade, but also to assume additional childcare responsibilities.²⁸ A large number of women stayed enslaved within Africa, serving to increase agricultural productivity, but also to expand kinship and consolidate rights in persons or wealth in people.²⁹ Enslaved women offered matrilineal societies the chance to expand lineages, since their children belonged to the father's kin. The offspring of free women, however, were incorporated into the mother's lineage, providing allegiance to the maternal uncle.³⁰ Besides the lineage expansion, women's labour and market value enriched militarily successful states, for example in Kongo, Mbailundu or the Bete country.³¹ Enslaved female labour played an important role in communities on the Gambia River, in the interior of Benguela and along the Gold Coast, as chapters in this volume show. Even in places established as colonies of freedom, such as Freetown and Libreville, enslaved women were of crucial economic importance.³²

While power and labour clearly form important components in any history of women in Africa, a series of discussions has led us to the conclusion that other aspects require more attention. A double panel on 'Atlantic encounters and female strategies: West and West Central African women in early colonial settings' at the African Studies Association of the UK conference (2014), organised by Mariana Candido and Silke Strickrodt, was followed by two panels on 'Women and Land: Historical Perspec-

---

²⁷ See also Beth Greene, 'The Institution of Woman-Marriage in Africa: A Cross-Cultural Analysis', *Ethnology* 37, no. 4 (1998): 395–412; Sandra E. Greene, 'Family Concerns: Gender and Ethnicity in Pre-Colonial West Africa', *International Review of Social History* 44 (1999): 15–31; Megan Vaughan, *Creating the Creole Island: Slavery in Eighteenth-Century Mauritius* (Durham, NC: Duke University Press, 2005), 150–1.

²⁸ It is impossible to estimate the numbers affected: see David Henige, 'Measuring the Immeasurable: The Atlantic Slave Trade, West African Population and the Pyrrhonian Critic', *The Journal of African History* 27 (1986): 300–301.

²⁹ Jan Vansina, *Paths in the Rainforests: Toward a History of Political Tradition in Equatorial Africa* (Madison: University of Wisconsin Press, 1990), 250–51; Miers and Kopytoff, eds, *Slavery in Africa*, 7–9; Ifi Amadiume, *Male Daughters, Female Husbands: Gender and Sex in an African Society* (London: Zed Books, 1987), 30–31; Assan Sarr, 'Land, Power, and Dependency along the Gambia River, Late Eighteenth to Early Nineteenth Centuries', *African Studies Review* 57, no. 3 (2014): 102–3.

³⁰ Joseph C. Miller, 'Women as Slaves and Owners of Slaves: Experiences from Africa, the Indian Ocean World, and the Early Atlantic', *Women and Slavery*, ed. Gwyn Campbell, Suzanne Miers and Joseph C. Miller, vol. 1 (Athens, OH: Ohio University Press, 2007), 12.

³¹ Osborn, *Our New Husbands Are Here*, 48–50 and 92–3.

³² Jean-Baptiste, *Conjugal Rights*, 13; Paul E. Lovejoy and Suzanne Schwarz, eds, *Slavery, Abolition and the Transition to Colonialism in Sierra Leone* (Trenton, NJ: Africa World Press, 2015).

tives on Access, Rights, and Property in West and West Central Africa', organised by Mariana Candido at the African Studies Association annual meeting. Finally, in 2017, a workshop in Dublin brought together a dozen case studies. From these discussions, three aspects – overlapping yet each important in its own right – emerged: mobility, property and vulnerability. Each aspect raises issues of agency. Let us deal with them in turn.

Property

Perhaps the major revelation of this book is the extent to which some of the African women involved in the Atlantic world in the eighteenth and nineteenth centuries owned property of various kinds.

It has of course been known for a long time that certain African women might own 'wealth in persons' as influential members of a matrilineage. A few studies have been devoted to women who owned slaves, for example on the Gold Coast, and to those who traded in slaves.[33] Further light is shed on such women in this volume: Assan Sarr mentions women who owned as many as 30 slaves on the lower Gambia River in the mid-nineteenth century, while most of the Gold Coast women whose stories are recounted by Natalie Everts seem to have had their own slaves. According to Mariana Candido, one woman in Benguela had 53 slaves (including 31 women) when she died in 1854.

Free individuals sought to exploit the economic opportunities and the comparative freedom offered by the growing urban centres. Natalie Everts mentions a woman in Elmina on the Gold Coast to whom the Dutch director-general transferred the ownership of a house when he returned to Europe. In Benguela, Saint Louis and Lagos, landed property became a major form of security and investment in the early nineteenth century, and by the 1830s a substantial number of properties in urban colonial centres were owned by African women who acted as landladies to immigrants and visitors.[34]

Various contemporary travellers' accounts referred to extravagant jewellery worn by some women on the coast, particularly the *signares* of Senegambia, and this has been noted in the literature. Hilary Jones has

[33] Adam Jones, 'Female Slave-Owners on the Gold Coast: Just a Matter of Money?' Stephan Palmié, ed., *Slave Cultures and the Cultures of Slavery* (Knoxville: University of Tennessee Press, 1996), 100–11; Bruce L. Mouser, 'Women Slavers of Guinea-Conakry', *Women and Slavery in Africa*, ed. Claire C. Robertson and Martin A. Klein (Madison: University of Wisconsin Press, 1983), 320–39; Ipsen, *Daughters of the Trade*.

[34] Mann, 'Women, Land and Wealth'; Marie-Hélène Knight, 'Gorée au XVIIIe siècle du sol', *Revue française d'histoire d'outre-mer* 64, no. 234 (1977): 33–54; Hilary Jones, *The Métis of Senegal: Urban Life and Politics in French West Africa* (Bloomington: Indiana University Press, 2013), 56; Mariana P. Candido, 'Women, Family, and Landed Property in Nineteenth-Century Benguela', *African Economic History* 43 (2015), 136–61.

demonstrated how the ownership of property (including slaves) served to consolidate group identity and how 'civilising goods', such as dresses, tea sets, shoes and hats, affected women's economic and social mobility.[35] Following this lead, chapters in this volume extend the discussion of links between consumption and identity to other parts of Africa's Atlantic coast. The main protagonist in Kristin Mann's chapter, who moved from Brazil to Lagos and had a number of dependants there, owned gold and silver chains as well as cloth, despite not being an elite woman. The wills and post-mortem inventories for Benguela, analysed by Mariana Candido, reveal an extraordinary amount of imported furniture, Chinese paintings, Western-style clothing, silk handkerchiefs, gold ornaments and other forms of property in the possession of elite women – all serving to enhance their prestige and establish a certain identity.

Female traders, both on local markets and in long-distance commerce, have received some attention, albeit rather limited.[36] In this book we encounter traders such as Betje Hamilton of Elmina on the Gold Coast in the mid-eighteenth century or Marie Pellegrin on the island of Gorée (Senegal) in the late nineteenth century. They were evidently of considerable wealth. Suzanne Schwarz's chapter on the Freetown peninsula recounts how early women settlers – including the 'recaptives' released from the slave ships – rejected European plans for a primarily agricultural economy in favour of commerce, selling products (and even slaves) on local markets or further afield.

That this made more sense from the perspective of a woman interested in autonomy is made clear in Esteban Salas' chapter on Catumbela, where much of the food consumed in Benguela and on slave ships that called there was produced. While women played a key role in agricultural production in Catumbela, serious obstacles prevented them from mobilising sufficient labour (through control of dependants) and gaining sufficient access to land, so that in comparison with African men the women had 'fewer possibilities of accumulating wealth through agricultural production'.

Until recently, little attention has been paid (except in the case of *signares* of Senegambia who bought land upon which to build a house) to women who managed to acquire landed property and use it to extract a surplus. In the mid-nineteenth century, some women took advantage of changing notions of landed property and were able to persuade the local authorities to recognise their claims to such land, enabling them to transmit it to their descendants.[37] In this volume, Assan Sarr discusses at length how both

---

[35] Jones, *The Métis of Senegal*, 73–95.
[36] E. Frances White, *Sierra Leone's Settler Women Traders: Women on the Afro-European Frontier* (Ann Arbor: University of Michigan Press, 1987).
[37] Elisabeth McMahon, *Slavery and Emancipation in Islamic East Africa: From Honor to Respectability* (New York: Cambridge University Press, 2013); Candido, 'Women, Family, and Landed Property'.

Mandinka and Jola women on the River Gambia either owned agricultural land themselves or had 'considerable control' over such land. In some cases, he writes, the land was 'part of their bridewealth'; in others it was passed down from mother to daughter. In the course of the second half of the nineteenth century, however, women lost much of this control or ownership, mainly because the growing importance of peanut cultivation led to a shift of agricultural production towards upland areas, but also because accelerated Islamisation posed a challenge to existing inheritance patterns.

Kristin Mann tells the story of Ajatu, an African woman who returned from Brazil and bought land in the Brazilian quarter of the city of Lagos. Mariana Candido refers to a woman in Benguela (originating from the interior) who invested in landed property in the 1850s. In the same period, as Vanessa Oliveira tells us, the 'natural daughter' of a deceased Portuguese man in Luanda inherited not only his captives and land but also the property of her first husband, who died soon after she reached the legal age of marriage. For African women who married Portuguese or Brazilian traders, she argues, it proved advisable to devise marriage contracts which would enable them to preserve their wealth.

The acquisition of landed property by African women was not confined to the African continent. In Lorelle Semley's chapter we learn of a woman from Senegal who in 1786, fifteen years after emigrating to St Domingue, was able to give her daughter upon the occasion of her marriage land as well as enslaved persons – despite (or indeed due to) having no husband herself.

Vulnerability

Yet behind the many stories of prosperity lie a sub-plot of almost continual insecurity, pressure and vulnerability. Although Madam Esperance rose from humble beginnings to become one of the richest persons on the lower Gambia in the late seventeenth century, her journey towards this achievement was, as Colleen Kriger shows in her chapter, beset with challenges and setbacks, not least from Englishmen who sought to deprive her of the wealth inherited from her English husband.

Similar stories from a century later are told by Natalie Everts in her chapter on the Gold Coast. Using records of the Dutch West India Company, she describes four cases of African women who on the one hand made good use of their relationship with European men but on the other faced numerous attempts by members of the African societies in which they lived to enslave, blackmail or even kill them. Merely to insinuate that a woman was descended from a female slave was enough to undermine her position.

Vulnerability could apply also to the question of racial identity. Everts argues that, for a woman, being of mixed descent was a considerable advantage when dealing with European officials in the forts on the Gold Coast. Hilary Jones shows that in Senegal those of mixed race benefited from access to education. But descent from a European in itself was no guarantee of being secure. As Lorelle Semley reminds us in the case of the 'natural daughter' of a Frenchman who had lived in Senegal, 'the claims to whiteness could be fragile'. While this particular woman was successful in making such claims, it may be assumed that many others failed.

One aspect which emerges clearly from Semley's account is the crucial importance of building networks in order for a woman to be more secure. While Semley describes how someone could benefit from 'three overlapping networks: continental, oceanic and ideological', using 'the language of belonging and the rhetoric of empire' to secure leverage within the *Ancien Régime*, Everts provides ample evidence of Akan women seeking to reduce their vulnerability by using ties with various branches of their matrilineage as well as with both Dutch and British officials in the coastal forts of the Gold Coast. Not all were successful in this, however. In the case of Luanda, as Vanessa Oliveira argues (and as Kristin Mann has shown for Lagos in a slightly later period[38]), it was mainly through marriage that women created advantageous networks for themselves.

Almost the same applies to Ademide Adelusi-Adeluyi's chapter on what is today south-western Nigeria in the period when attempts were being made to end the Atlantic slave trade. She offers us two narratives of female figures who 'found freedom' in Lagos. The first is of a girl called Alabon, who – depending on our perspective – was either enslaved or pawned by the merchant woman Madam Tinubu, then given by her to the wife of an English trader to cover a debt, then, in 1851, given a 'certificate of freedom', but was moved along the lagoon to Badagry (30 miles away) without her consent, and finally, having returned to Lagos as a British subject with a new British name, seems to have gained some kind of security after intervention by the British. In other words, she moved back and forth along the lagoons, as well as between slavery and emancipation. The second story, which took place a decade later, is that of a woman called Awa, bought as a slave in Ibadan and taken to Abeokuta, where she was used as a concubine and a domestic worker until she was locked up in a cell for a minor misdemeanour and then sold by her owner's principal wife to a man in Porto Novo (on the coast), from whom she escaped via the lagoon to Lagos.

Dealing with Lagos in almost the same period, Kristin Mann traces the vicissitudes in the tempestuous life of an African woman who in Brazil

---

[38] Kristin Mann, *Marrying Well: Marriage, Status and Social Change among the Educated Elite in Colonial Lagos* (Cambridge: Cambridge University Press, 1985).

was called Ajifoluke, then Luisa, then Ajatu (a Muslim name). Having gained manumission, she was able to return to Lagos in the 1850s or 1860s. The focus of the chapter, however, is on her murder in 1871 by a dependent young Muslim man, referred to as her 'son' although she was probably childless. The murder seems to have been the culmination of long quarrels between these two persons regarding authority within the house in which they lived – a conflict between male and female, but also 'inter-generational'. Besides the murder itself the robbery that accompanied it provides evidence of the insecurity and vulnerability that characterised the life of Ajatu, despite the fact that Lagos had been a British colony for a decade.

Sexual vulnerability is discussed in Adam Jones' chapter, which deals with women on the Gold Coast (today Ghana) who, in the late seventeenth century, found themselves obliged to place themselves at the services of the unmarried African men in their village. As he shows, the sources that we have concerning this institution are highly ambiguous, but they certainly suggest that some women had very limited room for manoeuvre in sexual matters.

Mobility

As already argued, Africa's Atlantic coast was a contact zone, where local people interacted with strangers. Direct Afro-European trade began in the late fifteenth century, in some cases accompanied by Christian missionary activities and small-scale European colonisation. All three phenomena – trade, mission and colonisation – involved movement back and forth. Chapters in this volume examine different types of mobility: the physical movement of women between rural and urban centres, as well as the journeys of slave and free women across the Atlantic, examined by Lorelle Semley and Kristin Mann, or between Europe and the African coast, as in the contribution of Colleen Kriger. While much attention has been paid to the forced migration of enslaved Africans, not much has been written on Africans who crossed the Atlantic as free people.[39] Physical mobility was a characteristic of the Atlantic world: before the nineteenth century, of course, the majority of those who crossed the Atlantic westward were enslaved Africans, but the movement of merchants and colonial officials, although far less significant in quantitative terms, likewise served to

[39] For studies on free Africans see Roquinaldo Amaral Ferreira, 'Atlantic Microhistories: Mobility, Personal Ties, and Slaving in the Black Atlantic World (Angola and Brazil)', *Cultures of the Lusophone Black Atlantic*, ed. Nancy Prisci Naro, Ro Sansi-Roca and D. Treece (New York: Palgrave Macmillan, 2007), 99–127; Júnia Ferreira Furtado, 'Lives on the Seas: Women's Trajectories in Port Cities of the Portuguese Overseas Empire', *Women in Port*, Catterall and Campbell, 251–86.

connect different ports with one another. Yet African societies too were characterised by considerable mobility in this period, with individuals and groups migrating towards new lands and resources, as well as to places less endangered by warfare.[40] Displaced people, including many women, were incorporated into host societies or migrated to coastal centres where they could engage in new economic opportunities which contact with the Atlantic world offered. Mobility affected physical geography, population size, as well as the circulation of ideas.

Two decades ago, as Kathleen Sheldon pointed out, urban colonial histories had relatively little to say about gender. Since then many studies have focused on African women migrating to colonial cities in search of wage labour in the formal or informal economy.[41] Yet we still know little about women's mobility before the twentieth century. The early modern Atlantic was shaped by the circulation of people, ideas, goods and crops. This circulation, particularly evident in port cities, transformed economies and facilitated the integration of women in new urban activities, such as the production and commercialisation of food, as well as the commercialisation of services such as washing and sewing. New economic activities facilitated the social mobility of African women.[42]

Vanessa Oliveira and Natalie Everts explore how African women took advantage of their roles as intermediaries between African populations and European traders or colonial officers to improve their own economic and social standing and protect their relatives and loved ones.[43] In empha-

---

[40] See, for example, the works of Jan Vansina and others on Bantu expansion and early long-distance trade.

[41] See Sheldon, *Pounders of Grain*. For female labour in urban centres see Judith Byfield, 'Women, Marriage, Divorce, and the Emerging Colonial State in Abeokuta (Nigeria), 1892–1904', *'Wicked' Women and the Reconfiguration of Gender in Africa*, ed. Dorothy L. Hodgson and Sheryl A. McCurdy (Portsmouth, NH: Heinemann, 2001), 27–46; M. Anne Pitcher, 'Conflict and Cooperation: Gendered Roles and Responsibilities within Cotton Households in Northern Mozambique', *African Studies Review* 39, no. 3 (1996); 81; Henrietta L. Moore and Megan Vaughan, *Cutting down Trees: Gender, Nutrition, and Agricultural Change in the Northern Province of Zambia, 1890–1990* (Portsmouth, NH: Heinemann, 1994); Carina E. Ray, *Crossing the Color Line: Race, Sex, and the Contested Politics of Colonialism in Ghana* (Athens, OH: Ohio University Press); Jean-Baptiste, *Conjugal Rights*.

[42] Havik, 'Women and Trade', 83–120; George E. Brooks, 'A Nhara of the Guinea-Bissau Region: Mãe Aurélia Correia', *Women and Slavery in Africa*, ed. Claire C. Robertson and Martin A. Klein (Madison: University of Wisconsin Press, 1983), 295–319; Selma Pantoja, 'Donas de 'arimos': um negócio feminino no abastecimento de gêneros alimentícios em Luanda (séculos XVIII e XIX)', *Entre Áfricas e Brasis*, ed. Selma Pantoja (Brasilia: Paralelo, 2001), 35–49; Vanessa S. Oliveira, 'Gender, Foodstuff Production and Trade in Late-Eighteenth Century Luanda', *African Economic History* 43 (2015): 57–81.

[43] Ipsen, 'The Christened Mulatresses'. Not all were successful: See Mariana P. Candido, 'African Freedom Suits and Portuguese Vassal Status: Legal Mechanisms for Fighting Enslavement in Benguela, Angola, 1800–1830', *Slavery & Abolition* 32, no. 3 (2011): 447–59; Mariana P. Candido, 'The Transatlantic Slave Trade and the Vulnerability of Free Blacks in Benguela, Angola, 1780–1830', *Atlantic Biographies: Individuals and Peoples in the Atlantic World*, ed. Mark Meuwese and Jeffrey A. Fortin (Leiden: Brill, 2013), 193–210.

sising relationships between African women and European men, we do not intend to overlook the disparity of power in these relationships. Sexual violence was, of course, inherent to the encounter between Europeans and Others.[44]

One central theme in the contributions of Schwarz, Adelusi-Adeluyi and Kriger is the slippage between girl/women categories. These authors examine the constructions and deployments around the idea of girls as vulnerable, indicating some of the difficulties involved in delineating a boundary between childhood and womanhood. In some instances, age mattered for the construction of gender and status, allowing girls to be differentiated from women.[45] Categories, however, have always been unstable, similar to the concepts of wife, concubine and prostitute explored in the chapters by Oliveira, Semley, Everts, Hilary Jones and Adam Jones.

Property, vulnerability, mobility: these three aspects of women's history on Africa's Atlantic coast before 1880 have received too little emphasis in the literature. Taken together, they draw attention to a number of contradictions: to own property normally implies being stationary, and people who are vulnerable have difficulty in accumulating property – be it land, slaves or jewellery. Such contradictions underlie many of the narratives uncovered in this volume; and even when the contradictions are not visible, we must assume that this is because our sources tend to shed light only upon one side of the story.

The chapters in this volume demonstrate the exciting nature of research on women in Atlantic Africa before the Berlin Conference. By employing a wide variety of sources, including oral interviews, population censuses, court minutes, maps, inventories and ecclesiastical records, the contributors make an important methodological contribution and, hopefully, will inspire more research in this field. The case studies shed light not only upon women's history but also upon the history of work conditions, access to property, presence in urban spaces and migration expe-

---

[44] For criticism of the naturalisation of the sexual nature of the colonial encounter see Anne McClintock, *Imperial Leather: Race, Gender and Sexuality in the Colonial Contest* (New York: Routledge, 1995); Isabel P. B. Fêo Rodrigues, 'Islands of Sexuality: Theories and Histories of Creolization in Cape Verde', *The International Journal of African Historical Studies* 36 (2003), 83–103; Ray, *Crossing the Color Line*, 5–6. For rape and sexual violence as a conquest and colonial strategy of control see, among others, Pamela Scully, 'Malintzin, Pocahontas, and Krotoa: Indigenous Women and Myth Models of the Atlantic World', *Journal of Colonialism and Colonial History* 6, no. 3 (2005); Pamela Scully, 'Rape, Race, and Colonial Culture: The Sexual Politics of Identity in the Nineteenth-Century Cape Colony, South Africa', *The American Historical Review* 100, no. 2 (1995), 335–59.

[45] Abosede A George, *Making Modern Girls: A History of Girlhood, Labor, and Social Development in Colonial Lagos* (Athens: Ohio University Press, 2015). For influential studies on African childhood see Audra Diptee, *From Africa to Jamaica: The Making of an Atlantic Slave Society, 1775–1807* (Gainsville: University Press of Florida, 2012); Benjamin Nicholas Lawrance, *Amistad's Orphans: An Atlantic Story of Children, Slavery, and Smuggling* (New Haven, CT: Yale University Press, 2015).

riences. Several chapters take a biographical approach, and the resulting African perspective on Atlantic history shifts the focus towards a more people-centred kind of narrative. The volume as a whole focuses on the plurality of experiences, bringing rural and urban spaces into dialogue and stressing women's varied backgrounds, as well as their different interactions with outsiders. By putting African women at the centre of the narrative and stressing their multiple identities, we aim to deprovincialise a particular period of African history and emancipate it from the national and disciplinary silos to which it has often been confined. As the contributors show, African women were part of a larger set of transformations involving property, vulnerability and mobility that affected African societies in the seventeenth to nineteenth centuries.

Part One
Property

1

Adaptation in the Aftermath of Slavery
Women, Trade & Property in Sierra Leone, c. 1790–1812[1]

SUZANNE SCHWARZ

The diverse roles played by entrepreneurial women in trade and agriculture in pre-colonial Africa have been the subject of a number of studies in the last four decades.[2] This scholarship has focused particularly on elite merchant women – *donas* (wealthy African and Eurafrican women), *signares* and *nharas* (both words, 'from the Portuguese *senhora* … signified women of wealth and influence') – although the experiences of poor and enslaved women have recently been traced through parish records in Angola.[3] The planting of a new port town at Freetown on the Sierra Leone peninsula in the closing decade of the eighteenth century opened up opportunities for neighbouring Temne women, as well as newly arrived migrant women of African origin and descent, to generate income through food cultivation, trade, commerce and service provision.

This chapter explores how uprooted and displaced women, who had already experienced multiple forms of migration, drew on skills from

---

[1] I would like to thank Barbara Bush, Kathryn Ellis, Nicholas Evans, Jane Landers, Robin Law, Paul Lovejoy, Bruce Mouser, Vanessa Oliveira, Judith Spicksley and Silke Strickrodt for their advice on issues discussed in this chapter. An earlier version was presented as a keynote lecture at the Twentieth Annual Workshop of the Women's Committee of the Economic History Society: 'Free Labour? Women and Work in Slave and Post-Slave Societies', Wilberforce Institute for the study of Slavery and Emancipation, University of Hull, November 2009.

[2] Edna G. Bay, ed., *Women and Work in Africa* (Boulder, CO: Westview Press, 1982); Bruce L. Mouser, 'Women Slavers of Guinea-Conakry', *Women and Slavery in Africa*, ed. Claire C. Robertson and Martin A. Klein (Madison: University of Wisconsin Press, 1983), 320–39; George E. Brooks, 'The *Signares* of Saint-Louis and Gorée: Women Entrepreneurs in Eighteenth-Century Senegal', *Women in Africa: Studies in Social and Economic Change*, ed. Nancy J. Hafkin and Edna G. Bay (Stanford, CA: Stanford University Press, 1976), 19–44.

[3] George E. Brooks, 'A Nhara of the Guinea-Bissau Region: Mãe Aurélia Correia', *Women and Slavery*, Robertson and Klein, 295–317, 295; Mariana P. Candido, 'Engendering West Central African History: The Role of Urban Women in Benguela in the Nineteenth Century', *History in Africa* 42 (2015), 7–36.

their earlier lives to exploit economic opportunities in West Africa. The settlers' migrant origins placed constraints on their capacity to conduct long-distance trade and to profit from the accumulation of slave labour. Freetown was not an indigenous African settlement, and its distinctive abolitionist agenda meant that the experiences of women in this new town were markedly different to those of coastal merchant women in other settings. In contrast to trading women in Benguela, Luanda and Saint Louis, women in Freetown were prohibited, in theory if not always in practice, from slave trading or owning enslaved Africans.[4] The arrival of 'recaptive' Africans after 1808 altered the situation, and settler women were able to capitalise on a new supply of labour to support their economic enterprises (see Map 2).[5] As these female settlers were also outsiders and 'strangers' with no contacts to inland societies, their opportunities for wealth accumulation were more limited than those of entrepreneurial women in other coastal settings.

By the turn of the nineteenth century, the convergence of various streams of Atlantic migration on Sierra Leone resulted in an intermixing of women from diverse cultures with different life experiences of freedom and enslavement in America, Africa, the West Indies and Europe. As the chapters by Hilary Jones and Kristin Mann in this volume demonstrate, inward migration shaped the cosmopolitan character of other coastal towns in West Africa. However, each urban community developed a distinctive social composition depending on the economic function of the town and the sources of inward migration. Among the women resident in Freetown by the early nineteenth century were individuals with first-hand experience of American slave systems, Jamaican Maroons (runaway slaves and their descendants) and local Africans. Prior to the large-scale influx of 'captured Negroes' (also referred to as 'recaptives' and 'liberated Africans') starting in 1808, Sierra Leone's population already included a substantial number of former slave women who had secured their freedom by different means. These settlers interacted with Temne women in Freetown's hinterland, as well as a small number of European women resident in Freetown in the late eighteenth and early nineteenth centuries.[6]

In its early phases of development preceding transfer to British Crown control in 1808 the 'infant colony' provides an exceptionally rich and

---

[4] Mariana P. Candido, *An African Slaving Port and the Atlantic World: Benguela and Its Hinterland* (New York: Cambridge University Press, 2013), 113–14, 116–17, 129. For a discussion of Senegal, see the chapter by Hilary Jones in this volume.

[5] The 'Disposal' column in the Registers of Liberated Africans records the names of settlers and colonial officials to whom 'recaptives' were allocated: Sierra Leone National Archives (SLNA), Registers of Liberated Africans, 1808–1812.

[6] For a discussion of the early history of the colony, see Christopher Fyfe, *A History of Sierra Leone* (London: Oxford University Press, 1962), 13–151; Paul E. Lovejoy and Suzanne Schwarz, eds, *Slavery, Abolition and the Transition to Colonialism in Sierra Leone* (Trenton, NJ: Africa World Press, 2015).

Adaptation in the Aftermath of Slavery: Women, Trade & Property in Sierra Leone • 21

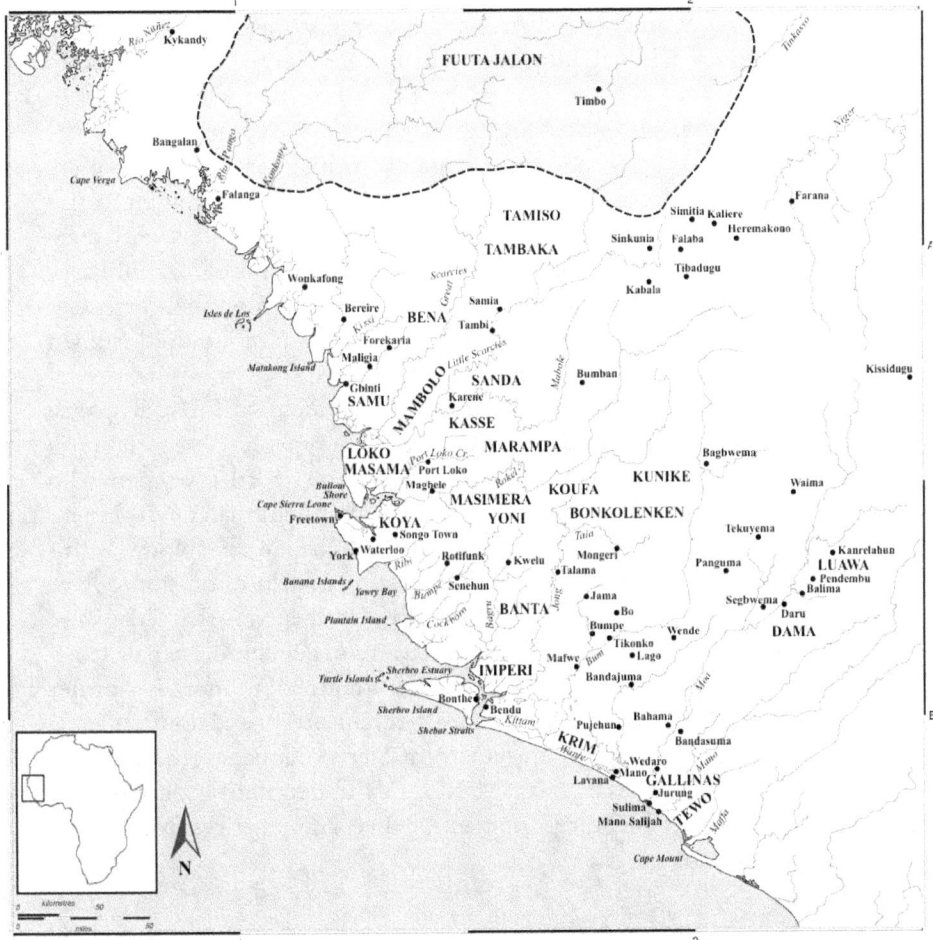

Map 2 The Upper Guinea Coast, 1820
(Source: Henry B. Lovejoy, Africa Diaspora Maps)

distinctive context in which to examine how women of African origin and descent adapted to new economic and social circumstances in the aftermath of slavery. The forced relocation of Africans to Freetown following their release from slave ships intercepted by Royal Navy patrols led to a marked shift in labour relations from 1808 – a situation which was taken advantage of by existing female settlers. The shifting demographic make-up of the settlement after 1808 offered the opportunity for settler women to acquire new sources of labour, even if this was more limited than in other comparable urban contexts in West Africa.

With the notable exception of E. Frances White's study of *Sierra Leone's Settler Women Traders* published thirty years ago, little attention has been paid to women and gender in the processes by which tens of thousands of recaptive Africans adapted to their forced resettlement in the British

Crown colony.[7] Women are even less visible in historical literature on the earlier phases of colonial administration by the Sierra Leone Company between 1791 and 1807. Although the Black Loyalists who resettled in Sierra Leone from Nova Scotia in 1792 have been the subject of extensive study, there is only sporadic comment in this literature on women, individually or collectively, and the overall experience of women in this 'infant colony' remains in shadow.[8] The 550 Jamaican Maroons who resettled in the colony in 1800 are usually mentioned in terms of male military action in suppressing an uprising by the Nova Scotians on their arrival at Freetown, and little notice has been taken of almost four hundred women and children among this body of settlers.[9]

As a new trading enclave in West Africa, Freetown offered diverse opportunities for wealth accumulation; but this involved negotiating a complex social, economic and political landscape. Settler women who attempted to utilise their trading skills in this unfamiliar environment were at risk of re-enslavement if they ventured outside the colony, as this new town had been established in the midst of an area of on-going slave supply.[10] Another potential obstacle faced by women was that they were exposed to diverse and conflicting expectations of gender roles; male colonial officials of an evangelical turn of mind attempted to moralise former slave women and impose European ideals of femininity and domesticity.[11] Even so, in adapting to circumstances in Sierra Leone, women among the Nova Scotians and Jamaican Maroons exhibited fluid economic and cultural identities, which drew on skills, beliefs and practices from earlier phases of their lives.[12]

Demographic Composition

Females comprised just under half of the population of Freetown and Granville Town (771 of 1,673 individuals) in 1802, although the male component was increased by ninety 'crewmen' (Kru) and ninety-two

---

[7] E. Frances White, *Sierra Leone's Settler Women Traders. Women on the Afro-European Frontier* (Ann Arbor: University of Michigan Press 1987), 1–16.

[8] A study of Mary Perth, one of the Nova Scotian settlers, is a notable exception: Cassandra Pybus, '"One Militant Saint": The Much Traveled Life of Mary Perth', *Journal of Colonialism and Colonial History* 9, no. 3 (2008): n.p.; White, *Sierra Leone's Settler Women Traders*, 16–26.

[9] Fyfe, *History*, 85–6.

[10] This danger was also present in Benguela: Mariana P. Candido, 'African Freedom Suits and Portuguese Vassal Status: Legal Mechanisms for Fighting Enslavement in Benguela, Angola, 1800–1830', *Slavery & Abolition* 32, no. 3 (2011): 447–59.

[11] Edna G. Bay, 'Introduction', *Women and Work*, ed. Bay, 5, 7, 10.

[12] Kathleen Wilson, 'The Performance of Freedom: Maroons and the Colonial Order in Eighteenth-Century Jamaica and the Atlantic Sound', *William and Mary Quarterly*, 3rd series, 66, no. 1 (2009): 53.

individuals in the African Corps.[13] This overproportion of males resembled the situation in plantation slave societies, where there was usually a majority of men, unlike Ouidah, Accra, Luanda and Benguela, which had more women than men.[14] As Lorelle Semley's chapter in this volume indicates, women also outnumbered men on Gorée in the eighteenth century.

Among the Nova Scotian and Maroon settlers, however, women and girls were in a majority and accounted for 53 per cent of the settler population of 1,406 individuals. Children accounted for just under half of the settler population (659 of 1,406). Taking the adult population in isolation indicates that women were in the majority among the Jamaican Maroons and accounted for 161 of 299 adults listed in the census of 1802 (54 per cent). Women also slightly outnumbered men among the Nova Scotian settlers, as 235 of 448 adults listed in 1802 were female (52 per cent).[15] The adult females recorded in Freetown in 1802 also included 22 Muslim women among 'Dalla Moodoo's people' and four European women.[16]

Settlement patterns point to a strong cluster of female-headed households among the settlers classified as 'Nova Scotians': just under one-third of 297 households were headed by women.[17] This pattern can be traced at least in part to the original composition of the group on its departure from Halifax in 1792, although the death of spouses in Freetown increased the number of widows. This social make-up featured a substantial number of households in which single and widowed women were responsible for the economic control of the family or kinship unit. By 1802 Martha March was left with six children upon the death of her husband, and Affy Channel headed a household with five children following the death of Scipio Channel. Other households with dependent children were headed by single women. There is little comment on occupational skills, and the notes appended to their names by colonial administrators typically focused on their marital status and sometimes their sexual behaviour. Alice Bacchus was described as a 'Lady of easy virtue' as it was noted that she had two daughters 'by as many fathers'. Concern with the status and stability of family relationships also emerges in some of the entries for

[13] The National Archives, United Kingdom (TNA), WO 1/352, War Department In-Letters and papers, iv, Sierra Leone: Sierra Leone Company.
[14] Hilary McD. Beckles, 'Female Enslavement and Gender Ideologies in the Caribbean', *Identity in the Shadow of Slavery*, ed. Paul E. Lovejoy (2nd ed, London: Continuum 2009), 164; Robin Law, *Ouidah: The Social History of a West African Slaving 'Port' 1727–1892* (Athens: Ohio University Press 2004), p. 76; Vanessa S. Oliveira, 'Gender, Foodstuff Production and Trade in Late-Eighteenth Century Luanda', *African Economic History* 43 (2015): 60.
[15] Fyfe, *History*, 216.
[16] TNA, WO 1/352, War Department In-Letters and papers, iv. Sierra Leone: Sierra Leone Company; Bruce L. Mouser, 'The Expulsion of Dalu Modu: A Muslim Trader in Anti-Slavery Freetown', *African Voices of Slavery and the Slave Trade*, ed. Alice Bellagamba, Sandra Greene and Martin Klein (New York: Cambridge University Press 2012), 334–41.
[17] A few other individuals of different origins were included with the Nova Scotians, including 'Sarah (a native)'.

men, and there is one instance where an unmarried man, John Hickford, was noted as having 'a spurious offspring'. The term 'Infamous' entered next to the names of Mary James and Sarah Almond may reflect concerns about prostitution expressed in contemporary accounts.[18]

Dora Lawson was the only female head of household among more than one hundred Maroon households. More typical among the Maroon settlers were large male-headed households with more than one adult female. Captain Andrew Smith's household of fifteen included two men, five women, five boys and three girls. The census does not break down the nature of the family relationships within households. Company officials complained frequently about polygamy among the Maroons, but the presence of several females did not necessarily imply a polygamous household. No female heads were among the listing of European households.

Nine years later, the census of 1811 indicates that women outnumbered men in thirteen of the fifteen streets in Freetown. This is suggestive of networks of female support, which offered advantages in facilitating childcare and releasing women to engage in fieldwork and trade outside the boundaries of the colony.[19] Rawdon Street exhibited a strong cluster of women, with eighty-two women and only forty-six men. Water Street also exhibited a mix of seventeen Nova Scotian women, nine Maroons, five Africans and just one European.[20] The interaction between these women in the 'concealed domain' of private households is not revealed through the statistical record, but the scope for social contact can be inferred from the close proximity of women in the same streets.[21] This interaction was not necessarily harmonious, and Francis Spilsbury on his visit to Freetown in February 1806 identified some residual hostility between the different groups of women: 'As to the American settlers, they have not nor ever will forget the shock they felt on the landing of the Maroons; their savage warlike appearance struck them with dismay; even the girls still scarcely speak to each other with common civility.'[22]

---

[18] The categorisation of women according to their sexual behaviour reflects contemporary views of slave women as licentious. Barbara Bush, *Slave Women in Caribbean Society 1650–1838* (London: Heinemann 1990), 53; Henrice Altink, 'Deviant and Dangerous: Pro-Slavery Representations of Jamaican Slave Women's Sexuality, c. 1780–1834', *Slavery & Abolition* 26, no. 2 (2005): 271–88; Gwyn Campbell, Suzanne Miers and Joseph C. Miller, eds, *Women and Slavery: The Modern Atlantic, Volume 2* (Athens: Ohio University Press 2008), 2, 15.

[19] Gwyn Campbell, Suzanne Miers & Joseph C. Miller, 'Women in Western Systems of Slavery: Introduction', *Slavery & Abolition* 26, no. 2 (2005): 167–8, 171–2.

[20] House of Commons Parliamentary Papers Online, 'Houses and Population within the Walls of Sierra Leone, taken by Order of Governor Columbine, April 1811', *Extracts from Report of Commissioners Appointed for Investigating the State of the Settlements and Governments on the Coast of Africa* (1812), 8.

[21] Campbell, Miers and Miller, *Women and Slavery*, xvii.

[22] F. B. Spilsbury, *Account of a Voyage to the Western Coast of Africa; Performed by His Majesty's Sloop Favourite in the Year 1805* (London: R. Philips 1807), 30.

The numerical pattern revealed in the 1811 census indicates that within the streets of Freetown, modelled on a North American colonial grid plan, different female traditions co-existed in close proximity. The influence of European women was limited, as the censuses of 1802 and 1811 both point to a ratio of over 100 adult black females to every adult European woman. Although Nova Scotian and Maroon women were associated with slave communities that had actively secured their own liberation, there were important distinctions in their experience. In contrast to women drawn from the free Maroon communities of Jamaica, the Nova Scotians had recent first-hand experience of enslavement, mostly in the southern states of Georgia, South Carolina, North Carolina and Virginia.[23] Spilsbury perceived differences in their behaviour: 'In the Maroon girl you evidently see the consciousness of freedom, while the unfortunate American, in her mind, feels yet the lash of an unfeeling master.'[24]

Land

The presence of over ninety female-headed households sheds light on the 'multiple and inseparable' roles of women as 'producers' and 'reproducers' in early nineteenth-century Freetown.[25] Women in the census included not just the wealthier members of Freetown society, but also the poorest. The resourcefulness of the Nova Scotian and Maroon women in maintaining their independence before their arrival in Sierra Leone influenced their adaptability to economic conditions in West Africa, and many adopted dual or multiple occupations in their pursuit of economic security and social mobility. Farming and trade were interdependent, as surplus agricultural products provided a basis for food preparation and marketing. Both groups of women had experienced the pressures of land hunger and placed a high value on acquiring freehold land as the basis for financial self-sufficiency and social autonomy.[26]

For women as well as men among the Black Loyalists, the offer of land by the Sierra Leone Company was one of the most powerful factors persuading them to migrate to West Africa. Two female heads of household listed among the Nova Scotians leaving Birchtown were described

---

[23] Ellen Gibson Wilson, *The Loyal Blacks* (New York: Putnam 1976), 69.

[24] Ibid.; Mavis C. Campbell, *The Maroons of Jamaica, 1655–1796: A History of Resistance, Collaboration and Betrayal* (Granby, MA: Bergin & Garvey, 1988), 3; Lucille Mathurin Mair, *The Rebel Woman in the British West Indies during Slavery* (Kingston: Institute of Jamaica 2007), 1–2.

[25] Bay, 'Introduction', *Women and Work*, Bay, 5.

[26] Mavis C. Campbell, *Back to Africa. George Ross and the Maroons: From Nova Scotia to Sierra Leone* (Trenton, NJ: Africa World Press 1993), xiv; James W. St. G. Walker, *The Black Loyalists: The Search for a Promised Land in Nova Scotia and Sierra Leone, 1783–1870* (Toronto: University of Toronto Press 1999 [London, 1976]), xi, 18.

as widows and farmers, and their equipment included axes, hoes, spades and a pickaxe. Lucy Banbury, aged 43, had access to a ten-acre lot, 'part improved'; but this may have been owned by the government. Abby Roger, aged 36, had access to the use of a 'Town Lot improved Govt' prior to her emigration from Nova Scotia.[27] Speaking from Moses Wilkinson's Methodist pulpit, Lieutenant Clarkson informed the settlers of the Company's offer of twenty acres for every man, ten for his wife and five for every child. Female heads of families were entitled to the same allocation as males, and the offer of land also extended to unmarried women 'going with families', who were also entitled to ten acres.[28] Women joined in the protest when the land had not been allocated fourteen months after their arrival at Freetown, and a plan of plots indicates that the typical allocations for males and females were far lower than originally promised.[29] Although a petition sent to the Court of Directors in October 1793 was delivered by two men, it was written on behalf of all 'the Black Settlers of this Place', who expressed concern at their inability to 'make a Crop to support us next year'.[30] The value of land as a basis for a self-sustaining community had also been driven home forcefully to the Maroons by land shortages, which had threatened their autonomous existence in Jamaica.[31]

Women had access to land in and around Freetown through grants made by the colonial authorities, as part of the initiative to encourage settler cultivation. This points to the private ownership of land by women, a pattern which has also been traced in other colonial settings in East and West Africa in the eighteenth and nineteenth centuries.[32] Women's legal entitlement to individual ownership of plots was recorded in registers, maps and charts drawn up by the authorities in Freetown.[33] After the transfer to Crown control, settlers were required to provide proof of their entitlement to specific plots. Women were prominent among those who submitted written and oral testimony to support their rights to land granted in the 1790s, as well as land purchased or inherited from other

---

[27] TNA, CO 217/63, 'List of the blacks in Birch Town who gave in their Names for Sierra Leone in November 1791', 362–3.
[28] *Substance of the Report Delivered by the Court of Directors of the Sierra Leone Company, to the General Court of Proprietors, on Thursday the 27th March, 1794* (London: J. Philips & Son 1795), 5.
[29] SLNA, 'Names of Settlers Located on the 1st Nova Scotian Allotment'.
[30] Christopher Fyfe, *'Our Children Free and Happy': Letters from Black Settlers in Africa in the 1790s* (Edinburgh: Edinburgh University Press 1991), 36.
[31] Campbell, *Back to Africa*, 58.
[32] Mariana Candido and Eugénia Rodrigues, 'African Women's Access and Rights to Property in the Portuguese Empire', *African Economic History* 43 (2015): 4–8; Eugénia Rodrigues, 'Women, Land, and Power in the Zambezi Valley of the Eighteenth Century', *African Economic History* 43 (2015): 30–35; Oliveira, 'Gender, Foodstuff Production and Trade', 58–9; Mariana Candido, 'Women, Family and Landed Property in Nineteenth-Century Benguela', *African Economic History* 43 (2015): 138–9; Kristin Mann, *Slavery and the Birth of an African City. Lagos, 1760–1900* (Bloomington: Indiana University Press 2007), 270.
[33] Candido, 'Women, Family and Landed Property', 142–3, 151.

inhabitants. Ann Dwight, a spinster, claimed possession of two acres of land allocated in the 1st Nova Scotian allotment. Although she had lost all her papers in the 'Great Fire' in 1810, the authorities granted her request after checking land records in Freetown.[34]

Women are recorded as the owners of 122 of 490 plots (25 per cent) distributed to Nova Scotian settlers. Although the number of plots corresponds broadly with the distribution of female-headed households, it is still a far lower proportion than the number of adult females in the population. The plots of land allocated to women were typically smaller than those distributed to men, usually accounting for two acres. Some were allocated larger plots; Catherine Anthony's plot extended to six acres, while Phillis King occupied the largest plot allocated to a woman, covering eight acres.[35]

Land tenure was highly contested, however, for both males and females as the colonial authorities attempted to impose charges on the land through quit rent in 1796 and 1797. The imposition of charges was fiercely resisted: quit rent was viewed as weakening their independence, as non-payment could result in confiscation of the land. Settlers regarded the imposition as a first step back into slavery.[36]

For those women who secured land grants, the plots of several acres indicate small-scale cultivation as a regular feature of women's work, a pattern consistent with gender divisions of labour in West African society, which designated this type of agricultural work as fit for low-status women and slaves.[37] Plots owned by females were clustered together in some instances, which may point to mutual support in cultivation methods. Gender expectations of labour among the Jamaican Maroons were likewise closely aligned to West African practices. Maroon women were agriculturalists who had experience of cultivating a diverse range of foodstuffs for the domestic market in Jamaica including yams, coffee, plantains, cocoa and fruits, as well as raising small livestock, and this experience was readily adapted to conditions in Sierra Leone.[38]

On their arrival in Sierra Leone, Company officials expected male and female Maroons to engage in farming, and it was resolved in January 1801 that individuals aged between fourteen and twenty-one should each be

[34] TNA, CO 270/13, Sierra Leone Sessional Papers. Council, 1811–1813, 43–4.
[35] SLNA, 'Names of Settlers Located on the 1st Nova Scotian Allotment'. Some of the names are illegible.
[36] Fyfe, 'Our Children', 13, 53–4.
[37] Bush, *Slave Women*, 33; Carol P. MacCormack, 'Control of Land, Labor and Capital in Rural Southern Sierra Leone', *Women and Work*, ed. Bay, 37, 41, 48; Claire C. Robertson and Martin A. Klein, 'Women's Importance in African Slave Systems', *Women and Slavery*, Robertson and Klein, 10.
[38] Lucille Mathurin Mair, *A Historical Study of Women in Jamaica, 1655–1844*, ed. Hilary McD. Beckles and Verene A. Shepherd (Kingston: University of West Indies Press 2006), 9–60; Mair, *The Rebel Woman*, 42; Campbell, *Maroons*, 4, 222.

allotted two acres for cultivation. In reality, the plots distributed were far smaller, with land allocations of less than one acre for men and women. Of the 112 plots allocated to Maroon settlers, only seven were registered to women.[39] Importantly, though, this land could be sold or bequeathed by the female owner, and as such contributed to wealth accumulation among the children of settlers. Nancy Perkins, allocated two-thirds of an acre at King Tom's Point, bequeathed this land to her daughter Betsey Bailey, who later sold it to Charles Benjamin Jones.[40] Although land distribution was heavily weighted in favour of men, it is likely that land allocated to male Maroons would have been cultivated by women and girls in their households.[41]

In addition to the plots allocated by the Company, some women acquired additional land through purchases from male and female settlers. In 1812, the Governor and Council confirmed Ann Dwight's rights to a town plot purchased from Samuel Ogden for twenty-four dollars. Her landholdings in town had been increased further by purchases from Phebe Lynch.[42]

Trade and Production

Petty trade and small-scale manufacturing provided additional and alternative forms of income for females. In mid-to-late nineteenth-century Sierra Leone, 'recaptive' Yoruba women released in the colony developed an important role as traders in foodstuffs, cotton goods, tobacco, palm oil and kola nuts.[43] Successful women traders can, however, be traced back to a much earlier phase of the colony's development: in their pursuit of economic independence Nova Scotian and Maroon women exploited diverse opportunities within the public spheres of trade and commerce. In common with what happened in other urban contexts in West Africa and the West Indies, retail trade and the supply of commercial services offered a source of wealth accumulation for women.[44] The busy port town also

[39] SLNA, 'Plan of 1st Maroon Allotment'.
[40] National Archives of Scotland, GD1/1135/6/2, No. 621. Transfer of land from Betsy Bailey of two thirds of an acre of land on King Tom's Point 'numbered in the register and a plan of the First Maroon Allotment One' to Charles Benjamin Jones and then Charles Heddle of Freetown, 26 October 1858. I am grateful to Nicholas Evans for this information.
[41] It was noted that the 'women are much employed in cultivating the town lots'. TNA, CO 270/6, Sierra Leone Sessional Papers. Council, 28 April 1801, 79.
[42] TNA, CO 270/13, Sierra Leone Sessional Papers. Council, 1811–1813, 49.
[43] White, *Sierra Leone's Settler Women Traders*, 35–58; E. Frances White, 'Creole Women Traders in the Nineteenth Century', *International Journal of African Historical Studies* 14, no. 4 (1981): 626–42.
[44] Nancy J. Hafkin and Edna G. Bay, 'Introduction', *Women in Africa*, Hafkin and Bay, 6; Women also featured prominently in petty trading in towns in the West Indies: Campbell, Miers and Miller, 'Women in Western Systems of Slavery', 164; Dominique Rogers and

offered opportunities for the supply of sexual services. In 1798, Governor Macaulay recorded his moral outrage that married and single women were prostituting themselves to visiting sailors.[45]

Women's resistance to Company efforts to impose a predominantly agricultural economy is reflected in their preference for trading.[46] Women were central to the development of a cash economy, and some became influential as independent traders. Three of the first six shops established by Company licence in Freetown in 1794 were run by Nova Scotian women: Mary Perth, Sophia Small and Martha Hazeley. Small also kept one of two taverns opened in Freetown in 1795, and eight of the twenty-seven spirit licences were held by women in 1811.[47] Spilsbury recorded in 1806 how he and a number of fellow crew 'all supped at Mrs. Small's, by whom we were most kindly treated'.[48] These three traders were not listed among the females allocated land plots by the colonial authorities, which suggests that their trading was prompted by their initial lack of access to land.[49]

As Maroon women had commercial experience of selling foodstuffs and livestock in Jamaican markets, they would have been well placed to respond to trading opportunities in Freetown and its hinterland. Female settlers among the Nova Scotians also undertook small-scale cultivation of surplus foodstuffs for the local market. According to the Company report of 1804, only half of the total population of 1,200 settlers derived their support from farming.[50] Assuming that the twenty or twenty-five settlers who earned a living from fishing were men, there would have been opportunities for women and girls to process and market the surplus produce.[51] From Spilsbury's account, Illustration 1, showing female settlers, is suggestive of small-scale marketing, as the women are pictured with a basket of produce containing foodstuffs.[52]

Women also took advantage of the marketing opportunities presented by the regular arrival of ships. Spilsbury reported how 'this day some women came on board to barter oranges, lemons &c.'[53] As most of the

---

(contd) Stewart King, 'Housekeepers, Merchants, Rentières: Free Women of Color in the Port Cities of Colonial Saint-Domingue, 1750–1790', *Women in Port: Gendering Communities, Economies, and Social Networks in Atlantic Port Cities, 1500–1800*, ed. Douglas Catterall and Jodi Campbell (Leiden: Brill 2012), 376; Oliveira, 'Gender, Foodstuff Production and Trade', 73.
[45] James Sidbury, *Becoming African in America: Race and Nation in the Early Black Atlantic* (Oxford: Oxford University Press 2007), 117, 236 n. 82.
[46] Bush, *Slave Women*, 46–9.
[47] Fyfe, *History*, 101–2.
[48] Spilsbury, *Voyage*, 34.
[49] SLNA, 'Names of Settlers Located on the 1st Nova Scotian Allotment'.
[50] *Substance of the Report Delivered by the Court of Directors of the Sierra Leone Company, to the General Court of Proprietors, on Thursday the 29th March, 1804* (London: J. Philips & Son 1804), 7–8.
[51] MacCormack, 'Land', 49.
[52] Spilsbury, *Voyage*, 38.
[53] Ibid., 19.

30 • *Property*

Illustration 1 Female settlers in Freetown, 1805
(Source: 'Negresses of Sierra Leone', Francis B. Spilsbury, *Account of a voyage to the Western coast of Africa; performed by His Majesty's sloop Favourite, in the year 1805* (London, 1807), facing p. 21; copy in Special Collections Department, University of Virginia Library)

vessels visiting Freetown were engaged in the transatlantic slave trade, this practice of shipboard huckstering carried with it the risk of re-enslavement.

From an early stage, Temne women exploited benefits arising from the Company presence in Freetown. Queen Yamacoubra, an influential local woman, regularly visited Freetown and requested presents from the Company.[54] Trading with settlers at Freetown also offered an opportunity to acquire high-status European goods, in much the same way that Fetu and Fante female traders at Cape Coast could benefit from the presence of European slave traders.[55] Traders coming to Freetown included petty traders of goods. Shortly after his arrival, Lieutenant Clarkson, superintendent at Freetown, described how 'the Natives both Male & Female flock every day to the Settlement in great numbers, bringing with them such fruit as they find in the woods, which principally consist of Ananas, Bananas, Plantains, Limes, oranges, Cassadas &c.' ('Ananas' = pineapple; 'Cassada' = manioc/cassava).[56] The market potential in Freetown was considerable: the Company reported in 1804 how between one and two hundred Africans visited the settlement each day to exchange their produce for British manufactured goods.[57] In Freetown, women of African descent came into regular contact with Temne, Mende and Sherbro women engaged in marketing. When Hanna, the African wife of Robin Dick, was to be tried by red water[58] in 1796, a large number of women from Freetown, including Mary Perth, travelled to Pa Demba's town in the Temne country to witness the trial. The Company botanist noted that she 'was well known in town, where she came almost every day for trade's sake'.[59]

The potential for obtaining European goods at Freetown also attracted female traders from further afield. In 1796 Macaulay recorded how 'A Lady of the name of Aredyana, the wife of the Port Logo chief Namina modou' had been in Freetown for several days. She had 'come with her Husband's rice &c to market' and 'brought with her a boy & a girl whom she left to be educated "white man's fashion"'.[60] The Company report of 1798 acknowledged the role played by Betsey Heard, a Eurafrican slave

---

[54] Henry E. Huntington Library, San Marino, California (HL), Diary of Zachary Macaulay, Thursday 1 August 1793 – Wednesday 16 April 1794, entry for 4 December 1793.
[55] Ty M. Reese, 'Wives, Brokers, and Laborers: Women at Cape Coast, 1750–1807', *Women in Port*, ed. Catterall and Campbell, 291–4, 299–300.
[56] Charles Bruce Fergusson, ed., *Clarkson's Mission to America 1791–1792* (Halifax, NS: Public Archives of Nova Scotia 1971), 174.
[57] *Substance of the Report, 1804*, 8.
[58] The red water or sasswood ordeal, imposed upon suspected sorcerers, involved having to drink a quantity of water mixed with a poisonous tree-bark.
[59] Alexander Peter Kup, ed., *Adam Afzelius Sierra Leone Journal, 1795–1796* (Uppsala: Institutionen för allmän och jämförande etnografi 1967), 63.
[60] HL, MY418(13), Zachary Macaulay's journal, 26 July–26 September 1796, 4.

trader, in facilitating trade with the 'Mandingo country' located to the north of the colony.[61] Those settler women who came into contact with Heard would have observed the behaviour of a powerful independent trader who owned slaves, had been educated in Liverpool, spoke English and was the ruler at Bereira, to the north of Freetown.[62]

For entrepreneurial women among the settlers, this inward flow of Africans presented opportunities for exchange in rice, camwood, livestock, yams, mats, gum copal, oranges and pineapples. Women also ventured outside Freetown as itinerant traders, walking or travelling by boat to surrounding villages. This may explain why the census of 1802 recorded that Aberdeen Turner's wife 'had died lately at Bullom Shore'.[63] Up to fifteen Nova Scotians owned small vessels, which, although Company reports did not specify ownership, undoubtedly provided a means through which female traders gained access to settlements north and south of the colony. These boats played a vital role in keeping the colony supplied with livestock and foodstuffs and could carry between two and eight tons of produce.[64]

Other women left on a more permanent basis to pursue trade, and such women 'crossed ethnic boundaries' and exploited their dual knowledge of African and European forms of trade to identify economic opportunities.[65] Following the death of Abraham Moore, his widow went to the north of Freetown to engage in trade.[66] In recounting a tale of poisoning carried out by African women, Spilsbury drew attention to how another female settler had developed trading opportunities in the colony's hinterland: 'A black chief who lives near Sierra Leone married a settler of this colony, an American black; who by her attention and industry by trading for him up the rivers, not only procured him riches, but respect and attention from the colony.'[67] By marrying an African trader, the Nova Scotian woman secured access to internal markets in much the same way as Portuguese men benefited from marriage to African and Eurafrican women in Luanda, Benguela and Senegal.[68] The

[61] *Substance of the Report, Delivered, by the Court of Directors of the Sierra Leone Company, to the General Court of Proprietors, on Thursday the 29th March, 1798* (London: J. Philips & Son 1798), 5.
[62] Mouser, 'Women Slavers', 320–5; Fyfe, *History*, 67, 90.
[63] TNA, WO 1/352, War Department In-Letters and Papers, iv. Sierra Leone: Sierra Leone Company.
[64] *Substance of the Report, 1798*, 5–6; Women in Saint-Domingue and Luanda owned boats. Oliveira, 'Gender, Foodstuff Production and Trade', 58. Rogers and King, 'Housekeepers', 374.
[65] E. Frances White, 'Women, Work, and Ethnicity: The Sierra Leone Case', *Women and Work*, Bay, 20, 21, 29.
[66] Fyfe, *History*, 102.
[67] Spilsbury, *Voyage*, 21.
[68] Brooks, 'The *Signares* of Saint-Louis and Gorée', 44; Candido, *An African Slaving Port*, 131–7.

relationship was mutually beneficial, as the Nova Scotian's experience in North America meant that she could act as a commercial intermediary with American and European slave traders. The presence of the trading colony and the influx of female Nova Scotian settlers meant that this intermediary role took a different form from the more usual pattern of African and Eurafrican women acting as 'cultural intermediaries' through marriage to European traders.[69]

Women from Freetown were drawn into slave trading, although the trade was usually under male control. At Crawford's Island, Spilsbury met Betsey Walker, a Nova Scotian, who was managing a slave factory for James Carr, formerly the Sierra Leone Company accountant.[70]

The most prosperous women in Freetown were those who operated shops and invested their profits in property. Two years after acquiring a licence for shopkeeping, Sophia Small had accrued sufficient funds to build a two-storied house on Water Street, regarded as one of the most prestigious locations in the settlement. She generated further income as a landlady by renting out the house to five Scottish missionaries in 1796.[71] Within three years of beginning to trade as a licensed shopkeeper, Mary Perth, a widow and former slave from Norfolk Virginia, had built up surplus capital of £150 from multiple occupations. Before she was granted a shopkeeping licence she operated a 'kind of boarding house and chophouse by the wharves', and her customers included slave ship mariners.[72]

In contrast to Senegal, the Gold Coast and Angola, marriage with a European official or trader was not a common source of enrichment for settler women in Freetown.[73] In view of the small number of European women in the settlement, it is likely that concubinage and informal 'marriages' with African and Afro-descendant women were not uncommon. Although marriage and sexual relationships with female settlers were actively discouraged by the Company, such relationships did exist.[74] William Cowling, a schoolmaster, was dismissed in June 1794 for having 'entered into an improper connexion with a woman in the Town',

---

[69] Brooks, 'A Nhara of the Guinea-Bissau Region', 295–9; Mouser, 'Women Slavers of Guinea-Conakry', 320–9; Bay, 'Introduction', *Women and Work*, Bay, 7–8; Lindsey Gish, 'Breaking Down African Hierarchies through Gendered Atlantic Trade: Free and Enslaved Female Entrepreneurs of Saint Louis Senegal in the 18th and 19th Centuries', Paper presented at Annual Meeting of the African Studies Association, San Diego, Nov. 2015.

[70] Spilsbury, *Voyage*, 23.

[71] Fyfe, *History*, 102–3; Rental of houses and warehouses provided income for free black women in Saint-Domingue in the eighteenth century: Rogers and King, 'Housekeepers', 368–9, 372.

[72] Fyfe, *History*, 60, 101–2; Pybus, '"One Militant Saint"'.

[73] Brooks, '*Signares* of Saint Louis and Gorée', 21–2, 34, 36, 42; Gish, 'Breaking Down African Hierarchies'.

[74] In Senegal, restrictions on marriage and relationships were ignored: Brooks, '*Signares* of Saint Louis and Gorée', 22–3, 28.

and a case of alleged infanticide in 1808 focused on a child born to a Nova Scotian woman and fathered by an assistant surgeon in the employ of the Company.[75]

Labour Supply

Compared with wealth accumulation by other female coastal traders in West Africa, a major constraint faced by women in Freetown was the prohibition on slave ownership and slave trading. Unlike female slave owners on the Gold Coast, Freetown women could not legally own slaves to assist in cultivation, sell merchandise or provide domestic labour in the household.[76] In contrast to wealthy *donas* in Benguela and Luanda, settler women would have been unable to use a large number of slaves to cultivate crops and sell them at urban markets. There was no scope to build up the level of slave ownership of the type associated with Caty Louette (or Cati Louet, see Chapter 10), the 'richest woman on Gorée', who owned sixty-eight domestic slaves, or even D. Catarina Pereira Lisboa in Benguela who owned nineteen slaves in 1798.[77]

Various devices were used by women to circumvent these restrictions and acquire labour during the period of Company control. In 1802, the households of a number of female heads included African children and adults who could have provided a source of unfree or dependent labour. Ann Smith's household had 'a Nat[ive] Boy and Girl', while 'Betsey Gold, a native' lived with Mary Porter. Cases of illegal slave sales during the Company period of control also came to light in 1809.[78] These forms of labour acquisition, although transformative for the individuals concerned, were small scale and could not compete with scale of slave ownership among local women coming into Freetown with their own slaves. Even if Freetown settlers did acquire coerced labour under this much criticised apprenticeship system developed in the Company phase before 1807, this can only have been on a relatively minor scale.

Circumstances for the acquisition of new forms of household labour changed markedly after 1807. The transfer of Sierra Leone to Crown control on 1 January 1808 was followed swiftly by the deployment of Royal Navy vessels at Freetown with instructions to intercept slave ships en route to the Americas. Although the number of ships inter-

[75] University of Illinois Chicago, Sierra Leone Collection, Box 2, Folder 10, Columbine, Edward H., 'Memo ... Voyage to Africa 1809–1811', 51–5, 59.
[76] Adam Jones, 'Female Slave-Owners on the Gold-Coast. Just a Matter of Money?' *Slave Cultures and the Cultures of Slavery*, Stephen Palmié (Knoxville: University of Tennessee Press 1995), 100–6.
[77] Brooks, '*Signares* of Saint Louis and Gorée', 30; Candido, *An African Slaving Port*, 135.
[78] *African Herald*, 11 (2 December 1809).

cepted in the initial years of suppression activity was small, the release of 'Captured Negroes' had a major impact on the gender structure and the supply of labour in the colony. By the end of 1812, 4,201 individuals had been released in the colony, more than double the number of Freetown's population in 1808. Women and girls accounted for 1,231 of these coerced migrants (29 per cent).[79] By 1809, a fierce controversy had arisen concerning the allocation of African 'recaptives' as apprentices to Nova Scotian settlers, Jamaican Maroons and colonial officials, because this was viewed as representing another form of enslavement.[80] Certainly, Nova Scotian and Maroon women saw the arrival of these Africans as an opportunity to acquire cheap additional labour and were among those who clamoured to hand over twenty dollars a head for men, women and children disembarked by HMS *Derwent* in March 1808.[81]

According to the Registers of Liberated Africans in the Sierra Leone National Archives, women were prominent among the settlers who acquired multiple individuals from slave ships in the early years of suppression activity. Some female settlers acquired adult males as apprentices: Pompey, a man aged 16, was apprenticed to Mary Harding, described as a married woman.[82] It was more typical, however, for female settlers to take on women and boys and girls in their households. Most females were apprenticed to learn housewifery, some for periods of more than a decade.[83] Even though a majority of recaptives were acquired by male settlers, women within their households must have been able to use this unfree labour.[84]

In the first few years of suppression activity, a high proportion of recaptives were taken off ships which had embarked Africans in the immediate hinterland of Freetown.[85] As a result, recaptives apprenticed to settlers included Temne and Mende females, who made an important contribution as unpaid labour to the economic development of the colony. Their knowledge of inland societies must have assisted the Nova Scotian and Jamaican Maroon women in accumulating intelligence of trading opportunities in Freetown's wider hinterland. Other women and girls released

[79] I am grateful to Erika Melek Delgado for this information.
[80] Michael J. Turner, 'The Limits of Abolition: Government, Saints and the "African Question"', c. 1780–1820', *English Historical Review* 112, no. 446 (1997): 319–57.
[81] Suzanne Schwarz, 'Reconstructing the Life Histories of Liberated Africans: Sierra Leone in the Early Nineteenth Century', *History in Africa* 39 (2012): 193–204.
[82] SLNA, Register of Liberated Africans, 1808–1812, number 131.
[83] TNA, CO 267/31, 'List of Captured Negroes on Hand December 31st 1810 and of those Received, Enlisted, Apprenticed, Disposed of to December 31st 1812'.
[84] The 'distinction between ownership and usage rights' of slaves was highlighted by Robertson and Klein in 'Women's Importance in African Slave Systems', 3.
[85] Gibril R. Cole, 'Re-thinking the Demographic Make-up of Krio Society', *New Perspectives on the Sierra Leone Krio*, ed. Mac Dixon-Fyle and Gibril Cole (New York: Peter Lang, 2006), 33–51.

in Freetown expressed their resistance to their forced resettlement by running away.

Conclusion

For many women who resettled at Freetown, the colony presented new opportunities for social mobility and economic diversification. They developed roles which adapted practical skills from their places of origin, as well as from the Americas. The diverse range of entrepreneurial activity by women was transformative for the individuals, as well as for the port town. Entrepreneurial women and female petty traders were central to the emergence of Freetown as a market centre and 'emporium of commerce'.[86] With the resettlement of a large number of former slave women in a European-controlled colony, Sierra Leone emerged not only as a site of conflict between abolitionist and anti-abolitionist ideas, but also as an important site of discourse about the roles of women. The situation was complicated still further by the fact that Freetown was neither a slave society nor a fully post-slavery society, and its uneasy position between the two was fraught with contradictions. Even so, the Company's emphasis on developing agricultural cultivation and 'honourable' trade with neighbouring African societies provided a fluid environment, in which females could accumulate land and other property.

Opportunities for female enrichment were far more constrained in Freetown than in other colonial settings in East and West Africa. In this early phase of colonial development there is little evidence for the emergence of a group of elite merchant women who had wealth and connections of the type exhibited by *donas* in Angola and Mozambique. In Freetown, individual ownership of land by women was commonplace, but the plots were small. In contrast to other areas, women among the Nova Scotian and Maroon settlers could not build up a large number of slaves or dependent labourers. They could not amass the degree of wealth in people demonstrated in the Zambezi Valley by D. Catarina de Faria Leitão and D. Francisca Josefa de Moura Meneses, who each owned more than a thousand slaves.[87]

The forced resettlement of 'Captured Negroes' after 1808 removed some of the constraints on labour, enabling female and male settlers to accumulate many dependants and a supply of cheap coerced labour. By the

---

[86] This phrase was used by Company directors to describe their achievements in Sierra Leone: *Substance of the Report Delivered by the Court of Directors of the Sierra Leone Company, To the General Court of Proprietors, on Thursday the 24th of March, 1808* (London: J. Philips & Son, 1808), 13–15.
[87] Rodrigues, 'Women, Land, and Power', 30–5; Candido, *An African Slaving Port*, 116–17.

second decade of the nineteenth century, the number of recaptive females in the colony exceeded that of women among the Nova Scotians and Jamaican Maroons. The controversial allocation of recaptives to settlers through 'apprenticeship' arrangements altered this social structure and enabled female settlers to utilise forms of cheap coerced labour to accrue wealth. Despite their own earlier experiences in enslavement, several court cases reported in the colony newspapers in 1808 and 1809 suggest that Nova Scotian and Maroon women regarded females apprenticed to them as property and enslaved labour.[88]

[88] Schwarz, 'Reconstructing', 203–5.

2

Women, Land & Power in the Lower Gambia River Region

ASSAN SARR

Before the mid-nineteenth century, women in the lower Gambia River region appear to have had access to land, to a greater extent than in the late nineteenth century. While men controlled the millet and Guinea-corn fields, Mandinka women exercised influence over the control of rice-lands located in the swamps.[1] This chapter will focus on women's shifting access to land and how this was linked to the transformation from food crop production to the cultivation of peanuts.

Throughout this chapter, I analyse instances where a few prominent women exercised some influence in land matters in the late eighteenth and the nineteenth centuries. Drawing on a wide range of oral sources, as well as information from travellers' accounts and colonial records, I attempt to locate the life stories of three prominent women, Wuleng Jabbi Jarsey, Jebu Sonko and Fatou Jobba, in their wider networks of power, and discuss their ability to control land. Furthermore, the chapter stresses the important roles that Islam and spiritual beliefs in jinns and other spirits played in shaping power dynamics and mobility. These influenced the ability of people to access land and whether a certain site should be abandoned or settled. The chapter reveals, mostly through the stories of the three women, that family dynamics and not just gender influenced land access. Women who controlled the land and the labour of enslaved and poor dependants overturned patriarchal power and the ideology that perpetuated it.

Historical research on pre-colonial African women 'landowners' is still very limited.[2] With regard to the Gambia, Isatou Touray has written

---

[1] Robert M. Baum, *Shrines of the Slave Trade: Diola Religion and Society in Precolonial Senegambia* (New York and Oxford: Oxford University Press, 1999), 29.
[2] Isatou Touray, 'Gender and Land Dynamics in the Gambia: The Struggle for Citizenship, Democracy Calling for the Agency of the Poor', in Sam Moyo, Dzodzi Tsikata and Yakham Diop (eds), *Land in the Struggles for Citizenship in Africa* (Dakar: CODESRIA, 2015), 145.

on the concept of ownership in Mandinka societies. She contends that 'traditionally, the Mandinka women' were able to access land but they did 'not own it',[3] yet overlooks the fact that Mandinka households held land under two broad forms. Michael Watts has identified the collective (*maruo*) fields, usually under the control of male heads (the *korrdaatiyolu*), on which family members were expected to work to provide domestic subsistence and the individual fields the Mandinka called *kamanyango*. The household or *kabilo* heads granted family members the plots they used.[4] Mandinka women cultivated rice on both the individual and collective fields, and swamp clearance usually conferred ownership (see Map 3).[5] Over the past few decades, many scholars have examined heightening inter-gender and intra-gender conflicts over land in the Gambia, which have been attributed to the introduction of mechanisation, the growth of commercial agriculture including the expansion of market gardening by women, privatisation and drought.[6] Little attention has been paid to women's shifting access to land and how this was linked to the transformation from food crop production to the cultivation of peanuts. This chapter seeks to fill this important gap.

Agriculture, Gender and Family Dynamics

Mandinka gender relations were complex. While women exercised some authority, where the goals of men and women conflicted, men usually came out as the winners. Colonial reports suggest that Mand-

---

[3] Michael J. Watts, 'Idioms of Land and Labor: Producing Politics and Rice in Senegambia', in Thomas J. Bassett and Donald E. Crummey (ed.), *Land in African Agrarian Systems* (Madison: University of Wisconsin Press, 1993), 176

[4] See, for examples: Richard A. Schroeder, '"Re-claiming" Land in the Gambia: Gendered Property Rights and Environmental Intervention', *Annals of the Association of American Geographers* 87, no. 3 (September 1997), 487–508; Pamela Kea, 'Maintaining Difference and Managing Change: Female Agrarian Clientelist Relations in a Gambian Community', *Africa: Journal of the International African Institute* 74, no. 3 (2004): 361–82; Peter Mark, 'Urban Migration, Cash Cropping, and Calamity: The Spread of Islam Among the Diola of Boulouf (Senegal), 1900–1940', *African Studies Review* XXI, no. 2 (September 1978): 1–14; Kenneth Swindell and Alieu Jeng, *Migrants, Credit and Climate: The Gambian Groundnut Trade, 1834–1934* (Leiden and Boston: Brill: 2006); Peter M. Weil, 'Slavery, Groundnuts, and Capitalism in the Wuli Kingdom of Senegambia, 1820–1930', *Research in Economic Anthropology* 6 (1984): 77–119; Watts, 'Idioms of Land and Labor', 157–193; Judith Carney, 'Landscapes of Technology Transfer: Rice Cultivation and African Continuities', *Technology and Culture* 27, no. 1 (January 1996): 5–35; Judith Carney, 'Converting the Wetlands, Engendering the Environment: The Intersection of Gender with Agrarian Change in the Gambia', *Economic Geography* 69, no. 4, Environment and Development, Part 2 (October 1993): 329–48.

[5] National Records Service, Banjul (hereafter NRS), CSO (Colonial Secretariat Office) 2/94-The Laws and Customs of the Mandingoes of the North Bank, 1906

[6] Mungo Park, *Travels in the Interior of Africa: First Journey 1795–1797* (Edinburgh: Adam and Charles Black, 1878 [reprint]), 400–1.

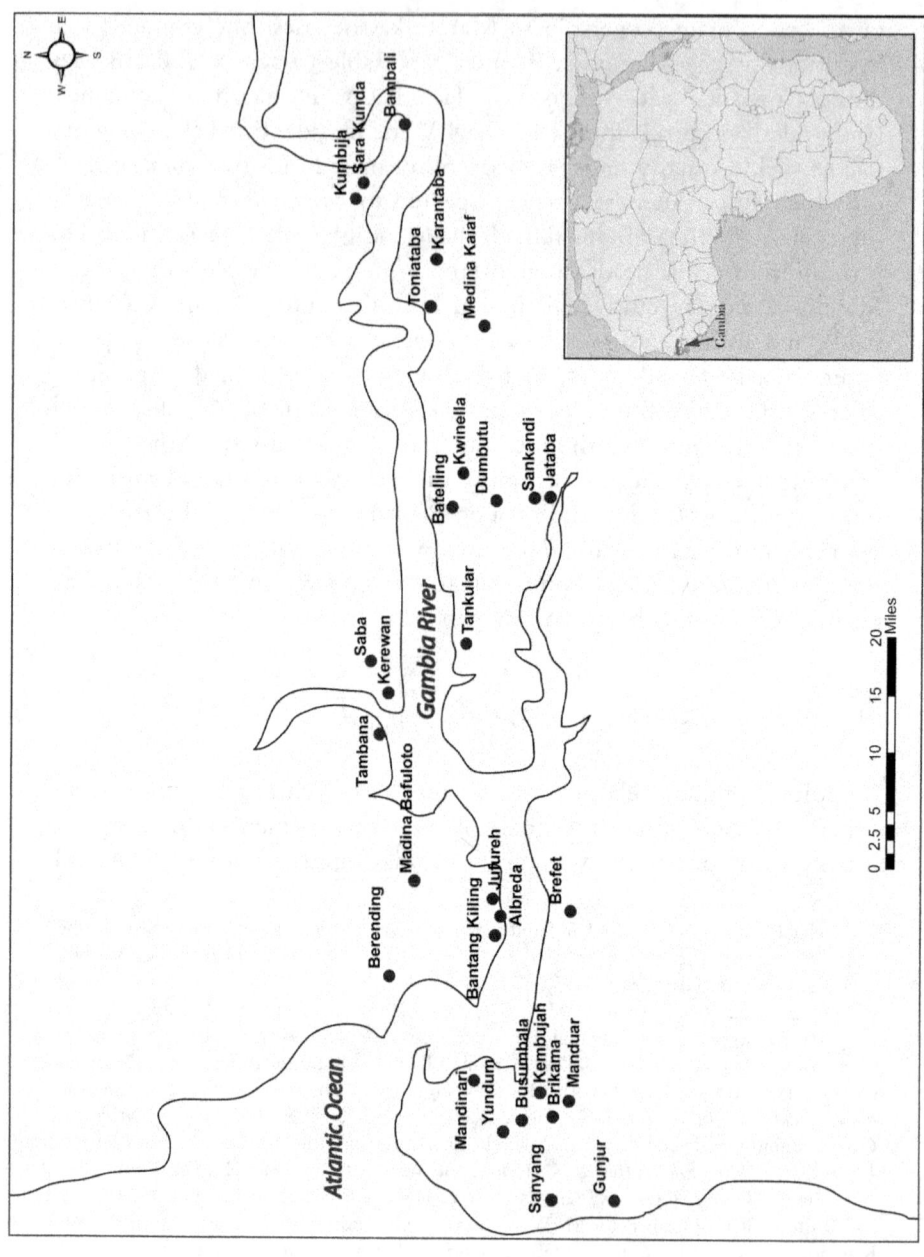

Map 3
The Gambia River
(Source: Nick Kroncke
at Ohio University)

inka women were almost all subordinate to their male counterparts. Few women, if any, were acknowledged as family heads. The oldest man in a family was always regarded as the head of the family. A married woman could not inherit property in her husband's household. Instead, it was the uncle who acted as guardian to the children until they came of age. Polygamy was widely established in Mandinka society, which was heavily influenced by Islam. Islamic law stipulates that men are allowed to marry only four freeborn wives, 'but poor men have sometimes only one or two wives, rich and powerful men have eight or nine and sometimes more'.[7] While this quotation is from a 1906 colonial source, there is no reason to doubt that this same state of affairs existed in the precolonial era.

Nevertheless, male dominance in Mandinka society co-existed with a degree of power for women. As Mungo Park observed in the 1790s,

> though the African husbands are possessed of great authority over their wives, I did not observe that in general they treat them cruelty … [T]hey permit their wives to partake of all public domains. When the wives quarrel among themselves, a circumstance, which, for the nature of their situation, must frequently happen, the husband decides between them. But if any one of the ladies complain[ed] to the chief of the town, that her husband has unjustly punished her, and shewn an undue partiality to some other of his wives[,] the affair is brought to a public trial.[8]

According to Park, married women, not men, officiated at these 'palavers'. Moreover, in all polygamous households, there was always a head wife, the husband's first wife.[9] As a rule, she took charge of the stores of rice and grain and held responsibility for distributing grain to the other wives when it was needed. The junior wives worked three days a week on the head wife's rice farm and worked for themselves on the remaining days. The head wife also took charge of the husband's house when he was away.

While the centrality of land in agricultural production cannot be overestimated, the value of land went far beyond its materiality. In the Gambia region every village had two types of field, one for their maize and the

---

[7] National Records Service, Banjul (hereafter NRS), CSO (Colonial Secretariat Office) 2/94, 'The Laws and Customs of the Mandingoes of the North Bank', 1906.
[8] Mungo Park, *Travels in the Interior of Africa: First Journey 1795–1797* (Edinburgh: Adam and Charles Black, 1878 [reprint]), 400–1.
[9] For more on Mandinka concepts of family and marriage, see NRS, CSO 2/94, 'The Laws and Customs of the Mandingoes of the North Bank', 1906; NRS, CSO 2/94, 'Reports on the Jolah People: Their customs and habits', 1906.

other for their rice.¹⁰ Mungo Park listed a variety of grains including *sanio,* rice and maize (*Toubab-nio* in Mandinka).¹¹ The two types of millet grown were *sanio,* and *suno,* which is smaller and is usually planted first. The Mandinka also cultivated Guinea corn, which they called *basso*¹² as well as Fonio (the normal name for this small variety of millet, *Digitaria exilis*) known locally as *findo.*

In the 1790s, these varieties of cereal were cultivated in 'considerable quantities' by people living along the banks of the Gambia River.¹³ While most of the harvest was meant for subsistence, surplus grain was also exchanged for much needed commodities. Slave traders, for example, depended significantly on the agricultural surpluses that Senegambian farmers sold them.¹⁴ European slavers working for companies based in Gorée Island purchased tons of grain from farmers in order to feed their captives about to be shipped to the New World.¹⁵ Grains came from Futa Toro (in the middle Senegal River), Sine, Saloum and around Kajoor and Bawol. Traders also acquired rice from the Gambia and Casamance regions, where the rains were more abundant and rice yields were higher than in northern Senegambia.

Women were important producers of grains.¹⁶ Rice was a principal crop for the Mandinka and Jola, and women played a crucial role in its production. Before cash-crop production expanded in the second half of the nineteenth century, agriculture was highly gendered. While Mandinka men cultivated *basso* (Guinea corn), *findo,* sorghum, millet and maize, women cultivated rice.¹⁷ We do not know when rice farming in Mandinka societies became an important female activity, but it certainly remained important for many Mandinka women for centuries. Even when peanut production took off in the 1840s, women continued to cultivate their fields. Ownership of the peanut farms was confined to the male members of the family, just as ownership of the *faro* (or fields) continued to be in the hands of the women. According to Reverend John Morgan, the cultivation of rice devolved on the women, who dug

---

[10] Francis Moore, *Travels into the Inland Parts of Africa* (London: J. Stagg, 1738), 90.

[11] *Toubab-nio* means white man's millet. Maize was brought to the region sometime in the sixteenth century. For more on grains, see Park, *Travels in the Interior of Africa,* 9.

[12] NRS, ARP (Annual Reports for the Provinces) 32/3 North Bank (1923–32), 6.

[13] Park, *Travels,* 9.

[14] Judith Carney, *Black Rice: The African Origins of Rice Cultivation in the Americas* (Cambridge, MA: Harvard University Press, 2001), 11.

[15] James F. Searing, *West African Slavery and Atlantic Commerce: The Senegal River Valley, 1700–1860* (Cambridge: Cambridge University Press, 1993), 85–7.

[16] See Olga F. Linares, 'From Tidal Swamp to Inland Valley: On the Social Organization of Wet Rice Cultivation among the Diola of Senegal', *Africa: Journal of the International African Institute* 51, no. 2 (1981): 557–95; Carney, *Black Rice*; Robert Baum, *Shrines of the Slave Trade: Diola Religion and Society in Precolonial Senegambia* (Oxford: Oxford University Press, 1999).

[17] Moore, *Travels into the Inland Parts of Africa,* 90.

the land when it was 'overspread with water, and sow[ed] the rice on the water'.[18]

Lack of mechanisation meant that cultivation of crops relied heavily on family labour, though slave labour was also used by those who could afford it. In the 1630s, Richard Jobson observed that people cultivated the land 'with their hands', which was 'painful and laborious'.[19] Mungo Park likewise noted: 'The application of animal labour to the purposes of agriculture is no where adopted; the plough, therefore, is wholly unknown. The chief implement used in husbandry is the hoe, which varies in form in different districts.'[20] In the 1820s, John Morgan pointed out that the people of the region had no knowledge of the 'use of horses or oxen in cultivating the land'.[21] Family and slave labour – the Mandinka used the term *dabadalu* to describe such a social unit – undertook the clearing, weeding, planting and harvesting of farmlands together. Often, young men assisted their male and female counterparts in tilling the land.[22]

Women and Land in Precolonial Gambian Society

The examples of West and West Central African women property owners discussed in this volume lend support to the work of Senegambian historians, demonstrating that some women accumulated wealth by purchasing or inheriting land and building houses.[23] Likewise Colleen Kriger's chapter in this volume tells the remarkable story of how a woman from the lower Gambia River rose from being a slave girl to become the widow of a Royal African Company agent and a property owner in her own right. My own chapter focuses on those women whose stories rarely made it into European documentary sources to show how, while the *kabilo*'s power over the distribution and manage-

---

[18] John Morgan, *Reminiscences of the Founding of a Christian Mission on the Gambia* (London: Wesleyan Mission House, 1864): 121.

[19] Richard Jobson, *The Golden Trade: Or, A Discovery of The River Gambra, and the Golden Trade of the Aethiopians* (London: Nicholas Okes, 1623), 158.

[20] Parks, *Travels*, 17.

[21] Morgan, *Reminiscences*, 121.

[22] Ibid, 121–2

[23] See Colleen Kriger, *Making Money: Life, Death and Early Modern Trade on Africa's Guinea Coast* (Athens: Ohio University Press, 2017); Hilary Jones, *The Métis of Senegal: Urban Life and Politics in French West Africa* (Bloomington and Indianapolis: Indiana University Press, 2013), 31, 40, 42; Lillian Ashcraft-Eason, '"She voluntarily hath come": A Gambian woman trader in colonial Georgia in the eighteenth century', in Paul E. Lovejoy (ed.) *Identity in the Shadow of Slavery*, (London and New York: Continuum, 2000), 202–21; George E. Brooks, 'The Signares of Saint-Louis and Goree: Women entrepreneurs in eighteenth century Senegal', in Nancy J. Hafkin and Edna G. Bay (eds) *Women in Africa: Studies in Social and Economic Change*, (Stanford, CA: Stanford University Press, 1976), 19–44.

ment of land was superior, control of land was not the sole prerogative of men.

The story of three local women may illustrate this. The first, Wuleng Jabbi Jarsey, features in oral accounts concerning Mandinka migration and settlement in the Gambia River region. Just before the arrival of the Mandinka migrants in Kombo, Jabbi, who was probably a Bainunka, ruled as the 'Queen of Sanyang'. Not only did she control Sanyang, but her people owned Kombo's land, which until the eighteenth century comprised extensive forests. As 'landlord' or host, she welcomed Karafa Yali Jatta, a noted Mandinka warrior and hunter from *tilibo* (meaning the 'east'), to settle there.[24] He founded Busumbala, which eventually became the capital of a new polity called Kombo. After Yali and Jabbi struck a marriage alliance between their families, Yali's family gained access to the land. In sum, this account tells the story of a man who came into the region as a stranger, and later joined the political class that founded and ruled the Gambian Mandinka state of Kombo. It is a well-established oral tradition recited by griots in Kombo.

The 'king list' of the Mandinka state of Niumi, located on the Gambia's north bank, includes thirteen 'muso mansa' (female rulers).[25] While the authenticity of such lists is hard to establish, research published in the last two decades indicates that many precolonial West and West Central African societies had female rulers. Where women did not rule the states, they performed roles similar to what Ifi Amadiume has called 'male daughters'. For instance, the marriage between Madibba Bojang (the daughter of the Kombo king) and a noted Muslim cleric from Pakao (the middle Casamance region) enabled that marabout, Moriba Ceesay, to found his own village, Mandinari, on the Gambia's south bank,[26] as well as allowing him to be exempted from paying taxes or tribute to the rulers of Kombo, who were at this time based in Yundum. Around the 1850s or 1860s, a similar marriage occurred between Jebu Sonko, daughter of the ruler of Niumi, Mansa Demba Sonko, and Masamba Koke Jobe, a warrior from the Wolof state of Kajoor. After the marriage, King Demba Sonko permitted Masamba to establish his village in the Toubabkolong forest known as Bantang Killing.[27]

Another prominent woman, Fatou Jobba (Jim) Bah, owned land and over thirty slaves.[28] Jobba was the daughter of Maba Bah and a sister of

---

[24] *Alkalo* Bakary Kutu Jatta, interview with Bakary Sidebe; Alhagie Bai Kunteh, 'History of Kombo', RDD tape catalogue #321 (1976).
[25] Donald Wright, interview with Ansumana Sonko and Karamo Sonko, Badume, Jarra, 20 January 1975 (Donald Wright papers, 1–59, Michigan State University Libraries).
[26] Alhagie Faa Ceesay, interview, Mandinari, Kombo, Western Region, 8 August 2008.
[27] Alhagie Mangkodou Sarr, interview, Kerr Cherno, Upper Niumi (2006); Imam Alhagie Momodou Lamin Bah, interview, Serrekunda, 30 June 2006.
[28] Imam Alhagie Momodou Lamin Bah, interview, Serrekunda, 30 June 2006.

Ibra Mariam – one of Maba's sons who founded the village of Pakao Ngogu in Upper Niumi.[29] At Medina, where she was married and worked as a local trader, she acquired a plot of land at the *faro*. She was also a *jeefulbe* – a nickname for Fula women who had many cattle. She used her slaves to cultivate her peanut and cotton fields. In some ways, Madibba Bojang, Jebu Sonko and Fatou Jobba are similar to women in Nnobi, south-eastern Nigeria, who owned land as 'male daughters'. By virtue of their birth they had been accorded the right to own land. It seems they were safeguarding their father's lineage and the property associated with it.[30]

Mandinka women were often given rice farms as part of their dowry, making marriage another route to land accumulation.[31] If the woman's husband's family did not have land to give her, she often acquired a plot from her father. A woman could continue

> to enjoy the right of use of her father's rice farms after her marriage, possibly in a neighbouring village; the woman's daughters who bear their father's name then continue to use this same land with the result that the mother's family is in danger of losing all interest in it, unless they continually reiterate their claim.[32]

Wuleng Jabbi Jarsey, Jebu Sonko and Fatou Jobba had influence as members of the *bankotiyolu* ('lords of the land', or landlords) because they came from elite families. They controlled both land and labour and commanded a great deal of respect. Although separated by over a century, Fatou Jobba's story is similar to that of the many *signares* of Senegambia who had property.

Jola women too cultivated upland rice farms and had considerable control over such lands. The upland rice fields depended on rainfall, though Jola men also constructed ridges to capture and store water for irrigation. While men used the *kajando*, a farm implement with a long handle, to construct the ridges, women followed to plant the rice seedlings. Jola women living in communities around the Bintang *bolong* (river), the Urambang Creek, the Brefet Creek and nearby swamps also utilised

---

[29] Maba was one of the jihadists who waged war against the rulers of Baddibu, Niumi, Saloum, Sine and Kajoor in the mid-nineteenth century. For more on Maba, see Philip D. Curtin, *Economic Change in Precolonial Africa: Senegambia in the Era of the Slave Trade* (Madison: University of Wisconsin Press, 1975), 57–8.
[30] Ife Amadiume, *Male Daughters, Female Husbands: Gender and Sex in an African Society* (London and New Jersey: Zed Books, 1987), 34.
[31] Kenneth Swindell and Alieu Jeng, *Migrants, Credit and Climate: The Gambian Groundnut Trade, 1834–1934* (Leiden and Boston: Brill, 2006), 84.
[32] NRS, CSO 10/71, Letter from Commissioner North Bank Province (hereafter CNBP) to Colonial Secretary, Bathurst, 26 June 1942.

rice swamps, just as Mandinka women did.[33] Unlike Mandinka families, however, Jola households were much smaller and land was much more individuated. In Foni, Jola women inherited land which they passed on to their daughters.[34] According to Banna Sanneh,

> women owned land just as men in ancient Jola society and rice cultivation was a major subsistence farming system. Women owned the swampy lands, locally called 'Bitab'. Mothers trained their daughters how to cultivate rice cultivation and this was necessary for the purpose of inheritance and ensuring a sustainable livelihood.[35]

Kenneth Swindell and Alieu Jeng note that rice land could be kept within a man's compound when husbands gave the rice farms of their mothers to their wives.[36] However, as seen above, many women also inherited rice swamps from their mothers. As explained in one report, 'rice swamps and the right of use descends in the female line … [I]f a woman marries out of the village, if her new home is not far away, she will continue to cultivate her own rice farm in her natal village.'[37] In practice, the land would continue to be the property of the woman (and by consequence her husband's family) so long as the marriage was in force and the woman had children who could inherit from her after she died. Ownership of such land could be a factor of conflict not just between the families but also between their villages when a divorce occurred.

An important piece of oral history documented by the Colonial Secretary's office in 1942 states that the ownership of rice fields had in the past been 'more or less perpetual … and the right of use descended in the female line. If a woman married out of the village and if her new home was not too far away, she often continued to cultivate her own rice farm in her natal village.'[38] The control of these rice fields, as noted by one European observer in the early twentieth century, 'nearly approximated lands held as freehold property'.[39] Often, these rice fields were 'jealously guarded' and 'from time to time, cases of dispute [over rice fields] … are brought before the courts of the province.'[40] Since paddies are productive for generations, Jola and especially Mandinka villagers valued their rice fields. There was also a stronger sense of memory built around percep-

---

[33] The Bintang *bolong* is one of the main tributaries of the River Gambia situated on the western side of the Gambia's south bank. It was one of the natural barriers that divided Foni from the Mandinka state of Kiang.
[34] Lamin Jatta, interview, Dassilami-Kombo, 14 July 2016.
[35] Banna Sanneh, interview, Brikama, 15 July 2016.
[36] Swindell and Jeng, *Migrants, Credit and Climate*, 85.
[37] NRS, CSO 10/71, Letter from CNBP to Colonial Secretary, Bathurst, 26 June 1942.
[38] Ibid.
[39] Ibid.
[40] Ibid.

tions of ownership than in areas where shifting cultivation tended to be the norm.

Along the river banks and behind the mangroves lie broad swamps, flooded by fresh water from the Gambia River. These swamps, commonly called the '*banta faros*', were also much used for planting rice. In Mandinka, the upland rice fields, located around or near creeks or marshes,[41] are often referred to as *tendako* (*tandako* in Jola)[42]; the tidal saline and freshwater swamps where wet or paddy rice grows are known as *bafaro* and *wamifaro* respectively.[43] Swamplands (locally known as *faros*) were valuable because they were well watered even during the long dry seasons. The Mandinka and Jola considered the swamps or floodplains the most fertile areas.

Most of the areas where rice was grown are lands which in the distant past were regularly flooded.[44] The Colonial Secretary's report mentioned above indicates that

> most of the areas where rice is … grown are lands which in the distant past were regularly inundated by the river and have slowly silted up until they are beyond the reach of tidal, and frequently river flood, effect. Commonly known as … *faros*, this marginal strip of land is divided up into irregularly shaped portions by low bunds made of weeds. These bunds act as boundaries and at the same time assist in holding rainfall water on the paddy fields.[45]

These details were recorded only in the mid-twentieth century by the district officer and commissioner but they seem to speak to its continuation into the colonial period. The commissioners were observant and often curious. Many devoted themselves fully to what they thought (however misguided some of their assumptions) was an operation that would benefit their subjects. As such, the commissioner's report had 'a historic and ethnographic' value.[46]

Some wealthy Fula and Wolof women were also able to own cattle, slaves and land. Although women of all social classes might own livestock, elite women were probably in a better position to accumulate property and

---

[41] NRS, ARP 28/1 Travelling Commissioner's Report, South Bank Province, 1894.
[42] Lamin Jatta, interview, Dassilami-Kombo, 14 July 2016.
[43] Carney and Watts, 'Disciplining Women? Rice, Mechanization, and the Evolution of Mandinka Gender Relations in Senegambia', *Signs* 16, no. 4 (1991): 654; Webb, 'Ecological and Economic Change', 547; Carney and Watts, 'Disciplining Women?', 654.
[44] K.W. Blackburne, Development and Welfare in the Gambia; Sessional Paper no. 2, 1943.
[45] Ibid.
[46] Alice Bellagamba, 'Slavery and Emancipation in the Colonial Archives: British Officials, Slave-Owners, and Slaves in the Protectorate of the Gambia (1890–1936)', *Canadian Journal of African Studies / Revue Canadienne des Études Africaines* 39, no. 1 (2005): 14.

inherit land and slaves. They were mostly descended from those who had either first settled important villages or assumed political authority through conquest. In Senegambian societies, the founding of a village was an important step in establishing authority.[47] It was a manifestation of independence.[48] Aja Kaddy Njie, a descendant of the Sonko royal family of Niumi, told me that her grandmother, who might have been Fatou Jobba's contemporary, owned many rice fields in Essau and Bakindik villages. Upon her death, she passed on these rice *faros* to her daughters (one of them was Njie's mother).[49] Aja Takko Taal, the *alkalo* (village head) of Juffure village, likewise told me the history of her ancestors who founded her village. From the times of her ancestors, women in her family had inherited the rice fields, as they still do today.[50] In Bambali too, Aja Tida Touray claimed that in her family women, not men, inherited and controlled the rice fields.[51]

Changes from the Mid-nineteenth Century

By the beginning of the 1880s, women appear to have lost much of the privileged access to land that they had previously enjoyed. In many ways, women's loss of control over rice fields speaks to another level of disruption that came with the change to cash-crop peanut production. When this started, women began to work to supplement the earnings of their husbands and lost some of their economic independence. As peanut production expanded, virtually all of the resources of a family (the labour, money for the seeds and agricultural inputs such as the animals and the animal-drawn implements) were invested in it. This led to the neglect and marginalisation of rice farming. Rice was no longer the 'king's crop'.[52]

While the *basso* and *kinto* harvests were very good in the latter half of the nineteenth century, these grains had ceased to be cultivated widely by Mandinka and other farmers. For growing peanuts men preferred lands located in the *jeeri* (upland areas), which made it more difficult for women rice growers to access their *faros*.[53] Many villages near the river with access to the swamps also abandoned their old sites in favour of locations near the main roads or the peanut trading centres – 'wharf towns' such as Kaur, Kansalla and Sami Wharf Town. For example, in the last decades of the 1800s, the *alkalo* and

---

[47] Cheikh Anta Babou, *Fighting the Greater Jihad: Amadu Bamba and the Founding of the Muridiyya of Senegal, 1853–1913* (Athens: Ohio University Press, 2007), 69.
[48] Ibid., 36
[49] Aja Kaddy Njie, interview, Essau, Lower Niumi, 15 June 2006.
[50] Aja Tako Taal, *Alkalo*, Juffure village, Upper Niumi, interview, 23 July 2006.
[51] Aja Tida Touray, Bambali village, Sabach-Sanjal, 21 April 2008.
[52] Here I borrow Ugo Nwokeji's phrase. For more on this see, G. Ugo Nwokeji, 'African conceptions of Gender and the Slave Traffic', *William and Mary Quarterly* LVIII (2001): 47–69.
[53] The Mandinka refer to the *jeeri* as *santo*.

imam of Panchang led their people in establishing a new town called Makka or New Panchang, abandoning the village's old site.[54] In consequence, the rice growers and custodians of the rice fields were now forced to walk several miles every day to their fields. This probably served as a disincentive for many women to cultivate their rice fields.

While none of the early nineteenth-century sources indicate women's ownership of land among the Mandinka, a close reading of some of the oral sources suggests that the shift from rice cultivation to peanuts significantly impacted women's rights to own rice fields, albeit gradually. The rapid Islamisation of the region also affected inheritance practices and intensified long-standing conflicts which threatened women's access to land in southern Senegambia[55] Moreover, the political and social fragmentation that accompanied the mid-nineteenth century jihads put pressure on communities to find ways to try to defend those lands where their women farmed.

One of the first such conflicts over the control of rice fields occurred in the north bank village of Sikka, partly because of tensions between the Muslims and the Soninke population of the village. The Soninke had monopolised control of both land and power; but by the 1860s this monopoly was being challenged by Muslim elements in the village population. The British, who saw these as a threat, intervened in 1866, attacking the Muslims and driving them out of the town. Within a year, Foday Sonko, a native of Sikka and a Muslim, returned to seize control of the village. He commanded his blacksmiths to 'rebuild the stockade' and gave permission to the women of Sikka to cultivate rice on 'their old ground'.[56] In June 1867, the British administrator Admiral Patey summoned Sonko and his chief marabout, Cherno Say, to Albreda for a meeting. Sonko refused to meet Patey, and so superintendent Richard A. Stewart travelled the four miles from Albreda to Sikka. According to Stewart, Sonko told him that he had returned to his own father's land and could not travel to meet the Governor, because he was 'hungry' and working hard on his land.[57] Sonko insisted that 'Sicca was the land of their forefathers [and] they had no wish to leave it.'[58] Stewart wrote numerous letters seeking intervention from Bathurst (the capital, later Banjul), but

---

[54] NRS, ARP 32 (Vol. 1 North Bank 1893–1898) Travelling Commissioner Reports – North Bank (60).
[55] For how Islam transformed inheritance, see Youssouf Guèye, 'Essai sur les causes et les conséquences de la micropropriété au Fouta Toro', Bulletin de l'I. F.A.N. XIX, sér. B, no. 3 1–2 (1957), 98; Boubacar Barry, Senegambia and the Atlantic Slave Trade (Cambridge: Cambridge University Press, 1998), 27.
[56] NRS, Banjul, CSO 1/14, Administrator in Chief's letter, Government House, Bathurst, Gambia, 31 August 1867.
[57] NRS, CSO 1/14, Extract of a letter from Richard A Stewart, Corporal of Police, to His Excellency Major Anton, Acting Administrator, British Albreda, 29 June 1867; NRS, CSO 1/14, Letter from British Albreda, 13 July 1867, Richard A. Stewart, Corporal of Police.
[58] Ibid.

the Governor advised him 'not to make any dispute but to live in peace with the marabouts'.[59]

In the 1870s and 1880s, conflicts threatened the ability of women in Sarrakunda to access their 'traditional' rice swamps. Residents of the village claimed that the land was seized from them with the help of Biran Ceesay: 'the Sarrakunda people are trying to get back some of the farms at Tendito [Tandaito village] which belonged to their ancestors and were taken away from them in the war with Biram Sisi.'[60] Biran Ceesay, one of Maba Bah's generals and a native of the commercial town of Kaur, had become important after the death of Maba in 1867 and during the civil war in Baddibu (1877–85).[61] Around the same time that Ceesay seized Sarrakunda's rice fields, Sarrakunda was on the verge of losing other parts of its land to people residing in the village of Kumbija. According to the commissioner's report of 1898, the land in question had originally belonged to the father of the *alkalo* of Sarrakunda, but 'in one of the small wars, this Alcaide's father was driven out of the town and had to seek refuge elsewhere'. Subsequently, the land fell into the hands of Chief Nderri Raumi, a Wolof chief residing in neighbouring French Senegal, who leased it to the *alkalo* of Kumbija. When the French administration of Senegal recalled Raumi, the *alkalo* of Kumbija appropriated the land and worked it without interference. The land encompassed about half an acre and was located outside the town of Kumbija, two miles from Sarrakunda. Commissioner Ozanne noted that it was a good spot for houses and several people were anxious to build on it.

These two land disputes re-emerged shortly after Commissioner Ozanne was appointed to administer the newly created North Bank Province in 1893. Upon hearing of the commissioner's appointment, the *alkalo* of Sarrakunda 'sent one of his wives to work a farm belonging to Tendito and the Alcaide of Tendito took away her hoe and sent her back'. Tension between the two villages forced Ozanne to instruct 'the Alcaide of Sarrakundu that we could not make the people give up lands that had been given to them by Biram Sisi and worked by them for some years'.[62] In June 1892, the Sarrakunda's *alkalo* also 'put in his claim' for the land seized by Kumbija.[63]

The question of women's inheritance also lay at the heart of a long-standing quarrel that erupted at the end of the nineteenth century between the south bank villages of Jattaba and Sankandi after a Sankandi woman,

---

[59] NRS, CSO 1/14 Essau, Barra Point, 30 August 1867 by Sumar of Essau.
[60] NRS, Banjul, ARP 32 Travelling Commissioner Reports – North Bank, 1893–1932 (60).
[61] Charlotte A. Quinn, *Mandingo Kingdoms of the Senegambia: Traditionalism, Islam, and European Expansion* (Evanston, IL: Northwestern University Press, 1972), 195.
[62] NRS, Banjul, ARP 32/1 Travelling Commissioner Reports – North Bank, 1893–1932 (60).
[63] NRS, ARP 32/1 (Vol. 1 North Bank 1893–1898) Travelling Commissioner Reports, 1893–98.

Mariama Darboe, went to marry Lang Seyfo, a man in the village of Jattaba.⁶⁴ Mariama had been given the land as a gift from her parents upon her marriage. According to custom, she was expected to use the land to cultivate rice to support her new family, Lang Seyfo's family in Jattaba. However, tradition claims that she conceived no children during her marriage. When she died, her uncle in Sankandi requested return of the land, noting that it had only been lent to her for the support of her family. But Lang Seyfo's family declined to give it back, arguing that they were not aware of how the rice field had become the property of the Darboe family of Sankandi.

Mansa Koto was the chief of the newly created district at the time of the dispute. As such, when the dispute intensified in 1899, Mansa Koto and his elders, Tumani Messeng and Bakary Kumba Santang, held a meeting in Sankandi. It was decided that the land belonged to Jattaba; but the people of Sankandi rejected the verdict,⁶⁵ insisting that the land was theirs and that they were determined to 'go to war' if it was not restored to them. A year later, the dispute was referred to the British commissioner, Sitwell, who according to oral sources from Sankandi, gave his judgement in favour of Jattaba.⁶⁶ Some say, however, that during his first judgement, the commissioner had ruled that use of the disputed property should be rotated between the two villages: Sankandi would use it for a year, then pass it on to Jattaba for use the following year. At any rate, Dari Bana Darboe, Sankandi's *alkalo*, and his close associates, again refused to accept Sitwell's proposal. In the end, the commissioner travelled to Sankandi to deal with the problem in person, accompanied by Assistant Commissioner Silva, Mansa Koto and six police constables. When they arrived, they ordered the village elders to meet them on the outskirts of the village to discuss the problem. This outraged the elders of Sankandi, who believed that Mansa Koto and the European commissioner did not accord them appropriate respect, because the proper place to settle a problem was in a *bantango* or *bantaba* (village meeting ground).⁶⁷ The village elders of Sankandi employed a blacksmith, Bollo Jobe, to mix gunpowder in preparation for conflict.

---

⁶⁴ In Sankandi, the Darboe *kabilo* are among the founder lineages of the village. They were the holders of the title of Alkali in Sankandi. By virtue of their position in the Sankandi community they controlled a lot of land. See National Centre for Arts & Culture, Banjul (hereafter NCAC), tape recording, Battelling, Kiang West, Lower River Region, 3 November 2001: transcription of interview available at the RDD collection in Fajara as Tape No. 5178. RDD is the section of the NCAC's Research and Documentation Division where all the oral history collections of the Centre are kept.
⁶⁵ RDD collection in Fajara as Tape No. 5177, NCAC staff, tape recording, Jattaba, Kiang West, Lower River Region, 3 November 2001.
⁶⁶ Government Publications Relating to the Gambia (Colonial Annual Report, 1901), Michigan State University Library.
⁶⁷ For more on *bentang*, see Mungo Park, *Travels*, 19.

With the gunpowder in hand, the men of Sankandi lay in ambush, waiting for the commissioner's entourage.[68] When he attempted to use force against the defiant population of Sankandi, the commissioner, his assistant, and the six police constables were murdered. Mansa Koto too sustained severe injuries and died later.

Foday Kabba Dumbaya, the man who waged a 'holy war' against numerous communities in Kombo, Foni and Kiang, took advantage of the conflict. In January 1901, the British sent a large expeditionary force from Sierra Leone with the mission to 'punish the towns implicated in the murder of the two travelling commissioner[s] and six constables in the previous year'.[69] Many of the village residents sought refuge in Medina Suumakunda, where Foday Kabba had his capital at the time, but Dari Bana Darboe and two others from the village of Sankandi were caught by the French near the border and handed over to the British, who tried and executed them. In the end, the British suppressed the dispute and it is not clear if the land issue was resolved, although in most cases the disputes over rice swamps that arose from time to time were mediated by elders while some led to spiritual fights where parties employed diviners and sorcerers to harm one another.[70]

These conflicts and the growth of peanut cultivation do, though, appear to have exacerbated women's loss of access to land. The nineteenth and twentieth centuries brought tremendous changes to women's power and standing in society. By the twentieth century, women had lost many of the rights they once had: 'land cannot be held by females'.[71] Another twentieth-century source states, 'No female holds any lands in her own right. They always work the rice fields but neither the land nor its fruits are considered their personal property; all is the property of the husband.'[72] And among the Jola, 'no female holds any lands in her own right', though they continued to cultivate the rice fields. All farms belonged to the male head, called *alefanow* or the 'big man' of the stockade.

Conclusion

As this chapter has shown in relation to the Gambia, the ability of women to gain access or control to land was often challenged in the latter half of the nineteenth century. From the mid-nineteenth century women's ability to access 'traditional swamplands' began to weaken due to a shift

---

[68] Government Publications Relating to the Gambia (Colonial Annual Report, 1901), Michigan State University Library.
[69] Ibid.
[70] Jali Ngali Mbye, interview, Brikama, 31 October 2015.
[71] NRS, CSO 2/94-The Laws and Customs of the Mandingoes of the North Bank, 1906.
[72] NRS, CSO 10/71, Letter from CNBP to Colonial Secretary dated 26 June 1942.

in the regional economy, which changed from grain cultivation to cash-crop farming. Following this change, many rice-producing villages relocated from the swamps to the inland *jeeri*, which were ideal for the peanut crop but meant women's power declined. This points to the importance of geographical mobility and shifting power dynamics among African women in Atlantic Africa, reflecting on key themes of this volume. The transformation was part of a broader shift from slave trading to an economic system based on exchanging non-slave items. It had important consequences for many Mandinka and Jola women in rural villages.

54 • Property

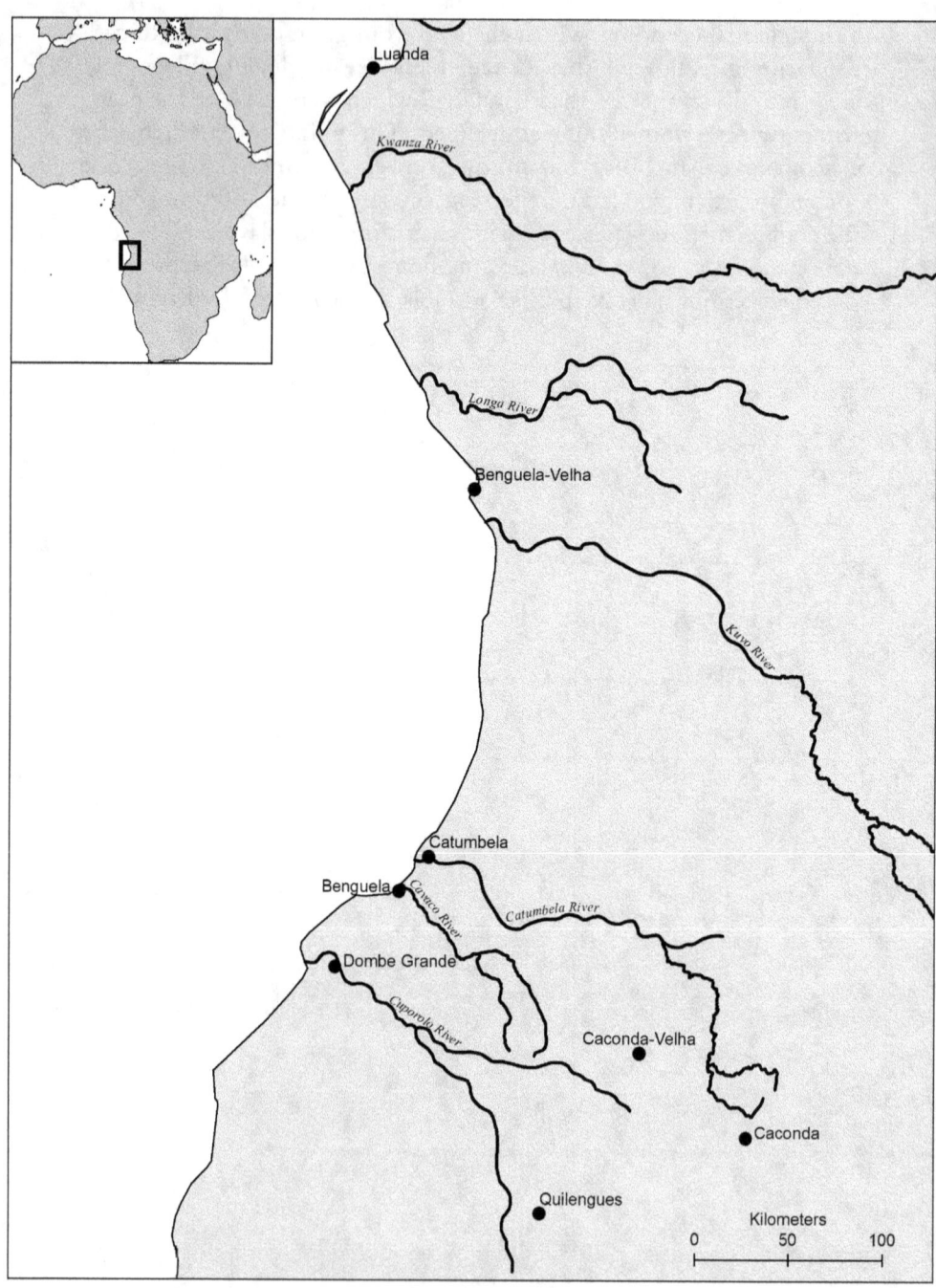

Map 4 West Central Africa, 1850
(Source: Center for Digital Scholarship, University of Notre Dame, 2017)

3

Women & Food Production
Agriculture, Demography & Access to Land in Late Eighteenth-Century Catumbela[1]

ESTEBAN A. SALAS

Dona Joana Ribeiro enjoyed extensive access to land and agricultural production in late eighteenth-century Catumbela – on the bank of the Catumbela River, some three miles from the Atlantic coast and some 10 miles north of Benguela (see Map 4 'West Central Africa, 1850'). She had four plots of land and three farms, where she produced 98 *cazongueis* – totalling around 3,234 lb (pounds) – of maize (corn) and beans in 1798. These numbers surpassed the average of 2,515 lb of crops generated per farmer in Catumbela in the same year.[2] Dona Joana belonged to a group of elite African women – one-third of the landowners – who accumulated wealth through access to land, control of dependants and agricultural production in the *presídio* (interior administrative outpost) of Catumbela.[3] Yet the ability

---

[1] This chapter was made possible thanks to the Luso-American Foundation, which supported my research in the Arquivo Nacional Torre do Tombo (ANTT) – the Portuguese National Archive – in Lisbon in 2016. My special gratitude to Dr Miguel Vaz, director of the Luso-American Foundation, Dr Silvestre Lacerda, director of the Arquivo Nacional Torre do Tombo, and Drs José Furtado and Maria dos Remédios Amaral. The Department of History of the University of Notre Dame awarded me a grant for archival research in the Arquivo Histórico Ultramarino (AHU) in Portugal.

[2] The *cazonguel* (plural *cazongueis*) was a unit of measurement used in Angola, Brazil and Portugal that meant different volumes in each of these places. In Angola two *cazongueis* equaled half an *exeque*, another measurement in the Lusophone Atlantic; see Joseph Miller, *Way of Death: Merchant Capitalism and the Angolan Slave Trade, 1730–1830* (Madison: University of Wisconsin Press, 1988), 415–17. An *exeque* equaled 132 lb or about 60 kg; this measure was used for grains; see José Carlos Venâncio, *A economia de Luanda e hinterland no século XVIII: um estudo de sociologia histórica* (Lisbon: Editorial Estampa, 1996), 56; Vanessa Oliveira, 'Gender, Foodstuff Production and Trade in Late-Eighteenth Century Luanda', *African Economic History* 43 (2015): 57.

[3] A similar case of a woman with access to land and agricultural production in Catumbela was that of Catarina Pereira Lisboa, who had nine plots of land, eight farms and 361 *cazongueis* of production. Dona Catarina did not reside in Catumbela but in Benguela, where she developed links with both the transatlantic slave trade and the colonial state; see Mariana Candido, *An African Slaving Port and the Atlantic World: Benguela and Its Hinterland* (New York: Cambridge

of African women to control land or food production did not constitute their main economic role in Catumbela: more important was their participation as labourers in agricultural production. Most of them were in a situation of economic dependency, often including slavery. Women represented two-thirds of the total number of free and enslaved dependants – i.e. either free or enslaved people whose labour was controlled by people with access to land. The higher number of women than men in this central economic activity supports the thesis that villages like Catumbela were immersed in the supply of enslaved people, mostly men, for the transatlantic slave trade, despite the fact that they were located in coastal areas.[4] In addition, this chapter shows that access to land consolidated rights and the accumulation of dependent labour, despite the lack of land titles. Some African women were able to benefit from land distribution.

Scholars interested in women's agency in pre-colonial and colonial Africa have paid attention to agricultural and other types of production in the private and public spheres.[5] Scholars have tended to generalise the predominant role of women in agricultural production, blurring the power distinctions entailed in the different activities involved. This chapter examines women's and men's control of dependents, access to land and agricultural production in Catumbela, as well as their personal connections in Benguela. I distinguish between women who were dependants and women who had access to land and labourers and controlled food production. Women did not constitute a homogeneous group in Catumbela and, moreover, there was a disparity between women's and men's opportunities to accumulate wealth.

Catumbela constituted the main supplier of foodstuffs for Benguela, which in tandem with its interior and coastal areas became the third-largest port of the transatlantic slave trade in the late eighteenth century.[6]

(contd) University Press, 2013), 263; Mariana Candido, 'Género, classificações, e comércio, as donas de Benguela, 1750–1850', *Actas do III Encontro Internacional de História de Angola* 2, no. 1 (2015): 264–5.

[4] Candido, *An African Slaving Port and the Atlantic World*.

[5] Jean Marie Allman, Susan Geiger and Nakanyike Musisi, *Women in African Colonial Histories* (Bloomington: Indiana University Press, 2002); Edna Bay, *Wives of the Leopard: Gender, Politics and Culture in the Kingdom of Dahomey* (Charlottesville: University of Virginia Press, 1998); Philip Havik, *Silences and Soundbytes: The Gendered Dynamics of Trade and Brokerage in the Pre-Colonial Guinea-Bissau Region* (Münster: LIT, 2004); Emily Lynn Osborn, *Our New Husbands Are Here: Households, Gender, and Politics in a West African State from the Slave Trade to Colonial Rule* (Athens: Ohio University Press, 2011); Mariana Candido and Eugénia Rodrigues, 'African Women's Access and Rights to Property in the Portuguese Empire', *African Economic History* 43 (2015).

[6] Candido, *Fronteras de esclavización*, 103. West Central Africa was the region with the highest export of slaves during the late eighteenth century. Of more than 12.5 million enslaved people from Africa who arrived in the Americas between 1501 and 1876, more than 2 million were delivered between 1776 and 1800; see David Eltis and Martin Halbert, 'The Transatlantic Slave Trade Database', consulted 29 January 2017, www.slavevoyages.org; Candido, *An African Slaving Port*, 152. The debate on the roles of African ports in the transformation of African societies has paid special attention to relations between coastal and interior areas with the aim of transcending

The slave trade involved the internal transformation of African societies, drawing them into the dynamics of the Atlantic world.[7] There are some cases of urban centres relying on agricultural production in the interior to supply their residents and people in transit, such as Ouidah, Lagos, Little Popo, and Luanda. The agricultural production of Catumbela served to supply the residents of the *presídio*, Benguela, as well as the caravans moving between the coast and the interior with enslaved Africans as well as ivory, wax and other commodities.[8] Catumbela benefited from having easy access to land and dependants, along with permanent access to water.[9] Like other towns such as Caconda and Quilengues, it constituted an entrepôt due to its multiple economic activities.[10] Joseph Miller describes Catumbela as a 'lesser peripheral outlet used mostly for smuggling', located on one of the routes of trade of slaves brought from the hinterland of Benguela.[11] Salt-mine production also stood out as an important activity of Catumbela, at least from the 1760s, when the colonial government monopolised that business.[12]

Due to its location near the Catumbela River, the place was also an important military outpost. In terms of political administration, Catumbela was an interior *presídio* at the end of the eighteenth century. The name of the colonial administrator, the *Capitão-Mor*, does not feature in any records from this period; yet the Benguela administration tried to maintain tight control over inland markets such as Catumbela, resulting in a series of documents like the *Relação de Moradores de Catumbela*.[13] Just

---

(contd) the understanding of the agency of Africans during this period as being determined solely by their interactions with Europeans. Other key works for this topic are: Robin Law, *Ouidah: The Social History of a West African Slaving 'Port', 1727–1892* (Athens: Ohio University Press, 2004); Kristin Mann, *Slavery and the Birth of an African City: Lagos, 1760–1900* (Bloomington: Indiana University Press, 2007).

[7] For more on the role of the transatlantic slave trade in the transformation of African societies, see Paul Lovejoy, *Transformations in Slavery: A History of Slavery in Africa* (New York: Cambridge University Press, 1983). See David Northrup, *Trade without Rulers: Pre-Colonial Economic Development in South-Eastern Nigeria* (Oxford: Clarendon Press, 1978); Mann, 'African and European Initiatives'; Strickrodt, *Afro-European Trade in the Atlantic World*; Oliveira, 'The Donas of Luanda, c. 1770–1867: From Atlantic Slave Trading to "Legitimate" Commerce'; Oliveira, 'Gender, Foodstuff Production and Trade'.

[8] Arquivo Histórico Ultramarino (AHU), Angola, Cx. 88, D. 58.

[9] Biblioteca Nacional do Rio de Janeiro (BNRJ), I-28, 28, 29; AHU, Angola, Cx. 93A, D. 11, November 6, 1799.

[10] For the political reconfiguration of Caconda during Portuguese colonial rule see Candido, *An African Slaving Port*, Chapter 5.

[11] Miller, *Way of Death*, 208.

[12] AHU, Angola, Caixa (Cx.) 88, Document (D.) 58, December 3, 1798, f. 15; Arquivo Nacional da Torre do Tombo (ANTT), Ministério do Reino, Maço (Mç.) 606, Document (D.) 20, 1768.

[13] The *Relação de Moradores de Catumbela*, a list of the residents collected in 1797, contains the names, gender and civil status of the people who had access to land and their dependants who laboured in agricultural production, IHGB (Instituto Histórico Geográfico Brasileiro), DL32, 02, 07, 'Relação de Moradores de Catumbela', 1798.

the year before the collection of the *Relação,* a source identified Catumbela as a *sobado vassalo* (vassal chiefdom).[14] Perhaps the entire area was changing status back and forth as the colonial forces and local African rulers disputed control of the territory. In the 1840s Catumbela was still a sobado vassalo, which entailed continuity in the legal condition of Catumbela as being under Portuguese colonial rule. At that time, the soba Francisco Pedro de Moraes ruled Catumbela.[15] In the first half of the eighteenth century the governor and general captain of Angola called Catumbela 'o reino de Catumbela' – the Kingdom of Catumbela, but the accuracy of this title remains doubtful.[16] Here I will exclusively examine the *presídio*'s population located on the Catumbela River, and not the chiefdoms or *sobado* states located nearby.

People with Access to Land and their Dependants

Women performed most of the agricultural labour in the production of foodstuffs for domestic consumption and local trade in several places in Atlantic Africa both within and outside areas under colonial administration.[17] Travellers also observed women's economic roles, as can be seen in Illustration 2. Some scholars have emphasised the gendered dimension of the transatlantic slave trade as one of the main reasons for the gendered nature of agricultural production. A majority of the enslaved people sent out of West Central Africa in the late eighteenth and early nineteenth centuries were men, while most of those who remained and continued to work as agricultural labourers were women.[18] This was less the case for a port like Benguela, where in 1797 women represented 61 per cent of the total population and only 53 per cent in the following year.[19] Benguela

[14] ANTT, Ministério do Reino, Mç. (Maço) 604, Document (D.) 5, 1796. For the definition of *sobado* as chiefdom – *Häuptlingstum* – see: Beatrix Heintze, *Studien zur Geschichte Angolas im 16 und 17 Jahrhundert: ein Lesebuch* (Köln: Rüdiger Köppe, 1996), 73, 77–79.

[15] Candido, *An African Slaving Port and the Atlantic World*, 291.

[16] AHU, Angola, Cx. 23, D. 43, 10 June, 1726.

[17] Several authors have shown the central role of women in agricultural production in precolonial West Central Africa: John Thornton, 'The Slave Trade in Eighteenth Century Angola: Effects on Demographic Structures', *Canadian Journal of African Studies* 14, no. 3 (1980): 417–427; Linda Heywood, 'Production, Trade and Power: The Political Economy of Central Angola, 1850–1930' (Columbia University, 1984); Miller, *Way of Death*; Linda Heywood, *Contested Power in Angola, 1840s to the Present* (Rochester, NY: University of Rochester Press, 2000); José Curto and Raymond Gervais, 'The Population History of Luanda during the Late Atlantic Slave Trade, 1781–1844', *African Economic History* 29 (2001): 1–59; Oliveira, 'Gender, Foodstuff Production and Trade'; Vanessa Oliveira, 'The Donas of Luanda, c. 1770–1867: From Atlantic Slave Trading to "Legitimate" Commerce' (Toronto: York University, 2016).

[18] Thornton, 'The Slave Trade'; Miller, *Way of Death*, 136; Curto and Gervais, 'The Population History of Luanda', 29.

[19] Mariana Candido, *Fronteras de esclavización: esclavitud, comercio e identidad en Benguela, 1780–1850* (México D.F.: El Colegio de México, Centro de Estudios de Asia y África, 2011), 90.

Illustration 2 Woman in Angola pounding grain with a mortar and pestle and wearing bead necklaces and a bead headband
(Source: 'Muchicongos', Jean-Baptiste Douville, *Voyage au Congo et dans l'Afrique équinoxiale dans les années 1828, 1829 et 1830* (Paris: J. Renouard, 1832); Copy in Bibliothèque nationale de France)

was not primarily a place of agricultural production and had to import foodstuffs from Catumbela and nearby places. By the first decade of the nineteenth century only about 2 per cent of the total Benguela population worked in agricultural production.[20]

By contrast, in Catumbela the demographic imbalance between women and men can be attributed to the specialisation of this place in agricultural production. The *Relação* lists a total of 1,154 residents in Catumbela: 714 women and 440 men.[21] Women constituted 62 per cent of the population, while men accounted for the remaining 38 per cent.[22] Thus demographic and gender variations within the West-Central African population can only be understood if we pay attention to the interplay between places and populations.

Recently, the distinction between those who farmed and those who had control over the land has gained importance in the debate on women's participation in agricultural production.[23] The distinction between women with access to land and those who were dependants is crucial in understanding the varying degrees to which agriculture involved women in different places in Africa, as well as the multiple roles they performed. As Assan Sarr has shown, the concept of wealth-in-people can be helpful in understanding how societies in pre-colonial Africa regulated access to wealth through the distribution of land.[24] The more dependants a person with access to land controlled, the greater the chances of higher revenue and accumulation. Vanessa Oliveira distinguishes between producers and labourers in the case of Luanda, centring her analysis on the African women known as *donas*, who had access to land and control of dependants.[25] *Donas* played a central role in agricultural production and commercialisation, yet women's participation in agricultural production varied according to their social position and their opportunities of making use of land.

Dependants included enslaved and free people who provided labour. Although the sources are not explicit about this aspect, this category could even include relatives of the persons with control of dependants, as long as these relatives laboured in agricultural production.[26] A total of 186 people,

---

[20] Candido, *Fronteras de esclavización*, 103–4.
[21] Eight people were listed without an identified sex. I do not take them into account in the analysis of the differences between women and men.
[22] The *Relação* did not include the ages; therefore there is no indication of the extent of child labour in agricultural production.
[23] Northrup, *Trade without Rulers*, 214–23; Walter Hawthorne, *Planting Rice and Harvesting Slaves: Transformations along the Guinea-Bissau Coast, 1400–1900* (Portsmouth, NH: Heinemann, 2003), 159–71; Law, *Ouidah*, 76–77. Heywood has also made this case for the nineteenth century: Heywood, *Contested Power in Angola, 1840s to the Present*, 9, 41–5.
[24] Assan Sarr, 'Land, Power, and Dependency along the Gambia River, Late Eighteenth to Early Nineteenth Centuries', *African Studies Review* 57, no. 3 (2014): 101–21.
[25] Santos Oliveira, 'The Donas of Luanda, c. 1770–1867: From Atlantic Slave Trading to 'Legitimate' Commerce'.
[26] Sarr, 'Land, Power, and Dependency', 115.

i.e. 18 per cent of the Catumbela dependants, reported being in a condition of slavery; 70 per cent of them (numbering 127) were women.

One indication of the reliance on the labour of dependants in agricultural production was the fact that the *Relação* identified five men who reported that there was no agricultural production on their farms due to a lack of dependants.[27] Yet each of them had not only access to land but also the ownership of *arimos* (productive land plots); presumably they were engaged in subsistence and not in commercial farming. Clearly, the control of dependants was the key difference between agricultural production for subsistence and for making a profit.

Cases of subsistence farming without dependants were rare in Catumbela. Agricultural production for profit attracted free people with access to land more than other activities, leading them to refuse to do the work required by the colonial state in the salt mines. The state needed labourers to work in the salt mines, but free people claimed that the payment for that work amounted only to 'one tenth of half an *alqueire* [bushel] of manioc flour, one inch of tobacco, and a little bottle of alcohol', which made it unprofitable.[28] Free people ran away from the salt mines and returned to their land plots in order to keep producing crops. The colonial government of Benguela responded by forcing the Catumbela residents to make their enslaved people work in the mines. The demand for the labour of dependants in activities other than farming diminished the labour force available, and limited the opportunities for people with access to land in Catumbela to accumulate wealth through agricultural production.

Although women formed almost two-thirds of the workforce in Catumbela, most of them did not have control over dependants and were themselves dependants of wealthier residents (see Chart 1 'Agricultural Producers of Catumbela'). Most of the dependent population, 68.6 per cent or 661 persons, were women. In addition, women controlled fewer dependants than did men. Out of the 131 persons who controlled labour, only 40 (30.53 per cent) were women. Those with dependants had an average of 9.48 of them, but the average among women only was significantly lower, standing at only 7.48 dependants.

John Thornton has suggested that the higher number of women than men in coastal areas of West Central Africa was probably due to the gender imbalance of the transatlantic slave trade, and that, as a result, more women remained in the interior areas where people were subject to raids and enslavement.[29] These women would have stayed in the coastal areas after being displaced from their zones of origin but would not have been

---

[27] IHGB, 'Relação de Moradores de Catumbela', ff. 6, 14, 16v, 18v, 19.
[28] ANTT, Ministério do Reino, Mç. 604, Doc. 5.
[29] John Thornton, 'Sexual Demography: The Impact of the Slave Trade on Family Structure', in *Women and Slavery in Africa* (Portsmouth, NH: Heinemann, 1997), 39–48.

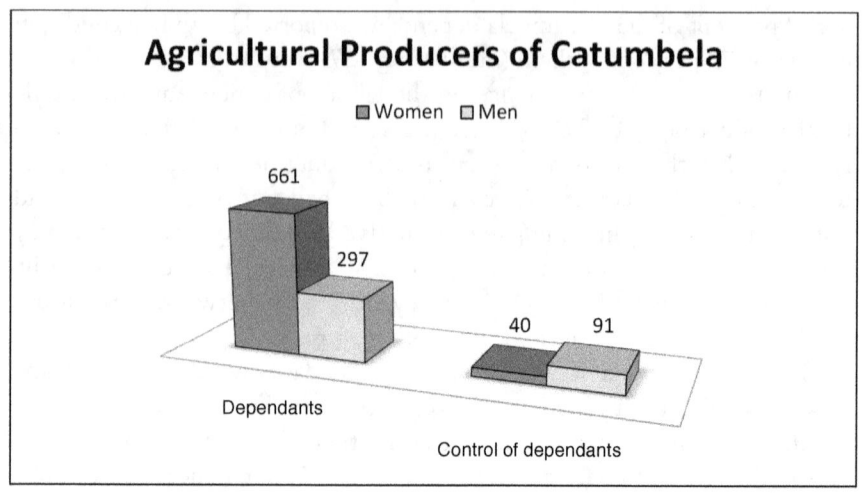

Chart 1 Agricultural Producers of Catumbela
(Source: Instituto Histórico Geográfico Brasileiro (IHGB), DL32, 02, 07,
'Relação de Moradores de Catumbela', 1798)

sent across the Atlantic. More recently, however, Mariana Candido and Daniel Domingues da Silva have shown that in this part of West Central Africa most of the people enslaved by the end of the eighteenth century originated from the coastal areas, contrary to the assumption that the slave frontier had moved further inland progressively.[30] The higher number of dependent women involved in agricultural production in Catumbela was related to the enslavement of men, but also to the ability of Catumbela residents to attract impoverished and landless peasants affected by warfare, raids and political instability in nearby places.

Access to Land and Agricultural Production

Along with the control of dependants, land access determined the wealth a person could accumulate in relation to agricultural production. Land occupation and farming had played a central economic role in the overseas territories of the Portuguese empire since the sixteenth century.[31] The Portuguese monarchy offered land grants to any Portuguese subject willing to cultivate and produce foodstuffs. A 1676 law stipulated that anyone willing to cultivate land could have access to land in the Portuguese-controlled 'Kingdom of Angola'. This law made it possible to expel

---

[30] Candido, *An African Slaving Port;* Daniel Domingues da Silva, *The Atlantic Slave Trade from West Central Africa, 1780–1867* (Cambridge: Cambridge University Press, 2017).
[31] Mariana Candido and Eugénia Rodrigues, 'African Women's Access and Rights to Property in the Portuguese Empire', *African Economic History* 43 (2015): 1–18.

local inhabitants who did not engage in farming and to withdraw land concessions previously made to colonial settlers who failed to make their plots productive within five years.[32] Implicit in the law was the removal of local communities from their own lands in order to make space available to Portuguese settlers. In this way, the colonial state positioned itself as the regulator of access to land in the territories under its nominal domain, and violence became a legitimate means of making the new rules effective. To maintain their rights over the land plots in late eighteenth-century Catumbela, African men and women and Portuguese settlers had to keep producing food and making their plots productive in accordance with colonial ideas regarding land use and occupation.

The notion of individual land tenure was not new to African colonial societies. The legal corpus for regulating land tenure existed in many colonial societies throughout Africa by the end of the eighteenth century, and some mechanisms had been developed to control the access of individuals to land within vassal territories.[33] Half a century ago, A. G. Hopkins argued that the commercialisation of land occurred significantly only after the prohibition of the transatlantic slave trade in the early nineteenth century and the consequent increase in cash-crop production.[34] This, however, was not the case all over the continent. Gareth Austin has argued that land ownership for the Asante was not a relevant issue, because what mattered was the control of the production that came out of the land concerned, and the rise of cash-crop production in the nineteenth century did not change this.[35] In some African societies the importance of private tenure of land had already increased before formal colonialism and the prohibition of the transatlantic slave trade. In some places communal land rights for extended families and chiefdoms had constituted indigenous frameworks for access to land, rather than remaining constrained to European conceptions of land ownership.[36] This assured the control of production in the hands of the politico-administrative lineage, serving as

---

[32] AHU, 'Index dos regimentos do governo e mais ordens expedidas para o Reino de Angola', February 12, 1676.

[33] Kristin Mann, 'Women, Landed Property, and the Accumulation of Wealth in Early Colonial Lagos', *Signs* 16, no. 4 (1991): 682–706; Eugénia Rodrigues, *Do Atlântico ao Índico: percursos da mandioca em Moçambique no século XVIII* (Maputo: Sociedades Costeiras, 1998); Mariana Candido, 'Conquest, Occupation, Colonialism and Exclusion: Land Disputes in Angola', in *Property Rights, Land and Territory in the European Oversees Empire* (Lisboa CEHC, ISCTE-IUL, 2014), 223–34; Sarr, *Islam, Power, and Dependency*.

[34] A. G. Hopkins, *An Economic History of West Africa* (New York: Columbia University Press, 1973), 126.

[35] Gareth Austin, *Labour, Land and Capital in Ghana: From Slavery to Free Labor in Asante, 1807–1956* (Rochester, NY: University of Rochester Press, 2005).

[36] Mann, *Slavery and the Birth of an African City*, 237–75; Kristin Mann, 'African and European Initiatives in the Transformation of Land Tenure in Colonial Lagos (West Africa), 1840–1920', in *Native Claims: Indigenous Law against Empire, 1500–1920*, ed. Saliha Belmessous (Oxford, 2011), 223–47; Northrup, *Trade without Rulers*, 11–12.

a base for the reproduction of political power.[37] Thus, different conceptions of land ownership flourished in West African societies according to the availability of lands for cultivation.

In colonial Angola, as Vanessa Oliveira has shown, people could own individual lands when they could prove that the land was productive.[38] The colonisation of territory in Angola started in the sixteenth century, and by the second half of the eighteenth century people in the interior supplied the public market with foodstuffs produced on their land.[39]

Although no documents exist recognising land in Catumbela as individual property, it is clear that access was restricted to those with the means to cultivate and with sufficient dependents for that purpose. As a territory under Portuguese colonial rule, Catumbela did not represent an exception to these regulations. Among the 1,162 residents of Catumbela, the *Relação* identified 223 people with access to land – less than one-fifth of the residents. Out of 222 land plots registered, 216 reported agricultural production. Only six plots did not report farming, but even these produced some crops.

The economic roles of women and men in agricultural production appeared similar in the intersection between access to land and control of dependants.[40] From the beginning of the seventeenth century, the Portuguese empire did not legally prevent women from having access to land in territories under colonial rule. The Portuguese *Ordenações Filipinas* established that 'women had rights of inheritance to family property as heirs and wives. Women owned half of the property held in marriage and at death, regardless of any will, daughters were entitled to an equal share of their parents' property'.[41] The *Ordenações* became the formal framework that made it possible for African women to gain access to individual land plots in Luanda, Benguela, Catumbela and elsewhere. In Catumbela, women represented only around one-third of the people with access to land, i.e. 70 women among the 223 people with land access (see Chart 2 'Access to land in Catumbela').

As centres of small-scale agricultural production, households were crucial in the distribution of power among women and men due to the centrality of food production for the economy.[42] Land access also meant the possibility of breeding cattle.[43] The limited information regarding the

[37] Sarr, 'Land, Power, and Dependency'.
[38] Oliveira, 'The Donas of Luanda', 67.
[39] Oliveira, 'The Donas of Luanda', 71.
[40] See Candido, 'Women, Family, and Landed Property', 136–61; Rodrigues, 'Women, Land, and Power', Oliveira, 'Gender, Foodstuff Production'.
[41] Candido and Rodrigues, 'African Women's Access and Rights to Property', 4.
[42] See for example the case of Baté of the Milo River, West Africa, where women could influence local politics in the realm of their households before formal colonialism began. Osborn, *Our New Husbands Are Here*, 44–8.
[43] BNRJ (Biblioteca Nacional de Rio de Janeiro), I-28, 28, 29, 1797.

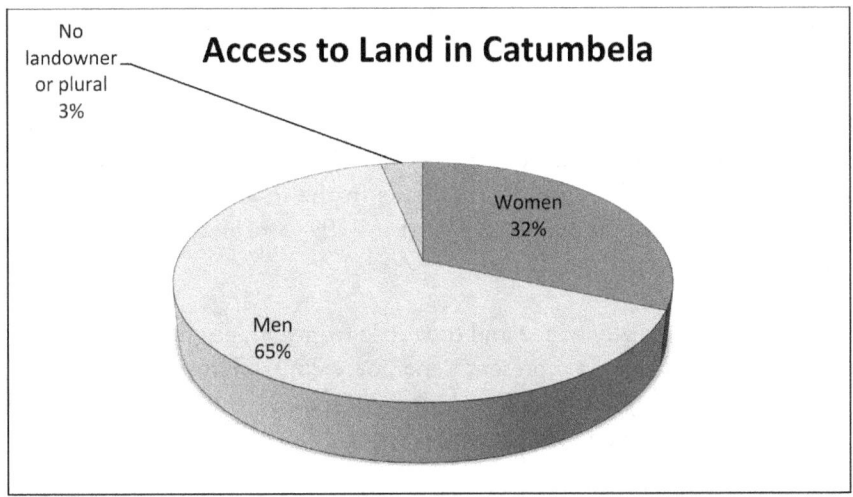

Chart 2 Access to land in Catumbela
(Source: Instituto Histórico Geográfico Brasileiro (IHGB), DL32, 02, 07,
'Relação de Moradores de Catumbela', 1798)

accumulation of animals in Catumbela farms suggests that the function of cattle as a source of meat for local consumption was secondary to the accumulation of wealth by their owners. However, when the owners passed away, their dependants and other people living nearby were allowed to eat the meat and distribute it for consumption.

Maize, Beans and Portuguese Control of Agricultural Production

The colonial authorities of Benguela measured the agricultural production of Catumbela as part of the Portuguese empire's attempts to consolidate control over its overseas territories. During the second half of the eighteenth century, the Portuguese empire developed a bureaucratic apparatus to keep track of information pertaining to the peoples, labour, access to land and production in the territories under its rule. This was part of the *Pombalinas* reforms, legal mandates established between 1750 and 1777. Madeira Santos has shown that the Portuguese empire collected information on the residents of its colonial possessions in Angola and their production in agriculture with the aim of spreading the ideas of civilisation that prevailed in Europe. These reforms also aimed to achieve

> the territorialization of the colonial state, increased white settlement and the foundation of cities in the hinterland of Luanda and Benguela to replace the military fortresses in the long term; the development of

agriculture and industries; and the bureaucratization of the state and the systematic use of writing and archives.[44]

At the beginning of the 1790s, Benguela's authorities were concerned about Catumbela's low agricultural production and used this as justification for counting the resources available in the town and measuring the productivity of its population. A report in 1797 informed the government of Benguela:

> The tithes are really scarce and the cattle from Quilengues and from the people of Catumbela represent a mediocre contribution to the colonial treasury in Benguela ... Agriculture, in spite of the generous natural conditions of the country, remains limited.[45]

This report linked low tax revenues to the low level of production. Both factors justified the same project: to measure the relevance of farming for wealth accumulation among Catumbela residents and land users. The scarcity of foodstuffs in Benguela seems to have persisted throughout the late 1790s.[46] The *Relação* embodied one of the mechanisms that the Portuguese colonial administration used to increase information about agricultural production, which they required due to the demand for foodstuffs. The *Relação de Moradores*, collected in 1797–98, emerged as part of Portugal's colonisation of Catumbela's territory and the effort to control its population and productivity.

Maize and beans constituted the two largest crops in Catumbela and two of the major agricultural products across Africa. Maize, along with cassava (manioc), had revolutionised agricultural production across Africa since the continent entered commercial exchange with the Americas in the fifteenth century.[47] By the eighteenth century, maize and cassava had become two of Africa's major agricultural products.[48] New types of bean

---

[44] Catarina Madeira Santos, 'Administrative Knowledge in a Colonial Context: Angola in the Eighteenth Century', *The British Journal for the History of Science* 43 (2010): 539–56.

[45] AHU-CU (Conselho Ultramarino), Angola, Cx. 76, D. 43, 21 June 1791, ff. 6v–7.

[46] Nielson Rosa Bezerra, *Escravidão, farinha e comércio*, 130–9; Mariza de Carvalho Soares and Nielson Rosa Bezerra, *Escravidão africana no Recôncavo da Guanabara (séculos XVII–XIX)* (Niterói, RJ: Editora da UFF, 2011), 212–15.

[47] For discussion about the agricultural revolution that took place in Africa after the rise of the commercial triangle with Europe and the Americas in the fifteenth century see Marvin Miracle, *The Introduction and Spread of Maize in Africa*, 1977; P. E. H. Hair, 'Milho: Meixoeira and Other Foodstuffs of the Sofala Garnison: 1505–1525,' *Cahiers d'Etudes africaines* 17 (1977): 353–63; Miller, *Way of Death*; Eugénia Rodrigues, *DoAtlântico ao Índico*; Silke Strickrodt, *Afro-European Trade in the Atlantic World: The Western Slave Coast, c.1550–c.1885* (Woodbridge: James Currey, 2015), 56–7, 197.

[48] Christopher Ehret, *The Civilizations of Africa: A History to 1800*, 2nd edn, Charlottesville: University Press of Virginia, 2016), 342; James McCann, *Maize and Grace: Africa's Encounter with a New World Crop 1500–1920* (Cambridge, MA.: Harvard University Press 2007).

coming from the Americas had joined beans that existed in Africa before the first contacts with Europeans.[49] Stanley Alpern has argued that the discussion about the introduction of new crops in Africa during the transatlantic slave trade cannot be limited to just some two or three of the major ones, since a total of 86 new crops were introduced during this period.[50] Among these, maize and beans became central to the diet of many African societies, in particular in areas fed by Catumbela residents. A total output of 9,552 *cazongueis* was reported in the *Relação* from the land of Catumbela. Maize production accounted for 5,299 *cazongueis* and beans for the remaining 4,253 *cazongueis*.

Women were once again at a disadvantage in comparison with men, in this case with regard to the control of crop production, mainly because they had less access to land and fewer dependants. They represented 31.3 per cent of those controlling the production of maize and beans, generating 2,520 *cazongueis* of maize and beans, i.e. 27 per cent of the total production of these crops.

Connections with Benguela

The fact that some people had residency, business and dependants in both Catumbela and Benguela reveals the connections between these two centres. The governor of Benguela, Francisco Paim da Câmara e Ornelas, visited Catumbela three times between September 1794 and January 1795.[51] Although the documentation does not show the reason behind his visits, it suggests the importance of Catumbela as a place of business for high-ranking people from Benguela. Câmara e Ornelas may have been involved in the production and trade of agricultural goods or even in the trade of enslaved people passing through Catumbela on their way to Benguela. The Portuguese chief officer of the Benguela royal treasury, António José da Costa,[52] not only visited Catumbela but also controlled land there in 1797, even though he resided in Benguela.

Not surprisingly, African women tended not to be mentioned by name or occupation in colonial records, making it difficult to identify those who moved between Catumbela and Benguela. Nevertheless, 17 out of the 25 persons who had land access in Catumbela but resided in Benguela

---

[49] Jan Vansina, *Paths in the Rainforests: Toward a History of Political Tradition in Equatorial Africa* (Madison: University of Wisconsin Press, 1990), 215.
[50] Stanley Alpern, 'Exotic Plants of Western Africa: Where They Came from and When', *History in Africa* 35 (2008): 63–102.
[51] AHU-Angola, Cx. 80, D. 52–55, 31 September 1794, 80; AHU-Angola, Cx. 80, D. 60 E 51, 14 October 1794; AHU-Angola, Cx. 81, D. 5 E 21, 20 January 1795.
[52] Roquinaldo Ferreira, *Cross-Cultural Exchange in the Atlantic World: Angola and Brazil during the Era of the Slave Trade* (New York: Cambridge University Press, 2012), 214–15.

were women, suggesting that they had connections and wealth in both places and were more involved in trading between these markets than were men.[53]

Three such women appeared in death records of Benguela from the period 1794–1832, showing that they moved between the business centre Benguela and their farms in Catumbela. One of them, *dona* Leonor Pereira da Costa, resided in Catumbela in 1797, but died in Benguela on 25 February 1800.[54] The title *dona*, employed to distinguish wealthy African women from other free women, solidified their social and economic recognition within colonial society.[55] Another elite woman was *dona* Teresa Vieira de Lima, who lived in Benguela and buried three of her slaves and a niece there before she herself died on 30 July 1799.[56] Another resident of Catumbela in 1797, Maria Ramos died in Benguela on 27 February 1806.[57] She too had buried two of her slaves in Benguela before that, suggesting that elite women and men maintained dependants and slaves in both centres – further confirmation of economic links between Benguela and cultivating centres, such as Catumbela.[58]

Although qualitative sources such as ecclesiastical data provide information about fewer people than the demographic data of the *Relação*, it is possible to conclude that the *donas* and other elite women were probably more involved in the trade of foodstuffs from Catumbela to Benguela than their male counterparts, since the number of women controlling land in Catumbela and having residency in Benguela was higher. Hence, although women had fewer free or enslaved dependants, as well as fewer land plots, in Catumbela, they played a central role in the supply of foodstuffs to Benguela.

Conclusion

Most of the farmers in Catumbela were women, but men accumulated most of the wealth derived from agricultural production. While women represented two-thirds of the dependants, they accounted for only one-third of the people who controlled dependants, had access to land

---

[53] IHGB, 'Relação de Moradores de Catumbela', ff. 1, 1v, 2, 2v, 3, 4, 5v, 6, 6v, 7v, 8, 8v, 9, 9v, 10, 10v, 14, 17v, 18.
[54] Arquivo do Bispado de Luanda (ABL), 'Óbitos Benguela 1770–1876', f. 11, 25 January 1800.
[55] Candido, 'Género, classificações, e comércio', 251–74.
[56] ABL, 'Óbitos Benguela', f. 85, 31 November 1795; f. 190–190v, 20 June 1793; 195–195v, 1 February 1794; and 73, 14 October 1796. For her burial record see ABL, 'Óbitos Benguela', f. 10, 30 July 1799.
[57] ABL, 'Óbitos Benguela', f. 48, 27 February 1806.
[58] ABL, 'Óbitos Benguela', f. 158, 29 April 1791.

and produced crops. The management of dependants enhanced agricultural output, since production relied heavily on their labour. Farming crops which were in demand in colonial towns, such as maize and beans, represented a way to gain access to land and control of dependants, and hence an opportunity to accumulate wealth. This explains why almost all land registered in the *Relação* was identified as being for agricultural production. Colonial officials were less concerned about controlling cattle ownership. Women had fewer opportunities to control land and dependants than men and their ability to accumulate wealth through agricultural production was also smaller. Yet they profited from their ability to connect the two centres as suppliers of maize and beans. Catumbela became a key to Benguela's rise to the position of the third-largest port in the transatlantic slave trade in the late eighteenth century, since it fed Benguela's population. The transatlantic slave trade was the catalyst for major transformations in African societies between the fifteenth and the nineteenth centuries, and places like Catumbela made possible the emergence of port towns focusing mainly on the slave trade and relying on the labour of women in agricultural production elsewhere.

4

Women's Material World in Nineteenth-Century Benguela[1]

MARIANA P. CANDIDO

This chapter examines consumption and trade, and women's central role as consumers of imported goods, including furniture, clothing, textiles and jewellery. In this study I will look at nineteenth-century wills and inventories available at the *Tribunal da Província de Benguela* in Angola to ascertain what kind of goods African women of Benguela acquired during their life time. Wills and post-mortem inventories list the material possessions women accumulated, helping us to determine how they lived. These sources allow us to imagine the interior of their homes and analyse their consumption habits and desires, providing information about private lives. Looking at the material world offers us the chance to place women at the centre of our analysis. Like Hilary Jones and Lorelle Semley, I stress how African women were connected to markets located as far away as Gujarat, Macau, Rio de Janeiro and Porto.

As Vanessa Oliveira and Esteban Salas show in this volume, African women were important economic actors in West Central Africa. Free or enslaved, they produced food, sold water and food in urban centres and assumed active roles in long-distance caravans.[2] However, we know little about their consumption patterns and their integration into global markets. Long-distance trade was part of the experience of societies living close to the coast as well as in the interiors, which allowed people in the central highlands to consume alcohol and textiles from elsewhere in exchange for copper, salt, ivory or human beings.[3] The contact with the

---

[1] Lorelle Semley, Daniel Domingues da Silva and Robin Law read an earlier version and provided important feedback. I am grateful for their suggestions.
[2] Besides the contributions in this volume see Selma Pantoja, 'Gênero e comércio: as traficantes de escravos na região de Angola', *Travessias* 4/5 (2004), 79–97; Vanessa S. Oliveira, 'Gender, Foodstuff Production and Trade in Late-Eighteenth Century Luanda', *African Economic History* 43, no. 1 (2015): 57–81.
[3] Jan Vansina, 'Long-Distance Trade-Routes in Central Africa', *The Journal of African History*

Atlantic world created new markets, desires and objects of consumption. It also transformed local production, the landscape and market practices.[4]

The trade goods listed in inventories offer a glimpse to what women collected in their houses. In some households the belongings were sparse, while other residents of Benguela lived at a level of comfort and luxury. These goods reveal connections within the Atlantic world and reinforce the idea that the engagement in the slave trade and, later, in legitimate commerce allowed Africans to become global consumers. Local societies produced wax, copper rings, ivory and animal skins, which were sold to European traders.[5] They developed techniques to exploit these natural resources and transport them to markets where they were consumed. With the end of slave exports, cultivation of sugarcane and coffee increased, alongside the exports of natural resources such as ivory, wax, and rubber.[6] This expansion was rendered possible by the existence of very organised long-distance trade routes that connected markets of the interior with the coast.[7] Thus tracing

---

(contd) 3, no. 3 (1962), 375–90; Linda M. Heywood, *Contested Power in Angola, 1840s to the Present* (Rochester, NY: University of Rochester Press, 2000); Beatrix Heintze, *Pioneiros Africanos: caravanas de carregadores na África Centro-Ocidental: entre 1850 e 1890* (Lisbon: Caminho, 2004).

[4] For more on this see Phyllis Martin, *The External Trade of the Loango Coast, 1576–1870: The Effects of Changing Commercial Relations on the Vili Kingdom of Loango* (Oxford: Clarendon Press, 1972); Colleen E. Kriger, *Cloth in West African History* (Lanham, MD: Rowman AltaMira, 2006); David Eltis and Lawrence C. Jennings, 'Trade between Western Africa and the Atlantic World in the Pre-Colonial Era', *The American Historical Review* 93, no. 4 (1988): 936–59; David Richardson, 'Consuming Goods, Consuming People: Reflections on the Transatlantic Slave Trade', *The Rise and Demise of Slavery and the Slave Trade in the Atlantic World*, ed. Philip Misevich and Kristin Mann (Rochester, NY: University of Rochester Press, 2016), 32–63.

[5] Joseph C. Miller, *Way of Death: Merchant Capitalism and the Angolan Slave Trade, 1730–1830* (Madison: University of Wisconsin Press, 1988), 105–15; Beatrix Heintze, *Angola nos séculos XVI e XVII: Estudo sobre fontes, métodos e história* (Luanda: Kilombelombe, 2007); Mariana Candido, *An African Slaving Port and the Atlantic World: Benguela and Its Hinterland* (New York: Cambridge University Press, 2013), 31–87.

[6] David Birmingham, 'Question of Coffee: Black Enterprise in Angola', *Canadian Journal of African Studies* 16, no. 2 (1982): 343–46; W.G. Clarence-Smith, *Slaves, Peasants, and Capitalists in Southern Angola, 1840–1926* (Cambridge: Cambridge University Press, 1979); Aida Freudenthal, *Arimos e fazendas: a transição agrária em Angola, 1850–1880* (Luanda: Chá de Caxinde, 2005); Linda M Heywood, 'Slavery and Forced Labor in the Changing Political Economy of Central Angola, 1850–1949', *The End of Slavery in Africa*, ed. Suzanne Miers and Richard Roberts (Madison: Wisconsin University Press, 1988), 415–35; Roquinaldo Amaral Ferreira, 'Agricultural Enterprise and Unfree Labour in Nineteenth Century Angola', *Commercial Agriculture, the Slave Trade and Slavery in Atlantic Africa*, ed. Robin Law, Suzanne Schwarz and Silke Strickrodt (Woodbridge: James Currey, 2013), 225–42; Jelmer Vos, *Kongo in the Age of Empire, 1860–1913: The Breakdown of a Moral Order* (Madison: University of Wisconsin Press, 2015).

[7] Jill R. Dias, 'Changing Patterns of Power in the Luanda Hinterland: The Impact of Trade and Colonisation on the Mbundu ca. 1845–1920', *Paideuma* 32 (1986), 285–318; Valentim Alexandre and Jill Dias, *O Império africano* (Lisbon: Estampa, 1998); Beatrix Heintze, 'Long-Distance Caravans and Communication beyond the Kwango (c. 1850–1890)', *Angola on the Move: Transport Routes, Communications, and History*, ed. Beatrix Heintze and Achim von Oppen (Frankfurt am Main: Lembeck, 2008), 144–62; Mariana P. Candido, 'Merchants and the Business of the Slave Trade at Benguela, 1750–1850', *African Economic History* 35 (2007): 1–30.

the history of commodity exchange and consumption practices provides tools for further examining the economic and social history of this region and its societies.[8] In addition, it allows us to understand the ideologies that governed the economic and social activities of women and men.[9]

This chapter examines the demands of African women as consumers of global products and in the process challenges scholars who have argued that the goods introduced by the Atlantic commerce had little impact on African everyday life.[10] The importation of iron bars improved farming; yet, as other scholars have shown, the importation of goods such as textiles and guns had a destructive effect on local manufacturing,[11] and I interrogate the motivations of African consumption of imported goods. I emphasise the insertion of African women into the global economy, not only as providers of human labour during the era of the transatlantic slave trade, but also as agents who shaped production in other parts of the world in response to African demands. A focus on what African women consumed and accumulated during the nineteenth century suggests their participation in economic life, as agents in the long-distance trade connecting their communities to places as distant as Brazil, India and China, but also their participation in global movements of commodities and ideas.[12]

Benguela as Part of the Global Economy

Africans were interested in material goods produced somewhere else and had a sophisticated taste for exotic commodities.[13] Merchants and political

---

[8] George Metcalf, 'A Microcosm of Why Africans sold Slaves: Akan Consumption Patterns in the 1770s', *Journal of African History* 28, no. 3 (1987); 387; Stanley Alpern, 'What Africans got for their Slaves: A Master List of European Trade Goods', *History in Africa* 22 (1995), 5–43.

[9] Ifi Amadiume, *Male Daughters, Female Husbands: Gender and Sex in an African Society* (London: Zed Books, 1987), 27–31; Miriam Goheen, *Men Own the Fields, Women Own the Crops: Gender and Power in the Cameroon Grassfields* (Madison: University of Wisconsin Press, 1996), 8–9.

[10] For more on this see Eltis and Jennings, 'Trade between Western Africa', 936–59. See also Kristin Mann and Philip Misevich, 'Introduction', *The Rise and Demise of Slavery and the Slave Trade in the Atlantic World*, ed. Philip Misevich and Kristin Mann (Rochester, NY: University of Rochester Press, 2016), 10–11.

[11] Edward A. Alpers, *Ivory and Slaves: Changing Pattern of International Trade in East Central Africa to the Later Nineteenth Century* (Los Angeles: University of California Press, 1975); Martin, *External Trade of the Loango*; Paul E. Lovejoy, *Transformations in Slavery* (New York: Cambridge University Press, 2000).

[12] Hilary Jones, *The Métis of Senegal: Urban Life and Politics in French West Africa* (Indiana University Press, 2013); Phyllis M. Martin, 'Power, Cloth and Currency on the Loango Coast', *African Economic History* no. 15 (1986): 1–12; Colleen E. Kriger, 'Mapping the History of Cotton Textile Production in Precolonial West Africa', *African Economic History* 33 (2005): 87–116.; Jeremy Prestholdt, *Domesticating the World: African Consumerism and the Genealogies of Globalization* (Berkeley: University of California Press, 2008).

[13] See David Richardson, 'West African Consumption Patterns and Their Influence on the Eighteenth-Century English Slave Trade', *Uncommon Market: Essays in the Economic History of*

elites of Benguela and its interior were connected to traders from different parts of the globe since the seventeenth century, and we should not underestimate the importance of Portuguese manufactures in these trade relationships.[14] Customs records reveal that Portuguese manufactured goods, such as wool textiles, beads, paper, and a miscellany of other items were imported into Benguela and, in the early nineteenth century, Brazil replaced Portugal as the main source of goods. These imports affected local industries.[15] Rogéria Alves has examined the commercialisation and carving of ivory to assess how Africans responded to the imports offered by Brazilian and Portuguese traders.[16] Crislayne Alfagali has analysed iron smelting technology and the importance of local techniques in the production of iron bars and tools in Angola.[17] It is difficult to quantify the exports of Central African natural resources and products, but their existence reveals that trade between Europeans and Africans was not simply a matter of exchanging alcohol, guns and textiles for enslaved bodies. From the earliest contacts between the Portuguese and Africans onwards, the former hoped to acquire gold and other metals, such as copper, and in the process bought, bartered and seized ivory, leather, wax and gum arabic.[18] The inventories analysed here reveal that not only rulers, but also urban and rural African women acquired imported commodities.

The sources used in this chapter are a selection of the 321 inventories available at the *Tribunal da Província de Benguela* (TPB) identified and

(contd) *the Atlantic Slave Trade*, ed. Henry A. Gemery and Jan S. Hogendorn (New York: Academic Press, 1979), 303–30; Daniel Domingues, *The Atlantic Slave Trade from West Central Africa, 1780–1867* (New York: Cambridge University Press, 2017), 122–41; Jones, *The Métis of Senegal*, 89–95; Kriger, 'Mapping the History of Cotton Textile,' 98–105; Roquinaldo Ferreira, 'Dinâmica do comércio intracolonial: gerebitas, panos asiáticos e guerra no tráfico angolano de escravos, século XVIII', *O Antigo Regime nos Trópicos: A dinâmica imperial portuguesa, séculos XVI–XVIII*, ed. João Luís Ribe Fragoso, Maria de Fátima Gouvêa and Maria Fernanda Bicalho (Rio de Janeiro: Civilização Brasileira, 2001), 339–78.

[14] For more on this see Gustavo Acioli Lopes and Maximiliano Mac Menz, 'Resgate e Mercadorias: uma análise comparada do tráfico luso-brasileiro de escravos em Angola e na Costa da Mina (Século XVIII)', *Afro-Ásia* 37 (2008): 43–72.

[15] Mariana P. Candido, *Fronteras de esclavización: Esclavitud, comercio e identidade em Benguela, 1780–1850* (Mexico City: Colegio de Mexico, 2011), 39–40; Martin, 'Power, Cloth and Currency', 1–12; John K. Thornton, 'Precolonial African Industry and the Atlantic Trade, 1500–1800', *African Economic History* 19 (1990): 1–19. See also John K. Thornton, *Africa and Africans in the Making of the Atlantic World, 1400–1800* (New York: Cambridge University Press, 1998), 7–45; Miller, *Way of Death*, 78–81.

[16] Rogéria Cristina Alves, 'Marfins africanos em trânsito: apontamentos sobre o comércio numa perspectiva atlântica (Angola, Benguela, Lisboa e Brasil), séculos XVIII–XIX', *Faces da História* 3, no. 2 (2016): 8–21.

[17] Crislayne Alfagali, *Ferreiros e Fundidores da Ilamba: Uma história social da fabricação de ferro e da Real Fábrica de Nova Oeiras* (Angola, segunda metade do séc. XVIII) (Luanda: Fundação Agostinho Neto, 2018).

[18] Harvey M. Feinberg, *Africans and Europeans in West Africa: Elminans and Dutchmen on the Gold Coast during the Eighteenth Century* (Philadelphia, PA: American Philosophical Society, 1989); Thornton, *A Cultural History*, 63–5.

consulted in 2003, 2016 and 2017. Of these 321 documents, 50 of them are inventories of women (see Table 1). I select seven inventories of women and ten of men, privileging wills and inventories produced between 1850 and 1867, after the end of the slave trade. The number of women recorded as living in Benguela rose from 1,235 in 1844 to 2,908 in 1860, but fell to 2,075 in 1878.[19] The number of European women remained very small (less than seven individuals) throughout this period. Although restricted to a small percentage of the female population, the wills and inventories offer insights into the experiences of urban and rural elites. In the context of colonial statecraft and colonial control, African women managed to use these sites of power to protect their interests and write their existence into history.[20]

The cases I discuss refer to locally born women, despite their Portuguese names. They were classified as black or of mixed race. The wills and inventories reveal the material objects and the people African women owned, where they lived, what they stored in their houses, and what was considered part of their estate and worth passing on to their heirs. They tell us about their social relationships and economic roles in their households and communities. Through their material possessions we can make inferences about their role in agriculture, weaving, trade, domestic service and cooking. A comparison with the inventories of men might reveal that African women did not own as much, yet their belongings reveal ingenuity and adaptability to external and internal changes. Besides, they show how African women who lived in Benguela, Caconda and Catumbela were integrated into a global economy by the mid-nineteenth century (see Map 4 at the beginning of Chapter 3).

---

[19] See, respectively, José Joaquim Lopes de Lima, *Ensaios sobre a statistica das possessões portuguezas na Africa occidental e oriental; na Asia occidental; na China, e na Oceania* (Lisbon: Imprensa nacional, 1844), 4A; *Almanak statistico da Provincia d'Angola e suas dependencias para o anno de 1852* (Luanda: Imprensa do Governo, 1851), 9; Arquivo Histórico Ultramarino, Angola, Pasta 48. There is a growing literature on the population estimates in the Portuguese possessions in Africa. For more on this see Paulo Teodoro de Matos and Jelmer Vos, 'Demografia e relações de trabalho em Angola C.1800: um ensaio metodológico', *Diálogos* 17, no. 3 (2014): 807–34; Paulo Teodoro de Matos, 'Population Censuses in the Portuguese Empire', *Romanian Journal of Population Studies* 1 (2013): 5–26; Daniel B. Domingues da Silva, 'The Early Population Charts of Portuguese Angola, 1776–1830: A Preliminary Assessment', *Anais de História de Além-Mar* 6 (2015): 107–24; Filipa Ribeiro da Silva, 'From Church Records to Royal Population Charts: The Birth of 'Modern Demographic Statistics' in Mozambique, 1720s–1820s', *Anais de História de Além-Mar* 6 (2015): 125–50.

[20] Ann Laura Stoler, 'Colonial Archives and the Arts of Governance', *Archival Science* 2 (2002): 87–109; Peter Pels, 'The Anthropology of Colonialism: Culture, History, and the Emergence of Western Governmentality', *Annual Review of Anthropology* 26 (1997): 163–83; Bhavani Raman, *Document Raj: Writing and Scribes in Early Colonial South India* (Chicago, IL: University of Chicago Press, 2012); Karen Graubart, *With Our Labor and Sweat: Indigenous Women and the Formation of Colonial Society in Peru, 1550–1700* (Stanford, CA: Stanford University Press, 2007).

Table 1 Inventories available at Tribunal da Província de Benguela

	Men	Women	NI	Total
1850s	78	12	1	91
1860s	54	10	1	65
1870s	30	6	4	40
1880s	41	6	2	49
1890s	32	7	1	40
1900s	16	6	1	23
1910s	0	0	1	1
1920s		1	0	1
1920s	2	1	0	3
Date Not Identified	7	1	0	8
Total	260	50	11	321

(Source: Tribunal da Província de Benguela)
NI = date not identified

Property and Consumption

While scholars have paid attention to the trade in alcohol and textile, we know very little about the consumption of items such as chairs, beads, socks or shoes, even though political and economic elites dressed in a Western fashion.[21] Usefulness, price and status might explain why certain goods were acquired; but goods also have a relationship with notions of modernity and 'civilisation' championed by colonial officials and missionaries.[22]

While some of the women discussed here lived in Benguela (such as Joana Rodrigues da Costa, a widow, and Teresa de Jesus Barros e Cunha, a widow who lived with another partner), others lived away from the coastal settlement: Maria José Martins and Josefa Manoel Pereira da Silva lived in Catumbela, 30 kilometres north of Benguela; and Florência José do Cadaval was from Caconda, more than 200 kilometres inland. Their property included land, houses, gardens, cattle, furniture, jewellery, textiles, weapons, tools and items of trade, such as beads and textiles, but also goods of a very different nature, such as gunpowder and knives. They

---

[21] Miller, *Way of Death*, 71–104; Ferreira, 'Dinâmica do comércio intracolonial', 339–78; Domingues, *Atlantic Slave Trade*, 122–41.
[22] For more on this see Arjun Appadurai, *The Social Life of Things: Commodities in Cultural Perspective* (Cambridge: Cambridge University Press, 2013); Arnold J. Bauer, *Goods, Power, History: Latin America's Material Culture* (New York: Cambridge University Press, 2001).

controlled significant numbers of enslaved people, who worked for them in their gardens, houses and businesses. The wills and inventories offer a glimpse of the tastes of consumers in Benguela and its interior and provide an indication of what was valuable, since people would leave some possessions to loved ones, including relatives, friends and former slaves. Their goods help us to understand consumers' preferences and tastes, suggesting how cultural and economic 'factors shaped commercial transactions in the Atlantic slave trade'.[23]

Wills and post-mortem inventories reveal that African women acquired land and houses. The shape, size, building material and location of the houses indicates the wealth of the owners as well as their insertion into colonial society. I focus first on immovable goods that people accumulated in their lifetime. Consumption mediates human relationships and can strengthen social claims and identities. The ability of West Central African women to buy imported goods helped them to secure and affirm status. It also suggests the importance of commodities in strategies of distinction.[24] African women in Benguela consumed imported products, spoke Portuguese, dressed in a Western fashion and thereby asserted their belonging to a colonial elite. In the process they projected the idea that they were closer to the Portuguese and different from neighbours who did not dress like them, did not have the same furniture or clothes and were not baptised. Individuals' taste and style were shaped by local understandings but also by imposed ones that might or might not be subverted. Nineteenth-century decisions regarding what to wear and what to buy facilitated the creation of a distinct group of Africans.[25]

FURNITURE

Individuals who dictated wills, or colonial officers who listed inventories, paid close attention to the description of furniture, describing their material, their use, their state of conservation, and their place of origin. Furniture was generally handmade; unfortunately, we do not know much about the process of assembling pieces and who were the carpenters. African men and women acquired tables, chests, rocking chairs, wardrobes and grandfather clocks brought from Portugal, Brazil or China. António da Silva Porto, a Portuguese-born trader who lived in Benguela's interior from 1846 to 1890, recorded that in Bihé there was an important ironwork and carpentry industry and trade in the 1860s. Bihé carpenters

---

[23] Kriger, 'Mapping the History of Cotton Textile', 88.
[24] Pierre Bourdieu, *Pascalian Meditations* (Stanford: Stanford University Press, 2000), 193–98; Prestholdt, *Domesticating the World*; Graubart, *With Our Labor and Sweat*, 63–5; Amy M. Porter, *Their Lives, Their Wills: Women in the Borderlands, 1750–1846* (Lubbock: Texas Tech University Press, 2015).
[25] Jones, *The Métis of Senegal*, 90–91; Prestholdt, *Domesticating the World*, 13–15.

manufactured 'chairs, beds, windows, tables, and doors. While the chairs could be sold for a piece of textile, the remaining items were worth four to eight pieces of textile each.'[26] Thus some of the furniture listed in inventories could have been produced in the central highlands.

Let us look at the furniture collected by Teresa Jesus de Barros e Cunha, who died in 1861, two weeks after giving birth to her son, Manoel de Barros e Cunha Van-Dunen. Although she was not legally married to Guilherme Van-Dunen, they lived together, and he was put in charge of identifying her belongings after her premature death. It is important to note that all items belonged to her, not to her surviving partner or her deceased husband. Among 23 items of furniture were a well-kept sofa set, eight chairs and two small benches, all handmade with straw-style seats imported from Porto in Portugal, estimated to be worth 21 thousand and 700 réis (written 21$700), the currency employed in the Portuguese empire in the nineteenth century.[27] The 21$700 réis was the equivalent to less than GBP £5 in 1861. She also owned a large mirror estimated at 4$000 (a little less than £1); four good chairs made of 'American wood'; a used rocking chair; an iron bed frame; three Chinese paintings; a dining table with four rounded wooden-finished legs and five drawers; a bedside table; a washbasin made of iron with a broken leg; a writing desk in the French style, and a jacaranda-wood table with two drawers. She also had a variety of chests used to store her clothing and other valuables.[28] The emphasis on the material, carving and style suggest these items were not common. Barros e Cunha's furniture stands out when compared with that of other residents, suggesting she was a wealthy resident. Josefa Manoel Pereira da Silva, for example, had five furniture items listed in her 1865 inventory. Pereira da Silva had a chest with drawers and a mirror worth 2$000 réis, a pinewood table in good condition, another pinewood table with four drawers, an old chest, and a small wooden bed frame with copper details estimated to be worth 16$000, or something over £3 at the time.[29] This was modest when compared with the furniture of Barros e Cunha. Both women acquired furniture produced elsewhere. While

---

[26] Biblioteca de Sociedade de Geografia de Lisboa, Lisbon, Portugal (BSGL), Res – 2-C-7, 'Silva Porto, notas para retocar a minha obra logo que as circunstâncias permitam', 1 April 1866, ff. 74, 28–29.

[27] The Portuguese currency, rei or réis, in plural, the symbol $ is used to indicate thousands. By the 1850s–1870s, a British pound was worth 4$500 réis. See Gervase Clarence-Smith, *The Third Portuguese Empire, 1825–1975* (Manchester, UK: Manchester University Press, 1985), Annex 1, 227. £1 in 1860 is equivalent to £59.13 in 2017 according to the currency converter available at The National Archives website, www.nationalarchives.gov.uk/currency. I am very thankful to Eugénia Rodrigues and Suzanne Schwarz for their help and suggestion in navigating currency conversion and price-level adjustments.

[28] Tribunal da Província de Benguela, Benguela, Angola (TPB), 'Autos cívis do inventário de Teresa de Jesus Barros e Cunha', 14 October 1861, ff. 16v–17v.

[29] TPB, 'Autos cívis do inventário de Josefa Manoel Pereira da Silva', 18 April 1865.

pine trees are common in Portugal and Jacaranda wood in Brazil, neither grow in Angola, suggesting that these items were imported. Besides, it is interesting that Barros e Cunha owned a writing desk in a town that had no permanent school until the mid-1860s.[30]

The reference to three Chinese paintings is curious but not unique. Narciso José Pacheco Lages, who lived in Catumbela, also had two Chinese paintings in his house.[31] Portuguese traders were active on sea routes connecting Goa and Macau, which might explain the appearance of these luxury items as well as silk in the inventories of Benguela residents. Travellers coming from China stopped at Benguela and Luanda and offered goods to residents.[32] In other cases, furniture is not even listed in the inventories, suggesting it had little monetary value or that people had not acquired any during their life.

CLOTHING AND JEWELLERY

Benguela residents who left wills or officers who compiled inventories paid careful attention to clothing and jewellery. Men owned and valued their shirts, socks, uniforms and coats, bequeathing some of these items to their heirs. Women invested in Western-style dresses, shoes, shawls and shirts, differing in the quality of the textile used.[33] Clothes were markers of identity and status and, in some cases, were the most valuable property people owned. Officials noted if the items had been used, if they were in good maintenance, and the type of material (cotton, wool, silk).[34] Florência José do Cadaval's inventory is an interesting one. She lived in Caconda, a village located 220 kilometres inland, where her home probably served as an entrepôt in one of the most important inland slave markets. When she died on May 21, 1854, her personal clothing included: four used coloured dresses (16$000), 22 used printed calico dresses (44$000, about £10 in the 1860s), six printed calico dresses in good condition (18$000), six used woollen shawls (24$000), 10 used shirts (20$000), 12 shirts of good quality made of unidentified textiles (30$000), 15 silk handkerchiefs of different colours (22$000), 6 used pairs

---

[30] Carlos Pacheco, 'Leituras e bibliotecas em Angola na primeira metade do século XIX', *Locus (Juiz de Fora)* 6, no. 2 (2000): 30.

[31] TPB, 'Autos cívis do inventário de Narciso José Pacheco Lages', 19 October 1863, f. 10v.

[32] Carlos José Caldeira, *Apontamentos de uma viagem de Lisbon a China*, vol. 2 of 2 (Lisbon: Castro & Irmão, 1853), 177–79. I am thankful to Vanessa Oliveira for bringing to my attention Caldeira's travel accounts. For more on thse trade connections see A. J. R Russell-Wood, *A World on the Move: The Portuguese in Africa, Asia, and America, 1415–1808* (Manchester, UK: Carcanet, 1992), 30–32.

[33] Other scholars have noted similar behaviour along the western coast: George E. Brooks, *Eurafricans in Western Africa* (Ohio University Press, 2003), 122–60; Jones, *The Métis of Senegal*; Pernille Ipsen, *Daughters of the Trade: Atlantic Slavers and Interracial Marriage on the Gold Coast* (Philadelphia: University of Pennsylvania Press, 2015).

[34] This is like other contexts in Africa but also elsewhere. See, for example, Bauer, *Goods, Power, History*, 69–70; Porter, *Their Lives, Their Wills*, 27–48.

of shoes (4$800), a coat of a light textile (1$500) and 20 silk socks (1$800).[35] It is not clear whether Florência José do Cadaval made her own clothes or employed some of her slaves (22 men and 31 women) to do so. Perhaps she had bought the items in one of the few shops available in Benguela or even from long-distance traders moving imported goods in their caravans.[36]

After the end of slave exports and the expansion of legitimate commerce, women continued to invest in Western-style clothing, blending it with local styles of clothing. Joana Mendes de Moraes, from Libolo, for example, owned nine pairs of socks ($450), four blouses (5$150), six jackets (3$000), and 112 pieces of worn textiles (33$000) used for wrapping around the waist or torso. She seems to have combined blouses and jackets with wrap skirts and head-wrappers. Also listed in Joana Mendes de Moraes's inventory were five new silk handkerchiefs (2$000), eight cotton handkerchiefs ($800), two cotton belts ($600), and five handkerchiefs of undetermined textile and quality ($250).[37] Some of them could have been sewn to make dresses, waist-cloths or head-wrappers (see Illustration 3). In her inventory no dresses or shoes were listed, although among her possessions were wooden shoe forms, indicating that she had the ability to produce footwear. Maybe she learned how to make shoes in Bihé or from an artisan from there – a Messeve (the Umbundu term for sandal-maker) or Oloaco (espadrille maker).[38] Although Joana Mendes de Moraes was from the interior, she lived in Benguela. Her belongings suggest she was not as concerned about accumulating Western-style clothes as Florinda José do Cadaval. Although clothing was a sign of status and economic distinction,[39] Joana

---

[35] TPB, 'Autos cívis do inventario de Florencia Jose do Cadaval', 15 June 1854. For more on Caconda see Candido, *An African Slaving Port*, 257–64.

[36] For the caravans connecting Caconda to the coast see Miller, *Way of Death*, 150–51; Aida Freudenthal, 'Benguela – da feitoria à cidade colonial', *Fontes & Estudos* 6–7 (2011): 197–229; Mariana P. Candido, 'Trade, Slavery and Migration in the Interior of Benguela: The Case of the Caconda, 1830–1870', *Angola on the Move: Transport Routes, Communications, and History*, ed. Beatrix Heintze and Achim von Oppen (Frankfurt am Main: Lembeck, 2008), 63–84; Roberto Guedes and Caroline S. Pontes, 'Notícias do presídio de Caconda (1797): moradores, escravatura, tutores e órfãos', África e Brasil no Mundo Moderno, ed. Eduardo França Paiva and Vanicléia Santos (Belo Horizonte, Brazil: Annablume, 2013), 153–80.

[37] TPB, 'Autos cívis do inventario de Joana Mendes de Moraes', 3 July 1861, ff. 20v–24. For the importance of trade in textile and their use see Miller, *Way of Death*, 81–3; Telma Gonçalves Santos, 'Comércio de tecidos europeus e asiáticos na África centro-ocidental: Fraudes e contrabandos no terceiro quartel do século XVIII' (unpublished M.A. dissertation, Universidade de Lisboa/Lisbon, 2014).

[38] BSGL, Res– 2-C-7, 'Silva Porto, notas para retocar a minha obra logo que as circunstâncias permitam', 1 April 1866, f. 79. The current spelling in Umbundu is Utongi Oluhaku for Shoemaker, Oluhaku for shoes and Olunuase for sandals. See H. Etaungo Daniel, *Dicionário Português-Umbundu* (Luanda: Mayamba, 2015), 786 and 785.

[39] For more on this see Heintze, *Angola nos séculos XVI e XVII*, 576–592; Silvia Hunold Lara, 'The Signs of Color: Women's Dress and Racial Relations in Salvador and Rio de Janeiro, ca 1750–1815', *Colonial Latin American Review* 6, no. 2 (1997), 205.

Illustration 3 Two women identified as baptised, Benguela, 1820s, wearing bead necklaces, head wraps and dresses decorated with beads and belts; both wear no shoes and carry calabashes and wooden sticks; one has a basket, while the other carries her infant strapped to her back

(Source: 'Negresses baptisées', Jean-Baptiste Douville *Voyage au Congo et dans l'Afrique équinoxiale dans les années 1828, 1829 et 1830* (Paris: J. Renouard, 1832); Copy in Arquivo Histórico Ultramarino, ICONI-001-OOD-00285_c0001)

Mendes de Moraes invested her wealth mainly in landed property, slaves and jewellery.

By the 1860s printed advertisements in the *Boletim Oficial da Província Geral de Angola*, the colonial gazette, announced the sale of certain items, such as socks and dresses, in specific shops in Luanda.[40] It is not clear if shops in Benguela also sold Italian straw hats for women, girls and children, or clothing and adornment coming from Europe.[41] The elite was always in search of new items, demanding that traders introduced textiles of different colours, patterns, qualities and textures. Raffia and bark clothes had lost importance as items of prestige and were quickly being replaced by Indian textiles.[42]

Some of the residents also had retail businesses. The trader Francisco Pacheco de Sousa Silva probably maintained a shop in Benguela or some type of business attending the consumer demands for imported goods. In his inventory he had a variety of women's dresses, probably sewn by some of his 76 slaves, who included Jacinto, a tailor, and Maria Quilombo, a seamstress who also ironed clothes.[43] Among Francisco Pacheco de Sousa e Silva's possessions were five dozen reels of wool, ten thousand sewing needles of different sizes, seven scissors and large amounts of cotton, Indian blue cotton cloth and *pano das costa,* West African textiles in demand in West Central Africa. His material possessions suggest that he had a tailoring business. Besides finished clothes, he also sold gold rings and earrings, since his inventory listed 17 boxes of brand new pairs of earrings. Among the retail items in his inventory, there were 15 dresses of different textiles (cotton, silk and camlet) and 29 blouses, 45 buckets for women; 37 women's belts, 3 women's silk capes and eight skirts, besides dozens of gloves, and 32 pairs of women's shoes. His business sought to meet the demand of Benguela residents eager to buy clothing associated with Westernisation and inclusion into colonial society. While most of the population of Benguela could not consume imported goods, a small elite had access to finer clothes and luxury items that differentiated them from the rest of the population. Through dresses and jewellery strangers could perceive economic power and social prestige of African women through a 'visual language of hierarchy'.[44]

---

[40] Boletim Oficial do Governo Geral da Província de Angola (BOGGPA), n. 1, 1 January 1865, p. 41 'Annúncios de meias para senhoras', and p. 75 'Anúncio de Grinaldas para senhoras a 6$500 reis'.

[41] BOGGPA, n1, 1 January 1865, p. 75, 'Annúncio recebidos da França'.

[42] Martin, *The External Trade*, 105–8; Miller, *Way of Death*, 82–3.

[43] TPB, 'Autos cívis do inventario de Francisco Pacheco de Sousa e Silva', 7 August 1865, ff. 8 and 8v.

[44] Lara, 'The Signs of Color', 205. For the importance of clothing in differentiating people see Sheryl McCurdy, 'Fashioning Sexuality: Desire, Manyema Ethnicity, and the Creation of the "Kanga," ca. 1880–1900', *The International Journal of African Historical Studies* 39, no. 3 (2006): 441–69; Thornton, 'Precolonial African Industry', 17–18.

Women also invested in jewellery and items of adornment, such as necklaces or hairpins of gold or silver, as can be seen in Illustration 4. Carlos Caldeira, who visited Benguela in 1851, described black women 'covered in textiles like those worn in Mozambique, but with more beads around their neck.'[45] Florência José do Cadaval, discussed earlier, had three pairs of gold earrings, six necklaces of different quality and purity of gold, four gold rings with different precious stones, a golden brooch and 209$880 in silver, the equivalent to £46 in 1860.[46]

In the 1860s, Joana Mendes de Moraes owned three gold earrings, one of which had diamond stones; two of the gold earrings were estimated at 1$250 réis, while the one with diamond stones was worth 27$000 (£6 in 1860). She also owned several gold bows of different quality, a gold ring with topaz stones (4$800 réis), a necklace with a gold crucifix (52$000, or £11) and a copper crucifix without monetary value.[47] Her jewellery also included five pairs of silver earrings (4$300) and a copper necklace (1$000). While the copper items were probably manufactured locally (copper was mined in the interior of Central Africa), the gold and silver jewellery probably arrived from Brazil, due to the close connection between Brazilian and Benguela-based traders.[48] Jewellery and luxury items could also be bought from other traders in need of cash. In 1865, for example, Dona Maria do Carmo Silveira announced the sale of her jewellery.[49]

Another Benguela resident in the 1860s, Josefa Manoel Pereira da Silva, also owned jewellery, which she bequeathed to her daughter Maria Augusta. In her inventory, a variety of jewellery was listed: a hairpin with golden details; six different qualities of golden hairpins; an image of Our Lady of Light in gold, a statue of Our Lady of Conception covered in gold; seven golden rings, five pairs of golden earrings, and three golden necklaces.[50] Wealthy African men and women felt the need to show their wealth to differentiate themselves from the poor and enslaved people, but also from those considered to be heathen or 'uncivilised'.

TEXTILES

The material culture detailed in the inventories gives some indication of the range of women's economic activities. These goods could also be commercialised and generate more profit. This is the case for textiles,

---

[45] Caldeira, *Apontamentos*, 2, 178.
[46] TPB, 'Autos cívis do inventário de Florência José do Cadaval', 15 June 1854, ff. 12–12v.
[47] TPB, 'Autos cívis do inventário de Joana Mendes de Moraes', ff. 25v–27.
[48] Eugenia W. Herbert, *Red Gold of Africa: Copper in Precolonial History and Culture* (Madison: University of Wisconsin Press, 1984); Colleen E. Kriger, *Pride of Men: Ironworking in 19th Century West Central Africa* (Portsmouth, NH: Heinemann, 1999).
[49] BOGGPA, n1, 1 January 1865, 6.
[50] TPB, 'Autos cívis do inventário de Josefa Manoel Pereira da Silva', 18 April 1865, ff. 8–9v.

Illustration 4 Benguela woman with gold earrings, different types of necklaces and bracelets; she wears an elaborate dress with several layers of different textiles

(Source: 'Costumes de Benguela', Arquivo Nacional de Angola P-1-40)

used as currency in some parts of West Central Africa.[51] If not used as currency, they could become dresses, shirts or trousers.

Inventories from mid-nineteenth century Benguela reveal that textiles continued to be important in commerce after the end of slave exports. Joseph Miller has argued that 'Africans sold people for imported goods',[52] and the inventories from the 1850s and 1860s suggest that afterwards cloth remained important as a commodity. After centuries of consumption, Benguela residents still wanted to accumulate large numbers of textiles from different parts of the world. Indian blue cotton cloth (*zuarte*), baize,

---

[51] Adriano Parreira, *Economia e sociedade na época da Rainha Jinga (século XVII)* (Lisbon: Estampa, 1997), 115–16; Ferreira, 'Dinâmica do comércio intracolonial'; Martin, 'Power, Cloth and Currency on the Loango Coast'; Gonçalves Santos, 'Comércio de tecidos europeus e asiáticos'.

[52] Miller, *Way of Death*, 82.

a kind of woollen textile (*baeta*), wool, cotton, West African cloth (*pano da costa*), printed calico (*chita*) circulated in Benguela and its interior in various sizes and assortments. *Covados*, for example, were 68 centimetres or three-quarters of a yard long. *Palmos* were a quarter of an ell, a measure of length used for textiles (45 inches).[53] Besides the external influences, there is a long history of association of cloth and power in different African societies that needs to be further investigated.[54]

The post-mortem inventory of goods of Joana Rodrigues da Costa, resident in Caconda, offers a glimpse of the kinds of textiles that circulated in the interior of Benguela in the mid-nineteenth century. Among the textiles in her home there were a piece of Indian blue cotton cloth (*zuarte*) estimated to be worth 6$000, 13 pieces of printed calico (2$109), four blue napkins (1$500), an assortment of cloths (*panos de garras*, 1$092), six *cavados* of baize, and white cloth ($640).[55] Dona Florência José do Cadaval's inventory listed a variety of textiles, including 71 pieces of Indian blue cotton cloth (390$500), 31 blue napkins (72$600), 30 blue napkins of lower quality (54$000), seven pieces of West African cloth (105$000), 19 pieces of American cotton (104$500), 160 yards of American cotton (28$000) a piece of printed calico (5$000), a piece of red calico (4$500), 46 pieces of white cloth (101$200), and thread for sewing (1$800).[56] Her belongings included textiles coming from West Africa, India and the Americas.

During her life Joana Mendes de Moraes acquired bundles of printed and white cotton cloth, silk napkins, cloth from West Africa and striped calico cloth.[57] The inventories from male residents likewise reveal a large quantity of textiles coming from India, Europe and West Africa, reflecting the internal demand for cloth, but also the participation of Benguela residents in global markets. Having thus travelled hundreds of miles before reaching Benguela, Caconda or Catumbela, these textiles were carefully stored in local homes.

Conclusion

The income earned by women involved in long-distance trade allowed them to consume goods perceived as valuable in the African context, such

---

[53] For more on textiles and their measurement see the glossary in Linda A. Newson and Susie Minchin, *From Capture to Sale: The Portuguese Slave Trade to Spanish South America in the Early Seventeenth Century* (Leiden: Brill, 2007).
[54] Thomas Bowdich, *An Account of the Discoveries of the Portuguese in the Interior of Angola and Mozambique* (London: J. Booth, 1824), 30. See also Martin, 'Power, Cloth and Currency', 5–7; Kriger, 'Mapping the History of Cotton', 105–07.
[55] TPB, 'Autos cívis do inventário de Joana Rodriges de Costa', 2 March 1850, ff. 13–14v.
[56] TPB, 'Autos cívis do inventário de Dona Florencia do Cadaval', 15 June 1854, ff. 7–8v.
[57] TPB, 'Autos cívis do inventário de Joana Mendes de Moraes', ff. 20v–22.

as silk blouses, shawls, socks and shoes, bowls, textiles from India and tea sets from China. These patterns of consumption indicate that even women in the far interior were fully integrated into a global economy, even though imports had to be transported over as much as two hundred kilometres from the coast. Both on the coast and in the interior, women invested in ostentatious jewellery and clothing. They also invested in enslaved people, who freed them from some work and provided economic and social prestige.[58]

It is essential to examine the material items people surrounded themselves with if we are to understand their social and economic lives. Most African women might not have owned much; but inventories of the elite point to women's creativity, economic activity and accumulation of goods in the attempt to make their homes both attractive and productive. Everywhere, the inventories highlight the exotic and the importance of passing on items considered valuable and worth to bequeath to heirs and here Benguela is no exception. The differences between men and women regarding the ownership of weapons, clothing, furniture and natural resources indicate that the material world of nineteenth-century West Central Africa was gendered. The wills and inventories reveal the material objects and the people African women owned, where they lived, what they stored in their houses, and what was considered part of their estate. They provide clues concerning the social relationships and economic roles of African women. They also reveal a great deal about household organisation and networks. It is through women's material possessions that we can infer something about their role in agriculture, weaving, trade and cooking. A comparison with the inventories of men might reveal that African women did not own as much, yet their belongings do reveal considerable ingenuity and adaptability to external and internal changes. Besides, they show how some of the African women who lived in Benguela, Caconda and Catumbela were integrated into the global economy.

---

[58] See Philip J. Havik, 'Women and Trade in the Guinea Bissau Region', *Studia* 52 (1994): 83–120; Eugénia Rodrigues, 'As donas de prazos do Zambeze: Políticas imperiais e estratégias locais', Magnus R. de Mello Pereira, Antonio Cesar de Almeida Santos, Maria Luiz Andreazza and Sergio Odilon Nadalin (eds), *VI Jornadas Setecentistas: conferências e comunicações* (Curitiba, Brazil: Aos Quatro Ventos, 2006), 15–34.

Part Two
Vulnerability

5

Prostitution, Polyandry or Rape?
On the Ambiguity of European Sources for the West African Coast 1660–1860

ADAM JONES

Early European travellers' accounts[1] mention prostitution on various parts of the West African coast, mostly with Europeans as the clients. However, a few also describe something different: an institution providing sexual services exclusively for African men, located on the coast of what is now south-western Ghana. In this chapter, using comparative material as well as source criticism, I examine what the evidence tells us about these women. Does it warrant using the term 'prostitution'? Did the women exercise any agency in the services they offered? Or should we rather view their sexual exploitation as evidence of girls' and women's extreme vulnerability, perhaps even justifying the term 'rape'?

The region is inhabited by speakers of four dialects of western Akan: Esuma, Nzima, Evalue and Ahanta. Little is known about the history of this area before 1800, because in commercial terms it had less to offer outsiders than the central or eastern Gold Coast, even though it did play a role in the gold trade.[2] It was forested, politically decentralised and, in relation to areas further east, sparsely inhabited.[3]

---

[1] This chapter is a translation (abridged and with modifications) of one published in German in *Außereuropäische Frauengeschichte*, ed. Adam Jones (Pfaffenweiler: Centaurus 1992), 123–58. For comments on the use of sources written by European men for the precolonial history of African women, see Adam Jones, *Zur Quellenproblematik der Geschichte Westafrikas 1450–1900* (Stuttgart: Franz Steiner, 1990), 81–4.
[2] Pierluigi Valsecchi, *Power and State Formation in West Africa: Appolonia from the 16th to the 18th Century* (Basingstoke: Palgrave Macmillan, 2011).
[3] Axim, with 500 inhabitants in about 1660 and 700–800 in 1860, was the largest settlement: Ray A. Kea, *Settlements, Trade, and Polities in the Seventeenth Century Gold Coast* (Baltimore: Johns Hopkins University Press, 1982), 38, 79–85; Albert van Dantzig, 'The Ankobra Gold Interest', *Transactions of the Historical Society of Ghana* 14 (1973): 169–85.

The Sources

Two early Dutch sources describe the initiation of women referred to as 'whores'. Using an unidentified source probably relating to the early 1660s, the geographer Olfert Dapper wrote in 1668:[4]

> Although the Blacks along the coast and in the interior are allowed to marry as many wives as they can maintain, Atzin [= Axim] and all the surrounding areas as far as the Quaqua Coast[5] have the custom that every village maintains two or three whores, called *abrakrees*. These whores are appointed and initiated into their status as whores by the village authorities in the presence of a large crowd of people in the following manner. First, these whores, who are purchased slaves, display themselves on a straw mat with all kinds of absurd gestures. Then the oldest among them takes a young hen, cuts off its beak and lets several drops of its blood drop on her head, shoulders and arms. Meanwhile they swear in an awful manner that they shall die if they do not accept as lovers every man as their wooer for three or four *kakraven*,[6] which are [the equivalent of] twelve or sixteen pennies, even if the man visiting them is very rich; indeed they do not even exclude their own blood relations ... As soon as they have sworn this oath, someone from the crowd is sent aside with one such whore. When he comes back, he testifies that he has found her to be a genuine woman. She takes her companion, namely another *abrakree* or whore, to her and is washed, after which a clean bed-sheet[7] is draped around her. Afterwards they sit down on a mat. There a string of glass beads is hung around her neck, and her shoulders, arms and breasts are smeared with lime or chalk. Finally two bachelors take these whores on their shoulders and run through the village with them, shouting out. The people dance and drink palm wine, and generally have fun. Thereupon she sits for eight consecutive days at the aforementioned place, and every passer-by must give her two or three *kakraven*.

Willem Bosman, whose account appeared 36 years later and who had lived on the Gold Coast from about 1688 to 1702, mainly in Axim, knew of Dapper's book, but does not seem to have used it. He noted that the institution was unknown in the 'countries of Commany, Fetu, Saboe,

---

[4] Olfert Dapper, *Naukeurige beschrijvinge der afrikaensche gewesten* (Amsterdam: Jacob van Meurs 1668), 479. See Adam Jones, 'Decompiling Dapper: A Preliminary Search for Evidence', *History in Africa* 17 (1990): 171–209.
[5] Eastern part of the Ivory Coast.
[6] Tiny pieces of gold, made of broken, low-carat trinkets, beaten flat and cut into little pieces: Timothy F. Garrard, *Akan Weights and the Gold Trade* (London: Longmans, 1980), 88.
[7] Used bed linen was exported from the Netherlands to West Africa and used for clothing.

Fantyn etc.', i.e. in today's Fante. His account of the initiation echoes Dapper's in some respects, but there are also contradictions:

> When the *mancevos*[8] resolve that they desire a public whore (*algemeene Hoer*) ... they go to the *caboceros*[9] and ask them to be so kind as to purchase one for the community. Thereupon these people or the *mancevos* themselves buy a female slave who is somewhat pretty (*wat hups*). The woman is brought to the public market place, accompanied by another woman, who is already qualified in this occupation and is to give her instruction about how to comport herself in future. When all of this has been done, the novice is smeared with earth and some sacrifices are made, so that she may be happy in her future position and earn a lot of money. Then a small boy comes ... and, in the presence of all the people, makes as if to have intercourse with her, thereby signifying that from this moment onwards she must receive all persons who approach her, without distinction, not even excluding small boys. After these revels a small hut is built for her slightly on one side, in which she must be secluded for eight or ten days and must have intercourse with every man who comes there. Afterwards she receives the honourable name of *abelcré* or *abelecré*, meaning 'public whore' (*algemeene, of openbare Hoer*). She is given a place to live near one of her masters or in a secluded part of the village. For the rest of her life she is obliged not to refuse any man the use of her body, even if he gives her only a tiny amount (seldom more than a *stuyver* [or 'stiver', a coin of very low value]) – unless she pleases someone so much that he gives her rather more; but he does so as a favour, and nobody is obliged to do this. Every village ... has one, two or three such wretched creatures (*elendige Schepels*), depending on the number of inhabitants.[10]

The two accounts correspond in many respects: both say that female slaves were purchased, placed in the care of someone who was already a 'whore' and put on display; an expiatory sacrifice was made and the woman was smeared with lime, chalk or earth. The Akan term *abrakree* or *abel(e)cré* is difficult to explain, but might conceivably represent a combination of *abáa*, *abéa* 'woman' and *akyére* 'poor soul, destined to die' in an Akan dialect.[11]

---

[8] Portuguese *mancebo*, 'youth'. These unmarried men were organised as a group (Dutch: *jongmanschap*) and had a collective voice in public affairs: Kea, *Settlements*, 131–4; Adam Jones, *Brandenburg Sources for West African History 1680–1700* (Stuttgart: Franz Steiner, 1985), 79–80, 147, 161, 178–9.

[9] *caboceers*, i.e. leading men.

[10] Willem Bosman, *Nauwkeurige beschryving van de Guinese Goud-, Tand- en Slave-kust* (Utrecht: Anthony Schouten, 1704; Amsterdam: J. Verheide, 1737), 203–4.

[11] Johann G. Christaller, *A Dictionary of the Asante and Fante Language Called Tshi (Chwee, Twi)* (Basel: privately printed, 1881), 2, 284–5. The 'r' or 'l' after the 'b' would be normal in the Nzima and Evalue dialects. For the meaning of *akyére* see Robert S. Rattray, *Religion and Art in Ashanti* (Oxford: Clarendon Press, 1927), 106. Of course, Rattray's interpretation need not

On the other hand, there are two discrepancies. Whereas Dapper says that a person was selected to verify that the prospective 'whore' was a woman, Bosman states that a small boy pretended to have sex with her in public. Secondly, Dapper writes that the 'whore' sat in the market place from the eighth day after her initiation and received small pieces of gold from passers-by, while according to Bosman she was shut up in a hut for eight to ten days and had to sleep with any man who came there. However, these discrepancies do not weaken the plausibility of the accounts.

We do not know what rights or duties such women had. Dapper claims that the 'whore' was obliged to receive any man for a nominal payment; yet even this tiny sum was not intended for her:

> Whatever she receives in this manner must be handed to the head of the village. On the other hand, they enjoy the liberty to take any food that they find in the houses or in the market – as much as they need for their maintenance; and no-one may forbid them.[12]

It is striking that potential 'clients' included the woman's blood relatives. Assuming that Dapper's informant was aware of the importance of matrilineal ties in this region, one wonders whether he was referring to members of the 'large' *abusua* (clan) or to the narrower 'small' *abusua* (matrilineal kin group).[13]

Bosman confirms that 'whores' were not allowed to keep the small payment they were given and implies that it was their 'masters' (*meesters*) who gave them enough for food and clothing. He too indicates that such women had no choice about which men they slept with, but adds that the men were mainly the unmarried *mancevos*, who collectively had a say in political matters:

> If our [Dutch] factor in Axim has a dispute with the Blacks under his authority, there is no way of bringing them to reason as effective and easy as by seizing these whores and holding them in custody within the fort; for as soon as this news reaches the ears of the *mancevos*, they hurry with full-blown sails to the *caboceros* and demand emphatically that they give the factor satisfaction ... The reason why they do this so actively is that while the whores are detained, the men who have no wives must suffer [sexual] hunger and might be obliged to sleep with the wife of another man.[14]

(contd) be relevant for an institution that existed outside Asante (Ashanti) two centuries earlier, but it suggests that the 'whores' were regarded as sacrifices.

[12] Dapper, *Naukeurige beschrijvinge*, 479.

[13] The *abusua* is exogamous: marriage and intercourse between its members are forbidden. But if the 'whores' were purchased slaves (rather than pawns), one would not expect them to have had any 'blood relatives'.

[14] Bosman, *Nauwkeurige beschryving*, 204.

The existence of an institution designed to meet the sexual needs of young, unmarried men is confirmed by a third source, referring to the small kingdom of Assinie, 100 kilometres west of Axim, whose inhabitants likewise spoke a dialect of Akan. A French adventurer, Godot, spent three months there in 1701.[15] In his manuscript Godot wrote three years later:

> Although these people are entirely idolatrous, the young men have such an aversion to immorality that they never fall prey to it. The king also takes measures to prevent it. For this purpose he keeps six wenches (*filles*)[16] in each village and town, to be at the services of those men who have no wives. Apart from these six, who are maintained by the king, the governor is obliged, depending on his resources, to maintain one or two [more]. These creatures go through the towns and villages and do not dare to reject anyone, for they would be punished … In order that they may be distinguished from other women, they wrap a piece of white linen around their head. They live outside the towns or villages, and all inhabitants are welcome there – that is to say, those who have no wives; for those who have wives and are accused of having intercourse with these creatures are severely punished and must in addition pay a fine to the king. These creatures are not allowed to accept anything from anyone, although that does not prevent them from receiving something if someone gives it to them; but it must be as a favour. If it were to become known that they received presents, they would be punished in an exemplary manner, just as if they were to reject a wooer (*courtesan*).[17]

Here again the 'wenches' enabled men who themselves had many wives – in this case the king and governors – to allay the discontent of young, unmarried men, whose loyalty was indispensable. Godot goes further than Bosman when he says that married men were forbidden to have intercourse with such 'wenches'.[18] Moreover, whereas Bosman believed that such women met a 'wretched' end, Godot writes: 'When they are too old to

---

[15] See Jean-Claude Nardin and Hermann Spirik, 'Un nouveau document pour l'étude des populations lagunaires de la Côte d'Ivoire du début du XVIIIe siècle: le voyage de Jean Godot à Assinie (1701)', *Proceedings of the 8th Interrnational Congress of Anthropological and Ethnological Sciences 1968*, 3 vols (Tokyo 1970), vol. 3, 78–81. Assinie, which today belongs to Côte d'Ivoire, was then part of the Gold Coast.

[16] The term 'wenches' was actually used on the Gold Coast in this period, albeit for a different institution – that of female 'castle slaves', who may (or may not) have been subject to sexual abuse in European forts: see Rebecca Shumway, 'Castle Slaves of the Eighteenth-Century Gold Coast (Ghana)', *Slavery & Abolition* 35 (2014): 84–98, 92–3.

[17] 'Voyages de Jean Godot', Bibliothèque Nationale (Paris), Ms français 13380–13381, ff. 278–9.

[18] Perhaps it would have been classified as adultery.

practise this sinful profession, the king makes a grant towards their upkeep (*augmente leur pension*), and they retire to wherever they like.'[19] Both authors wanted to make a moral point: for Bosman the women received their just deserts, whereas Godot thought they got off rather lightly.

I have found only one reference to 'whores' in the eighteenth century – a list of gifts by the Dutch West India Company to people of the town of Shama, 70 kilometres west of Axim, in 1793, including brandy, tobacco and two dozen pipes for 'the old and young whores (*hoeren*)', as well as 'textiles, brandy, tobacco and four dozen pipes for the wenches (*meiden*)'. The reference to 'old whores' echoes Godot's statement regarding a pension, but the distinction between 'whore' and 'wench' is difficult to explain.[20]

My final source relates to the country of Ahanta, lying between Axim and Shama, in 1851.[21] The Dutch West India Company's director-general on the Gold Coast, Van der Eb, wrote a memorandum about customs of this region, based on his experiences over at least fifteen years. It included a section on 'fetish wenches or public women' (*Fetische Meiden of openbare vrouwen*):

> Especially in the Ahanta country one finds these creatures. Most are slave women, purchased by wealthy men or women exclusively for this purpose or else who were from their childhood intended for it and were given to the public as a gift. Due to their clothing and hair-style (*opschik*) everyone can recognise them, and as soon as they are of nubile age (*huwbar*), they are initiated by the fetish priests and priestesses. For the payment of 1/12 *engels* in gold they are available to any man except the one who is the first to sleep with them after their initiation. This person is obliged to pay the usual fee (*vervalt in een te betalen kostuum*), which is used for the purchase of new girls intended for the profession. From their payment a certain portion must go to the man or woman who owns them. There is no regulation stipulating that the daughters must follow the profession of their mothers; normally this does not happen.[22]

[19] 'Voyages de Jean Godot', f. 279.
[20] Algemeen Rijksarchief (The Hague), NBKG 223. A Dutchman who spent many years on the Gold Coast a century after Bosman and knew his book commented that such 'public women' no longer existed: J. A. de Marrée, *Reizen op en beschrijving van de Goudkust van Guinea*, 2 vols (Amsterdam: Gebroeders Van Cleef, 1817–18), Vol. II, 127.
[21] Ahanta designated a much larger area than it does today: see C. W. Welman, *Native States of the Gold Coast, No. 2: Ahanta* (London: Dawson, 1930), 5.
[22] A. van der Eb, 'Inboorlingrecht van de kust van Guinea 1851', *Bijdragen tot de taal-, land- en volkenkunde van Nederlandsch-Indië* 88 (1931), 287–313, pp. 297–8. Van der Eb knew this area well: H. F. Tengbergen, *Verhaal van de reistogt en expeditie naar de nederlandsche bezittingen ter westkust van Afrika (kust van Guinea)* (The Hague: S. de Visser, 1839), 95–8. Although not published until 1931, Van der Eb's manuscript, including his remarks on 'fetish wenches', was plagiarised in J. S. G. Gramberg, *Schetsen van Afrika's Westkust* (Amsterdam: Weijting & Brave, 1861).

It seems that a few of the features recorded by Dapper and Bosman in the seventeenth century had survived intact: the purchase of slave girls exclusively to perform sexual services, the initiation ceremony and the obligation to hand over part of their income to their owners. On the other hand, Van der Eb mentions elements not found in earlier accounts: the special fee (presumably higher than normal) paid by the first client after the initiation, the religious aspect implicit in the term 'fetish wench'[23] and the fact that some of these people might be owned by women.

Interpretations[24]

While there are some discrepancies between the sources, both Dapper and Bosman attach importance to the ritual of initiation. Many aspects of it are difficult to explain, yet the importance attached to the colour white will be familiar to anyone who has studied Akan culture. Assuming that the sheet in which the whore was wrapped was white, this would have had significance in terms of the red-white dichotomy in Akan *rites de passage*. White clothing is worn mainly for joyful occasions, and depending on the context, white may symbolise purity, virtue, victory, God or ancestral spirits.[25]

Equally important was the smearing of the body of the 'whore' with white clay or chalk. Such practices can today serve various purposes, mainly connected with purity, integration and/or victory. In the eighteenth and nineteenth centuries it was usual to sprinkle white clay powder over the victorious party in a dispute or someone who had been acquitted of a charge – a custom known as 'making *foefoeterre*' or '*bo hyirew*'.[26] The same custom was used in the nineteenth century when a man announced that a slave woman whom he had married, together with her children, should henceforth have the status of free people.[27]

---

[23] In Ahanta there was a stronger link between secular and sacred power than in other Akan areas. In the eighteenth century, wars were led by persons whom the Dutch called 'fetish priests'.

[24] For earlier attempts to interpret one or other of these sources see Kenneth Little, *African Women in Towns: An Aspect of Africa's Social Revolution* (Cambridge: Cambridge University Press), 89 note 16; John K. Thornton, 'Sexual Demography: The Impact of the Slave Trade on Family Structure', *Women and Slavery in Africa*, ed. Claire Robertson and Martin A. Klein (Madison: University of Wisconsin Press, 1983), 39–48, 46. See also Emmanuel Akyeampong, 'Sexuality and Prostitution among the Akan of the Gold Coast c. 1650–1950', *Past and Present* 156 (1997): 144–73, where 146–9 summarise my German article of 1992.

[25] Peter Sarpong, *Girls' Nubility Rites in Ashanti* (Tema: Ghana Publishing Corporation 1977), 70.

[26] Van der Eb, 'Inboorlingrecht', 312–3; *Royal Gold Coast Gazette*, 11 March 1823; Kofi Antubam, *Ghana's Heritage of Culture* (Leipzig: Köhler & Amelang, 1963), 81. '*Foefeterre*' may have been a combination of the Twi/Akan word *fufu*, 'white', and Portuguese *terra*, 'earth'. For *hyirêw* 'white clay' see Christaller, *Dictionary*, 208.

[27] Marrée, *Reizen*, Vol. I, 122–3. White clay also has significance in divorce ritual.

But the most striking parallels lie in two other kinds of initiation: those for a chief (*ohene*) and a nubile girl. Visitors to the central Gold Coast observed in the early seventeenth century how a 'new nobleman' was smeared with white earth and carried through his village on a chair. A similar custom is performed today in the vicinity of Axim when an *ohene* is elected or during the puberty rites of a girl. In both cases there follows a phase of transition, lasting several days – a *rite de passage* –, during which the persons concerned are shut up in one place, just as Dapper's and Bosman's 'whores' were.[28] Dapper's statement that the 'whore' sat upon a mat after her initiation might be compared with the rule forbidding an *ohene* (at any time) or a girl (during her nubility rites) to touch the earth.

Taken together, these elements suggest that the 'whore' was far from being, like European prostitutes, a *demi-mondaine*. True, she did not choose her profession, and her status was probably low; yet the 'absurd ceremonies' were not designed to humiliate her, but rather to give her a recognised position within the community. This is why she had to be rendered ritually pure (through the hen's blood, the washing and the anointment with chalk), but not because she had somehow been sullied; it also explains why she was displayed in public and celebrated.[29] In this sense she did not fit Meillassoux's generalisation about female slavery: 'The depersonalisation and desocialisation which were the fate of slaves in general go along here with a joint process of desexualisation.'[30]

Thus in seeking to understand such institutions one must take into account the power relations within the society concerned. One decisive factor was the ability of 'big men', most of whom were old, to lay claim to a large number of women; another was the fact that unmarried young men could exercise some pressure on the way the village community was organised.[31] Admittedly, the western Gold Coast was not unusual in this respect. Why did similar institutions not emerge elsewhere?[32] Possibly this was connected with the economic and social disadvantages they would have entailed for certain people. In West Africa's rainforest zone it is not unusual for rich men to exploit the extramarital escapades of their young

---

[28] Adam Jones, *German Sources for West African History 1599–1669* (Wiesbaden: Franz Steiner, 1983), 32; Pieter de Marees, *Description and Historical Account of the Gold Kingdom of Guinea (1602)*, ed. Albert van Dantzig & Adam Jones (London: Oxford University Press, 1987), 85b, 86b; cf. Welman, *Native States*, 83; Sarpong, *Nubility Rites*, 38ff, 52.

[29] For possible parallels in nubility and *kyiriba* rites see Sarpong, *Nubility Rites*, 37f, 50–4.

[30] Claude Meillassoux, 'Female Slavery', *Women and Slavery in Africa*, ed. Claire Robertson and Martin A. Klein (Madison: University of Wisconsin Press, 1983), 49–66, 65. Both Godot and Van der Eb mentioned that the 'whores' were recognisable by their clothing (cf. the Twi term *aguaman-tám*, 'clothing of a whore': Christaller, *Dictionary*, 586). This might suggest that they were not fully integrated. But since a similar distinction was made between the clothing of married and unmarried women, the opposite may have been the case.

[31] Bosman, *Nauwkeurige beschryving*, 155.

[32] See, however, the evidence from the Slave Coast discussed below.

wives, placing young men in a position of obligation. In the past this was a method of acquiring non-kin dependants or slaves for export.[33] The fact that on the western Gold Coast 'whores' were made available for single men suggests either that rich men had no need to procure labour in this manner or – more plausibly – that every man who visited such a woman incurred obligations vis-à-vis her owner.

A further factor may have been the size of settlements. In a village with only a hundred inhabitants a slight shift in gender ratios would have had more drastic repercussions than in a town. If, for instance, five of the most powerful men each married five women, only a small number of sexual partners remained for the rest of the male population.[34]

Different West African Case: The Central Slave Coast

In the same book as his report on the 'whores' of Axim, Bosman wrote about 'public whores' (*algemeene hoeren*) whom he had seen in the 1690s in Ouidah, in the south of what is today Benin, 500 kilometres east of Axim,[35] and who, he believed, could be found 'in all the Ardra [= Allada] countries' of the vicinity:

> In the country of Fida [Ouidah] I have seen a number of huts, no more than ten foot (*voeten*) long and about six wide, placed near the large roads throughout the country. In these such women are obliged to serve any man whom it pleases on fixed days in the week ... I was assured that some, who were beautiful (*fray van leeft*), had intercourse with no less than thirty men within one day ... Their fee is three small shells, called *boesjes* there and cowries in our country, which are worth about two *duyts* there. This is a fixed price, from which they must feed themselves, unless they are in the position to do some handicraft and thereby earn a little more ... It is usual among some of the principal or wealthiest ladies (*wyven*), when they lie on their deathbed, to buy some foreign slave women, in order to donate them to the community (*gemeen*) for this purpose ... This serves the same purpose as a requiem mass among the Papists.[36]

[33] Susan B. Kaplow, 'Primitive Accumulation and Traditional Social Relations on the Nineteenth Century Gold Coast', *Canadian Journal of African Studies* 12 (1978): 19–36, 33–4; Caroline Bledsoe, *Women and Marriage in Kpelle Society* (Stanford: Stanford University Press 1980).
[34] Unless some men had chosen a male partner. For marriage between two men see I. Signorini, '*Agonwole Agyale*: The Marriage between Two Persons of the Same Sex among the Nzema of Southwestern Ghana', *Journal de la Société des Africanistes* 43 (1973): 221–34.
[35] See Robin Law, *Ouidah: The Social History of a West African Slaving 'Port', 1727–1892* (Athens: Ohio University Press, 2004).
[36] Bosman, *Nauwkeurige beschryving*, 203.

Here too prostitution was evidently not something for European clients; nor was it a private matter. Whether or not we credit Bosman's vision of slave women being donated to the community by rich ladies on their deathbed (not inconceivable, although he often allowed himself poetic license), they must have been organised by someone. Quite apart from the fact that Bosman uses the term 'obliged', he goes on to note that, as on the western Gold Coast, the women had to meet the sexual needs of unmarried men, in particular those of slaves: 'Since these countries are very populous, the slaves very numerous and the married women kept under strict control ... these women must tolerate a great deal on those days.'[37]

This emphasis on the strict control to which married women were subject is important. As Bosman states elsewhere, unmarried men in the Ouidah region who wanted to seduce a married woman ran a high risk:

> The men here are so strangely jealous of their wives that on the least suspicion in the world they sell them to the Europeans for deportation, unlike the Blacks of the Gold Coast, who have no scruple about driving a public trade with their wives' bodies.[38]

Bosman's report is corroborated by an anonymous French description of Ouidah, written in about 1714:

> For the security of their wives and for the use of unmarried men there are in every village a certain number of licentious wenches (*filles abandonnées*), to whom it is forbidden to reject anything and who are paid with five cowries (*bouges*), worth five *deniers* ... All these debauched wenches (*filles débauchées*) pay tribute to the king: one of his senior wives is responsible for this, and she is called their captain. In the market places there stands a small hut into which no more than two persons fit. One of these wenches is put on show (*exposée*) there for the duration of the market. If a Black comes, he places his straw hat on a stick in the entrance, thereby showing that the place is occupied. Nobody disturbs him, and when he comes out, he gives the wench five *deniers*. One can best compare her with a breeding stallion which is put on show at a fair.[39]

Most of this corresponds with Bosman's account: the small huts, the low (and fixed) fee and the implication that such a woman received many men on her appointed day. The most important additional information is the

---

[37] Ibid., 203.
[38] Ibid., Chapter XVIII.
[39] Aix-en-Provence, Archives Nationales d'Outre-Mer, Dépôt des Fortifications des colonies, Côtes d'Afrique, Ms. 105 (undated), 'Relation du Royaume de Judas en Guinée', ff. 47–8.

statement that the 'wenches' were under the king's control and paid taxes to one of his wives. Later authors made similar remarks. Interestingly, as in Bosman's report on Axim, the market place is mentioned – perhaps an indication that sex was regarded as a commodity, or at any rate not as a purely private matter.

It is not known whether similar institutions existed in the interior at this time, since the sources available are limited. An Englishman who was held prisoner in Abomey, the inland capital of Dahomey, in 1734 wrote in a letter that King Agadja was interested in acquiring a 'whore, either white or Mullatoe ... either to be his wife or else practice her old Trade'.[40] It seems possible that Agadja already had other 'whores', whose position was distinguished from those of his wives and other women. This would fit the report of another Englishman, Robert Norris, who visited the capital of Dahomey in 1772 and witnessed a procession of 250 prostitutes 'by royal appointment':

> In every town there is a certain number of women, proportioned to its size, who are to be obliging to every customer that offers; the price of their favours is regulated, and very moderate; and though these poor creatures pay a heavy tax annually, which was the occasion of their being convened at present, yet by having small beer, and breeding poultry added to what their occupation brings in, they are enabled to live; and I am inclined to think that there are wretches in the world, of the same profession, more miserable than they are.[41]

Like Bosman, Norris explains the purpose of the institution in terms of satisfying the sexual cravings of unmarried men – a serious problem in Dahomey, since the king and senior dignitaries strictly reserved a large portion of the women for themselves:

> This is a precaution taken by the government to prevent the peace of private families being violated, and is perhaps more necessary here, than in any other state; as ... every indiscretion of gallantry exposes the delinquents to death or slavery; especially too, as the people of rank engross the major part of the women. The king's seraglio consists of between 3 and 4 thousand; his principal men have from 1 to 3 or 4 hundred wives each; and people in humbler stations from half a dozen to twenty; from this unequal distribution ... the lower class remain unprovided with female companions.[42]

---

[40] William Smith, *A New Voyage to Guinea* (London: John Nourse, 1744), 183.
[41] Robert Norris, *Memoirs of the Reign of Bossa Ahádee, King of Dahomy, an Inland Country of Guiny* (London: W. Lowndes, 1789), 98.
[42] Ibid., 98–9.

Norris' statement about the extremely unequal distribution of wives in Dahomey was confirmed by nineteenth-century visitors and may explain why a form of officially sanctioned prostitution survived until the introduction of colonial rule in the late nineteenth century. Most authors even imply that it was the monarchy that had introduced the institution. In a book published in 1819 an English trader with long experience of West Africa wrote concerning Dahomey:

> Houses are licensed by royal authority, to prevent those evils which are so very prevalent in other countries, where the youth are allured by the women. Persons keeping houses so licensed are bound under severe penalties to keep good order.[43]

Other authors, however, emphasised the religious aspects of such 'houses'. The German missionary Schlegel wrote in his dictionary of the Ewe language (1857):

> All along the Slave Coast in every town there is at least one institute in which the finest Black girls, some of them from the age of 10–12 upwards, reside for about three years as *kosio*, 'consecrated persons' (*geweihte*) ... During these three years they support themselves by begging. When these years of living in the institute are over, they become common whores, having been made this by the *edro* [= 'idol'], or rather, by its priest. There are also male institutes, likewise called *kosi*, 'consecrated ones', but these are less common; they later become the priests of idols. These youths are from time to time allowed to visit the whore-houses (for that is what such establishments are) ... Such women, made into common whores by the priests, are then really like a public brothel. And all along the Slave Coast, from the Volta (Amu) almost as far as the Niger, it is with such persons that the so-called, self-styled Christians, who think themselves civilised – merchants, captains etc. – have dealings.[44]

It almost sounds as if Schlegel had accommodated what he learned about the Slave Coast to what he knew about prostitutes with European clients and about temple prostitution in other parts of the world. Yet some elements of his description of the *kosi* are plausible. Schlegel may have mixed up material concerning prostitution with reports concerning girls'

---

[43] George A. Robertson, *Notes on Africa* (London: Sherwood, Neely & Jones, 1819), 274.
[44] J. B. Schlegel, *Schlüssel zur Ewe-Sprache* (Bremen: W. Valett, 1857), 280–1. This passage and Norris' report were plagiarised together in A. B. Ellis, *The Ewe-Speaking Peoples of the Slave Coast of West Africa* (London: Chapman & Hall, 1890), 141. Jacques Marcireau, *Histoire des rites sexuels* (Paris: Robert Laffont, 1971) offers a misleading summary of the (secondary) account of Ellis, which he mistakenly applies to the 'Tshi', i.e. Akan.

initiation schools, which were a separate institution,[45] although one eighteenth-century source suggests that such schools were often connected with promiscuity, even if this was officially disapproved of.[46]

A few years after Schlegel's book appeared, Richard Burton visited Dahomey's capital Abomey on behalf of the British government but had little to say about this topic – surprisingly, considering his interest in African women: 'A small party of *Ko-si*, or *filles de joie*, 'for man side' and 'for woman side', all dark and very plain, sang before the royal tent, and walked about amongst the males'.[47] This terse account referred to the fact that, like many other elements in the socio-political organisation of Dahomey, the *kosi* were divided into two groups of equal status, one of which lived outside the palace, while the other was responsible for the 'inside'. This second group, as Skertchly, another Englishman, remarked after visiting Abomey in 1871, represented a 'rather curious circumstance, since there is not a single man within the palatial walls'.[48] It is difficult to imagine what function these women might have had apart from upholding the symmetry of ideological symbolism.[49] Perhaps Agadja's request for a 'white or mulatto whore' 150 years earlier was referring to the same kind of symmetrical arrangement.

Skertchly proceeded to offer a useful description:

> These women are a public institution in Dahomey, and receive licence from the king to practise their trade. They are under the orders of the *Meu* and his Amazonian double,[50] whose duty is to keep up the supply of these somewhat superfluous ladies in a land where polygamy is rife. The initiation is performed by an old hag, who takes the neophyte into her confidence, and when fully instructed leaves her in a small hut, where she is forced to receive gratis the attentions

---

[45] See Le Sieur d'Elbée, 'Journal du voyage des isles, dans la coste de Guinée', in J. de Clodoré, *Relation de ce qui s'est passé dans les isles & terre-ferme de l'Amerique pendant la dernière guerre avec l'Angleterre...* (Paris: Gervais Clovzier, 1671), 347–558, 444–6; Bosman, *Nauwkeurige beschryving*, Part 2, 158.

[46] John Atkins, *A Voyage to Guinea, Brasil and the West-Indies* (London: Ward & Chandler, 1735), 114–5. Schlegel was not the only missionary in this area to see a connection between prostitution and religion: see A.J.N. Tremearne, 'Extracts from the Diary of the Late Reverend John Martin, Wesleyan Missionary in West Africa, 1843–48', *Man* 12/74 (1912): 140.

[47] Richard Burton, *A Mission to Gelele, King of Dahome*, 2nd edn, 2 vols (London: Tinsley Brothers, 1864), Vol. II, 257.

[48] J.A. Skertchly, *Dahomey as it is* (London: Chapman & Hall, 1874), 283.

[49] For this symmetry see Edna Bay, 'Servitude and Worldly Success in the Palace of Dahomey', *Women and Slavery in Africa*, ed. Claire Robertson and Martin A. Klein (Madison: University of Wisconsin Press 1983), 340–67, 343–4.

[50] The *meu* was one of the highest-ranking persons in Dahomey, responsible for the annual festivities. Like other officials outside the court, he shared his office with a woman inside the palace.

of all gentlemen who may please to visit her for seven days. At the expiration of this period she is entitled to a fee of about two strings of cowries, and is obliged to submit to the embraces of any person who pays the honorarium.

Apart from Skertchly's illogical remark about polygamy and superfluity, this report complements those of Bosman and Norris. Skertchly describes a dance, 'so truly Dahoman in its duality', performed by the *kosi* under the supervision of a 'female captain':

> These ladies have the exclusive privilege of playing a large drum called *Addugba*, and they exhibit themselves with all the nonchalance of their trade. The *Addugba* drum is the accompanying music to a peculiar dance, more like a quadrille than anything else. A soldier stood opposite each *ko-si*, and when the music struck up, the couples commenced a wild corybantic display, having no beauty whatever in its movements. After a few moments the couples crossed over and changed sides, and repeated the figure. All wore long white turbans, and carried round brass fans, like small frying-pans … At the conclusion of the dance, the inside *Ko-si* made a similar display, the place of the male dancers being taken by girls dressed in men's costume. These inside *meretrices* wore blue robes and scarlet turbans, while the officer was clothed in a yellow and crimson striped tunic.[51]

It is uncertain whether these reports from the Slave Coast all referred to the same institution. Even if they did, it would be wrong to regard it simply as a variant of what existed on the Gold Coast, though Bosman and Skertchly stressed the similarities.[52] One difference lay in the manner in which girls were prepared: in Dahomey they underwent a long period of training, which was replaced on the Gold Coast by a public initiation. Moreover, 'whores' of the Gold Coast were 'owned' by influential persons of a village, whereas those of the Slave Coast on the one hand belonged to the community as a whole and on the other seem to have been relatively autonomous. Apart from Bosman no author spoke of the prostitutes of the Slave Coast as 'slaves', and he himself recognised differences between the two regions: 'Since they [the 'whores' in the Ouidah area] do not belong to anyone, nobody takes any trouble on their behalf, nor are they solemnly initiated, as they are on the Gold Coast.'[53]

---

[51] Skertchly, *Dahomey*, 283–4.
[52] Bosman, *Nauwkeurige beschryving*, 205; Skertchly, *Dahomey*, 283. Between the western Gold Coast and the central Slave Coast lay the well documented areas today inhabited by the Asante, Fante and Gã, in which no such institutions appear to have existed.
[53] Bosman, *Nauwkeurige beschryving*, 206.

Furthermore, as we have seen, Bosman believed that a wife on the Slave Coast was punished more severely for marital infidelity than on the western Gold Coast – partly, perhaps, because descent on the Slave Coast was patrilineal.[54] On the Gold Coast a man might be punished for adultery with a married woman; but the woman herself, unless she was the senior wife, might get off lightly. Hence one of the justifications for 'professional' prostitution on the Slave Coast – that the virtue of married women must at all costs be protected – played less of a role among Akan groups on the Gold Coast.

As far as the nineteenth century is concerned, an additional difference lay in the political systems. Political centralisation made it possible to organise hundreds of women from the capital of Dahomey, whereas in Ahanta and surrounding areas these women were probably organised at village level.

Nevertheless, in both cases the women were organised by the community – by the kingdom of Dahomey (or its predecessor Allada) or by a village on the Gold Coast – and were obliged to accept any unmarried man who approached them. In both the community thereby protected the interests of men who had many wives and were politically dominant.[55]

A further similarity lay in the fact that both on the western Gold Coast (in the seventeenth century) and in Dahomey (in the mid-nineteenth century) there was a transitional (or liminal?) period in which the new 'whore' received no payment for sexual services. Moreover, for both areas a religious element is hinted at, although the details are unclear.

A striking parallel may be noticed between the 'rich ladies' in Ouidah around 1690 and the female owners in Ahanta in the mid-nineteenth century. Clearly we cannot interpret organised prostitution solely as an institution used by polygynous men to avert the threat posed by single men, as Norris did. Nor can we in this case accept the general argument that African women owned female slaves because this gave them more leisure or raised their productivity.[56] Possibly the institution helped to raise their *reproductivity*, because they gave birth to children who may have then belonged to their owners, male or female; yet the same result could have been achieved if such women had been married to slave men.

Whatever the motives of the female owners were, it cannot have been the expectation of direct financial gain; since the fees in both areas were

---

[54] Ibid., Chapter XVIII.

[55] By offering 'communally regulated sexual intercourse', these men encountered the threat posed by younger men on the marriage market in a manner similar to that of middle-aged men in towns of south-east France in the fifteenth century: cf. Jacques Rossiaud, 'Prostitution, jeunesse et société dans les villes du sud-est au XVe siècle', *Annales: Economies, Sociétés, Civilisations* 31 (1976): 289–325.

[56] *Women and Slavery in Africa*, ed. Claire Robertson and Martin A. Klein (Madison: University of Wisconsin Press 1983), 15.

low. A woman who earned only three to five cowries from every man with whom she had intercourse would hardly have been able to maintain herself. One hen cost between 240 and 280 cowries.[57] Even if she did – *credat Judaeus Appella* – copulate with thirty men a day, as Bosman wrote, this would have left her poor, unless someone supported her. When Skertchly visited the Slave Coast in 1871, these women could claim two strings of cowries from each client, but this was the result of cowrie hyperinflation in the 1850s and 1860s. Given that the 'whores' had to give part of their earnings to their community or their owners, one wonders whether they improved their economic status by other activities. Brewing beer – often associated with prostitution elsewhere in Africa – would hardly have been possible in the forest around Axim, where people drank palm wine and its sale was a male monopoly.

One further common element was the risk of catching a venereal disease, which Bosman mentioned with reference to both areas. Such diseases were common by 1600 in Sierra Leone, on the central Gold Coast or at Cape Lopez, where European ships called frequently;[58] but it is unlikely that they were as widespread on the western Gold Coast or central Slave Coast. Nevertheless, although nobody confirmed Bosman's claim, it deserves to be taken seriously, because he was in a good position to know about this.

Polyandry?

A possible interpretation is that the authors who wrote about 'whores' were describing a form of polyandry. Edwin Ardener has argued with reference to post-independence Cameroun that 'prostitution' in small and medium-sized towns should really be called 'hyperpolyandry':

> Domestic privileges such as the provision of meals may be conceded to regular clients, who may themselves help to provide firewood or other amenities. The lack of anonymity, or impersonality, in prostitution

---

[57] Marion Johnson, 'The Cowrie Currencies of West Africa', *Journal of African History* 11 (1970), 17–50 and 331–54, 347. According to Bosman (*Nauwkeurige beschryving*, 206), the fee on the Slave Coast was somewhat lower than on the Gold Coast. Of course, incomes varied enormously within this region: see Kea, *Settlements*, 307–13. It is not inconceivable that the owners made a profit, but if so, it must have been small.

[58] Johnson, 'Cowrie Currencies', 339, 347. In Skertchly's day a string consisted of 50 cowries in Ouidah (on the coast), but only 46 in Abomey (the capital of Dahomey). The value of the cowrie had sunk by about a quarter in the previous twenty years. In 1850 a hen cost the same as in the early eighteenth century: between 200 and 280 cowries. If all other factors remained equal, this might suggest that the two strings of cowries that a woman received in 1871 had eight times as much purchasing power as the three cowries that a woman in Ouidah received in the 1690s, or five times as much as the five cowries that were paid in around 1714.

transactions in a 'stranger quarter' gives the relations with the client group some quasi-uxorial qualities.[59]

Similarly, the 'whores' had a set of clients which must have been much smaller than that of modern prostitutes: given the size of the villages, it can hardly have been more than a dozen men. It is possible that the 'whores' performed non-sexual services for some men. Cooking and sex are associated in Akan culture, and the woman who cooks for an unmarried man is often the one with whom he sleeps.

Polyandry is not a homogenous phenomenon and cannot be described everywhere in the same terms.[60] Here we confine ourselves to one African case. The Lele of the Democratic Republic of Congo share several features with the Akan: a tropical rainforest environment, rice as a staple food and a matrilineal emphasis in kinship. Mary Tew (later Douglas) described in 1951 an institution called *hohombe*, 'village-wife', which had been prohibited by the Belgians in 1947.[61] The 'village-wife' was acquired by the men of one age-set by violent abduction or a regulated transfer. During the first months she was treated with respect; then she received several 'house husbands', who had the right (in rotation) to sleep with her in her house. In the forest, however, every man of the village shared this right. The children of such women became 'children of the village'.

Tew depicts that *hohombe* as a 'safety valve', removing excessive pressure of the marriage system upon men and women. One wonders whether the same applied to the *abrakrees* of the Gold Coast. The fact that these were purchased as slaves need not be crucial: after all, the position of many female slaves in relation to their owners was not very different from that of junior wives. Like the *hohombe*, the *abrakree* was instructed in her duties and enjoyed a 'honeymoon' period. Moreover, the Lele, like the inhabitants of the western Gold Coast but unlike the Fon of Dahomey, never had a centralised state; indeed, Tew considers it unlikely that such an institution could have co-existed with centralised control.[62]

Nevertheless, there are striking differences. Although one might argue that the 'youngmen' constituted a sort of age-set, it was not possible on the Gold Coast for a man to be both polyandrous and polygynous. Tew rejects the terms 'village prostitute' and '*femme commune*' on the grounds that for a 'village-wife' (unlike a princess) the term adultery certainly had a meaning. This does not seem to have been the case on the Gold Coast. If we are to

---

[59] Ardener, *Divorce*, 21.
[60] Nancy E. Levine and Walter H. Sangree, eds, *Women with Many Husbands: Polyandrous Alliance and Marital Flexibility in Africa and Asia*. Special issue of the *Journal of Comparative Family Studies* XI, 3 (1980): 385–6.
[61] Mary Tew, 'A Form of Polyandry among the Lele of the Kasai', *Africa* 21 (1951): 1–12; Mary Douglas [née Tew], *The Lele of the Kasai* (London: Oxford University Press 1963).
[62] Douglas, *Lele*, 140.

believe Dapper, even the taboo on incest (as defined in this society) was ignored. At any rate the *hohombe* could reject certain men, while the *abrakree* could not. Furthermore, the *abrakree* probably did not have a fixed group of 'husbands', although our information is not clear on this.

The comparison with polyandry reveals gaps in what we know about the Gold Coast 'whores'. One wonders whether the normal division of labour was set aside, as it was for the 'village-wife' during the 'honeymoon' period,[63] and whether such women had to do weeding or fetch water for a particular man. In addition, assuming that the 'whores' must have had children, were they 'children of the village' or did they belong to the lineage of the man who had purchased their mother? Or was the question of paternity not settled until the woman actually bore a child, as in systems of secondary marriage in central Nigeria?[64] On the western Gold Coast children normally belonged to the matrilineage of their mother; but children of a slave woman married to a free man would have more obligations towards the matrilineage of their father.[65] Apart from Van der Eb's statement that daughters did not have to follow their mother's occupation, none of our authors mentions children. Was birth control or abortion practised?[66] Alternatively, women chosen for this task may have been considered infertile,[67] or their status and unsettled lifestyle may have reduced the probability of conception.[68]

Conclusion

One might conclude that what Europeans observed on the western Gold Coast represented a form of institutionalised rape: sexual exploitation of certain unfree women in the interests of the male elite of a primarily rural society. Yet to prove this, we would need less ambiguous evidence.

At least we can say something about what the institution was *not*. It had little to do with prostitution as practised in African towns today, and any

[63] Tew, 'Form of Polyandry', 3.
[64] In central Nigeria forms of cicisbeism used to exist, in which all children belonged to the man who had paid bridewealth, irrespective of the identity of the genitor.
[65] For different parts of southern Ghana see Robert S. Rattray, *Ashanti* (Oxford: Clarendon Press 1923), 43; Arthur Ffoulkes, 'Fanti marriage customs', *Journal of the African Society* 8 (1908–9), 31–49, 43; Mission 21 Archive (Basel), D-10,3.10, J. Mader 28 October 1868.
[66] We know little about birth control in precolonial Africa. On contraceptives, abortion and infanticide in West Central African history see Robert Harms, 'Sustaining the System: Trading Towns along the Middle Zaire', *Women and Slavery in Africa*, ed. Claire Robertson and Martin A. Klein (Madison: University of Wisconsin Press 1983), 95–110, 106–7. See also Wolf Bleek, 'Did the Akan Resort to Abortion in Pre-colonial Ghana?' *Africa* 60 (1990): 121–32.
[67] In West African towns in the mid-twentieth century women sometimes became prostitutes because they were infertile and hence excluded from marriage: Aidan Southall, ed., *Social Change in Modern Africa* (London: Oxford University Press 1961), 47.
[68] Cf. Ardener, *Divorce*, 54; Meillassoux, 'Female Slavery', 52–4.

attempt to explain the sources in terms of classical economics is unlikely to tell us much. The institution did bear some resemblance to what Europeans saw on the central Slave Coast, but here too there are marked differences, as well as aspects which remain unclear in the sources.

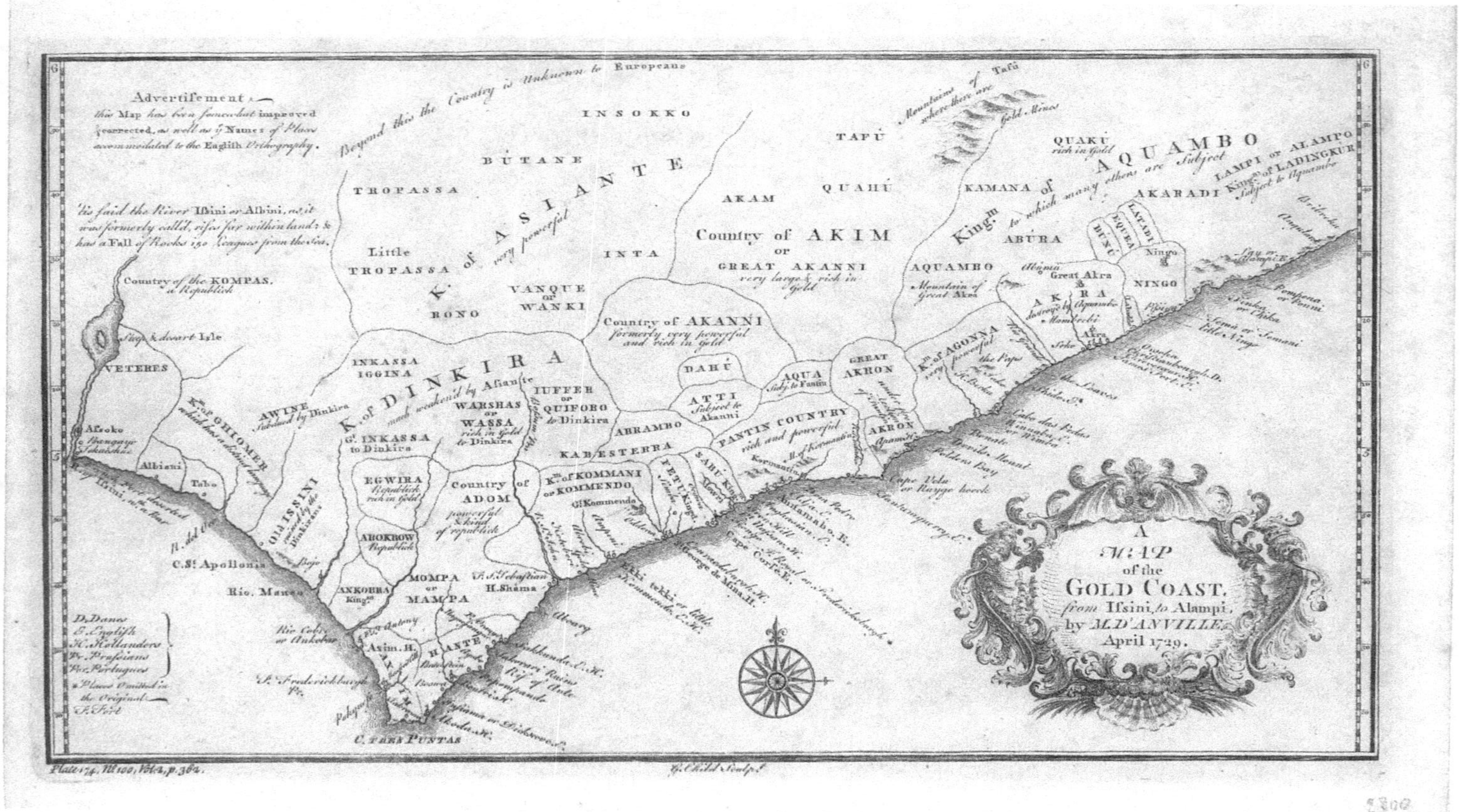

Map 5 The Gold Coast from Issini to Alampi, by M.D. Anville, April 1729 (Source: Natalie Everts, private collection)

6

Parrying Palavers
Coastal Akan Women & the Search for Security in the Eighteenth Century

NATALIE EVERTS

On Tuesday, 22 July 1788, Martin Watts, commander of the British slave-trading fort at Anomabo, sent a letter appealing to his superior, Governor Norris, at Cape Coast Castle: 'I am heartbroken and do not know what to do.'[1] The principal *caboceer* (headman), Amonu Kuma, 'one of the most powerful men in all the Fante states',[2] was pressing Watts to 'hand over' his locally born wife and children. Amonu had given him an ultimatum: 'Next Saturday will be the day I have to hand her over, and will be a spectator to the murdering of my wife and children, sacrificed to slavery.'[3]

While a crowd of Amonu's adherents showed bravado in front of the fort gate, reminding Watts that their master was not joking, Watts attempted to gain time. As some of his wife's family happened to be 'Dutch subjects', originating from nearby Mouri, and 'she herself, had lived for several years under Dutch rule', his wife felt entitled to appeal to 'His lordship the General of Elmina'. Compared with Norris, Watts' British superior, she deemed the director-general of the Dutch West India Company, stationed at Elmina Castle, better able to pass an impartial judgement on her case.

---

[1] National Archives, The Hague, the Netherlands (NL-HaNA), Nederlandse Bezittingen op de Kust van Guinea (NBKG) (Netherlands possessions on the Coast of Guinea), 1.05.14, 167, Correspondence, Watts to Norris, Anomabo, 22 July 1788. A guide to Dutch collections is Michel R. Doortmont and Jinna Smit, *Sources for the Mutual History of Ghana and the Netherlands, an Annotated Guide to the Dutch Archives relating to Ghana and West Africa in the Nationaal Archief, 1593–1960s* (Leiden and Boston: Brill, 2007).

[2] *Caboceer*: headman, derived from *cabeça*: head, in the lingua franca: Mary Esther Kropp Dakubu, 'The Portuguese Language on the Gold Coast, 1471–1807', *Ghana Journal of Linguistics* 1, no.1 (2012): 15–33, 26. British ally Amonu Kumu likely was *Omanhene* (Fante: *oman*: state; *ohene*: chief) or *Anomabohene* the paramount chief of Anomabo: Margaret Priestley, *West African Trade and Coast Society: A Family Study* (London: Oxford University Press, 1969), 15; Rebecca Shumway, *The Fante and the Transatlantic Slave Trade* (Rochester, NY: The University of Rochester Press, 2011), 60, 82–6.

[3] NL-HaNA, NBKG 167, Anomabo, 22 July 1788.

Therefore, Watts placed his hope in the hands of both governors so that they, with the *Terre Grandes* (principal headmen or elders) of Cape Coast, could act 'to bring this *palaver* to an end'. His wife had convinced him that only a joint effort in diplomacy at the very top level could save their children and herself.[4]

Was Madam Watts, who was of Eurafrican descent and married to the commander of a British trade fort according to the 'customs of the country', really in danger of being reduced to slavery with her children, or did her husband – he even spoke of 'murder' – dramatise the precariousness of her situation? Although he appeared to be panic-stricken by Amonu Kumu's intimidating conduct, she apparently managed to keep a cool head. It was she who, having been born and raised in the cosmopolitan coastal environment, came up with the idea of summoning the help of the senior Dutch authority.

Like all peoples belonging to the myriad of African Atlantic societies in the eighteenth century, the coastal Akan had to cope with disruptive effects derived from the intensification of the trade in enslaved human beings. A tried and tested method to reduce people, either of slave status or free birth, to poverty, pushing them farther into dependency, was 'the stretching of palavers' (from Portuguese *palavra*: dispute).[5] The Reverend Philip Quaque, called as a minister to Cape Coast Castle, witnessed how wealthy merchants ensnared civilians by pinning upon them false claims for a debt that it would have been impossible to pay off.[6] This forced household heads to pawn to a creditor someone from among their family slaves or direct kin, whom they were subsequently seldom able to redeem. In the introduction to her volume *Fighting the Slave Trade*, Sylviane Diouf discusses the experiences of individual West Africans and the strategies they employed when confronted with arbitrariness and violence. These women and men should not be divided simply into perpetrators or victims, she argues. If someone managed to redeem a relative or family slave, for instance, the debtor had to offer the creditor another enslaved woman or man as a substitute.[7]

Little is known about the experiences of women living in the decentralised coastal Akan communities at the time. In addition to Madam Watts we discuss in depth the cases of Aquassiba, Betje and Catrijn. Although all

[4] Ibid.
[5] Willem Bosman, *Nauwkeurige Beschrijving van de Guinese Goud-, Tand- en Slavekust* (Amsterdam: J. Verheide 1737 [1704]),168, 172. Akosua Adoma Perbi, *A History of Indigenous Slavery in Ghana, from the 15th to the 19th century* (Legon, Ghana: Sub-Saharan Publishers, 2004), 62–66.
[6] Vincent Carretta and Ty M. Reese (eds), *The life and Letters of Philip Quaque, The first African Anglican Missionary* (Athens, GA and London: University of Georgia Press, 2010) 112–13.
[7] Sylviane A. Diouf (ed.), *Fighting the Slave Trade, West African Strategies* (Athens, OH: Ohio University Press; Oxford: James Currey, 2003), ix–x.

four were energetic entrepreneurs who were operating on the interface of cultures and familiar with the mechanisms of the Afro-European trade, their room for manoeuvre was limited.

Although all of these women were born and raised in an African environment, only Aquassiba is addressed by her Akan name[8] in the written sources. I will explore her battle in Elmina first, before returning to Madam Watts.

Aquassiba, Madam Watts and Betje each applied to European officials for help. They were in a position to request mediation on their behalf, because they were part of the same intercultural coastal network. Catrijn, the daughter of a Dutch father and an enslaved mother from Nzema, the most westerly Gold Coast region, spent most of her life among the residents of Axim Lower Town. In contrast to the others, she seems to have kept her connections with the successive commanders of Axim Fort to a minimum.

Apart from Aquassiba, who fell into trouble at a young age, the principal concern of each woman was for her household, including those with whom she shared her life. In the unsafe and highly competitive coastal environment, however, each operated in her own interest. Who challenged these women, and what tactics did they employ when they became embroiled in palavers?[9]

Women's Space in an Intercultural Setting

Both the British fort at Anomabo and Cape Coast Castle, the seat of the British Company of Merchants Trading to Africa, had been established in thriving commercial states that fell within the Fante sphere of influence. The leadership of the Edina *oman* (Elmina state) operated more or less independently, albeit in alliance with the Dutch stationed at the Castle São Jorge da Mina, which served as the West India Company's headquarters.[10] These Gold Coast hubs of the Atlantic slave trade were also locations

---

[8] Quassiba: Sunday born. In the text I maintain the spelling of the original documents.

[9] Following Carina Ray, *Crossing the Color Line, Race, Sex, and the Contested Politics of Colonialism in Ghana* (Athens: Ohio University Press), 5–7, these cases of women calling in help from stranger connections must be seen as part of a wide range of power relations between coastal women and European males.

[10] West India Company (WIC) official Bosman characterised Fante as a commonwealth of states: Bosman, *Beschrijving*, 3–5, 57–60. In the mid-eighteenth century, Anomabo, a major point of embarkation for enslaved Africans, was a Fante city state, whereas Oguaa (Cape Coast) had become autonomous of Fetu. See Robin Law, 'Fante Expansion Reconsidered: Seventeenth Century Origins', *Transactions of the Historical Society of Ghana*, New Series No.14 (2012), 41–78; Robin Law, 'The Government of Fante in the Seventeenth Century', *The Journal of African History* 54, no. 1 (2013): 31–51. For Elmina see: Harvey M. Feinberg, 'Africans and Europeans in West Africa: Elminians and Dutchmen on the Gold Coast during the Eighteenth Century', *Transactions of the American Philosophical Society*, 79, part 7 (1989).

112 • *Vulnerability*

Illustration 5 Woman of the Gold Coast, identified as being of mixed race, with bead jewellery, belt and anklets, carrying a parasol
(Source: 'A mulatto woman of the Gold Coast', William Hutton, *A voyage to Africa* (London: Longman, Hurst, Rees, Orme & Brown 1821), p. 92; Copy in Albert and Shirley Small Special Collections Library, University of Virginia)

where Africans – mostly Akan speakers – had been welcoming overseas traders since the arrival of the Portuguese in the fifteenth century. At certain sites, notably Elmina and Cape Coast, in the course of time partners in Afro-European commerce had created communities in which the intercultural overlap was regulated by rules and mores.[11]

Family elders, male and female alike, had become accustomed to marrying off both freeborn daughters and domestic slave girls to resident Europeans. Such an affiliation by kinship was called *casar* to marry in the local language of communication,[12] and served to strengthen the lineage concerned. As a rule, a mixed couple's Eurafrican children belonged to their mother's *abusua* or matrilineal descent group and inherited her status, either as a freeborn member or as a family slave.[13] In contrast to a trade slave (*odonko*: stranger originating from the hinterland), who had to do without an affiliation to an Akan lineage, a family slave was regarded as belonging to a house that served as residence to a group of members who belonged to the same *abusua*.[14]

Akan women's lives centred on their own segment of an *abusua*, whose living members knew they were united along the female bloodline with both the ancestors and future generations. Members made sustained efforts to safeguard the continuity of the line of descent, to the extent that daughters could be pressed to get married and have children. Adoption was also prevalent. Compared with the perpetual connection represented by the *abusua*, marital bonds were considered to be of a more temporary nature.[15]

The *abusua* not only afforded women a deeply felt sense of security: it also offered them opportunities to develop social and economic activities.

---

[11] On cultivating connections: Lisa A. Lindsay, 'Extraversion, Creolization, and Dependency in the Atlantic Slave Trade', *The Journal of African History* 55, no. 2 (2014): 135–45; for women's roles: Philip J. Havik, 'Female Entrepreneurship in West Africa: Trends and Trajectories', *Early Modern Women, an Interdisciplinary Journal* 10, no. 1 (Fall 2015): 164–77.

[12] Kropp Dakubu, 'The Portuguese Language', 27; Akan-speakers were barely receptive to Christianity and stuck to their own legal system. *Casar* marriages were concluded according to the rules of customary law. Feinberg, 'Africans and Europeans', 88–92, 97–98.

[13] The term Eurafrican emphasises the African identity of people of mixed descent: George E. Brooks, *Eurafricans in Western Africa: Commerce, Social Status, Gender, and Religious Observance from the Sixteenth to the Eighteenth Century* (Athens: Ohio University Press and Oxford: James Currey, 2003), xxi.; for the Gold Coast: Priestley, *West African Trade*, 3–24; Kwame Yeboa Daaku, *Trade and Politics on the Gold Coast, 1600–1720: A Study of the African Reaction to European Trade* (Oxford: Clarendon Press, 1970), 96–114; Pernille Ipsen, *Daughters of the Trade: Atlantic Slavers and Interracial Marriage on the Gold Coast* (Philadelphia: University of Pennsylvania Press, 2013). In addition to the *abusua*, patrilineal ties were essential too: James Boyd Christensen, *Double Descent among the Fanti* (New Haven, CT: Human Relations Area Files 11, 1954) 34–38, 97–123.

[14] Perbi, *A History of Indigenous Slavery*, 3, 99–100. An *abusua* was a localised lineage consisting of numerous segments with affiliation to an *abusuakuw* or larger clan. Christensen, *Double Descent*, 19–26.

[15] Ibid., 31, 37.

Enterprising females, like their male relatives, could accumulate possessions such as merchandise, gold and enslaved men or women; they could also establish a new household on the *abusua*'s landed property. The system functioned flexibly, yet everyone was subordinated to the collective interest.[16] A woman was esteemed when she could transfer the property she had accumulated during her lifetime to her children, thus contributing to the material strength of her matrilineage.

Aquassiba's Way Out of Dependency

Any Gold Coast woman could become embroiled in a palaver. However, although spouses of European traders, like Madam Watts, proved to be no exception, a husband with a connection to a fort could offer a way out of trouble. One example is Aquassiba's striking story, summarised in a note in the Elmina Castle minutes of 16 January 1762, which Adam Jones annexed in his classic article on female slave ownership.[17]

As a freeborn child, Aquassiba had been entrusted to the care of a woman called Tetjeba; but after her foster-mother's death she was claimed as a slave by Tetjeba's great-grandson and heir, Quacoe, on the basis of a claim his great-grandmother had once made on Aquassiba's relatives.

While Jones' focus was on Aquassiba's shifting status of dependence, I want to look at the initiative she took to negotiate her position. The writer of the note, her husband Walmbeek[18] – a slave trader – explains his wife's dispute to the West India Company General in meticulous detail. He must have done so on her behalf, for only she could have told him the particulars about her childhood.[19] Trouble had started years before, when Tetjeba claimed a sum in gold she said she had once advanced to

---

[16] M.R. Doortmont and N.C. Everts, 'Vrouwen, familie en eigendom op de Goudkust [Ghana]: De verwevenheid van Afrikaanse en Europese systemen van erfrecht in Elmina, 1760–1860', C. van Eijl (ed.), *Geld en Goed: Jaarboek voor Vrouwengeschiedenis* 17 (Amsterdam: IISG, 1997), 114–30, 117–18. Although they could not inherit from each other, marriage partners could transfer goods to each other in the presence of witnesses: Bosman, *Beschrijving*, 192–93. Maternal relatives of a deceased person were entitled to the estate, but powerful men sometimes tried 'to stretch the rules ... a little more than that they were entitled to'.

[17] Adam Jones, 'Female Slave-Owners on the Gold Coast, Just a Matter of Money?' Stephan Palmié, ed. *Slave Cultures and the Cultures of Slavery* (Knoxville, University of Tennessee Press, 1995), 100–11, 106–07, summarised from: NL-HaNA, NBKG 298, 115, Walmbeek to Erasmi, Elmina, 16 January 1762.

[18] Ibid. Walmbeek's 'heart's desire' was that 'if he was to die, he would be assured that his black wife and the children she might have by then, would be safeguarded from such extortions'.

[19] Walmbeek emphasises Aquassiba's status: her 'grandfather' was 'Teckie Ankan, prince of Great Commenda (Eguafo)'. 'Grandfather' can refer to any male relative of a previous generation: Jones, 'Female Slave-Owners', 109. A relative had brought her to Tetjeba, so she could '*crejaar*' (Portuguese: *criar*, to raise) her as if she was her own daughter.

one of the girl's relatives to buy her a female slave, but this man had failed to do so. Aquassiba's relatives refused to pay; but when they subsequently ordered the girl to return to them, her foster-mother sprinkled some earth on the ground and swore: 'If you run away to your relatives before I have received my payment, you must die, Aquassiba.' This '*jurament*' (Portuguese *juramento*: oath) frightened her so much that she did not dare to leave Tetjeba.[20]

On Aquassiba's wedding day, her Dutch groom went to Tetjeba to present the bridewealth, but she refused to accept it, saying: 'She is not my slave, and I am not the one who is entitled to receive the *costumes* (customs) for the *callesharen*.[21] Take it to her kinsfolk instead; I merely ask for my payment.' Although they accepted the *costumes*, Aquassiba's relatives insisted to Walmbeek that they were disavowing her on account of Tetjeba's claim to the value of a female slave,[22] but also because Aquassiba had disobeyed their order to return to them. Abandoned by her *abusua* and at the same time claimed by Quacoe, she found herself in a particularly vulnerable position.

On 20 January, when the dispute was brought before the Dutch court in the Castle for arbitration, Aquassiba conducted her own defence. Although the plaintiff Quacoe stated that she was his slave, the court decided in favour of the defendant, because she had 'provided perfect proof to the contrary'. This formally secured her freeborn status,[23] but she was ordered to pay Quacoe the 'costs amounting to two male slaves' to settle his late great-grandmother's claim and to 'make up for all time that had passed since the late Tetjeba had been deprived of the benefits of a female slave'. This final decision would surely have ruined Aquassiba, had she not been married to a European trader who could afford to pay. Not only had she found herself a partner who assisted her in regaining her freeborn status: he also delivered her from Tetjewa's oath on her life that must have been haunting her ever since. This cleared the way for her to establish a household and raise children of her own,[24] thereby creating a new power base that would enable her to set herself up as a trader and return to the bosom of her *abusua* as a full member, able to contribute to its collective interests.

---

[20] NL-HaNA, NBKG 298, 115.
[21] Dutch corruption of *casar, calisar* – marriage in accordance with customary law.
[22] Walmbeek wrote '*caveeren*': stand surety for someone else's payment.
[23] Ibid., 22 January 1762: a registered certificate served as proof against future claims.
[24] Walmbeek bequeathed gold to his wifes Abenaba and Adjuwa and their children, but Aquassiba had probably died before him, leaving no children: NL-HaNA, NBKG 335, 17, Elmina, 10 August 1765.

Illustration 6 Johanna Vitringa Coulon of Elmina with her daughter Mercy Hughes; Johanna was the daughter of Elmina-born Adjua Hogen and the Dutch colonial official Julius Vitringa Coulon, who served on the Gold Coast from 1853 to 1866. See http://let.rug.nl/doortmont/WebDocs/Images.
(Source: Copy in Collection National Museum van Wereldculturen, Amsterdam/Leiden, the Netherlands; Coll. no. TM-60024063. Images of the Gold Coast (West Africa) 1870–1890, collected by Hendrik Muller)

Madam Watts' Family Palaver

A dispute like Aquassiba's could easily escalate into a conflict between kin groups. The rulers of coastal towns had become accustomed to 'taking' possibly disruptive palavers 'to the forts'. European commanders, who strove to create a 'peaceful climate' beneficial to trade, were willing to act as arbiters on their behalf. Despite unremitting British-Dutch rivalry, when such a conflict loomed, the respective commanders tended to cooperate for the common good, exerting themselves to render this 'service' to the 'natives'. To that end, they could call in the assistance of an indigenous mediator, often someone registered as a 'broker' on a fort's payroll. His duty was to examine a dispute *in situ*, in consultation with all parties concerned, and to inform the European officials, who in turn tried to reconcile the dissenting parties in accordance with the procedures of customary law.[25]

One is inclined to think that mediation would have been easily available to the Eurafrican sons and daughters of local women and European fort personnel – as well as subsequent generations of descendants. However, due to the diversity of their origins and social status, many of a mixed line of descent had very little if any contact with Europeans. Notably Eurafrican women and girls born and raised in an Akan environment without having consciously known their stranger progenitors had to do without such a direct lifeline. They could, however, cultivate contacts or, as Aquassiba did, seek a marital alliance with a white man, preferably someone in the higher echelons.

Let us return to Anomabo Fort, where we left Madam Watts, with her husband in a panic and Amonu Kumu's men before the gate. Eventually she persuaded him to request assistance from his superior, the Dutch general at Elmina. In his cry for help of 22 July 1788, Martin Watts described the alarming situation in which his wife and children, as well as her sister and maternal uncle, found themselves. This conflict had surfaced around 1770, when his wife, who told him herself that she was from the Andemanfo (*fo*: people), was 'taken to be very rich, but of a household group not strong enough in number to take a stand in a palaver.'[26] A certain Apachie, who belonged to 'a family of the same name as my wife, named Andemanfo', grew envious of her material wealth. He must have been from another

---

[25] WIC officials euphemistically designated inhabitants of the towns near the forts 'our subjects'. In reality, the WIC did not exercise territorial power but merely operated as a commercial organisation: René Baesjou, 'Dutch "Irregular" Jurisdiction on the Nineteenth Century Gold Coast', in René Baesjou and Robert Ross (eds), *Palaver: European Interference in African Dispute Settlement* (Leiden: Afrika-Studiecentrum, African Perspectives, 1979), 2, 21–66.

[26] Wives of British officials were addressed by their husbands' names. Watts speaks of 'my wife'. Unfortunately, the document does not reveal what exactly made up her wealth.

branch of the extended family, which was scattered over various coastal towns.[27] By 1788, Watts was an old hand, well informed about indigenous customs. He confirmed that eighteen years earlier, his wife had been 'unjustly attacked' by Apachie because of a 'claim for some slaves'. It regularly occurred, he wrote, that some 'big man', in name of the family collective, would think himself entitled to the possessions accumulated by an individual member and would try to mobilise family opinion to enforce his claims. Back in 1770, Watts had written to the then British Governor, Mill, who had in his turn applied to 'Caboceer Cudjoe' (Cudjo), and 'Aggerij' for assistance.[28] Birempong (Fante: headman) Cudjo, had earned himself the reputation of being the senior broker and ally of the British on the coast. On Cudjo's authority, the claim made by Apachie was investigated and dismissed as false, and all had 'remained peace and quiet' for Madam Watts and her next-of-kin for many years.[29]

This had lasted until the moment Watts had accepted the appointment as commander of Anomabo Fort. When she arrived at her husband's new post, his wife had run into Amonu Kuma,[30] who had told her that he was the head of 'all of her Andemanfo' and immediately resurrected the old claim. Amonu was endowed with such 'great ability' to 'win someone's ears by a great many fabrications' that Watts feared 'that my wife and poor children are being brought to ruin'.

Shortly afterwards, Madam Watts had found Cudjo's successor, Aggerij, who also happened to be in Anomabo with his retinue, willing to do his best for her. Aggerij had managed to induce Amonu to agree that the woman 'should be done justice' and offer to 'sign a paper ... as an official guarantee [of her innocence]'.[31] However, Aggerij overplayed his hand when he had subsequently insisted that Amonu give Madam Watts '*foefe terre*',[32] the mixture of white clay she would put on her face when she performed the 'customary' ritual in public to demonstrate that she was cleared from the unlawful claim. This would have meant that she had to 'dance on the market square, on that occasion, so as to disappoint her enemy', and so, as Watts commented, Amonu feared being publicly

[27] NL-HaNA, NBKG 167, Watts to Norris, Anomabo, 22 July 1788.
[28] Birempon (Fante: wealthy through inheritance or trade) Cudjo (Kojo/Kodwo) became *ohene*, political leader of Cape Coast. Aggrey, his son and successor, died in 1793: Yann Deffontaine, 'Pouvoir monarchique et création étatique sur la Côte de l'Or au XVIII siècle: Brempong Kojo et la création de l'état d'Oguaa (Cape Coast)', *Mondes Akan/Akan Worlds, Identité et pouvoir en Afrique Occidentale/Identity and power in West Africa* (Paris, L'Harmattan, 1999), 187–13; Priestley, *West African Trade*, 15–16, 19–22; Shumway, *The Fante*, 36, 102.
[29] Deffontaine, 'Pouvoir', 200; NL-HaNA, NBKG 167, Anomabo, 22 July 1788.
[30] After Cudjo's death in 1777, Amonu Kuma was held to be the most powerful man in Fante: Shumway, *The Fante*, 60, 82–86.
[31] See note 22.
[32] *Fufu* (Fante: white), *terre* (French: earth, cf. Portuguese *terra*): a mixture of white clay, representing someone's innocence.

'disgraced'. Suddenly, while his adherents were shouting 'the palaver has begun again', he changed his mind altogether and refused to sign the document. Amonu's men chanted that since it was about a 'family palaver', Aggerij and his 'kinfolk' had to stay out, for it did not concern them.[33]

Madam Watts' position was threatened from within the Andemanfo, her own extended family: initially only on a local level by Apachie but subsequently, in 1788, by Amonu of Anomabo, who represented the superior authority of the collective at that moment. Her enduring marriage to a white man had enabled her to accumulate wealth, but in contrast to her powerful but distant relative, Amonu, she did not have a host of adherents to protect her kin against an aggressor. Naturally, she could have sought shelter in her husband's quarters in the fort, but Amonu could easily have blocked all incoming supplies.[34] Moreover, Amonu could order his men to apply the tested local practice of *panyaren* (from Portuguese *penhorar*, to seize as a pledge or security) to members of her household. In that case, she and all of her kin and domestic slaves would be in danger of being kidnapped by Amonu's men in Anomabo or anywhere else, which would have impeded all forms of commercial activity.

As she was a rich woman, why did she simply not buy off the claim? By paying a few slaves she might have safeguarded her children, sister, maternal uncle and herself. Watts did indeed suggest this course to her, but she refused to listen to him. From his letter it can be deduced that there was more to the matter. At a certain moment, the council of elders of her family had assembled, but she had not been invited, although because of her status, she should have been present. Apachie, the elder who had first lodged a claim against her, had died, and his son, *caboceer* Yansah, had succeeded his father as a council member. Yansah stated that he had a 'claim' on Madam Watts because 'his ancestors had once bought her great-grandmother'.[35]

From the moment Yansah's father had confronted her with this 'false claim', some two decades earlier, Madam Watts had insisted that she had never heard she might possibly be a descendant of a female slave. Nor had her mother or anyone else from previous generations of blood relations ever told her that they had once belonged to anyone. Moreover, she had 'always' paid for all commodities in advance 'out of her own pocket'. In fact, all expenses 'had been paid by her, but never by those who had lodged the claim on her people'. Although there was no indication in her family tradition that she herself or any of her preceding kin had ever been of a dependent status, she did not deny that Amonu stood 'at the head of all of her Andemanfo'.

[33] NL-HaNA, NBKG 167, Anomabo, 22 July 1788.
[34] He could have cursed his adversary by invocation, represented by an object (called '*fétiche*' by Europeans) put up before the gate: Law, 'The Government of Fante', 39–40.
[35] NL-HaNA, NBKG 167, Anomabo, 22 July 1788.

She acknowledged that old ties existed between Amonu's kinsfolk and her next-of-kin, but in the sense that they both descended from a lineage that, according to her 'information', had 'parted about two hundred years earlier'.[36] For a very long time, she had been providing for her kin, without ever having been indebted to Apachie, Yansah or Amonu. This was proof of her independence and free status. Therefore, Watts' proposal that she satisfy her detractors by paying them a redemption was unacceptable. Were she and her next-of-kin to submit like that, it would seem that there was some truth in the claim on them. To put it in her own words: 'Therefore, we are of the opinion that if we were to concede this point, we would be considered to be slaves subject to the orders of the Andamanfoes'.[37]

Over the years, Madam Watts had actively propagated her story. However, she lacked supporters. Only by insisting that her husband appeal to the Dutch Governor for assistance could she escape a dire fate. Upon the receipt of Watts' distress call, the British Governor passed the message on to Elmina. He appended a note saying that he believed he could manage 'to bring this dispute to an end', drawing upon 'the story as related by the woman herself'. His Dutch colleague fully endorsed this and sent an impartial Elmina envoy to urge Amonu to drop this palaver. Although Amonu agreed to do so, Yansah refused to give in. Thereupon, the British Governor had it announced along the coast that if Yansah were to 'practise any villainy against the woman or her kinfolk', he would order his Cape Coast allies – Aggerij and his men – 'to kidnap Anomabo folk everywhere in all of the seaside towns situated around British forts'. This method of coercion was in accordance with customary law. Such a retaliatory policy of repaying evil with evil – 'panyaring' a random number of inhabitants from Anomabo – would have harmed Amonu most. This would keep Yansah, who was clearly held in lower esteem than the *Anomabohene* (ruler), Amonu, from undertaking anything more.

Thus intercultural coastal diplomacy offered Madam Watts protection for the time being. The fact that a freeborn woman, who had been married to a European commander for years, found herself in such serious trouble offers food for thought. Despite the fact that she stood up for herself and specified her family tradition in detail, if she had not appealed for help to the British as well as the Dutch authorities, who in their turn called in the aid of formidable allies like Birempong Cudjo, Aggerij and a skilful anonymous mediator from Elmina, she would not have managed to carry it off.[38]

[36] Ibid.
[37] Ibid.
[38] NL-HaNA, NBKG 167, Norris to Van Bergen van der Grijp, Cape Coast, 23 July; 4 August 1788.

Betje Hamilton's Palaver

If we take a step back in time to the year 1756, we again come across Birempong Cudjo in Cape Coast. This time it is not altogether clear whether his role was that of a mediator or of a party in the dispute, in which the British and Dutch authorities found themselves on opposing sides.

Following the disappearance of some gold belonging to Cudjo and other persons, Cudjo had a domestic slave named Quoy, whom he suspected of being the thief, remanded in Cape Coast Castle.[39] The Acting Governor, Bell, informed his Dutch colleague in Elmina, Ulsen, about it, since Quoy belonged to 'the black woman Andoba, and her [daughter] Betje Hamilton, inhabitants of your village'. Bell also wrote that Quoy had already confessed to the theft of the gold and that he had taken it to Elmina, where he had handed it over to 'old Andoba'.

Andoba's daughter, Betje, responded that the allegation that anyone in her family had received that gold was ridiculous. In an attempt to solve the affair,[40] she made an appeal to her European connections. In September she asked Ulsen to write to a commander of an outer fort in Ahanta, to invite a 'renowned gold-finder and medium' to trace the gold for her in Elmina. Since this was to no avail, two months later she went to Cape Coast herself. At her request, Ulsen wrote a note to his British colleague Bell, in which he urged the latter to give Betje his protection and ensure that the Cape Coast indigenous authorities did their utmost to settle her palaver.[41] The next day Bell answered that he had received 'Madame Betje Volkmar' and would assist her to the best of his ability. In Bell's correspondence, Betje is referred to by the name of her previous husband, Volkmar, who had returned to Amsterdam in 1755.[42]

Both Ulsen and Bell treated Betje with civility for good reason: she and her mother, Andoba, were descended from the distinguished Cape Coast Andofo family.[43] Betje was a well-connected trader. She had been the country-wife of the British free trader Hamilton and, after his return to England, had settled down in Elmina with her mother and established

---

[39] NL-HaNA, NBKG 117, Bell to Ulsen, Cape Coast, 19 November 1756.

[40] An owner was liable for offences committed by a domestic slave: John Mensah Sarbah, *Fanti Customary Laws* (London: Frank Cass, 1968 [1897]), 39.

[41] NL-HaNA, NBKG 117, Ulsen to Bell, Elmina, 2 December 1756.

[42] NL-HaNA, NBKG 117, Cape Coast, 3 December 1756. Wives of Dutch officials were usually known by a first name, whereas the British used to address African wives by their husbands' names.

[43] They possibly descended from Ando, *Manfrohene* in 1690: Ray A.. Kea, *Settlements, Trade, and Polities in the Seventeenth Century Gold Coast* (Baltimore, MD: Johns Hopkins University Press, 1982), 229–30.

a new household.⁴⁴ There are indications that she had been *gecalisaard* with the Dutch director-general Baron De Petersen who, on the eve of his departure for Amsterdam, signed a deed by which he transferred the ownership of a house in town to her.⁴⁵ Betje had a son with Hamilton and most likely a daughter with De Petersen. Betje had agreed that her children would have a Christian upbringing in Europe, and both children accompanied their respective fathers to their countries of birth. Afterwards, Betje continued to live in Elmina with her mother. Her brother, Coffy, and sister, Amponesie, had managed the family house in Cape Coast and the domestic slaves who belonged to it.

Although Betje was treated with respect by both Dutch and British officials, from the outset they quarrelled about whether the dispute fell under the jurisdiction of Elmina or Cape Coast. The moment Bell had informed him about the apprehension of Betje's family slave, Quoy, Ulsen had consulted the Elmina *Grandes*, who agreed that, because it concerned a domestic slave belonging to an Elmina 'subject', he should be interrogated in Elmina. Only on neutral ground could it be determined if he had confessed to the theft under duress and if other accomplices had assisted him. Bell told Ulsen that he should stay out of the matter: 'Andoba, Bettie, as well as their slave, being born in Cape Coast, they happen to be our subjects.'⁴⁶

This dispute between the two governors resurfaced when it was found that Betje's sister, Amponesie, had fled from Cape Coast to Elmina, where she had found refuge in her sister's house.⁴⁷ Governor Senior, who had succeeded Bell, thought that Amponesie had attempted to bribe the Fante rulers with 'presents' to persuade them to side with her family. Since they represented a superior authority, this had caused Birempong Cudjo to feel so intimidated that he had thought it necessary to recruit a bodyguard. Since Cudjo had been treated unjustly, Senior urged the Dutch in Elmina to have Amponesie handed over to him, so that this new complication could be properly investigated in Cape Coast.⁴⁸

---

⁴⁴ George Hamilton managed a 'floating factory' at Anomabo (1737–1743) as agent of a London firm: Joseph E. Inikori, 'The Volume of the British Slave Trade, 1655–1807', *Cahiers d'Etudes africaines* 32, no. 128 (1992): 643–88, 666.

⁴⁵ *Gecalisaard*: married in accordance with customary law (cf. Note 21). NL-HaNA, NBKG 240, Register, April 1747, title deed. NL-HaNA, NBKG 301, minutes 1768, 122: in May 1768, Betje's brother Coffy gives account of 16 ounces in gold (worth about £300 in 2018) that he forwarded to De Petersen in Amsterdam: 'guardian' of Elisabeth Dorothea Hamilton, who was heir to her 'mother Betje, who died in 1766'.

⁴⁶ NL-HaNA, NBKG 118, Bell to Ulsen, Cape Coast, 18, 21 January 1757; Ulsen to Bell, Elmina, 19, 21 January 1757.

⁴⁷ NL-HaNA, 1.05.01.02, Second West India Company (WIC) 505, Resolutions, Elmina, 16 January 1760.

⁴⁸ NL-HaNA, NBKG 120, Senior to Huydecoper, Cape Coast, 26 August 1759. The Fante rulers mentioned might be those of Mankessim and/or Abura, see: Law, 'The Government of Fante', 49–51.

At Elmina Castle the ambitious Acting Governor Jan Huydecoper was angling for a permanent appointment as director-general. Aware that the man with the casting vote on the Company Board in Amsterdam was De Petersen, Betje's former husband, he seized the opportunity to act as her champion and that of her kin. He indicated to Senior that Cudjo was the reason Amponesie had been forced to seek refuge in Elmina, because it was he who had made her life a misery in Cape Coast. Huydecoper emphasised he would never hand over an innocent woman who had sought his protection.[49]

In the meantime, Betje had ordered some of her retinue to 'panyar' someone from Cudjo's domestic slaves, to hold as a hostage. Upon his arrival in Elmina, this man, Binyeah, was interrogated at the castle. He testified that it had been Cudjo himself who had instigated people to steal the gold. Moreover, Cudjo had made false accusations against Betje's sister, Amponesie, with the intention of ruining her family.[50] Binyeah's confession was in flat contradiction to the confession made earlier in Cape Coast by the accused Quoy. These contradictory statements had a paralysing effect on the Dutch authorities and their allies, the Elmina *Grandes*, who left the dispute unsettled for two years.[51]

In 1759 Cudjo took the role as mediator in the palaver over the stolen gold, and came with a proposal: although he had already spent over a hundred ounces[52] of gold on trade goods in that capacity, he was willing to content himself with a compensation of only 70 ounces in liquid gold. Governor Senior deemed Cudjo's offer very reasonable: he could well have demanded double the amount for all the trouble it had caused him.[53] Betje and Amponesie said they were inclined to meet Cudjo's proposal and pay him the sum requested, on condition that, if the stolen gold ever did resurface, they could keep it.[54] Cudjo refused to countenance this. It now turned out that the women did not have the 70 ounces Cudjo was demanding from them.[55]

Initially, Huydecoper, who apparently trusted Betje's creditworthiness, had indicated that he was willing to advance the sum to Cudjo on her behalf. However, there are indications that Huydecoper, who had entered into business transactions with Cudjo himself, hoped that he could thereby

---

[49] NL-HaNA, NBKG 120, Senior to Huydecoper, Cape Coast, [26] July, 5, 14 August 1759; Huydecoper to Senior, Elmina, 12 August 1759; WIC 505 Resolution, Elmina, 16 January 1760.
[50] Ibid.
[51] Ibid.
[52] Seventy ounces is worth about £1250.
[53] NL-HaNA, NBKG 120, Senior to Huydecoper, Cape Coast, 14 August 1759.
[54] Ibid. Huydecoper to Senior, Elmina, 21 August, 1759: Cudjo could not declare the exact value as he had not kept the gold in his house when it was stolen: Senior to Huydecoper, Cape Coast, 26 August.
[55] Ibid.

further his own commercial interests.[56] Be that as it may, at some point Huydecoper withdrew his offer to Betje.

In December 1759, when Betje and Amponesie had still not paid Cudjo, the situation got out of control. On 3 January 1760, Huydecoper asked Governor Senior why Cudjo had ordered his people to block the roads leading to Elmina, allowing no farmers to come into the fort. Senior replied that he could no longer stop Cudjo from taking the law into his own hands. Moreover, he warned Huydecoper that, if Betje and her sister kept on postponing the payment, Cudjo would force them to pay. Cudjo's son, Aggerij Bah, while paying a New Year's visit to Elmina, had been beaten up by someone from Betje's retinue. Nevertheless, in order to end the conflict, Cudjo would keep his end of the bargain, but now claimed compensation for his domestic slave, Binyeah, who had died in Elmina Castle, where he had been held hostage by Betje's family.

On 16 January, Huydecoper learned that Cudjo had issued directives all along the coast ordering that hostilities be commenced against indigenous inhabitants dwelling under Dutch authority, in retaliation for what Betje owed him. That same day it was unanimously decided at Elmina Castle to settle the dispute at once by 'friendly means' by a secret diplomatic mission. It is likely that Cudjo was persuaded to allow Betje to pay in instalments. The last trace we find in the documents is that Betje requested Huydecoper to advance her an enslaved man whom she could transfer to Cudjo, to make up for the deceased Binyeah.[57]

Catrijn's Dangerous Isolation: Violence in Lower Axim

On the morning of 26 August 1770, members of a ship's crew who had disembarked found the apparently lifeless bodies of three women and a girl in Axim Lower *krom* (from *kurow*: village).[58] Although it had always been the bustling home of fishermen, salt-makers, middlemen and *rimadoors* (canoe-men), the village now seemed deserted. The crew informed the fort Commander Fennekol, who sent his surgeon. The victims – the Eurafrican woman Catrijn, with her sister Anna, a young girl identified as 'Van Rhijn's child', and a female slave – had been poisoned. After being given an emetic, Catrijn, her sister and their servant regained consciousness. However, the girl was unable to vomit and died the same evening, 'swollen like a toad'.[59] In contrast to Betje Hamilton, Catrijn was clearly a

[56] By taking over the debt Huydecoper intended to clear a debt Cudjo owed him at the same time. When Cudjo did not respond, Huydecoper blamed Cudjo's 'deep rooted hatred' against the 'Andofo': NL-HaNA, NBKG 120, Huydecoper to Senior, Elmina, 21 August 1759.
[57] NL-HaNA, WIC 505 Resolution, Elmina, 5, 16 January 1760.
[58] NL-HaNA, NBKG 193, Fennekol to Woortman, Axim, 27 August 1770.
[59] Ibid.

woman who was fighting a losing battle, perhaps because she did not have the same kind of networking capabilities.

The girl, a daughter of either Catrijn or her sister Anna, had grown up without having known her father, Hendrick van Rhijn, who had served as a merchant at Axim Fort but returned to Holland in 1761.[60] Commander Fennekol considered it essential to mention his name in the brief report of the incident he sent to the director-general in Elmina, since in his eyes, the identity of the girl was still somehow connected to her absent father. For Catrijn and her sister, Anna, the loss of their daughter and niece dashed all hope that she would continue the bloodline of their small family unit.

The reason the *krom* was deserted at the moment of the assault was a serious palaver in which Commander Fennekol had become embroiled. Three weeks earlier, the inhabitants of that section of Axim, having lost trust in him, had run off *en masse*. Apart from blaming Fennekol and his men for stealing foodstuffs and merchandise, they accused two soldiers of hitting a passer-by on the head with a stone. Fennekol shrugged this off as the unfortunate result of playing a game 'who could throw farthest' in the bush. The person they had hit happened to be one of Catrijn's domestic slaves. Instead of 'bringing the *palaver* to the fort', Catrijn had at first attempted to settle the matter with the culprits herself. Only when her slave succumbed to his wound, had she gone up to see the commander. When Fennekol indicated he could no longer do anything for her, as she had already settled the case herself, she had become furious.[61] The encounter must have strengthened his impression that she was against him and had sided with the disaffected villagers.

Fennekol might well have read in the Axim correspondence that 21 years earlier, in 1749, Catrijn had stirred up a revolt against one of his predecessors.[62] At that time, Axim 'subjects' suspected the fort commander of being in league with a supplier of enslaved people and ivory, originating from the hinterland polity of Egila. Since many villagers in Lower Town earned their living as middlemen in the trade between the resident merchants or visiting ships and the inland suppliers, they felt they had been bypassed.[63]

The next morning, the commander learned that 'quarrelsome persons' from 'the An Donae quarter' were beating the alarm drum.[64] They were

---

[60] NL-HaNA, WIC 962, Elmina 12 January 1761.
[61] NL-HaNA, NBKG 193, Fennekol to Woortman, Axim, 11 August 1770.
[62] NL-HaNA, NBKG 110, Bacot to Van Voorst, Axim, 23 October 1749.
[63] Ibid. The small Nzema state of Axim consisted of Bolofo Solo (Upper Town) and Bolofo Aleze (Lower Town): Pierluigi Valsecchi, *Power and State Formation in West Africa, Appolonia from the Sixteenth to the Eighteenth Century* (New York, Palgrave Macmillan, 2011), 22, 27, 64–83; Michel Doortmont and Benedetta Savoldi, *The Castles of Ghana, Axim, Butre, Anomabu, Historical and Architectural Research on Three Ghanaian Forts* (Saonara: Il Prato, 2006) 21–75.
[64] For 'An Donae' see: Valsecchi, *Power and State Formation*, 64.

also abusing canoe-men and 'Company slaves' who served at the fort, but dwelled in town, calling them 'cowards and women'. When the quarter's fighting men appeared in front of the gate, the commander, who dismissed their allegations, invited them to confirm their mutual friendship with a sip of brandy. Catrijn and her retinue urged the war party not to accept the drinks he was offering, for he did so with 'ill intent'.[65] Catrijn emerges from this fragment as someone who dared to stand up for the collective interest. The commander recalled that years before, Catrijn's father had been executed in Elmina.[66] Consequently she had grown up in the environment of her mother, Adjuwa, who had been of a subordinate status. Yet Catrijn evidently radiated sufficient authority to keep the young fighting men from being taken in by a European commander. He even suspected her of being the one who had 'made them believe that I acted as their adversary'.[67]

Two days after the attempted murder of Catrijn and her closest kin, Commander Fennekol stated that he had discovered the source of the palaver in which he was involved with the Axim inhabitants. He suspected one Amo Tando, who had risen from goldsmith to *caboceer*, owning many slaves and pawns. Initially, Fennekol had offered Tando trade goods on consignment, but had never received 'anything in return'. Now he had discovered that Tando had exchanged this merchandise for trade slaves, but had sold them to foreign slavers instead of Dutchmen. As his fortune increased, Tando had acquired so many adherents that he had been raised to the status of *'primo noble'*.[68] Fennekol suspected that Tando was scheming to have him replaced by someone whom he could more easily deceive. By bribing people with presents, he had made them swear an oath that they no longer wanted to live near the fort as 'Dutch subjects'. They had proved to be willing to abscond with him and found a new *krom*, situated on the beach across the Ancober River.[69] The Company broker had tried in vain to keep the people from leaving Axim.

Fennekol suspected that Tando had incited the rebels to kill Catrijn. When they absconded, they had wanted 'to take Catrijn along with them',

---

[65] On women warriors: Adam Jones, 'My Arse for Okou:' 'A Wartime Ritual of Women on the Nineteenth-Century Gold Coast', *Cahiers d'Études africaines* 132 (1993), no. xxxiii, 545–66.

[66] NL-HaNA, NBKG 110, Bacot to Van Voorst, Axim, 23 October 1749. Her father was probably the merchant Jan Rijxborn, who was hanged for treason: NBKG 6, Minutes of the Council, 18 May 1725.

[67] NL-HaNA, NBKG 110, Bacot to Van Voorst, Axim, 23 October 1749.

[68] NL-HaNA, NBKG 193, Fennekol to Woortman, Axim, 29 August 1770. This probably refers to the award of the title *obirempon*, given by Akan polities in order to promote 'the ethic of achievement through accumulation': T.C. McCaskie, 'Accumulation, wealth and belief in Asante history, I: To the close of the nineteenth century', *Africa: Journal of the International African Institute* 53 (1983): 23–43. See also above, note 28.

[69] Ibid. For oath-taking see: Valsecchi, *Power and State Formation*, 177, 218, 266.

but she had refused. She had even offered them a redemption sum of 'one ounce of gold' to be allowed to stay.[70] However, there was more to the situation than Fennekol wanted to admit.

On 2 September, Fennekol left Axim as he had been summoned to Elmina, and a mediator arrived to investigate the palaver. This arbiter discovered more dissatisfied 'Dutch subjects', among them a group of forty canoe-men, who had been engaged in Fennekol's service but now refused to take up duties until a new commander had been appointed. Angry that he had failed to pay them their due – with the result that they had run up debts – they had incited the young men of their quarter to riot.[71] At the beginning of August, the *Grandes*, who wanted no part in the irregularities, had left for their temporary retreats in the bush.[72]

Catrijn could have gone with them and afterwards seemed to regret she had not done so. On 29 August, two days after the attempted poisoning, she informed Fennekol she had decided 'to let herself be carried into the bush', believing 'that the wrath of her deceased mother's spirit caused her misfortune, because she had not wanted to go with the *Grandes*'.[73]

Catrijn might have founded a household of her own and accumulated wealth as a trader, but she could still not deny her loyalty to the family to whom her mother had once belonged as a dependant. What made her decide to stay in the first place, instead of seeking a refuge in the bush, in the company of her family elders? Was it just reluctance to leave her house, merchandise and gold unprotected? Her decision cost her dearly.

Fennekol put it dryly: instead of 'the wrath of her mother's spirit' it had been 'the poison that brought her to the brink of death'. Fennekol reported that Catrijn had paid a redemption in gold to the big man, Tando, to be allowed to remain in her house. It was precisely this transaction that had stirred rumours among the rebellious villagers that she was keeping 'all her gold hidden in the *Salt krom*'.[74] The unsettled situation might also have given Tando an opportunity to rid himself of a competitor who had tried to evade domination and to appropriate her gold. Be that as it may, Catrijn had isolated herself, partly because she had neglected to cultivate contacts with subsequent commanders at the fort.

On 18 December 1770, the dispute between Fennekol and his 'subjects' was settled and everyone could return to Axim. However, he

[70] NL-HaNA, NBKG 193, Fennekol to Woortman, Axim, 27, 29 August 1770.
[71] Ibid., WIC 972, Dizi to Woortman, Hollandia, 2, September 1770. Many were related to the canoe-men. Fennekol did not report this conflict, probably because he had not paid them their due.
[72] NL-HaNA, WIC 972, Dizi to Woortman, Hollandia, 2 September 1770.
[73] NL-HaNA, NBKG 193, Fennekol to Woortman, Axim, 29 August 1770. As her choice had brought misfortune, she believed to have acted contrary to the rules: see Vinigi L. Grottanelli, *The Python killer, Stories of Nzema Life* (Chicago, IL: University of Chicago Press, 1988) 16–18.
[74] NL-HaNA, NBKG 193, Fennekol to Woortman, Axim, 29 August 1770.

sighed, another complicated dispute had to be settled – that of 'Catrijn's estate'.[75]

She must have passed away during her time in the bush. Two claimants stated they were entitled to the estate: the family of the Company broker from Axim and a certain Cudjo from nearby Ahanta. This time Fennekol promised the *Grandes* he would assist them in determining the legitimate heir. His superior, the general in Elmina, advised him to search for the person who 'had buried Catrijn's mother and performed the customary funeral rites for her', because he was the rightful heir.[76] However, Fennekol thought that it was all about tracing the person who had 'owned' Catrijn's mother Adjuwa.[77]

The estate, which apart from one female dependant, a house and what remained of her gold we can only guess about, must have been considerable. Assembled at the fort 'in conclave', it took the *Grandes* eight days of 'palavering' to settle it. Finally, the broker from Axim emerged triumphant, it was he who was designated as Catrijn's heir.[78]

Conclusion

This chapter has highlighted both women's vulnerability and their skill in countering the acts of violence they faced. Certainly they were part of a larger clan, but they spent their days within the smaller segment in the midst of their households. During such episodes in their lives as recounted above, their efforts were principally aimed at retaining their and their relatives' independence. The networks they built, both with powerful headmen from among their extended families and with local political authorities, were consciously oriented towards safeguarding the interest of their closest kin.

Coastal inhabitants were familiar with dispute settlement by resident European officials, and Akan women seem to have been astute in cultivating contacts with them. As can be gleaned from the texts that document their palavers, they could certainly benefit from such arbitration. It would appear that in their contacts with fort officials, mixed descent women had an advantage over others. Like Betje and Madam Watts, they were identified at the forts by the names given them by their fathers, or by their husbands' names. Their Akan names have not even come down to us. Even Catrijn, who had considerably fewer connections with commanders in her home town Axim, was known as the daughter of her long-dead European father.

[75] NL-HaNA, WIC, 973, Axim, 28 December 1770.
[76] Ibid.
[77] Ibid., Woortman to Fennekol, Elmina, 2 January 1771.
[78] Ibid., Fennekol to Woortman, Axim, 10, 16 January 1771.

Marital alliances with Europeans enabled both African and Eurafrican women to increase their prosperity, something that three of them – and perhaps Catrijn too – had experienced at certain points during their lives. Marriage even enabled Aquassiba to regain her freeborn – i.e. noble – status. Had she lived, she could have founded her own lineage. Madam Watts as well as Betje were descended from prominent families too. Catrijn, by contrast, the daughter of a mother who had belonged to a family in a subservient position, managed to become prominent in her community as a middle-woman in her own right.

Being Akan, these women may well have cherished the ideal of being commemorated after death as founding mothers and esteemed ancestors,[79] but the households they created and the possessions they amassed aroused the envy of more powerful members of their own clans or that of social upstarts. Demonstrating a sense of *local knowledge*, Madam Watts's husband acknowledged the precarious situation in which his wife was entangled. She had become wealthy, but lacked relatives and adherents to defend herself against those who challenged her. This goes to the heart of the matter, as it points towards the chronic insecurity that was prevalent in coastal societies of the time. Madam Watts appears to have been of free status, yet she, with her children and kin, had to do her utmost to refute the allegation that she was a slave.

Diouf discerns three strategies people used to resist the dangers that threatened them: they could act independently either offensively or defensively, or they could seek help from outside.[80] In the actions of the women examined, we see all these strategies in operation, with emphasis on the third option. Once Aquassiba was assisted by her new husband, she did not hesitate to conduct her own defence at the castle while he was the one who settled her late foster-mother's claim. Madam Watts and Betje summoned the help of both European and African allies, whereas Catrijn seems to have operated almost entirely on her own account without seeking help from anybody.

For Madam Watts, who was part of a many-branched family spread out along the central Gold Coast, the threats came from within the wider circle of her own relatives. Initially, as the wife of the commander of Anomabo Fort, she must have imagined herself protected. However, when she was challenged from two sides, she gradually lost control of the situation and was forced to take a defensive stand. In holding on to her conviction that she, just as her ancestors before her, was a freeborn member of the Andemanfo, she resolutely refused to meet her detractor's demand for a ransom. Her wish to call in the 'impartial' help of the Dutch general indicates that she feared that her formidable adversary, Amonu Kumu, ultimately

[79] Christensen, *Double Descent*, 34–38, 45; Grotanelli, *Stories of Nzema Life*, 3.
[80] Diouf, *Fighting the Slave Trade*, xi–xii.

could not be forced to back down by the British Governor and his broker, Aggerij, alone. Nevertheless, it was this governor who devised the offensive strategy that effectively divided her enemies.

Betje was confronted with an accusation of the theft of a considerable sum in gold by one of her domestic slaves, for which she, her ageing mother Andoba, and her siblings were held responsible. Betje had an extensive intercultural network of connections. Furthermore, her house in Elmina offered her and her relatives a refuge under the protection of subsequent Dutch directors-general and the *Terre Grandes*. Besides, she could count on a retinue of dependants who could not only come to her defence but, at times, could also make a stand against her adversaries. Perhaps Birempong Cudjo, preoccupied with expanding his own commercial empire in Cape Coast, was 'stretching a palaver'. Maybe it was convenient for him to try to weaken the position of members of the ancient Andofo. Nevertheless, he seems to have taken his role as intermediary with the British government seriously, for in the end he accepted a tactful solution. Like Aquassiba and Madam Watts, Betje also responded rationally, in line with the principles of customary law. Although she suffered loss, she adopted a sophisticated strategy devised to limit the damage. Eventually, Betje succeeded in keeping the possessions she had acquired intact, and was able to bequeath the house in Elmina, her gold and domestic slaves to her sister and heir, Amponesie.

Catrijn's story was a different matter. She was confronted with an adversary determined to eliminate her, her sister Anna, their little daughter/niece, and a domestic slave. The man after her blood, probably the upstart Amo Tando, might have had several motives: was it her gold he coveted, did he owe her a sum or did he want to eliminate a competitor? Notwithstanding her humble descent, Catrijn had seized the opportunity to establish herself as an independent trader, fully integrated into her quarter in Axim. Although she was still somehow connected to the *abusua* of her late mother Adjuwa, she was used to defending her own interests. Instead of cultivating contacts with Europeans, she adopted a reserved attitude towards them. When riots broke out and she decided to stay, instead of seeking refuge in the bush, she found herself in isolation. The attack that eventually proved fatal befell her at a moment when the traditional structures of her community had fallen apart. The harm that came Catrijn's way may well have befallen other women in eighteenth-century Atlantic West Africa. If so, Aquassiba, Madam Watts and Betje were the lucky exceptions.

7

To be Female & Free
Mapping Mobility & Emancipation in Lagos, Badagry & Abẹokuta 1853–1865

ADEMIDE ADELUSI-ADELUYI

When British gunboats bombarded Lagos twice in late 1851, they displaced not only the incumbent king but also the significance of local narratives around the event. The November bombardment was meant to end the city's reliance on the profits of the slave trade; but it failed. The December bombardment represented an effort to make up for this defeat and install a king amenable to British interests. Britain's success in this *ija agidingbi* or 'booming battle' is popularly interpreted as the first step in the process that ended with the cession of Lagos to Britain in 1861.

This chapter focuses on the effects of British intervention in Lagos in 1851, and again in 1861, on domestic slavery, especially on women who were enslaved. Historians have analysed the profits from the slave trades, as well as the processes of dismantling slavery and emancipating the formerly enslaved. The aftermath involved a variety of labour relationships whose conditions often mirrored slavery, including forced labour, pawnship, redemption, apprenticeship and indentured servitude.[1]

Known in the British records as the 'reduction of Lagos', the November and December bombardments of 1851 had repercussions which were felt as far east as Porto Novo (where slave dealers fled) and as far north as Abẹokuta, where Christian missionaries and their local allies celebrated the first strong step in British intervention. Within a decade of the bombardment,

[1] Pawnship: in this part of West Africa, pawnship developed as a system of exchange. In this context it refers to the situation where a person is given as collateral to secure a debt, or is offered in lieu of a monetary payment. Kristin Mann, *Slavery and the Birth of an African City: Lagos, 1760–1900* (Bloomington: Indiana University Press, 2007); E. Adeniyi Oroge, 'The Fugitive Slave Question in Anglo-Egba Relations 1861–1886', *Journal of the Historical Society of Nigeria Journal of the Historical Society of Nigeria* 8, no. 1 (1975): 61–80; Paul Lovejoy and Toyin Falola, eds, *Pawnship in Africa: Debt Bondage in Historical Perspective* (Boulder, CO: Westview Press, 1994); Gwyn Campbell and Alessandro Stanziani, eds, *Debt and Slavery in the Mediterranean and Atlantic Worlds* (London: Pickering & Chatto, 2013).

Lagos had become a formal colony. Drawing upon Foreign and Colonial Office correspondence,[2] maps and sketches, court testimonies, travel narratives and missionary journals, this chapter investigates two ways in which women and children were enslaved but then found and maintained their freedom. It also maps their itineraries, showing how Lagos became a focal point for freedom, first after the British bombardments in 1851 and again after it was annexed in 1861. I analyse how the experiences of two enslaved females shed light on female mobility and produce a spatial biography of these encounters. Of the many people enslaved in the Bight of Benin between 1851 and 1865, two female figures, Awa and Alabọn, come to life in the archival record. Both found freedom in Lagos. For Awa, emancipation came after she fled domestic slavery in Abẹokuta. She was one of many pawns in a moral and economic crisis over slavery in the 1860s involving John Glover, Lieutenant Governor of Lagos, and the 'Native Christians' who lived in Abẹokuta and Lagos.

Alabọn was set free after being 'dashed' (given) to a European merchant's wife in Badagry. For her, the path to freedom meant enduring a process of conversion to Christianity, and social reinvention as 'Rosa'. Despite this, she was kidnapped and taken to Lagos, where she was eventually set free again. For such women and children, the path to emancipation was uncertain and often dangerous. Emmanuel Ayandele noted in 1967 that the 'politics of the three towns (Lagos, Abẹokuta and Badagry) became a pro- and anti-missionary issue'.[3] As I shall show, the connections between Abẹokuta, Lagos and Badagry were brokered by the geography, cultures and policies surrounding emancipation.

Rather than treat women's biographies as briefly illustrative of a point about slavery, pawnage or concubinage, I focus on the fullness and contradictions of their experiences: Alabọn lived between pawnage and panyarring (arbitrary seizure), while Awa brings life to the debate on the 'fugitive slave question' that preoccupied consuls and governors in Lagos alike. Both narratives converge at Lagos. In ceding power in 1851 and territory in 1861, Lagos's ọbas inadvertently set the scene for Lagos to become a space of emancipation. Awa's circuitous journey from enslavement to liberty, which in this case meant travelling from Abẹokuta to Lagos, must be seen in the context of the struggle between British officials at Lagos and ethnic Saro merchants in Abẹokuta.

---

[2] Almost all the letters that refer to women were written by men. Only one document purports to give the perspective of a woman, Awa, and even here, the extent to which her deposition is entirely her own is unclear. In formatting, it resembles another deposition submitted in the case against Henry Robbin.

[3] Emmanuel Ayankanmi Ayandele, *The Missionary Impact on Modern Nigeria, 1842–1914: A Political and Social Analysis* (New York: Humanities Press, 1967), 9.

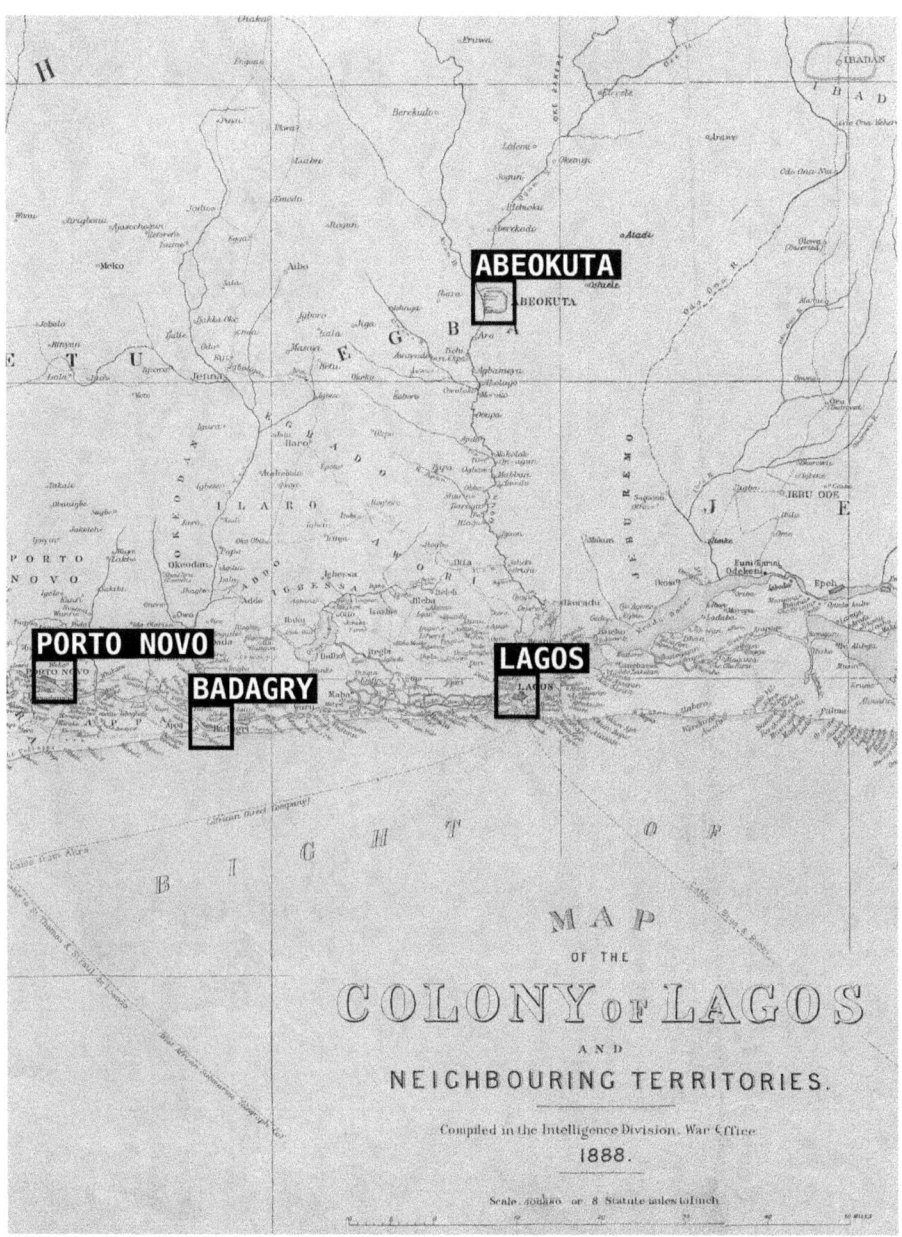

Map 6 The Colony of Lagos and Neighbouring Territories, 1888
(Source: The National Archives UK, Map CO 700/LAGOS 15, 'Map of the Colony of Lagos and Neighbouring Territories', 8 statute miles to 1 inch (Compiled in the Intelligence Division, War Office, 1888), 700)

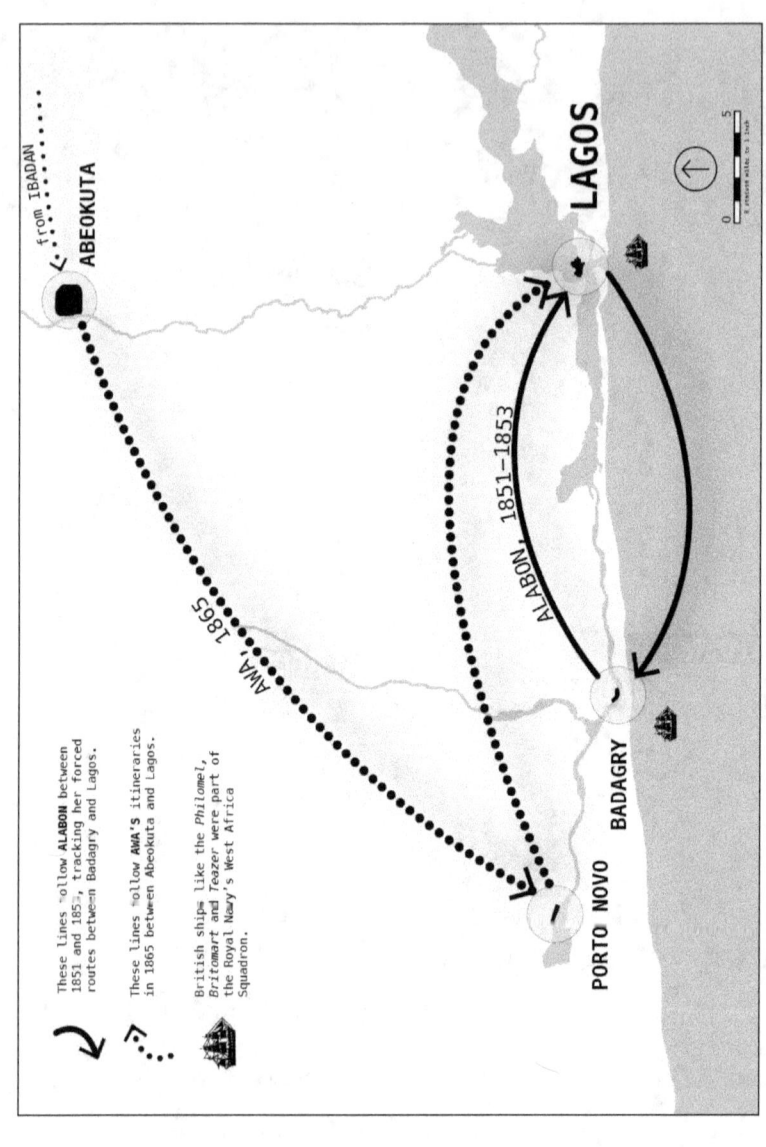

Map 7 Tracing Awa's and Alabon's routes
(Source: © Ademide Adelusi-Adeluyi)

Emancipation in Urban Space

The 'biographical turn' has led historians to pay attention to the lived experiences of little known people in the Africa and the Atlantic world. Similarly, the 'spatial turn' has made scholars more attentive to space, place and the ways that human interaction has shaped geographical environments, and vice versa. Lisa Lindsay and James Sweet have argued that 'by attaching names and faces to the broad processes such as slaving, enslavement, identity formation [and] emancipation, biography can illuminate the meanings of these large, impersonal forces for individuals'.[4] They point to the importance of biography as method, for the ways that it can provide an infrastructure for historical narratives. While the archival fragments used here do not permit full biographies of Awa and Alabǫn, they at least provide a template for narrating and mapping the story of their emancipation.

A sequence of lagoons, lakes, rivers and land routes connects the series of cities, towns and villages on the Bight of Benin,[5] four hundred miles of coastline between Cape St Paul in present-day Ghana and the outlet of the Niger River in Nigeria. The interior of the Bight of Benin is characterised by three ecological zones: a savannah, a rainforest belt and a narrow strip bordering the coastline, where the interconnected lagoons run parallel to the Atlantic. The network of towns in this region included Ibadan, Porto Novo, Badagry, Lagos and Abęokuta. This analysis is confined to the latter three towns for three important reasons. Most significantly, Lagos was the most prominent of the cities when it came to the emancipation of enslaved peoples. Secondly, both Awa and Rosa spent most of their time in these spaces, and were most frequently observed there.

While the lagoons run parallel to the ocean, there are a series of four rivers running to the coast. These rivers – from west to east, the Ouémé, Yewa, Ogun and Osun – are used in conjunction with a number of overland routes to provide access to such towns as Allada, Ota and Abęokuta.

---

[4] John Wood Sweet and Lisa A. Lindsay, eds, *Biography and the Black Atlantic* (Philadelphia: University of Pennsylvania Press, 2014), 1.

[5] Of his 1803 voyage, John M'Leod wrote: 'Along that line of coast from Cape St Paul to Cape Formosa (an extent of, at least, three hundred miles) an easy communication between the various countries is afforded by means of lakes and rivers, which run in a direction nearly parallel with the sea-beach': John M'Leod, *A Voyage to Africa; with Some Account of the Manners and Customs of the Dahomian People* (London: Frank Cass, 1971), 127. Almost fifty years later, in 1849, Commander Forbes wrote: 'On the west side the lagoons may be said to join the Volta, although in the dry season, at a little distance from the town of Godomey (fifteen miles from Whydah), a sandy neck divides the Lagoons of Lagos and Whydah. Emptying into these lagoons are several navigable rivers, as yet but imperfectly known, except to slave enterprise.' Frederick E. Forbes, *Dahomey and the Dahomans; Being the Journals of Two Missions to the King of Dahomey and Residence at His Capital in the Years 1849 and 1850*, vol. 1 (London: Frank Cass, 1966), 9.

Together, these water and land routes frame the settlements on the coast and in the interior of the Bight. Lagos sits at the centre of these land, lagoon and river routes. The issue of slavery has exerted an enormous influence on the historiography of the Bight and particularly of Lagos.[6]

Awa's case has received some scholarly attention, notably from the historians McIntosh and Shields, who discussed the impact of her concubinage and enslavement.[7] This chapter shifts the emphasis to Awa's attempt to liberate herself and her exercising her limited agency in choosing to flee to Lagos. The historian Abosede George, in arguing for 'girling the subject', points to ways in which African girls have been neglected in the historiography.[8] Alabǫn's narrative has received far less attention than Awa's, which is unsurprising given that she is stripped of agency in life, and is never allowed to represent herself in the archival record. Girling the subject in this case then suggests that we should be attentive to effects of these layers of silencing in her experience that are effectively a function of her gender, and then her youth.

Scholarship on pawnship and slavery has shown how formerly enslaved children were often collateral damage in the efforts to make slavery illegal; they were often forced to continue to labour as pawns.[9] Lindsay and Sweet posit that the 'Black Atlantic' is at once a 'space and an argument'.[10] Alan Baker, a geographer, has argued that 'there is more to geography than spatial relationships – and indeed more even than spatial relationships and environmental conditions'.[11] Examining routes taken by the people moving through the lagoon systems raises interesting questions about the relationship between history and geography. But is landscape simply a stage for the 'enactment' of history?[12]

In *A History of Spaces,* the geographer John Pickles suggests that mapping practices should be more than just following a subject, and that we should focus on the ways in which 'mapping and the cartographic gaze have coded subjects and produced identities'.[13] What insights can a spatial history introduce? Perhaps, in Alabǫn's case, it can begin to reconstruct her narrative as she 'moves' from Alabǫn to Rosa – in her case the distance between freedom

---

[6] See Kristin Mann, *Slavery and the Birth of an African City: Lagos, 1760–1900* (Bloomington: Indiana University Press, 2007).

[7] Marjorie Keniston McIntosh, *Yoruba Women, Work, and Social Change* (Bloomington: Indiana University Press, 2009); Francine Shields, 'Those Who Remained Behind: Women Slaves in Nineteenth-Century Yorubaland', in *Identity in the Shadow of Slavery*, ed. Paul E. Lovejoy (London and New York: Continuum, 2009), 183–201.

[8] Abosede A George, *Making Modern Girls: A History of Girlhood, Labor, and Social Development in Colonial Lagos* (Athens: Ohio University Press, 2014), 14.

[9] Lovejoy and Falola, *Pawnship in Africa*.

[10] Sweet and Lindsay, *Biography and the Black Atlantic*, 1.

[11] Baker, *Geography and History*, 24.

[12] See ibid., 18.

[13] John Pickles, *A History of Spaces: Cartographic Reason, Mapping, and the Geo-Coded World* (London: Psychology Press, 2004), 18.

and enslavement. No direct testimony from her exists. But numerous people spoke on her behalf: the British merchant James G. Sandeman and two of his African employees – Mary Coker, a Saro woman, and Samuel C. Austin, clerk to Sandeman in Badagry. Brian Harley, the historical geographer, once suggested that the 'map has become a graphic autobiography; it restores time to memory and it recreates for the inner eye the fabric and seasons of a former life.'[14] In this vein, a spatial history relies on interpreting and creating maps as a way of accessing and illustrating the past. I rely on maps and sketches to track mobility in the triangle formed by Lagos, Abẹokuta and Badagry. Commenting on the 'testimony of images', the cultural historian Peter Burke has argued that images should not be used as mere evidence of a previously drawn conclusion, but rather as a departure point for analysis: 'images allow us to "imagine" the past more vividly'.[15]

Maps, like other visual sources, have been recognised as socially constructed interpretations of reality that are 'argumentative in orientation' and therefore specifically 'propositional by nature'.[16] This chapter uses maps in a variety of ways. Some, such as Map 6, are used to establish geographical context and provide spatial data on relationships in the Bight of Benin. Some are annotated with data gleaned from other archival sources, including consular correspondence. I also offer two maps that are new illustrations of arguments around the fugitive slave question and on mapping gender and emancipation. There are drawbacks to this reliance on cartographic technology to reconstruct biographies, especially in the ways that itineraries become linear, with a start and destination encoded solidly in space, as if predetermined.

'Who Broke Lagos?'

> Ask any native who broke Badagry, and what is the answer? *Alapako* (Mr. Gollmer's country name). Who broke Lagos? *Alapako*.[17]

[14] J. B Harley, 'The Map as Biography: Thoughts on Ordnance Survey Map, Six-Inch Sheet Devonshire CIX, S.E., Newtown Abbot', *The Map Collector* 41 (1987): 18–20, quoted in Jeremy W. Crampton, *Mapping: A Critical Introduction to Cartography and GIS* (Hoboken, NJ: John Wiley & Sons, 2011), 96.
[15] Peter Burke, *Eyewitnessing: The Uses of Images as Historical Evidence*, Picturing History Series (London: Reaktion Books, 2001), 13.
[16] See J.B. Harley, 'Deconstructing the Map', *Cartographica: The International Journal for Geographic Information and Geovisualization* 26 (1998): 1–20; J. B. Harley, 'Historical Geography and the Cartographic Illusion', *Journal of Historical Geography* 15, no. 1 (January 1989): 80–91; J. B. Harley, 'Maps, Knowledge, and Power', ed. Denis Cosgrove and Stephen Daniels (Cambridge: Cambridge University Press, 1998).
[17] The National Archives, UK, hereafter TNA, FO 403/5, 'Consul Campbell to the Earl of Clarendon, Lagos, May 28, 1855', in *Correspondence Relative to the Dispute between Consul Campbell and the Agents of the Church Missionary Society at Lagos* (printed for the use of the Foreign Office, 1856), 5.

Several detailed accounts of the 'reduction of Lagos' exist.[18] Individual actors were swept up in the broader mechanisms of abolition, freedom and emancipation. The British attack on Lagos was launched from the sea, while Badagry and Abẹokuta served as bases for (King) Akitoye's forces. In Badagry, thirty miles away from the centre of the action, a different scene was unfolding. Alabọn, a young girl child of only twelve years, had disappeared from the home of her 'protector', James Sandeman, while he was setting up his new business in Lagos. The bombardment had spurred new business and other opportunities in the city, and Lagos saw a rapid influx of merchants and missionaries. Sandeman was part of the new exodus to Lagos. While powerful men in Abẹokuta and Dahomey sought ways to exploit the presence of British ships in the Bight of Benin, there were those who took advantage of the spotlight moving away from Badagry.

On 16 January 1853, Sandeman wrote to Louis Fraser, the newly appointed Vice Consul, about the missing girl. Fraser was not one who considered slavery in its domestic form a 'milder' form of bondage than its transatlantic variant. He wrote to the Foreign Office:

> My Lord, I consider it my imperative duty, to draw particular attention, to this glaring case of Kidnapping, breach of treaty and total defiance of all English authority. After the vast expenditure of life and property, to reduce Lagos, I cannot suppose that such things as the enslaving (if only for 22 days) of free blacks, are to be allowed, much more that British merchants should be subject to such insults and inconveniences. It will be remembered that during this girl's captivity, she had food she was not accustomed to, and was compelled to sleep on the ground. Subject to be sold and transported, nobody knows where, fetished, poisoned, violated or otherwise maltreated or murdered.[19]

Paul Lovejoy points to a distinction between kidnapping and 'arbitrary seizure' or panyarring – a West African term discussed in this volume by Natalie Everts.[20] Was Alabọn enslaved, a pawn or somehow both? The answer depended on the interpreter's perspective. In his article on the enslavement of Yoruba women, Olatunji Ojo suggests that Sandeman

---

[18] Martin Lynn, 'Consul and Kings: British Policy, "the Man on the Spot", and the Seizure of Lagos, 1851', *The Journal of Imperial and Commonwealth History* 10 (1982): 150–67; Robert Sydney Smith, *The Lagos Consulate: 1851–1861* (London: Macmillan, 1978).

[19] TNA FO 84/920, 'Vice Consul Louis Fraser to the Earl of Malmesbury, "Case of the Kidnapping at Lagos", Inclosure 1 in Slave Trade No. 2', 20 February 1853.

[20] Paul Lovejoy, 'Pawnship and Seizure for Debt in the Process of Enslavement in West Africa', in *Debt and Slavery in the Mediterranean and Atlantic Worlds*, ed. Gwyn Campbell and Alessandro Stanziani (London: Pickering & Chatto, 2013), 65. See also Robin Law, 'On Pawnship and Enslavement for Debt in the Pre-Colonial Slave Coast', in *Pawnship in Africa: Debt Bondage in Historical Perspective*, ed. Paul Lovejoy and Toyin Falola (Boulder, CO: Westview Press, 1994), 51–69.

may have 'accepted' Alabǫn from Madam Tinubu as a form of payment, fearing that he would otherwise have to write off her debt. Ojo interprets Alabǫn's predicament as a clear case of 'enslavement for debt'.[21] If we consider the whole period 1851–1853, we recognise that pawnship was simply one stage of her experience between slavery and freedom.

Few children in Lagos captured the colonial officials' imagination like Alabǫn or 'Rosa', as she was later christened.[22] She had been enslaved by Efunronye Tinubu (the popular merchant also known as Madam Tinubu), who in 1851 gave her as a 'dash' or gift to Sandeman's wife.[23] Because Tinubu was known at the time as a prominent slave trader, Sandeman freed the girl. Mrs Sandeman was dead by this time.[24] In recounting the episode, Vice Consul Fraser suspected that the entire ordeal was a result of Tinubu's escalating debt to Sandeman.[25] To solidify her emancipation, Sandeman acquired a 'Certificate of Freedom' for Alabǫn (signed by B. Cruikshank) a document which promised that she was 'unconditionally free'. It was later proved to have little effect on assuring her status.

Alabǫn only received her Certificate of Freedom on 31 December 1851, four days after the successful bombardment of Lagos.[26] Within the space of a year, she had been moved the 30 or so miles from Lagos to Badagry, most likely without her consent. Her case is illustrative of the decentralised control of slave trading in the region, and illustrates how people might be moved within the region. Alabǫn's own voice is not preserved in the archival record, but several others speak on her behalf. Vice Consul Fraser was her fiercest advocate, and it was he who pressured Akitoye to 'find' her. By Fraser's account, less than a year of being 'brought up European style' was enough to transform and distinguish her from other 'native' people. As Alabǫn, she was just a slave; as Rosa, 'the Black Girl', she was a 'free British subject'. She was taught to eat and dress in British style, and her honesty, 'so rare among Africans', made her well known.

In 1852 Louis Fraser came from Dahomey to Lagos, where he spent only a year and a half as consul.[27] In early January, informed that the girl had

---

[21] Olatunji Ojo, 'The Business of 'Trust' and the Enslavement of Yoruba Women and Children for Debt', in *Debt and Slavery in the Mediterranean and Atlantic Worlds*, ed. Gwyn Campbell and Alessandro Stanziani (London: Pickering & Chatto, 2013), 86.
[22] TNA FO 84/920, 'Vice Consul Louis Fraser to the Earl of Malmesbury, "Case of the Kidnapping at Lagos", Inclosure 1 in Slave Trade No. 2'.
[23] Ibid.
[24] TNA FO 84/920, 'Testimony of Mary Coker, Dated January 21 1853, Inclosure 2 in Slave Trade No. 2: Vice Consul Louis Fraser to the Earl of Malmesbury, "Case of the Kidnapping at Lagos",' 20 February 1853.
[25] TNA FO 84/920, 'Vice Consul Louis Fraser to the Earl of Malmesbury, "Case of the Kidnapping at Lagos", Inclosure 1 in Slave Trade No. 2'.
[26] Ibid.
[27] Louis Fraser, *Dahomey and the Ending of the Trans-Atlantic Slave Trade: The Journals and Correspondence of Vice-Consul Louis Fraser, 1851–1852*, ed. Robin Law (Oxford: Oxford University Press, 2012), 11.

been seen in Lagos, he immediately spoke to the king, Akitoye, who on 18 January flatly declared he would not interfere in the business between Tinubu and Sandeman. Fraser responded with threats of gunboats and men-of-war. Akitoye, in an uncharacteristically cool response, retorted, 'send for them'. Commander Heseltine, Senior Officer, refused to attack immediately and, having met with Akitoye on 24 January, gave him six days to 'produce the girl'.[28]

Eventually Alabọn was found, and by 1 February the news reached Fraser that she had been 'handed over to the king'. Two days later, she ran away to Sandeman's property. Both the transatlantic slave trade and domestic slavery in Lagos continued to flourish on Lagos Island and in surrounding towns, with the lagoons as a conduit. Alabọn's forced journeys, first to Badagry and then to Lagos, demonstrate the decentralised nature of slavery and enslavement in this region.

In Lagos, questions of slavery were linked to territoriality,[29] and Kristin Mann has shown how 'selective' consuls were when choosing to interfere with the fates of enslaved women and children. Martin Lynn points to the ways that British 'men on the spot' used their discretion when implementing British agendas in the context of thin budgets and little manpower. Four such officers feature here. First, John Beecroft, the British Consul for the Bights of Benin and Biafra, took the initiative to attack Lagos twice in 1851. Later, Fraser in 1853 began the process of pressing for Alabọn's release, citing irreparable harm done to a British subject being enslaved. In 1861, it was Acting Governor McCoskry, himself a former trader like Beecroft, who supervised the annexation of Lagos and the beginnings of an on-the-ground policy towards fugitive slaves. Finally, John Glover, another Acting Governor, used the idea of runaway slaves to counteract the influence of the Abẹokuta elite.

Sometimes, these city and coastal interventions were followed by personal ones. Fraser's interference in the Sandeman case has been interpreted as political, rather than humanitarian.[30] Alabọn's case resembles that of Sarah Forbes Bonnetta, who was rescued by another consul and whose original name, 'Aina', was likewise changed. George reminds us of the expectations that come burdened with names. For Alabọn, the unlikely but recorded translation of her name was 'keep the house clean'.[31] Later she became 'Rosa, the black girl'.

Alabọn's story is compelling for the way that she moved (and was moved) along the lagoons, as well as the manner in which these jour-

---

[28] TNA FO 84/920, 'Vice Consul Louis Fraser to the Earl of Malmesbury "Case of the Kidnapping at Lagos", Inclosure 1 in Slave Trade No. 2'.
[29] Mann, *Slavery and the Birth of an African City*, 177.
[30] Mann, *Slavery*, 164.
[31] TNA FO 84/920, Vice Consul Louis Fraser to the Earl of Malmesbury, "Case of the Kidnapping at Lagos", Inclosure 1 in Slave Trade No. 2'.

neys reflected her movement between slavery and emancipation. After the bombardments of Lagos, Sandeman had begun transferring his business concerns to Lagos, in order to take advantage of the growing British influence there. This was what had led Tinubu's people to capture the girl in order to sell her again. Vice Consul Fraser, in turn, had based his action on what he called the 'country law': 'if you have a slave, that slave cannot be taken away without proper intimation'.[32]

Reimagining Abẹokuta

Between 1853 and 1861, British officers stationed in Lagos and on the coast went through the motions of propping up ọba Akitoye and then his son Dosunmu, who was unable to govern effectively even with military assistance. By 1859 the British wanted a different set-up, one that would better reflect political reality. Robert Smith's *The Lagos Consulate*,[33] a diplomatic history of the decade after the bombardment in 1851, offers a detailed analysis of the consular actions leading up to annexation.

In William McCoskry's opinion, the annexation of Lagos was entirely necessary in order to preserve the peace required to maintain a successful trade in palm oil, since Dosunmu had demonstrated that he could not fulfil the terms his father Akitoye had agreed to in 1852. McCoskry was the British government's 'man on the spot' in Lagos. To him and other European observers, Dosunmu was a weak king, unable to maintain control over his own subjects and the diverse group of merchants, missionaries and returnees who already considered themselves outside of his jurisdiction.[34]

McCoskry was particularly vexed by the question what to do with enslaved people escaping to Lagos: he noted in 1861 that 'questions arising out of the domestic slavery existing among the natives are giving me more trouble than all the rest of the business together'.[35] McCoskry testified

[32] TNA FO 84/920. For the legal issues around the British abolition of slavery, see Silke Strickrodt, 'British Abolitionist Policy on the Ground in West Africa in the Mid-Nineteenth Century', in *The Changing Worlds of Atlantic Africa: Essays in Honor of Robin Law*, ed. Toyin Falola and Matt D. Childs (Durham, N.C.: Carolina Academic Press, 2009), 155–72.

[33] Robert Sydney Smith, *The Lagos Consulate: 1851–1861* (Berkeley: University of California Press, 1978).

[34] William McCoskry Esq. 'Testimony – April 6 1865', 412. Report from the Select Committee Appointed to Consider the State of British Establishments on the Western Coast of Africa; Together with the Proceedings of the Committee, Minutes of Evidence, and Appendix', in *Report from the Committees: Eight Volumes (Contents of the First Volume) Africa (Western Coast), Session 7 February–6 July 1865* (Ordered by the House of Commons to be Printed, 1865).

[35] TNA FO 84/1154, 'Acting Governor William McCoskry to the Earl Russell, Slave Trade No. 17', 1861.

that enslaved people were streaming to Lagos from all over the region, notably from Abẹokuta, Ouidah and Ibadan. They sought freedom in order to escape export, as well as ill treatment in domestic circumstances.

The Foreign Office supported the annexation and so, in July 1861, McCoskry invited Dosunmu aboard HMS *Prometheus*. McCoskry and Norman Bedingfield (head of the Navy in the Bight) informed Dosunmu that the British government had decided to annex Lagos. Dosunmu eventually acquiesced to their demands, but not without protest. To convince him, McCoskry and Bedingfield had pointed to the gunboats, anchored on the Lagos Lagoon within view of his palace, ready to fire on the town if he were to refuse. Richard Burton, the English explorer, was there when Britain formally claimed the territory:

> The 'Captain' read out an English proclamation, very intelligible to the natives, confirming 'the cession of Lagos and its dependencies' – a pleasantly vague frontier. Then followed a touching scene. One Union Jack was hoisted in the town, another on the beach. 'Prometheus Vinctus' saluted with twenty-one guns … Thus, Lagos rose.[36]

On August 6, 1861, Lagos became a British colony. Liora Bigon has described the British administration in the first two years as having a 'lightness of touch and looseness of control'. The newly empowered British administrators set about transforming Lagos.

> Q. 1586: Do you think it absolutely necessary to admit into the island of Lagos any number of fugitives that choose to present themselves? – A: They make their way there; they are there; you do not, in fact, admit them, they come there before you are aware; the Governor would probably find a fugitive at the foot of the stairs on his knees when he came down in the morning.[37]

Making Lagos British was a process that involved more than infrastructure. There could be no more slavery in the town. McCoskry, now Acting Governor (writing to the Colonial Office from what had become 'Government House'), appealed for funds:

---

[36] Richard F. Burton, *Wanderings in West Africa from Liverpool to Fernando Po: By a F. R. G. S. With Map & Illustration, in 2 Volumes*, vol. 2 (London: Tinsley Brothers, 1863), 216–17.

[37] 'Testimony of William McCoskry, Esq., April 6, 1865', in *(170) West Coast of Africa, Copy of the Report of Colonel Ord, the Commissioner Appointed to Inquire into the Condition of the British Settlements on the West Coast of Africa* (Colonial Office, 1865), Q. 1586, page 72;, 'Testimony of William McCoskry, Esq., April 6, 1865', in *Report from the Committees: Eight Volumes (Contents of the First Volume) Africa (Western Coast), Session 7 February–6 July 1865*, vol. 5 (Ordered by the House of Commons to be Printed, 1865), (Response to Question 1586), 72.

Since the cession, hundreds of slaves have made their escape to Lagos; many were sent by their masters to convey supplies: from their creditors, but on reaching Lagos took shelter within the Slave Court, and in course of time they were either liberated, apprenticed, or a compensation, in most cases not half the value of a slave, were given them. These liberated slaves became Government servants, either as policemen, armed police, or by being enlisted in the regular West India companies, or employed as farm labourers by Government Agents; such, then, are the various manners in which the native masters see their slave made use of.[38]

The discussion on fugitive slaves revolved around three sites: the Slave Court, the Slave Commission Court and the Liberated Africans' Yard. Adeniyi Oroge has documented how William McCoskry created an 'establishment for Liberated Slaves' in Lagos in 1861.[39] Within a year the new governor, Stanhope Freeman, renamed the initiative the 'Liberated Africans' Yard' (echoing the term used in Sierra Leone), despite the fact that most people who utilised it had been victims of domestic slavery, and were not immediately at risk of being sold abroad.[40] It was run by Mr Davies, a Saro. Later, a Slave Court sat every Tuesday to deal with issues relating to compensation and employment for these people. John Glover, Acting Governor, replaced this Slave Court with a Slave Commission Court in October 1864.[41] It was guided by 'political expediency': Glover determined that in some instances, people could be returned to their masters in the interior.[42]

Abẹokuta, the walled city east of the Ogun River, was home to numerous Saro merchants and European missionaries. In November 1865, Governor Glover brought accusations against Henry Robbin, a prominent indigenous Christian trader with cotton and palm oil businesses in Abẹokuta, as well as influence in Lagos. To Glover, Robbin was the archetype of the 'semi-civilised' native convert who oscillated between supposedly stable Christian and African values.

'I am Mr. Henry Robbin's slave at Abbeokuta [sic]'.[43] Awa's deposition began with this short declaration on 12 November 1865, before Ussher

---

[38] 'Appendix (D), Memorial of Sierra Leonean Merchants to His Excellency, Col. Ord., R.E., Her Majesty's Commissioner, Lagos, 27 December 1864', in *(170) West Coast of Africa, Copy of the Report of Colonel Ord, the Commissioner Appointed to Inquire into the Condition of the British Settlements on the West Coast of Africa* (Colonial Office, 1865), 46.
[39] Oroge, 'The Fugitive Slave Question', 67.
[40] Ibid.
[41] TNA CO 148/1, 'No. 13: An Ordinance to Confirm the Establishment of the Slave Commission Court', 28 October 1864.
[42] Oroge, 'The Fugitive Slave Question', 76.
[43] TNA FO 84/1250, 'Deposition of Awa, a Slave-Woman of Mr. Henry Robbin, at Abbeokuta' (Inclosure No. 1 in Slave Trade No. 25, 12 November 1865).

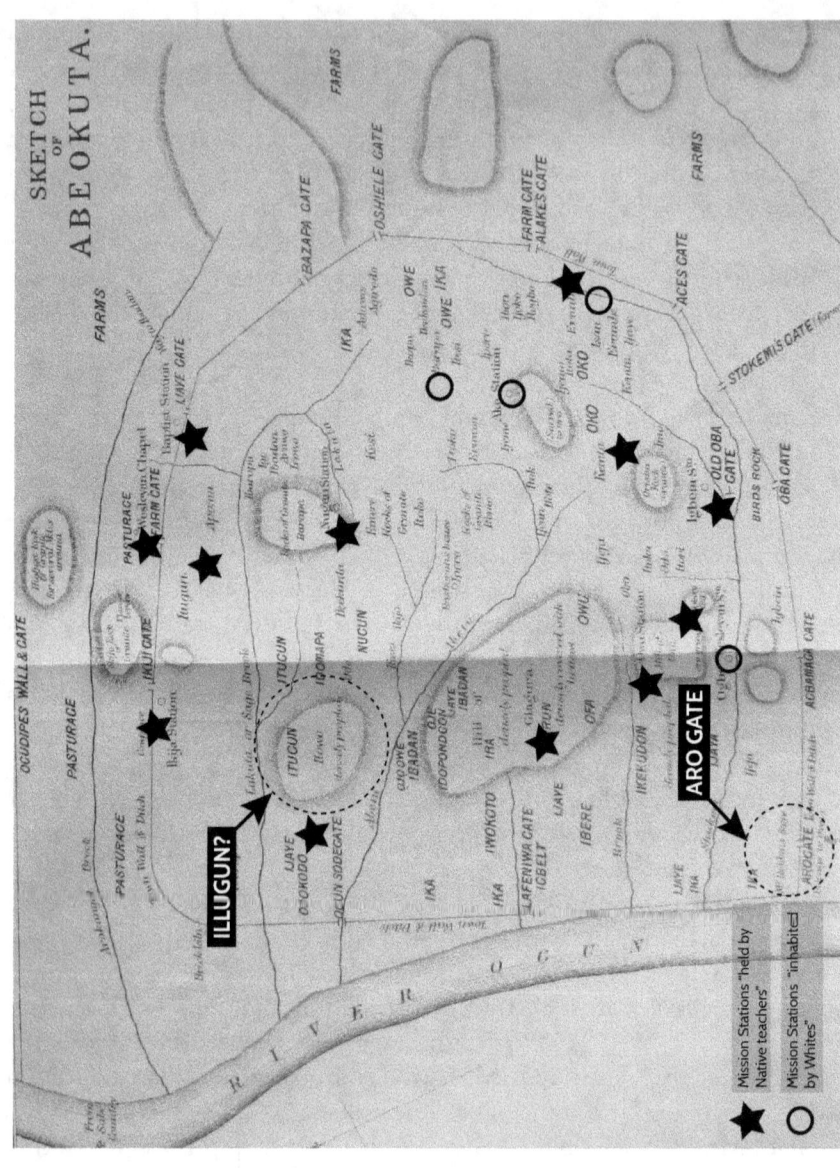

Map 8 Sketch of Abẹokuta, c. 1865, showing the quarters and racial make-up of the mission stations

(Source: The National Archives UK, sketch CO879/15/African#192; the information on the mission stations comes from another version of the map, 'Sketch map of Abeokuta, Nigeria, showing its position on the River Ogun', compiled separately (TNA MPG 1/850/2, Sketch Map of Abeokuta, Nigeria, showing its Position on the River Ogun, the Layout of the Town, Mission Stations, and Type of Country Surrounding the Settlement, July 1892, 2 inches to 1 mile))

and Pinkerton, Justices of the Peace in Lagos. She had escaped from Abẹokuta to Lagos. The conditions of her enslavement were unpleasant: punishments were swift and sudden, and Awa claimed she was used both as a concubine and as a domestic worker. In one instance, she was sent from Illugun with eight other enslaved women to Abẹokuta's Aro Gate to 'bring up cowries'. Their punishment, she said, for dallying too long was to be locked up in a cell under Robbin's bedroom floor where they had no light and little air. On another occasion, she was shackled to a post for six days after allegedly being rude and was denied food and drink. Awa's itinerary of enslavement had begun in Ibadan, where she claimed Henry Robbin bought her, from where he took her to Abẹokuta. Eventually Robbin's 'principal' wife, Osanyinpeju, sold her to a man in Porto Novo, where she was kept for two months ('moons'). It was here that she finally made her escape east along the lagoons to Lagos.

Evidently, Awa was kept in Illugun, in the north-west section of Abẹokuta. The sketch of the city reproduced in Map 8 illustrates how many mission stations were distant from those manned by Europeans, allowing a sense of plausible deniability about the activities around domestic slavery in the city.

Awa was able to escape from Porto Novo because of her association with Daniel Dọpẹmu, a man who, she claimed, had also been held in slavery with her by Robbin. Before his escape to Lagos, Dọpẹmu had been employed as a canoe man in Abẹokuta, plying his owner's trade mostly between Abẹokuta and Lagos, via the Ogun River. In his deposition, he claimed that he ran away from Robbin's establishment, after being chained for twelve days, to escape being resold over the case of a confiscated canoe. He was first chained for five days at Robbin's home and from there was taken to the home of Lumẹyẹ, a slave trader. Lumẹyẹ, instead of selling him at Oke Odan, a market town a few miles south-west of Abẹokuta, located on the Yewa River, as instructed by Robbin, decided to sell him to the King of Porto Novo on the coast. Explaining the circumstances of his escape from Lumẹyẹ, Dọpẹmu stated simply: 'I was glad to find on the night of the seventh day, that the chains fell off from me during a very strong wind that was then blowing.'[44] He left the chains in a bush at Illugun, after which he made his way to Lagos through the river: from Illugun, he went to Oko Oba and then Mokoloki, both towns on the bank of the Ogun River. From Mokoloki, he travelled down the Ogun River to Ọtta in a canoe and then took the overland route to Lagos. His escape took ten days.[45] In Lagos he managed to contact the Superintendent of Police and thus

[44] TNA FO 84/1250, 'Deposition of Daniel Dọpẹmu, a Christian Convert at Abbeokuta', Inclosure No. 1 in Slave Trade No. 23, 7 November 1865,.
[45] Ibid.

catch the attention of Glover. He eventually crossed paths with Awa in the streets of Lagos.

Henry Robbin (sometimes 'Robin'), born in 1835 in Sierra Leone, moved to Abẹokuta in 1857, where he was in charge of cotton production for the Church Missionary Society.[46] In Lagos he was responsible for supervising the Abẹokuta cotton.[47] There is some evidence that John Glover intended to manipulate the Slave Commission Court in order to wield influence over some of the Ẹgba (inhabitants of Abẹokuta). Glover was convinced that many of the elite merchants were still slave holders, and he used the testimonies of Awa and Dọpẹmu, who had escaped from Abẹokuta to Lagos and claimed to have been enslaved by one of these men, against them.

On 20 November 1865 Robbin called a meeting in Ake, in Abẹokuta to discuss the charges that Glover had made against him in Lagos. He was unwilling to go to Lagos to defend himself, and in his defence sent a summary of the meeting. At least four witnesses corroborated his story. He maintained that he was a practising Christian and therefore did not participate in the enslavement of others; that Dọpẹmu (and by extension Awa) was actually never enslaved but had been in pawn because of debt; and that he could not defend himself in person in Lagos because of Glover's 'strong prejudice'. Missionaries, fellow tradesmen and fellow Saro wrote a 'memorial' to the Colonial Office, vouching for Robbin in the case of Dọpẹmu. However, no such evidence has survived for Awa.

Conclusion

Despite treaties and ordinances designed to end participation in the trans-atlantic slave trade and check domestic slavery in Lagos, both continued to flourish on Lagos Island and in surrounding towns, with the lagoons functioning as a conduit. Alabọn's forced journeys, first to Badagry and then to Lagos, throw light on how women were still enslaved in this period. The subsequent lives of both Awa and Alabọn are not to be found in the archival record. Once Alabọn was found and safely returned, Fraser turned to more pressing matters: how to manage a 'quasi-consulate' and enforce various treaties. Similarly, the Colonial Office minutes indicate a lack of interest in Awa's redemption.

On the lagoons Lagos was imagined as a site where freedom could be gained and made permanent. Though Awa and Alabọn were pawns in

---

[46] Jean Herskovits Kopytoff, *A Preface to Modern Nigeria: The 'Sierra Leonians' in Yoruba, 1830–1890* (Madison: University of Wisconsin Press, 1965), 297–8.
[47] Saburi O. Biobaku, *The Egba and their Neighbours 1842–1872* (Oxford: The Clarendon Press, 1957), 58.

two senses of the word, their journeys through the towns framed by the Ogun River and the lagoons offer a perspective different from that of the depersonalised route surveys, soundings and maps drawn by the naval officers and missionaries who travelled along the same routes.

8

Gendered Authority, Gendered Violence
Family, Household & Identity in the Life & Death of a Brazilian Freed Woman in Lagos

KRISTIN MANN

Between 1821 and 1824 the young sisters Ajifoluke and Ayebomi and their male 'cousin' Shetolu were enslaved in Owu, an important kingdom in the southern part of the Yoruba-speaking world located in what is today south-western Nigeria.[1] One of the two little girls, Ayebomi, was sold to a woman in Ijebu Ode, about sixty miles away, where she lived as a slave for a number of years until redeemed and reunited with her mother. Perhaps because of their greater age, the child's older sister Ajifoluke and her male 'cousin' Shetolu were traded to the coast and sold to Brazilians or Portuguese.

It is likely that Shetolu, who became known in Brazil as Francisco Gomes de Andrade, was bought by a slave trader either in Lagos, then the leading port in the Bahian trade, or in Salvador. The man indicated years later that between 1827, when he spent six months in Lagos, and the mid-1840s he had travelled 'backwards and forwards' between the West African coastal town and Brazil.[2] Such mobility was characteristic of the significant number of Brazilian slaves who worked in the transatlantic slave trade. Although no document has come to light that definitively reveals Francisco Gomes de Andrade's owner, much circumstantial evidence points to a man named Luis Antônio de Andrade, who was

---

[1] On the destruction of Owu c. 1821/1822 and enslavement of many of its people see A. L. Mabogunje and J. Omer-Cooper, *Owu in Yoruba History* (Ibadan: University of Ibadan Press, 1971), chapters 4 and 5; The Rev. Samuel Johnson, *The History of the Yorubas* (1921; reprint, London: Routledge and Kegan Paul, 1969), 206–10.

[2] David Eltis and David Richardson, *Atlas of the Transatlantic Slave Trade* (New Haven, CT: Yale University Press, 2010), Map 78, 120; Lagos Supreme Court (hereafter LSC), Judge's Notebook Civil Cases (hereafter JNCC), *In the matter of Louisa Ajatu, deceased*, vol. 7, 216, 29 August 1887, and *In the matter of Ayebomi, deceased*, volume number lost, 101–110, 7 March 1889. These records are housed in the tower of the Lagos State High Court building, Lagos, Nigeria. I am grateful to Susan Rosenthal for a copy of the second document.

involved in the illegal slave trade at Lagos probably from the late 1820s until his death in the town in 1847. Francisco Gomes de Andrade's work and transatlantic travel in the slave trade enabled him to commence small-scale commerce of his own, probably in African commodities for which there was a demand among slaves and freed people in Bahia.

Through his labours he accumulated the capital to manumit himself, and around 1844 he returned to live permanently in Lagos, where he helped establish a community of Brazilian and Cuban freed slaves. There he continued to trade with Brazil, founded what grew into a large, polygynous family, and acquired land on which he built a substantial house in the area that developed into the Brazilian quarter. Although never a truly powerful man, Francisco's cultural mobility – his capacity to navigate African, Lusophone and British practices and institutions – enabled him by the 1850s to acquire influence with the local king Dosunmu as well as the British consul in the town, and to emerge as a leader of Lagos's Brazilian community. By that time the Brazilian slave traders had been expelled.[3]

Less is known about Ajifoluke's life as a Brazilian slave. After her sale into the transatlantic slave trade, she was probably transported from Lagos to Bahia, since the commerce between the Bight of Benin and other parts of Brazil was small in the 1820s.[4] Furthermore, Francisco Gomes de Andrade later said that in 1827 he had met Ayebomi and her mother Ayiku in Lagos and told them he had seen Ajifoluke in Brazil.[5] Given his connections with Bahia, he probably encountered his female cousin there. In Brazil Ajifoluke was baptised Luisa; but she converted to Islam, not Catholicism. On her conversion, she took the Muslim name Ajatu, by which she strongly preferred to be known for the rest of her

---

[3] Mary Hicks, 'The Sea and the Shackle: African and Creole Mariners and the Making of a Luso-African Atlantic Commercial Culture, 1721–1835' (Ph.D. dissertation, University of Virginia, 2015), chapters 3 and 4; Kristin Mann, 'The Illegal Slave Trade and One Yoruba Man's Transatlantic Passages from Slavery to Freedom', in *The Rise and Demise of Slavery and the Slave Trade in the Atlantic World,* ed. Philip Misevich and Kristin Mann (Rochester, NY: University of Rochester Press, 2016), 222–3; The National Archive (hereafter TNA), Merchants, traders, and residents of Lagos to Campbell, April 1, 1855, encl. in F.O. 84/976, Campbell to Clarendon, 28 May 1855; Sierra Leonean, Brazilian and Cuban emigrants to Adams, 10 October 1856, encl. in F.O. 84/1002, Campbell to Clarendon, November 29, 1856; Minutes of a Conference between the King of Lagos and Merchants, 10 February 1859, F.O. 2/28, Lodder to Malmesbury; Minutes of a Commercial Meeting, 6 January 1860, F.O. 2/35, Brand to Russell, 12 January 1860; Interview, Aduke Gomez and Professor Abosede George, Lagos, 15 June 2017.
[4] *Voyages: The Transatlantic Slave Trade Database*, Estimates, 1821–1830, Embarkation Region = Bight of Benin, Disembarkation Regions = Amazonia, Bahia, Pernambuco, South-eastern Brazil, Brazil unspecified (accessed 2 November 2017). David Eltis and David Richardson, 'A New Assessment of the Transatlantic Slave Trade', in *Extending the Frontiers: Essays on the New Transatlantic Slave Trade Database,* ed. David Eltis and David Richardson (New Haven, CT: Yale University Press, 2008), 15–21 and Table 8.1.
[5] *In the matter of Louisa Ajatu,* 216.

life and by which she will therefore be called for the remainder of this chapter. Finally, in the 1850s, Ajatu herself returned as a freed woman to Lagos. She came, however, not from Salvador but from Rio de Janeiro, suggesting either that at some point she was traded from Bahia to the prosperous and growing southern city in the intra-Brazilian slave trade or that after manumitting herself in Bahia she migrated voluntarily to Rio.[6]

Ironically, the woman's insistence on using a Muslim name, an expression of her Islamic faith and identity, has made tracing her in the Brazilian records very difficult. Brazilian scribes who documented bureaucratic and other encounters between African slaves or freed people and secular and ecclesiastical authorities almost never included African names in their records. In Bahia, Ajatu would have been identified as Luisa or possibly Luisa Nagô, and in Rio as Luisa or Luisa Mina.[7] Yet there were hundreds of Yoruba-speaking slaves named Luisa in Salvador alone during the period when the woman probably lived in Bahia. That number expands into the thousands if one includes the Recôncavo, where she may also have spent time, and Rio de Janeiro. Without a Brazilian *sobrenome*, of the sort that Shetolu acquired, taken usually from an owner, it is very difficult to trace individual African slaves and freed people in nineteenth-century Brazilian sources. Indeed, as Colleen Kriger's and Ademide Adelusi-Adeluye's chapters also show, coerced and voluntary name changes both within particular societies and across spatial, cultural and political frontiers pose real challenges in research on African women in the Atlantic world. The little that is known and is communicated in this chapter about Ajatu's life as a slave comes not from Brazilian sources but from the records of criminal and civil proceedings in colonial courts that Britain established in Lagos after colonising the town and surrounding area in 1861.[8]

---

[6] *In the matter of Louisa Ajatu*, 216; *In the matter of Ayebomi*, 104; and Criminal Court records, Lagos Colony, *Reg. v. Momo and others*, 106–37, 2 April 1871. The Criminal Court record remains in the possession of the Lagos State High Court, and I am indebted to Susan Rosenthal for a copy of it. On the intra-Brazilian slave trade see João José Reis and Carlos da Silva Jr., 'Introdução', and Richard Graham, 'Nos tumbeiros mais uma vez? O comércio interprovincial de escravos no Brasil', in *Atlântico de dor: Faces do tráfico de escravos*, ed. João José Reis and Carlos da Silva, Jr. (Salvador: EDUFRB; Belo Horizonte: Fino Traço, 2016), 25–6, 347–56, 360–9; and Herbert S. Klein and Francisco Vidal Luna, *Slavery in Brazil* (New York: Cambridge University Press, 2010), 74–6, 85, 96–101. Most work on the intra-Brazilian slave trade has focused on the period after 1850, by which time Ajatu had probably left Bahia. Mary C. Karasch, *Slave Life in Rio de Janeiro, 1808–1850* (Princeton, NJ: Princeton University Press, 1987), 25–6, 44–54, and passim, however, includes some discussion of the inter-provincial trade in the 1830s and 1840s; Sandra Lauderdale Graham, 'Being Yoruba in Nineteenth-Century Rio de Janeiro', *Slavery & Abolition* 32, no. 1 (2011): 1–26, reconstructs the lives and marriage of a Yoruba-speaking woman and man sold from Bahia to Rio around the same time as Ajatu.

[7] João José Reis and Beatriz Gallotti Mamigonian, 'Nagô and Mina: The Yoruba Diaspora in Brazil', in *The Yoruba Diaspora in the Atlantic World*, ed. Toyin Falola and Matt D. Childs (Bloomington: Indiana University Press, 2004), 77–110.

[8] See, in particular, the records of the three cases cited in notes 2 and 6.

British Colonial Court Records and Research on African Slaves and Freed People

Court records of different kinds from Britain's early West African colonies in Sierra Leone, the Gold Coast and Lagos preserve evidence about thousands of African women and men, including slaves and freed people. While some of the slaves, like Ayebomi, had been owned locally, others, such as Shetolu and Ajatu, had been sold into the Atlantic trade and later freed themselves and returned to the continent of their birth. At a moment of growing interest in researching the lives of Africans around the Atlantic basin, the narratives that women and men related in British colonial courts constitute a treasure trove rich with possibility.[9] Elsewhere, I have discussed how to read and interpret the civil records of the Lagos Supreme Court (LSC) established by the British after a major judicial reform in 1876. I have used these records to study patronage, slavery, emancipation, land ownership, labour relations and other subjects in the colony.[10] This chapter closely reads the record of a criminal proceeding in an earlier British colonial court that followed the murder of Ajatu in 1871 to see what it reveals about the woman's life after she returned to Lagos in the era of abolition and British colonisation. After her murder, Ajatu's property was seized and sold by the colonial government, which claimed the substantial proceeds of £329. A chain of events ensued that affected Ayebomi and Francisco Gomes de Andrade for the remainder of their lives, became a flash point in the British colonial government's uneasy relationship with the independent state of Abeokuta on its frontier, and included several civil proceedings in the LSC pertaining to the inheritance of Ajatu's estate.[11] Although these events lie

---

[9] For a discussion of some of these courts and their records see Kristin Mann and Richard Roberts, 'Slave Voices in African Colonial Courts', in *African Voices on Slavery and the Slave Trade*, vol. 2, *Essays on Sources and Methods*, ed. Alice Bellagamba, Sandra E. Greene and Martin A. Klein (New York: Cambridge University Press, 2016), 132–53.

[10] Kristin Mann, 'Interpreting Cases, Disentangling Disputes: Court Cases as a Source for Understanding Patron-Client Relationships in Early Colonial Lagos', in *Sources and Methods in African History: Spoken, Written, Unearthed*, ed. Toyin Falola and Christian Jennings (Rochester, NY: University of Rochester Press, 2003), 195–218; Kristin Mann, *Slavery and the Birth of an African City: Lagos, 1760–1900* (Bloomington: Indiana University Press, 2007), chapter 8. For examples of other new work on the transatlantic biographies of slaves and freed people that uses legal records in different ways see James H. Sweet, *Domingos Álvares, African Healing, and the Intellectual History of the Atlantic World* (Chapel Hill: University of North Carolina Press, 2011); João José Reis, Flávio dos Santos Gomes and Marcus J. M. de Carvalho, *O alufá Rufino: Tráfico, escravidão e liberdade no Atlântico Negro (c. 1822–c. 1853)* (São Paulo: Companhia Das Letras, 2010); Rebecca J. Scott and Jean M. Hébrard, *Freedom Papers: An Atlantic Odyssey in the Age of Emancipation* (Cambridge, MA: Harvard University Press, 2012); Lisa A. Lindsay, *Atlantic Bonds: A Nineteenth-Century Odyssey from America to Africa* (Chapel Hill: University of North Carolina Press, 2017).

[11] TNA, CO 147/61, Moloney to Holland, 12 December 1887, plus encls. The LSC did not finally conclude the long dispute over Ajatu's estate until March 1896, twenty-five years after her death: *Lagos Weekly Record*, 28 March and 27 June 1896.

mostly beyond the scope of this chapter, evidence contained in the LSC civil court records is incorporated into the analysis when relevant.

Much less is known about the operation of the pre-1876 British criminal and other courts than about the later LSC, because few records survive from them.[12] The thirty-one page record of the jury trial of the three men accused of Ajatu's murder was written by the Acting Chief Magistrate, G. F. Pike, who presided over it. The document summarises in detail the evidence given by the witnesses and accused who spoke in the courtroom. It also includes, unlike later Supreme Court records, questions that the Crown Prosecutor and jurors asked witnesses and the accused, as well as their responses. The Africans who appeared during the trial spoke different languages – some probably Yoruba alone, others Yoruba and Portuguese, and still others Yoruba and English. The text does not specify what language a particular African speaker used. The Acting Chief Magistrate, Crown Prosecutor, and some of the jurors probably spoke only English. While the record of the trial contains no indication that interpreters were used in the courtroom, the annual colonial estimates of expenses and lists of government colonial servants show that the pre-1876 colonial courts employed interpreters. Testimony in Yoruba, and perhaps some in Portuguese, was surely interpreted for jurors, the Crown Prosecutor and the Acting Chief Magistrate, who wrote notes on what was said exclusively in English. Thus much of the language in the courtroom was twice mediated – by one or more interpreters and by the Acting Chief Magistrate, who wrote the record of the case. In certain places, translations of specific Yoruba words into English can be inferred; more generally the words originally spoken cannot be determined.

Reading and interpreting the record of the case is further complicated by the fact that the cramped handwriting is difficult to decipher and names are spelled inconsistently throughout. In places, moreover, the paper has disintegrated and words or phrases are missing from the text. Given these challenges, what does the early criminal court record reveal, and why is the information significant?

Ajatu was not an elite woman. She apparently returned from Brazil with significant material resources, as the evidence will show, and not as a complete stranger. Her prominent cousin Francisco Gomes de Andrade was already living in the town, as were other *retornados* she had known in Brazil or met on board the ship sailing back to Africa. Even so, she arrived in Lagos as an outsider, who needed soon to provide housing, food and other basic necessities for herself. She also needed to construct a network of social relationships with people on whom she could rely for practical help and spiritual and emotional support. In sum, she required paths of incorporation into the economic, social, religious and political life of the town.

[12] For a brief discussion of Lagos's colonial courts before 1876 see Mann, *Slavery*, 105.

Because of Ajatu's marginality as an immigrant and outsider, this chapter responds to the editors' challenge to restore visibility to non-elite women. The record of the criminal trial yields insights into how such a woman constituted a family and established a household in Lagos. The latter accomplishment was a requirement for any woman or man who sought to minimise the demands of others on her/him for material and other support, as well as to create a residence where she/he would be remembered after death. The text reveals, moreover, how Ajatu acquired a younger male dependant, who lived in her household and laboured under her authority, contributing to her economic welfare. Further, the document illuminates the kinds of people with whom the woman forged networks of help, care and support in Lagos. In all of these areas, her gender and her multiple and overlapping identities as a Muslim, a Brazilian, and an Owu descendant proved pivotal. Ultimately, Ajatu's male dependant rebelled against her authority in the name of patriarchy, and when she resisted, he plotted to murder her. The criminal court record exposes how Ajatu's female and Brazilian supporters then used new British legal institutions to ensure that the perpetrators were caught and punished, avenging her violent death.

Ajatu's Family and Household in Lagos

When Ajatu returned to Lagos from Brazil, she probably stayed initially with her well-established kinsman Francisco Gomes de Andrade or another Brazilian she knew, who already had a residence in the town. Evidence in the LSC civil records shows that, very soon after her arrival, she sent a message to her mother and younger sister in Abeokuta, sixty miles away.[13] In the 1830s, they had joined other Owu refugees who were establishing their own quarter in the new, confederated Egba town.[14] Francisco was aware where Ayiku and Ayebomi were. If he had not already managed to communicate that information to Ajatu in Brazil, perhaps helping to awaken her desire to return to Africa, he would certainly have told her when she arrived in Lagos. The civil court records indicate that Ayebomi and her mother then travelled down to stay with Ajatu for a period of time, and she in turn visited them in Abeokuta.[15] These sojourns illuminate the importance of mobility between Abeokuta and Lagos, as well as across the Atlantic, in Ajatu's story. They enabled the mother and two daughters to renew family ties that had been interrupted, but clearly not broken, by

[13] *In the matter of Louisa Ajatu.*
[14] Saburi O. Biobaku, *The Egba and their Neighbours, 1842–1872* (Oxford: Clarendon Press, 1957), 4, 18.
[15] *In the matter of Louisa Ajatu.*

slaving and the slave trade at least three decades before. Through her sister and mother, Ajatu re-established important connections with other Owu people in Abeokuta.

Evidence in the civil court records also indicates that in Lagos Ajatu bought land on Bamgbose Street in the Brazilian quarter, near where Francisco lived, and built a substantial house on it. Her kinsman, who may have used his local knowledge and contacts to help Ajatu arrange the purchase and construction, as Ajatu herself would later do for another Brazilian freed woman, insisted in court that his cousin had paid for her land and house with money of her own that she had brought from Brazil.[16] This assertion was central to Ayebomi's later claim to be her deceased sister's heir. If it was true, then a significant transatlantic capital flow helped Ajatu establish a household in Lagos. After the woman acquired a residence, Ayebomi visited her intermittently, sometimes staying many weeks at a time and strengthening the family ties. Indeed, Ayebomi said she was in Lagos when, on the night of 26/27 February 1871, a man named Momo stabbed Ajatu to death in her sleep.[17]

Who was Momo? And why did he commit such a violent act? Answering these questions requires further consideration of the composition of Ajatu's family and household in Lagos. Evidence in the 1871 criminal court record reveals that in the second half of the 1860s Momo lived in the Bamgbose Street house with Ajatu and that she at least sometimes called him her son. In court, witnesses also spoke of the woman as Momo's mother. Another man, Adebambi, also accused and later convicted of Ajatu's murder, said when referring to his discussions with Momo before the crime that a second man lived in the house, whom Momo called 'father'[18]. This remark suggests that Ajatu may have had a husband. However, no-one else who spoke during the criminal trial mentioned this second man. It is possible that Momo invented the 'father' as part of a plan to draw Adebambi into Ajatu's murder.

On the other hand, it was customary in the 1850s for the *Jornal do Comércio*, then Rio de Janeiro's leading commercial newspaper, to publish police notices of individuals departing from the port. Between 1850 and 1859, it printed seventeen notices of African freed people leaving Rio for the *Costa da Mina*, as the littoral of the Bight of Benin was known in the southern city. There were five Luisas or Luizas among the 117 clear adults named in the entries, and four of them travelled with husbands.[19] It

[16] Francisco Gomes (de Andrade) had acquired a grant to land in the area that developed into Campos Square from Oba Dosunmu in 1856. Docemo's Crown Grants, Lagos State Land Registry.
[17] *In the matter of Louisa Ajatu*.
[18] *Reg. v. Momo*, 119–20.
[19] See *Jornal do Comércio*, The Brazilian National Library, www.bn.gov.br/en, for the departures of Antonio Joaquim Theodoro, his wife Luiza Joaquina Theodora, their daughter, and

is not certain that any of these women was Ajatu. One of them may have been, however, and only one among them travelled alone. In fact, only about 30 per cent of the African freed women named in the notices across the decade left the city unaccompanied by a husband. Thus the 'father' mentioned by Adebambi could plausibly have been a husband returned with Ajatu from Brazil.

One of the married Luizas departed from Rio in the 1850s with three minor sons. Overall, about 35 per cent of the adult freed women left for Africa with *filhos* or *filhas* – sons or daughters – or young dependants (*agregados*) of different kinds, commonly called '*crias*' or '*criados*' in the documents. It is certainly possible that in the 1850s Luisa, with or without a husband, brought the young male from Brazil to Lagos.[20] That said, no evidence in the Lagos court records, whether about his name, language or cultural practices associates Momo with Brazil. If he was a Brazilian creole, in the decade and a half or so since his arrival in Lagos, he had thoroughly acculturated, becoming fluent in Yoruba and forging a dense network of social relationships with locals there and in Abeokuta. Moreover, had he been Ajatu's biological son, it is unlikely that the conflict over the house and other property would have developed and then become as heated as it did.

In the absence of any clear evidence linking Momo to Brazil, I think it is most likely that he entered Ajatu's household only after she arrived in Lagos. Indeed, if a second, older, male also lived there, Ajatu may have established a relationship with him too after returning to Africa. By the time the woman reached Lagos, she was beyond childbearing age. When she arrived in the town and renewed contact with her kin and country folk in Owu quarter of Abeokuta, they probably arranged for a youth to be taken down to Lagos to be brought up under her authority and perform the sorts of labour and service that children in Yoruba households owed residents senior to them. That was the cultural norm. In the second half of the nineteenth century, there were few households in Lagos, whether inhabited by Brazilians, Saros or locals, without children in them who were not part of the immediate family or even of the wider kin group. Some of these children were slaves or, in any case, of slave origin. Others were strangers displaced from their communities of

(contd) a female minor (November 1851); Jaime José Ignacio and his wife Luiza Velloso (October 1853); Romão Fortunato, his wife Luisa Maria da Conceição, and three minor sons (March 1855); José Bernardo Pereira Soares and his wife Luiza Francisca (April 1856); and Luiza Maria (April 1856).

[20] Lisa Earl Castillo, 'Mapping the Nineteenth-Century Brazilian Returnee Movement: Demographics, Life Stories and the Question of Slavery', *Atlantic Studies: Global Currents* 13, no. 1 (2016): 34–7; and Luis Nicolau Parés, 'Afro-Catholic Baptism and the Articulation of a Merchant Community, Agoué 1840–1860', *History in Africa* 42 (2015): 186–7, document the departure of African freed people in Brazil for West Africa with children who were not their offspring.

origin, wards sent for training of one kind or another, or pawns placed in households to provide security for loans and cover the interest on them. Given Ajatu's and, as we shall see, Momo's Islamic religion, the young man may have come to the town to attend Koranic school. In all such cases, youths were expected to labour for those with whom they lived. Although there is no evidence about Ajatu's work, her prosperity indicates that she engaged in some type of economic activity, probably trade, a primary sphere of Yoruba women not only in Africa but also in Salvador and Rio.[21] A young male inside the household would have been expected to fetch water and firewood, run errands, and assist his mistress in her daily economic activities. The circulation of youths not only benefited women economically, it also provided a means for those without offspring to bring children into their households, in the hope, in some cases, that over time a filial relationship would develop between the woman and child. The linguistic convention was for kinship terminology to be applied to these relationships, even in the case of slavery.[22] If Momo was not Ajatu's biological son, but rather a dependent child imported from Abeokuta to live and work in her household, he would have referred to her on many occasions as his 'mother', and she would have called him her 'son'. In the court records these terms are English translations, almost certainly of the Yoruba words *iyá* and *omo*.

One piece of evidence in Momo's courtroom testimony confirms a fictive rather than narrower biological use of the term mother. When recounting events following Ajatu's death, the man said, 'people were passing and came to me … saying "Momo your mother die". I said, "which mother?"'[23]. This response suggests that Momo referred to more

[21] LaRay Denzer, 'Yoruba Women: A Historiographical Study', *International Journal of African Historical Studies* 27, no. 1 (1994): 2–3, 6–7; Marjorie Keniston McIntosh, *Yoruba Women, Work, and Social Change* (Bloomington: Indiana University Press, 2009), 127–33; Richard Graham, *Feeding the City: From Street Market to Liberal Reform in Salvador, Brazil, 1780–1860* (Austin: University of Texas Press, 2010), 35–42; Juliana Barreto Farias, *Mercados Minas: Africanos ocidentais na praça do merdado do Rio de Janeiro (1830–1890)* (Rio de Janeiro: Prefeitura do Rio/Casa Civil/Arquivo Geral da Cidade do Rio, 2015), 145–58.

[22] Kristin Mann, *Marrying Well: Marriage, Status, and Social Change among the Educated Elite in Colonial Lagos* (Cambridge: Cambridge University Press, 1985), 99, 106–07; Mann, *Slavery*, 65–9, 181–9; A.G. Hopkins, 'A Report on the Yoruba, 1910', *Journal of the Historical Society of Nigeria*, 5, no. 1 (1969): 77–9; N.A. Fadipe, *The Sociology of the Yoruba* (Ibadan: Ibadan University Press, 1970), 100, 149, 180–93; A.K. Ajisafe, *Laws and Customs of the Yoruba People* (Lagos: Kash and Klare Bookshop, 1946), 63–6; E. Adeniyi Oroge, 'Iwofa: An Historical Survey of the Yoruba Institution of Indenture', *African Economic History*, 14 (1985): 75–106; and Toyin Falola, 'Pawnship in Colonial Southwestern Nigeria', in *Pawnship in Africa: Debt Bondage in Historical Perspective*, ed. Toyin Falola and Paul E. Lovejoy (Boulder, CO: Westview Press, 1994), 245–66. For an analysis of the circulation of girls among Fon households in the colonial period see Jessica Catherine Reuther, 'Borrowed Children, Entrusted Girls: Encounters with Girlhood in French West Africa, c. 1900–1941' (Ph.D. dissertation, Emory University, 2016).

[23] *Reg. v. Momo*, 128.

than one older woman in his social world as *ìyá*, and that his use of the word did not imply a strictly familial relationship.

A further piece of evidence illuminates the shifting composition of Ajatu's household in Lagos. A Brazilian freed woman named Felicidade testified that she had known Ajatu in Rio de Janeiro and that when she arrived in Lagos, she lived in Ajatu's house for a while; perhaps paying rent. A rental market existed in Lagos by the 1870s, and Yoruba in Rio who owned or rented housing brought in important income by renting space to others.[24] After a while, however, Felicidade acquired sufficient funds to buy a house of her own, and she asked Ajatu to help her arrange the purchase, as Francisco Gomes de Andrade had probably earlier done for Ajatu herself. This vignette shows that Ajatu not only housed Brazilian freed women who arrived in Lagos after her, probably deriving income from the arrangement, but also used her local experience, knowledge and contacts to act as patron and intermediary on their behalf. Collectively, the evidence that Momo, at least one Brazilian freed woman and intermittently Ayebomi and her mother lived in Ajatu's residence shows that in Lagos the woman established a complex inter-generational household composed, from time to time, of kin and non-kin, male and female dependants of different kinds and persons from Abeokuta as well as Brazil. The composition of her household signals a woman striving for security, stability and even upward social mobility in Lagos, and it shows the role of both regional and transatlantic geographical mobility in her pursuit these goals.

The Conflict between Momo and Ajatu

According to Adebambi, in Momo's discussions with him before the murder, the young man claimed that in the 1860s his 'father' had died. Whether or not that was the case, conflict subsequently broke out between Momo and Ajatu over control of the house where they lived and authority within it. A witness who said she had been acquainted with Momo 'for a very long time', when asked if she knew of any quarrel between him and Ajatu, answered: 'Yes, they were always quarrelling'.[25] Another woman who said that she had known Momo for about twelve years, in response to the same question, replied: 'There was [animus] between mother and son'. The conflict grew so severe that in 1867 or 1868 Ajatu 'turned Momo out of her house and would not let him live with her any more'.[26] What was going on in this conflict?

[24] Mann, *Slavery*, 263–8; Graham, 'Being Yoruba', 11.
[25] *Reg. v. Momo*, 133.
[26] *Reg. v. Momo*, 135.

We do not know if, in fact, a husband lived in the dwelling with Ajatu and while alive would have claimed to own it with her. Under Brazilian law, in the absence of a will, a widow would have inherited a jointly owned dwelling, and the early colonial courts in Lagos would probably have ruled that way as well in a case involving two self-emancipated slaves from Brazil.[27] In Yoruba culture, on the other hand, spouses did not inherit from one another. A residence passed to children if there were any, with males generally taking precedence. If widows did not remarry, their sons normally allowed them to continue to live in the property, but under their authority.[28] By invoking a deceased 'father' but not one clearly identified with Brazil, Momo may have been seeking to turn Ajatu into a Yoruba widow and thereby establish grounds for plausibly claiming, in local culture, possession of her dwelling and authority over it. Had he been Ajatu's biological son, the pressure on him to act would not have been so great. As a biological son, he would have had secure rights in a house owned by his mother, and he would have known that if he bided his time the property would probably one day be his. Few mothers, moreover, would have wanted permanently to rupture relations with a biological son, from whom they anticipated care in old age, help with their all-important funeral and preservation of their dwelling after their death, so that they could be remembered and honoured there. The magnitude and totality of the breach between Ajatu and Momo lead me to believe that they were not a biological mother and son, but rather a female household head and male subordinate living and working under her authority.

Distance did nothing to heal the breach between the pair. Instead, Momo's grievance festered and grew toxic. Ajatu thought that he was plotting to take her house from her. A literate and influential Saro woman, Mary Davis, testified that two months before she was murdered Ajatu had come to her house and asked for advice. Ajatu had complained that her son was attempting to deprive her of the property. Mary interestingly replied, 'our society [will] assist [you]', and she promised that its headman would intervene with the Governor.[29] The court record contains no further information about the nature of the society; it was probably a Saro advocacy and self-help association headed by an influential merchant or well-placed colonial civil servant. Ajatu's turn to Mary Davis for advice reveals the importance of gender, literacy and Atlantic experience in her strategy for obtaining help in her conflict with Momo.

---

[27] Zepher L. Frank, *Dutra's World: Wealth and Family in Nineteenth-Century Rio de Janeio* (Albuquerque: University of New Mexico Press: 2004), 29–30; Katia de Queirós Mattoso, *Família e Sociedade na Bahia do Século XIX* (São Paulo: Corrupio, 1988), 414, 51–2.
[28] Mann, *Marrying Well*, 36, 51; 147, Note 7 cites additional relevant sources.
[29] *Reg. v. Momo*, 112,

The escalation of the inter-generational struggle between Ajatu and Momo suggests that he was seeking to redefine his relationship with her and, in the process, to transform his social and economic position in Lagos. It also shows that Ajatu resisted his efforts. So long as people in the town, especially those who were younger, depended on others for housing, they were subject to the demands of the household head for labour, service and other kinds of support. The only way to free oneself from such demands was to acquire a residence of one's own. Moreover, possession of urban real estate had other material, social and political advantages.[30] The conflict between Momo and Ajatu over control of the house on Bamgbose Street formed part of a broader struggle over the terms of the relationship between them, and it had major significance for the status and opportunities of each in the town.

By early 1871, Momo's ill-feeling toward Ajatu had grown so fierce that he plotted a course of action far worse than depriving the woman of her house. At the end of February, a trader from Abeokuta named Adebambi came to Lagos by canoe with a number of companions and some palm kernels for sale. Momo may earlier have sent the man a message urging him to come to town. Indeed, Momo's close relationship with Adebambi provides additional evidence that Abeokuta was Momo's place of origin. As it happened, Adebambi was indebted to a recently deceased Lagos trader named 'Rosao', whose name suggests that he was a Brazilian. This debt would ultimately be the undoing of both Adebambi and Momo. During the murder trial, Adebambi identified Ajatu as his 'sister', and others who gave evidence referred to him as her 'brother'.[31] Adebambi said that, when he came from the interior to Lagos, he went to see Ajatu. I suspect that this kinship terminology was used because Ajatu and Adebambi were both identified as Owu people, dispersed when the kingdom was destroyed in 1822. By then many such individuals had resettled in Owu quarter at Abeokuta. Others had migrated to Lagos or elsewhere on the coast, as Francisco Gomes de Andrade had done in 1844 and Ajatu about a decade later. They came not only from other parts of Yorubaland and Brazil, but also from Sierra Leone and Cuba.[32] The words sister and brother may also have implied some sort of fictive or real kinship between Ajatu and Adebambi, although I doubt they meant that the two were full or half siblings. The later Supreme Court civil records include information about Shetolu's,

---

[30] Mann, *Slavery*, 7, 70, 242–3, 262–74. For an analysis of the role of the control of urban real estate in the acquisition of clients and achievement of political power in twentieth century Lagos, see Sandra T. Barnes, *Patrons and Power: Creating a Political Community in Metropolitan Lagos* (Bloomington: Indiana University Press, 1986).

[31] *Reg. v. Momo*, 107, 119.

[32] Mabogunje and Omer-Cooper, *Owu*, chapters 4–6; Biobaku, *The Egba*, 13; and 'Òwu Wars' in *The Encyclopedia of the Yoruba*, ed. Toyin Falola and Akintunde Akinyemi (Bloomington: Indiana University Press, 2016), 259–60.

Ayebomi's and Ajatu's kin, and there is no reference in them to Adebambi. Whatever the relationship between Adebambi and Ajatu, that between him and Momo was more egalitarian than hierarchical, as events were to show.[33]

Soon after Adebambi reached Lagos, Momo drew him into a plot to murder Ajatu, although Adebambi later denied knowing that violence was being planned until after the fact. Momo complained to Adebambi that his 'father' had died three years ago, that 'the house his father had his mother took', and that his mother had then driven him out of the house. Adebambi admitted telling Momo that in 'palaver between mother and son', if the mother died the house would be his, Momo's. The son allegedly replied, 'the palaver is greater than that ... [All] that his mother had done did not hurt him so much as her taking the property belonging to his father', by which he apparently meant his father's personal possessions. According to Adebambi, Momo said that if he would go with him to Ajatu's house to recover his father's box, the debt that Adebambi owed 'would be paid'.[34] It was within boxes stored in the inner rooms of residences that Lagosians kept their important personal possessions.

At about 9 p.m. on the night of 26/27 February, Adebambi accompanied Momo to Ajatu's house. Adebambi stood watch outside while Momo went in and stabbed Ajatu to death in her sleep. Once the woman was dead, however, Momo did not retrieve a box containing goods belonging to a man but rather stole cloth together with gold and silver chains that belonged to Ajatu. Adebambi insisted throughout the trial that if Momo had told him he was going to kill somebody, he would not have gone with him.

Following the murder and robbery, Adebambi took the stolen goods to the house of Disu, an Owu trader in Lagos, where Momo was then living. The next morning, Adebambi's travelling companions from Abeokuta began pressing him to leave by canoe on the return journey home. Rather than depart, Adebambi went to see Momo and asked for some material reward. Momo gave him some of Ajatu's cloth and also the gold and silver chains that had been stolen, which Adebambi tied in his wrapper. Momo then cautioned Adebambi that he should leave town immediately and that if he said anything about what had happened, it would be very bad for them. Still, Adebambi hesitated, because he was 'troubled in mind', he said at the trial. His delay proved fateful.

On the night of 1 or 2 March, a woman named Ijuade reported Adebambi's presence in Lagos to the executors of his deceased creditor

---

[33] For a discussion of the importance of 'horizontal' or egalitarian relationships among Yoruba-speaking friends, companions and co-worshippers in the nineteenth century see J.D.Y. Peel, *Religious Encounter and the Making of the Yoruba* (Bloomington: Indiana University Press, 2003), 55–9.

[34] *Reg. v. Momo*, 119.

Rosao, and the police issued a writ for the man's arrest. The following morning Adebambi was arrested, and at 7 a.m. J.A. Otunba Payne, the Saro clerk of the Court of Requests, which was charged with enforcing creditor-debtor relations, ordered Adebambi to be brought immediately to the court.[35] Once there, Payne began pressing Adebambi about what goods he had to settle his debt. The Abeokuta trader offered cloth and gin received from the sale of his palm kernels. Payne insisted they would not suffice and told Adebambi that once they were seized he would be sent to the debtor's prison. Adebambi begged not to be put 'in the lock up'; in a desperate effort to avoid that calamity he offered Ajatu's cloth and then untied his wrapper and produced her gold and silver chains.[36]

Solidarity, Law and Justice: Ajatu's Gendered, Brazilian and Islamic Networks of Identity and Support

What happened next reveals the public, popular nature of law and justice in Lagos during the early colonial period. It also illuminates Ajatu's strong and specific networks of identity and support among women, Brazilians and Muslims in the town. Indeed, if members of all three of these groups who knew Ajatu, but most specifically women, had not mobilised as they did, it is possible the crimes against her would never have been solved.

Following Ajatu's murder, news of her violent death circulated quickly in her neighbourhood and beyond. She had a friend named Virginia Owomi, who lived not far from her at Tinubu Square. Like Ajatu, Virginia was a Muslim and she was probably also a Brazilian returnee, although she was never specifically identified that way in court. J.A. Otonba Payne described Virginia as a 'trading woman, and [an] honest woman, and a woman in [whom people] can...' and here the paper has disintegrated, silencing his further description.[37] The morning after the murder, a *lemomu*, or imam, sent word to Virginia of Ajatu's death and called her to see him, probably to discuss arrangements for the funeral and burial, which in keeping with Islamic practice needed to be arranged within twenty-four hours.[38]

That same morning the woman named Ijuade came to Virginia's house to 'sympathise' with her about Ajatu's murder. Virginia said at the inquest following the death and repeated during the murder trial that Ijuade had told her of Adebambi's arrest for debt. Ijuade communicated that when

---

[35] Two witnesses associated with the Court of Requests gave different dates for the issuance of the writ of summons and subsequent arrest: James M. Roberts swore they occurred on 1 and 2 March (108), while J.A.O. Payne gave the dates as 2 and 3 March (114–15).
[36] *Reg. v. Momo*, 115.
[37] *Reg. v. Momo*, 118.
[38] In fact, a post-mortem delayed the burial.

Adebambi was arrested, he gave a piece of cloth and also offered gold chains as security for his debt. Chains made of gold and silver were a common form of property and a minor repository of wealth in Rio de Janeiro and Salvador during the first half of the nineteenth century. Africans in those cities acquired them when they could and, a further sign of capital flows back across the Atlantic among freed slaves, took the valuable and easily transportable objects with them when they returned to Africa.[39] The reference to the gold chains aroused Virginia's suspicions, and she reported asking Ijuade, 'Where does an Egba man get gold chains to pay a debt?'[40] Virginia also remembered that Ajatu had told her she had a brother in Abeokuta named Adebambi. Alarmed by these two pieces of information, Virginia went immediately to the Court of Requests, asked to see the cloth and chains, and began questioning Adebambi about how they came to be in his possession. She then identified the chains as the property of the recently murdered Ajatu.

Still concerned about Adebambi's debt, the authorities at the Court of Requests ordered a bailiff, Police Constable Asan Omanu, to accompany Adebambi to the house of a Muslim woman named Felimina, where he had been staying since arriving in Lagos, and seize any of Adebambi's property that might be there. The constable's name suggests that he too was a Muslim. As the pair walked the short distance north from the courthouse at Tinubu Square to Massey Street, rumours circulated that Adebambi had murdered Ajatu, and a crowd formed that processed with the two men to Felimina's house. It significantly attracted two Brazilian men, one of them named Antonio Suse.[41]

En route, Adebambi either became frightened or his resolve weakened, because he began confessing to the police constable what had happened on the night of 26/27 February. When they reached Felimina's house, Asan Omanu locked Adebambi inside, away from the crowd, although somehow the two Brazilian men managed to gain entry, a sign of their identification with Ajatu and determination to learn more about her violent death. Within the compound walls, Adebambi continued to talk. When the constable heard Mr Payne outside, he admitted him to hear what Adebambi had to say. That same afternoon, Payne and Asan Omanu reported what Adebambi had told them to the Saro Inspector of Police, I.H. Willoughby, who sent constables to arrest Momo and Disu. Adebambi insistently implicated the latter man in the crime despite evidence showing that he was not in Lagos when it occurred.

[39] Frank, *Dutra's World*, 40; Karasch, *Slave Life in Rio*, 90; Graham, *Feeding the City*, 33–4. The careful itemisation and valuation of gold and silver jewellery and religious objects in inventories indicates their material and cultural significance.
[40] *Reg. v. Momo*, 106.
[41] 'Suse' may have been how the Acting Police Magistrate rendered Souza.

Three days later Momo, Adebambi and Disu were formally charged with Ajatu's murder.

This series of events underscores the importance of gender and relationships with strong women in Ajatu's life in Lagos. Indeed, the evidence indicates that there she inhabited a world of resourceful women, who took an interest in each other's affairs and supported one another, including in their conflicts with men. Whether or not Ajatu ever shared her Lagos house with a 'husband', she left behind a network of female friends and acquaintances who were committed to seeing her killers caught and punished. The determination of Ijuade and Virginia Owomi, a co-religionist and probably also a Brazilian freed woman, stand out. However, Mary Davis, a Saro acquaintance, also mobilised on Ajatu's behalf. Hearing the day after the murder that a woman had been killed, she went to see who it was. When Mary learned that the victim was Ajatu, who had come to see her seeking advice, she did not retreat to avoid involvement but immediately reported what Ajatu had said to her about Momo to the colonial legal authorities.

The murder trial also illuminates the importance of Ajatu's identity as a Brazilian freed person in Lagos. Beyond the specific evidence regarding Ajatu's relationship with Virginia Owomi and assistance to Felicidade lies the information about the two Brazilian men who followed the crowd to Felimina's house. These men may, of course, have known Ajatu in Brazil or Lagos, and they may have had some deeper and fuller relationship with her. The court record reveals only that they recognised her as a Brazilian like them and on that basis inserted themselves into the events following her murder. If they acknowledged a shared bond with Ajatu as a Brazilian, it is likely that she would have reciprocated. Returnees differed in many ways, such as by class, gender, religion and place of origin. Those who had been born in Africa, however, were all united by the shared experiences of having been violently enslaved, brutally transported across the Atlantic, owned as slaves in an alien land for many years, and then of having freed themselves against long odds and subsequently returned to West Africa, where they faced the challenge of re-forging their lives. The two Brazilian men's interest in Ajatu's death reflects, at the very least, an identification with her and concern for her born of these common experiences.

Significantly, a number of the women and the Brazilians who took an interest in Ajatu's murder used new colonial legal institutions when they mobilised on her behalf. Ijuade had first reported Adebambi's presence in Lagos to Rosao's executors. Virginia Owomi quickly and directly intervened at the Court of Requests to determine where Adebambi had obtained the cloth and chains in his possession and to identify them as Ajatu's property. Mary Davis communicated incriminating evidence to the colonial authorities, and the two Brazilian men made sure they were witnesses to Adebambi's confession. The Brazilians Virginia Owomi, Felicidade and Antonio Suse gave evidence during the murder trial, although their summons to the criminal court was surely not voluntary. The evidence indicates that these actors were familiar with colonial Lagos's new constables and courts, as well as some of its laws, and used them to good effect.

The murder trial, in addition, provides powerful evidence of the centrality of Islam in Ajatu's life and, indeed, in Lagos more generally. The woman's resolution to be known by a Muslim name bespeaks her strong and clear Islamic identity. Although she would in the 1880s be referred to by officials of the LSC by both her Christian baptismal name Luisa and her Muslim name Ajatu, those who spoke about her during the 1871 murder trial called her only Ajatu – without the Luisa and without a Brazilian surname. The particular name that Ajifoluke chose when she converted to Islam is also significant. Ajatu, short for Ajaratu, derives linguistically from the Arabic name Khadija, that of the Prophet's first wife, who was a source of early, constant and great support to him. The name signalled verbally a woman devoted to the teachings of the Prophet Muhammad and worship of Allah.[42]

The quick intervention of a *lemonu* following Ajatu's death indicates that she was known by an Islamic authority. There is no evidence at this point about the mosque where she worshipped or whether it was one of a number founded by Brazilians who returned to Lagos from Salvador and Rio de Janeiro, or the larger Central Mosque. There were in the second half of the nineteenth century several Brazilian mosques in Lagos, some within easy walking distance of Bamgbose Street.[43] H. O. Danmole suggests that by the early twentieth century the term *lemonu* was used in Lagos to refer to the Chief Imam of the Central Mosque.[44] If that was the case in 1871, it would mean that Ajatu was known in Lagos's Muslim community beyond a neighbourhood Brazilian mosque.

A rich associational life characterised a number of Lagos's neighbourhood mosques and its wider Muslim community. Ajatu and Virginia may

[42] Personal communication, Asan Saar, 10 March 2017. In some Muslim traditions, Muhammad's wives are referred to as 'mothers of believers', a phrase borrowed from the Qur'an, 33:6.
[43] According to L.B. Adams, ed., *Eko Dynasty, Colonial Administrators and the Light of Islam in Lagos* (Lagos: Eko Islamic Foundation, 2004), the mosques included, in the order of their founding, Salvador Mosque on Bamgbose/Joseph Street, Brazilian Olosun Mosque on Luther Street, Brazilian Oloro Mosque on Odunfa Street and Brazilian Inabere Mosque on Inabere Street. T.G.O. Gbadamosi, *The Growth of Islam among the Yoruba, 1841–1908* (Longman: London, 1978), 28–30, lists Salvador Mosque, Olosun Mosque, Alagbayun Mosque and Tairu Eko Mosque in his discussion of Muslims who returned to Lagos from Brazil. Further research is needed to establish which of these mosques existed in 1871. The current imam of Tairu Eko Mosque says that it was founded in 1882: personal communication, Sarah Katz, Ph.D. student, University of Michigan, 16 September 2017.
[44] 'A Visionary of the Lagos Muslim Community: Mustapha Adamu Animashaun, 1885–1968', *Lagos Historical Review* 5 (2005): 22–48.

have belonged to an association of Muslim women of the sort then being formed in Yoruba towns to promote the faith and support their members. If so, her companions in the organisation would have helped sustain her in life and have contributed meaningfully to her funeral.[45]

One further type of evidence points to the centrality of Islam not only in Ajatu's life but also in the world she inhabited in Lagos. All of the men charged with her murder were Muslims. Indeed, at the time of the murder Momo lived with Disu in a largely Muslim household. Two women who resided there were wives of an *alufa*, or Koranic teacher. Another woman who bore the Muslim name Rasamo/Rosomo said she had formerly 'eaten' and 'lived' with Momo, language that suggests a domestic or conjugal relationship.[46] During the trial, several of those who gave evidence dated the events surrounding Ajatu's death by saying that they had occurred just before a 'Mohammedan' festival, probably *Eid al Maulud* celebrating the birth of the Prophet Muhammad, which could fall around the end of February in the colonial, Christian calendar. When Virginia Owomi challenged Momo's possession of the chains at the Court of Requests, he defended himself by saying that Ajatu had given them to him to buy a ram, by implication to be killed during the festival.[47] During the murder trial he repeated the claim. When asked where he was around the time of the murder, Momo said he had been 'busy at home' sewing his gown, presumably to wear at the festival. Members of Muslim societies commonly wore to religious festivals clothing made especially for the occasion from identical fabric.[48] In addition, Momo referred to going to a '*missolagi/missolaji*', Yoruba renderings of the word mosque. Finally, most of the witnesses Momo called in his defence during the trial were Muslims, judging from their names.[49]

Adebambi's beliefs as a Muslim shaped his response to events following the murder, as in different ways did Momo's. In prison, Adebambi initi-

---

[45] Gbadamosi, *The Spread of Islam*, 53–8, 73; Hakeem A. Akitoye, 'Islam and Traditional Titles in Contemporary Lagos Society: A Historical Analysis', http://creativecommons.org/licenses/b4/4.0.

[46] *Reg. v. Momo*, 135.

[47] *Reg. v. Momo*, 107.

[48] *Reg. v. Momo*, 128. See also interviews with N.E.S. Adewale, 22 Glover Street, Lagos, July 1974, and I. L. Apatira, Apatira Street, Lagos, December 1973. J. D. Y. Peel, *Christianity, Islam, and Orișa Religion: Three Traditions in Comparison and Interaction* (Oakland: University of California Press, 2016), 130, notes that by the 1890s Islam claimed the allegiance of a majority of indigenous Lagosians. J.A.O. Payne, *Table of Principal Events in Yoruba History* (Lagos: Andrew M. Thomas, 1894), 25–6, lists the *Giwas*, or Heads, of Lagos's neighbourhood Islamic associations, and he includes the rules of one of them.

[49] I am grateful to Saheed Aderinto, personal communication, 16 February 2017, for assistance in identifying the Muslim names, translating '*missologi/missolaji*', and confirming that the Muslim festival was Eid al-Maulud. Disu said during the trial that he was returning from the '*missadoji*' when he was arrested. The spelling of Yoruba words varies with dialect, and the Acting Chief Magistrate also spelled words inconsistently.

ated a conversation with Disu and Momo about what had transpired. To Disu he said: 'Do you see things plainly like that and [deny it?] [Don't you fear God?]'. According to Adebambi, Momo was listening and swore by his Qur'an that if in court Adebambi would retract his story, he, Momo, would do 'whatever thing you want me to do for you'. Adebambi said that while in prison Momo told him he had sent sixty heads of cowries 'to an *alufa* to help … him in his palaver'. A police constable who worked in the jail, a Muslim like Asan Omanu, testified that Momo had asked him to go to the *alufa* and say that if he would 'attend to his case' and 'get him away from his trouble', Momo would give the *alufa* ten bags of cowries and the house that he wanted. The *alufa* allegedly asked the constable to tell Momo that he 'keeps awake every night praying' for him. The constable stated that he went to see the *alufa* a second time, but by then the learned man had changed his mind complaining that he was 'afraid to [do] anything for Momo for when he gets clear of the palaver, he will not pay'. Otherwise, said the *alufa*, 'he would have made a charm which he would have put under a [Icory] [stone] and he would have stood on the stone and prayed all night to get Momo clear'.[50] These data indicate that in Lagos Ajatu lived not exclusively, but centrally, in a community of Muslims.

The Owu Connection

Lastly, the evidence in the criminal trial record points to Ayebomi's, Ajatu's and Shetolu's enduring identity as Owu people, almost fifty years after that kingdom and its capital city had been destroyed by warfare and their populations dispersed into Egba territory, elsewhere in the region and across the Atlantic.[51] By 1827, Ayebomi had been redeemed from slavery in Ijebu Ode and reunited with her mother. In that year, the two of them were in Lagos, where they met their kinsman Shetolu, then a Brazilian slave. Soon after the 1834 founding of Owu quarter in Abeokuta, however, the pair left Lagos and joined their country folk in the new inland town, suggesting a desire to live among people they considered their own.[52] Moreover, when Ajatu returned to Lagos after a three-decade forced exile in Brazil, she not only re-established an on-going relationship with her mother and sister in Owu quarter, but also, judging from evidence in the murder trial record, with others living there. Her world in Lagos was populated by women and men, such as Disu and a witness called Aina, who were identified specifically as Owu.[53] Owu

[50] *Reg. v. Momo*, 124–6.
[51] 'Òwu wars', 259–60.
[52] *In the matter of Louisa Ajatu*.
[53] *Reg. v. Momo*, 132–3.

city before its destruction and Owu quarter of Abeokuta subsequently are both known to have had sizeable and important Muslim populations,[54] and Ajatu's identities as a Muslim and an Owu were mutually reinforcing. Francisco Gomes de Andrade, on the other hand, was a Catholic, but he too was thought of as an Owu man, including long after his death. In *The Torch Bearers or Old Brazilian Colony in Lagos,* published in 1943, for example, A.B. Laotan identified him as 'Senhor Francisco Gomez (Papae Seteolu Owu)'.[55]

When the British colonial government rejected a claim by Ayebomi to be her sister's heir in 1871, she returned to Owu quarter and sought the assistance of people there. Throughout a long struggle with the British over her sister's estate, Ayebomi maintained in her dealings with British executive and judicial officers that she was a resident of Owu quarter and a citizen of an independent and sovereign African state, Abeokuta. As such, she asserted, British courts in Lagos had no legal jurisdiction over her. By the end of her life in 1887, Ayebomi may have lost her taste for the struggle. The British authorities certainly believed that by then she was being manipulated by powerful men in Abeokuta.[56] Further research is needed to untangle the complex politics within Owu quarter and greater Abeokuta, as well as between Abeokuta and the British at Lagos, that shaped Ayebomi's experience following Ajatu's murder. Collectively, however, the evidence coheres to demonstrate a strong and enduring Owu identity among Ajatu, Ayebomi, Shetolu/Francisco Gomes de Andrade and many of the other actors in this story.

Ajatu's life and death in Lagos, reconstructed largely from evidence in British colonial court records, demonstrates that, after the freed woman returned from Brazil, her gender and her relationships – rooted in shared history and identity – with family members, Brazilian returnees, Muslim co-religionists and Owu descendants opened paths of incorporation into her new homeland. Through them, she built a new life in the city. Ties to women, Brazil, Islam and a re-imagined Owu hometown within Abeokuta all helped her survive her second transatlantic crossing. As it is now, Lagos was then an African and Atlantic urban space inhabited by many people for whom becoming Lagosian meant maintaining connections to other places. Tragically, the resistance of a younger male to the property rights and gendered authority Ajatu sought to protect and maintain in

[54] Gbadamosi, *The Spread of Islam*, 4; Percy Amaury Talbot, *The Peoples of Southern Nigeria*, vol. I (1926; reprint, London: Frank Cass, 1969), 137; Biobaku, *The Egba*, 25–6.
[55] Laotan, *The Torch Bearers* (Lagos: Ife-Olu Printing Works, 1943), 13. Catholic priests baptised fifteen of Francisco Gomes de Andrade's children between 1846 and 1871, indicating his Catholic identity: Archive, Society of African Missions House, Cork, Ireland, Lagos Baptism book.
[56] CO 147/20, Kennedy to Kimberley, 11 May 1871, plus enclosures; CO 147/61, Moloney to Holland, 12 December 1887, plus enclosures.

her household led to her violent murder and premature death by unnatural causes. Indeed, Ajatu has become visible in the historical record only because she was a property owner, a methodological constraint in research on Africa's Atlantic women noted by Colleen Kriger and Hilary Jones. Significantly, Momo expressed his resistance, to his accomplice at least, by invoking the loss of an earlier patriarch and, by extension, patriarchy. Whether that older male authority figure had, in fact, ever existed is, in a sense, irrelevant to my argument. In the end, Ajatu's female and Brazilian supporters and the young British colonial state avenged her death. After a fifteen-minute deliberation, the jury returned a verdict of guilty, and Momo and Adebambi were soon after hanged in the colonial prison. Disu was acquitted of the crime.

Part Three

Mobility

9

From Child Slave to Madam Esperance
One Woman's Career in the Anglo-African World c. 1675–1707

COLLEEN E. KRIGER

A young Luso-African child slave named Esperança (Hope) arrived at England's Royal African Company (RAC) fort on James Island in the Gambia River in the early 1680s. Precisely who took her there, who gave her the name Esperança, and whether she was a captive or born into slavery, are all unknowns. We learn of her approximate age from English court and parish records, which suggest she was born in about 1675.[1] She became a child slave of the RAC employee John Booker, whose time of arrival at the James Island fort is also uncertain. The first mention of him in the RAC account books comes in December 1680. A major change in staffing at the fort on 31 August 1683 brought Alexander Cleeve to the top position of company agent with Booker as his 'second', promotions that would situate both men at the centre of RAC trading operations on West Africa's Upper Guinea Coast.[2] During the late seventeenth century, when the company enjoyed a monopoly of English trade in Africa, Anglo-African commerce in Upper Guinea was organised primarily by the James Island agent and his assistants. Atlantic commerce and the socially fluid, multi-cultural world it generated would mark in very particular ways the lives of Booker, his child slave Hope, and others living on and around the island. This chapter focuses on the life and travels of Hope and what her experiences can

[1] PROB 18/24/11, 12 March 1696. The National Archives, United Kingdom (hereafter TNA); John Kennedy, *A History of the Parish of Leyton, Essex* (Leyton: Phelp Brothers, 1894), 117. In George Brooks' groundbreaking book on Eurafricans in West Africa, he mistakenly identifies Esperança (Hope) Booker as the wife of John Booker and conflates her with another woman, Esperança Vaz. The latter appears in later RAC records (1733–34) as the former slave of James Island agent Robert Plunkett (d. 1725). George Brooks, *Eurafricans in Western Africa: Commerce, Social Status, Gender, and Religious Observance from the Sixteenth to the Eighteenth Century* (Athens: Ohio University Press, 2003), 190, 222–23; T 70/1446 (November 1725); T 70/1451 (1733), TNA.

[2] T 70/831, 832, TNA. Booker's account at this time lists him as a surgeon.

reveal about social and economic prospects and constraints faced by Euro-African women in the early modern era. Those who attained high status, designated by titles such as *senhora* or *signare*, illustrate the career paths open to women as merchants, property owners and slave holders in Atlantic Africa.

James Island

Lying barren and exposed at the mouth of the Gambia River, this small, rocky outcrop was highly prized by merchants from a number of European countries for its strategically important location. The Gambia was a major artery in local and Atlantic trade, connecting inland commercial markets with coastal and maritime traffic (Map 9). Taken into English hands in 1661, James Island developed into an inter-continental trading hub especially after 1677, as the newly formed RAC established a station there and began to staff and supply it regularly.[3] But the company did not own the island. Permission to occupy it and to build and maintain a fort had to be negotiated periodically with the rulers of neighbouring kingdoms and nearby towns. Lacking arable land and a source of water, RAC men who lived on James Island were dependent on a variety of people on the mainland, especially villagers who lived along the river's northern bank. Offsetting these inconveniences, James Island offered an ideal vantage point for monitoring daily movements of people and vessels travelling on the Gambia and for defending the fort against unwanted or hostile intrusions.

Compared with the years of armed conflict after 1690, the 1680s were a time of relative peace and stability at James Island. Taking advantage of these favourable conditions, the RAC agent Cleeve devised and put into place an audacious fraud that lasted from 1683 to 1688. In violation of company rules prohibiting employees from engaging in private trade, Cleeve recruited a team of men to do just that. However, he cleverly arranged it so that the company itself would be profiting as well. To separate out the company's trades, he created a special account in the company books using the name of a fictitious person called 'Francisco Lopus'.[4] RAC employees contributed a share of their trades to that account, that is, to the company, and kept their own private profits hidden from the books. It was probably at this time, if not before, that Cleeve's assistant John Booker would have considered himself in need of a staff of personal slaves to oversee his improving and more private accommodations and also to assist

---

[3] John M. Gray, *A History of the Gambia* (1940; reprint, New York: Barnes and Noble, 1966), 87–88.
[4] T 70/832; T 70/50 London to Booker at James Island, 7 January 1690, TNA.

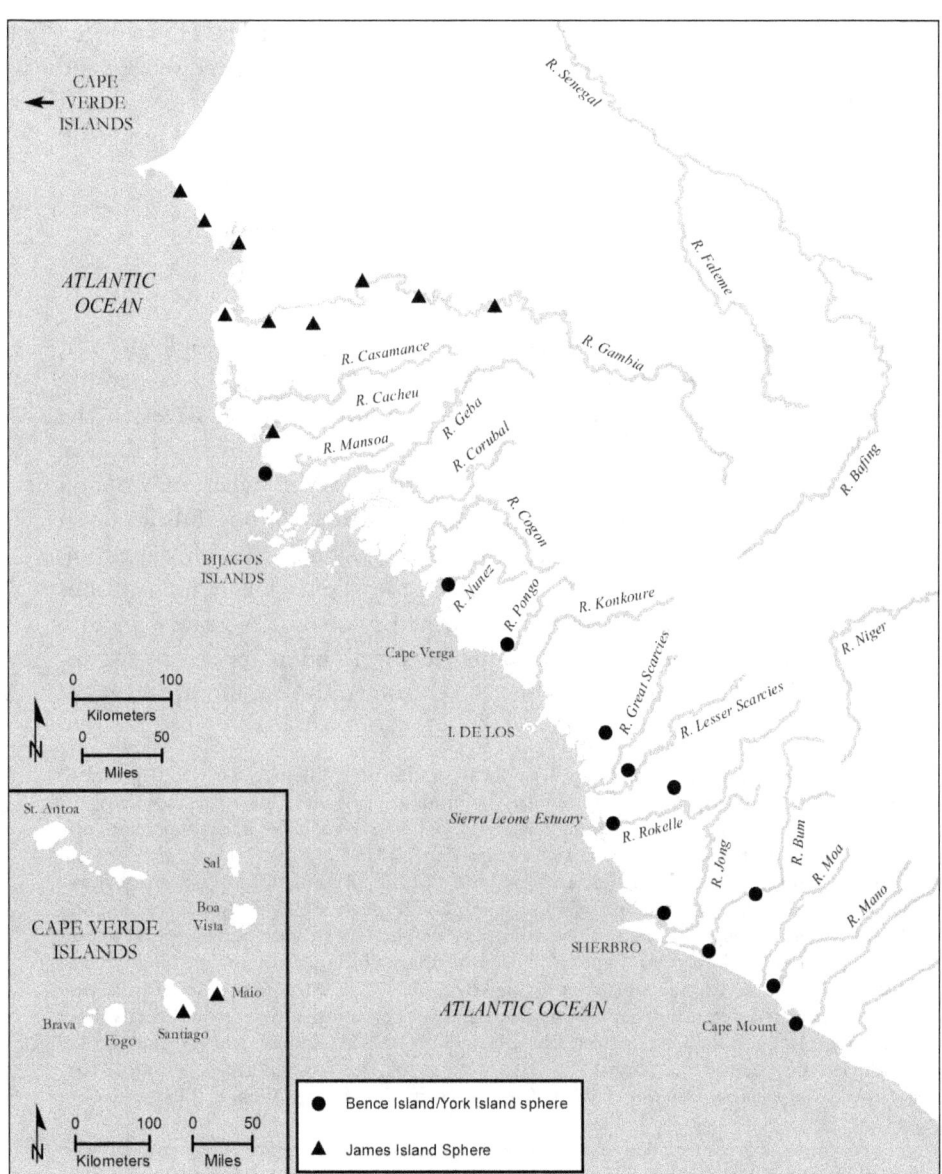

Map 9 Royal African Company trading sphere on the Upper Guinea Coast, late seventeenth century
(Source: Brian Edward Balsley, GISP)

him in his trading activities and expanding social contacts. He acquired his slave António Lopez, who probably served him as a messenger and commercial agent, and at some point he also acquired by purchase or gift at least two child slaves – the girl Esperança and a younger boy named Sanko.

Growing up Enslaved

Among English-speakers Esperança became known as Hope Booker, calling her by the surname of her owner – one of a variety of naming practices used by European and Euro-African owners of slaves in the early modern Atlantic.[5] Booker sent Hope to London to learn to read and write English. I have not been able to determine where in London he sent her for schooling, but there are any number of possibilities. John Booker's origins in England are stubbornly opaque – the only mention of any family members comes in a codicil to his will, where he mentions an uncle, John Willbee [Wilby?], who had two sons. A general picture of Booker's circle of friends and supporters in London appears in a security bond he had to provide to the RAC prior to his promotion to agent

---

[5] That Esperança had a Portuguese name is significant. Whether she was baptised or not, it suggests either a Christian identity or influence of some kind which set her apart from Sanko. See António de Almeida Mendes, 'Child Slaves in the Early North Atlantic Trade in the Fifteenth and Sixteenth Centuries' in *Children in Slavery through the Ages*, ed. Gwyn Campbell, Suzanne Miers and Joseph C. Miller (Athens: Ohio University Press, 2009), 20–22. A vivid example of slave naming and renaming is Jacobus Elisa Johannes Capitein, a mid-eighteenth-century child slave on the Gold Coast whose second master wanted him to be known as 'Captain'. That same master brought him to The Netherlands, where slavery was not recognised or defined by positive law. After four years of education he was baptised, retaining Capitein as a surname and taking the given names of his three sponsors: Jacob, his master/patron; Elisa, Jacob's sister; and Johannes, their female cousin by marriage. Grant Parker, transl., *The Agony of Asar: A Thesis on Slavery by the Former Slave, Jacobus Elisa Johannes Capitein, 1717–1747* (Princeton, NJ: Markus Wiener, 2001), 7–10, 86, 92.

For the issue of baptism designating someone as Christian and therefore not an infidel (who could be owned) under English law, see Michael Bundock, *The Fortunes of Francis Barber* (New Haven, CT: Yale University Press, 2015), 33–34.

In Luso-African communities on the Upper Guinea Coast, it was not unusual for slaves to be known by the surnames of their masters. A well-known example was one Gaspar Vaz, an enslaved Mandinka Muslim who had been owned by a tailor, Francisco Vaz, in the late sixteenth century. Gaspar Vaz had been instructed in the Catholic faith, spoke Portuguese, and was trained as a tailor. When his master freed him, he returned to his Muslim identity and homeland along the Gambia River. André Donelha, *An Account of Sierra Leone and the Rivers of Guinea of Cape Verde (1625)*, trans. and ed. A. Teixeira da Mota; P. E. H. Hair (Lisbon: Junta de Investigações Científicas do Ultramar, 1977), 149. More generally, bearing the surname of one's owner can be read not only as a sign of ownership and/or baptism but also as a possible deterrent to kidnapping and re-enslavement by another master.

in 1688. Four men pledged the sizeable sum of £1500: Thomas Sellon, ship handler; Edward Hawkins, sailmaker; Thomas Minge, schoolmaster; and Humphrey Dyke, merchant.[6] Where Minge taught and whether he taught Hope Booker cannot be determined, but there were boarding schools in and around the docklands east of the City of London in places like the parish of Saint Dunstan, Stepney, where Thomas Sellon and Humphrey Dyke lived. Some private schools run by schoolmasters themselves were known to specialise in teaching writing, arithmetic and other skills necessary for keeping the accounts of merchants working abroad or at sea.[7] Literacy in English would become for Hope an extremely useful vehicle for attaining social mobility and economic power during her life and career.

Booker had every reason to be carried away by his own growing ambition as he expanded his trading contacts and began amassing an impressive personal estate in Atlantic commerce. Participation in Cleeve's 'Lopus fraud' was effective and profitable training; and having Hope as his own household scribe to keep private records for him would have been an invaluable asset – all the more so after Cleeve departed for London in late 1688 and Booker succeeded him as RAC agent at James Island. In anticipation of the event, Booker had returned to England to arrange his security bond and also to make out a will, where he identified himself as merchant. Neither in his security bond nor in his will is there any mention of family members. He appointed as executors the merchant Humphrey Dyke and Dyke's young daughter Elizabeth, naming the child Elizabeth as his sole legatee.[8] One can only speculate about reasons for these cryptic choices. Perhaps they were a condition for Dyke's contribution to Booker's security bond. In any event, his London business completed, Booker returned to James Island just as tensions between England and France were mounting in Europe and the north Atlantic.

Hope was about thirteen years old when Booker's promotion to agent transformed their living and working conditions. In addition to handling Booker's household and personal accounts she and António would now have significant social and managerial responsibilities related to his wide-ranging commercial dealings. It is likely that Hope, as a female child slave, had been trained to perform a variety of women's domestic tasks, perhaps initially by the person who sold or gave her to Booker. But their 'Governor's Lodgings', situated at the centre of the fort, formed no ordi-

[6] T 70/1428, 24 July 1688. TNA.
[7] John Stow, *A Survey of the Cities of London and Westminster: Corrected, Improved, and Very Much Enlarged* (by John Strype, 1720), 2 vols (London: printed for A. Churchill, 1720), vol. 1, 172.
[8] PROB 11/420/298, TNA.

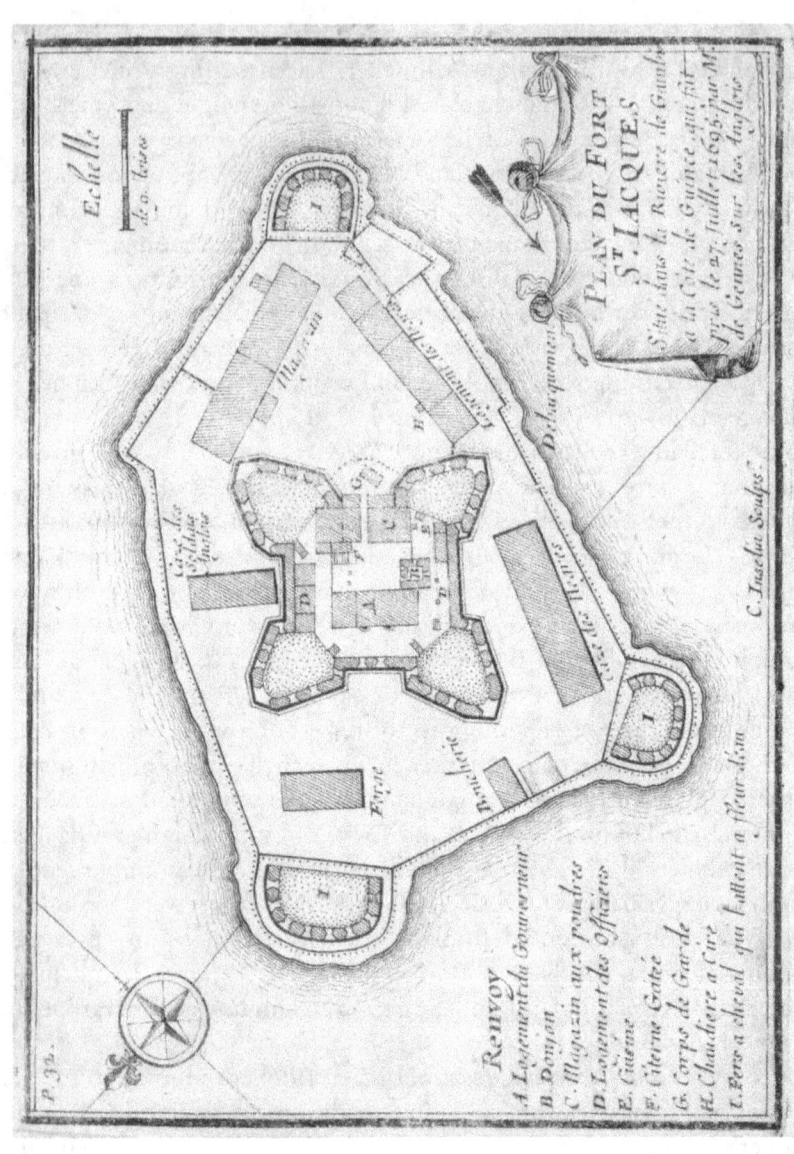

Map 10 Plan of James Island [image cropped and not to scale]

Source: François Froger, *Relation d'un Voyage fait en 1695, 1696, & 1697* (Paris: Michel Brunet 1698), 32, 'Plan du Fort St Jacques'; The Oliveira Lima Library, The Catholic University of America

nary household setting (see Map 10: 'A. Logement du Gouverneur'). Important meetings and entertainments were held nearby, and looming alongside the southern wall was a dungeon. Armed guards were stationed at the fort's entrance. In English court records Hope described her life briefly but without any reference to her birth family or to her arrival at James Island, her captivity or status as a slave, or what it was like living in James Island fort. She stated only that she was born in Guinea and was brought up by John Booker, that he was kind to her, and at his own expense sent her to England to be educated. Upon returning to James Island she remained there as a member of his household until his illness and death in 1693.[9]

Growing up at James Island she would have witnessed the day-to-day business of cross-cultural Atlantic commerce – the coming and going of merchantmen and captains from overseas, as well as locally based Euro-African and African suppliers in the import-export sector. Among these local merchants were successful and respected women who were socially recognised as such by the title *senhora*, some of them based upriver and others in coastal towns such as the Luso-African port of Cacheu. Hope would even have had opportunities to make the acquaintance of individual female merchants who visited the island. One example was known as Jane Vaz, whose father, Peter, had an account in the 1660s with The Royal Adventurers, the predecessor of the RAC, and who continued to deliver exports to the RAC at James Island until August 1683.[10] In the following month Jane took over the account and supplied the company with exports over the next ten years. In doing so, she mastered the specialised commercial knowledge and expertise that brought success in the import-export trade and regularly managed a male labour force to transport shipments of goods between her base at Cacheu and the RAC fort on James Island. Her recorded visits during that time numbered nineteen, and after a gap in the records between 1688 and 1692, her account shows her titled and married as Senhora Bernardo de Melo.[11] Thus in Hope's corner of the world it was not unusual for a woman to become an independent, respected, and successful import-export merchant.

Living on James Island, Hope also would have formulated through daily observation and experience a wide-ranging and complex understanding of the variable forms of late seventeenth-century Atlantic slavery. Map 10 shows James Island defended by batteries of cannon at three of the island's corners and the fort situated at its centre where the

---

[9] PROB 18/24/11, TNA.
[10] T 70/828, 830, 831, 832, TNA.
[11] T 70/832, 833, 546, 547, TNA. In this area of the Upper Guinea Coast the Portuguese forms *senhora* and *senhor* were used most often.

'Governor' (chief agent) and company officers resided. Outside the fort's walls were other buildings – a warehouse for trade goods, dormitories for housing company soldiers and 'company slaves', and a prison holding captives forced from their homelands in the West African interior to be exported across the Atlantic to be sold as chattel slaves in the Americas. Slave conditions on the island covered a broad spectrum. At one end of the spectrum were the nameless, unkempt, and predominantly male 'sale slaves', who suffered the daily degradations of imprisonment, poor diet, and the threat of violence. One wonders if Hope witnessed the large-scale insurrection of sale slaves at James Island on 24 April 1693 on a ship loaded for Jamaica, and what must have been terrible reprisals after its failure. Also on and around the island were male and female 'company slaves', called *grometos*, who had names, clothing and freedom of movement, living in better conditions and being paid on salary or by task. At the other end of the spectrum were RAC employees' personal slaves such as Hope herself and António Lopez – privileged house slaves who were trusted, had personal property of their own, were sometimes literate, and might someday be manumitted by their masters.[12] For these slaves it is not clear if there was a general or lasting stigma attached to their unfree pasts.

Hope's Manumission

The death of the RAC agent John Booker at the James Island fort in June 1693 set off a series of events and disputes involving a number of his acquaintances on the Upper Guinea Coast and in England over the following decade.[13] A codicil to his will, which he dictated the month before he died, gives a general indication of how much personal wealth he had accrued while working for himself and the company on James Island, providing also a richly detailed account of his multi-cultural social relationships. Its terms immediately and dramatically changed the lives of his private house slaves.

Following the customary religious preface where he bequeathed his soul to God and gave instructions for his burial, Booker requested his 'girle Speranca commonly known by the name Hope Booker' as his executrix to carry out his funeral arrangements. He bequeathed freedom to her 'without any scruple or conditions'. She also inherited moveable property – all her wardrobe and other possessions, including her valuable jewellery of gold, silver, and coral. Her 'brother', Sanko,

---

[12] This description of James Island is based on that in my book *Making Money: Life, Death, and Early Modern Trade on Africa's Guinea Coast* (Athens: Ohio University Press, 2017).
[13] T 70/11 Heath to London, 12 December 1693, TNA.

was not freed but was to be at Sperança's disposal. She inherited other house slaves and company slaves – *grometoe* men, women, boys, and girls – all of whom were to be held for her in the care of Senhora Bernardo de Melo until Sperança's further orders. It was Booker's intention that Sperança be sent to England, where she would be supported and cared for by his London executors while they arranged for her to receive out of his personal estate a lifetime annuity of £25 for her maintenance.[14] Booker's bequests reveal the complexity of his position toward his house slaves, as both slave master and self-appointed paterfamilias. He clearly considered Hope, who at that time was about eighteen years of age, an invaluable and trusted, though unfree, member of his household. With freedom, property and the gift of an annuity in pounds sterling he was readying her, English-style, for marriage.

Among the other people mentioned or given bequests by Booker – RAC employees and *grometos*, local friends and long-time acquaintances, relatives and associates in England – were several other slaves. To his trusted slave António he gave freedom without any conditions, clearly considering himself having the prerogative to do so; to a 'molatta' child called Betty, daughter of a local titled woman known as 'Billingary', he gave 'Two Negro girles', presumably emulating fashionable English gentry, who acquired child slaves of African descent to serve as conspicuously exotic companions for their own children. Whether these girls were his personal slaves is unclear, as is what kind of relationships he had with the child Betty and her mother.[15] Whatever the case, Booker's bequests provide us with rare glimpses of RAC men's unrecorded private trade and ownership of personal slaves. Company slaves and sale slaves were normally recorded in the RAC account books, while slaves owned privately by RAC employees were not.

Hope Booker's First Marriage

Upon the death of Booker, another RAC employee, William Heath, succeeded him as agent at James Island and assumed responsibilities as an executor of Booker's personal estate on the Upper Guinea Coast. This put him into close contact with Hope as they organised the burial and funeral of Booker and the sorting out of his property, assets, debts and company accounts. According to testimonies of witnesses, Hope was at this time a spinster without any matrimonial contract. Her freedom, her impressive personal qualities, and her inheritance – personal

---

[14] PROB 11/427/15, TNA. Hope's legacies and annuity at the time of Booker's death were estimated at around £2500. PROB 18/24/11, TNA.
[15] PROB 11/427/15, TNA.

property and annuity – certainly made Hope an attractive marriage prospect. William Heath began to court her ardently, urging her to marry him according to 'local custom' with the promise that later, whenever they should be in the vicinity of a Christian church, he would marry her again in a formal religious ceremony conducted by a priest or minister. The specificity of this pledge suggests that the condition had been proposed by Hope herself and that she had at least some familiarity with Christian religious practice and its importance in English jurisprudence. She accepted William's promise and their marriage took place on James Island in October 1693, four months after the death of John Booker.

Court records provide a detailed description of Hope and William's wedding ceremony as it was performed in accordance with 'local custom' on the Guinea Coast, a marriage that was later judged legal in England by the Prerogative Court of Canterbury. The couple planned a formal dinner and celebration within the protected enclosure of the fort, with invitations sent out to company employees and military officers, who would also serve as witnesses. Before the dinner they stood in front of their guests, each taking the other by the hand and solemnly pledging before God (indicating Sperança was a Christian and not an 'infidel') their love and lifelong devotion. Throughout the dinner, guests passed bowls of punch around the tables, drinking toasts to the bride and groom and wishing them good health and a long and happy marriage. Witnesses testified also that from that day on, Hope and William lived and slept together in the same quarters as lawful man and wife, testimony that was sufficient to prove also in an English court that William was indeed the father of their daughter Elizabeth.[16]

In March 1694, just six months after their marriage, Hope embarked on her second voyage to England. William was to follow her when he finished sorting out Booker's estate and his own affairs.[17] At the time of her departure, William made solemn protestations that he would never forsake her and swore an oath that as soon as he arrived in England they would marry again in a Church of England ceremony. The oath was in writing and he took care to show it to several of his acquaintances.[18] Hope gave birth to their daughter in November, at or near the home of

---

[16] PROB 18/24/11, TNA. What was meant by 'local custom' at this time and place appears to refer to the European-style ceremony itself, which took place in public and with witnesses but without the full sacramental legitimacy of a formal Christian rite. West African marriages were legitimised quite differently, primarily by a series of public bridewealth exchanges (in Mandinka, *furu-fe*) which in contrast to European 'dowry' transferred wealth primarily from the family of the prospective husband to the family of the prospective wife: Maurice Delafosse, *La Langue mandingue et ses dialects*, 2 vols (Paris: Geuthner, 1955), vol. 2, 232.

[17] T 70/11 Heath at James Island to London, 7 March 1694. TNA.

[18] PROB 18/24/11. TNA.

Humphrey Dyke in the hamlet of Ratcliff, Stepney. On 5 December at the parish church Saint Dunstan and All Saints she was baptised Elizabeth, daughter of William Heath, Agent of James Island in Africa and of Sperinda [sic], his wife.[19]

From the time of Hope's departure from James Island, Heath publicly expressed his love for his wife, drank to her health, and was overjoyed when he learned of their daughter's birth. Regretting that he was not yet able to be with them in England, he expressed concern about their health and welfare in letters he sent to Hope and to others – first from James Island and then from Lisbon, where he stopped off on his homeward voyage.[20] But having concluded his business and set out on the last leg of his journey, Heath died at sea in December.[21]

Living in London

When William Heath sent Hope to London, along with a '[Negro] boy and girl for himself', he had arranged for the merchant Humphrey Dyke to take responsibility for her care during her pregnancy ('laying in'). Why Heath did not send her to his own family is unclear. Dyke and his wife continued to support Hope during the first year of Elizabeth's life, providing nursing care, clothing, and other necessary assistance. It is not clear where exactly Hope and Elizabeth lived, but Dyke kept accounts of the expenditures he incurred in caring for Hope and her daughter and administering William Heath's estate, which came to a total of £297. What happened to Heath's two child slaves is not known. They apparently survived the voyage: Dyke paid the passage of Hope 'and two Negroes' when they arrived in London.[22] Possibly they were absorbed into the Dyke household.

One month after the news of William's death, Hope received another shock: Samuel Heath, elder brother of William, filed a bill of complaint in the Court of Chancery accusing 'Sparnissa' [sic] alias Hope Booker, Humphrey Dyke, William Collins [sic] and Richard Hutchinson, Esq. of defrauding him as 'rightful' heir to his brother's estate. He alleged that 'Sparnissa' had lived with William as his hired servant, not his wife, and had destroyed William's will in which Samuel was supposedly named as heir. The many factual inaccuracies contained in the complaint – such as referring to William as the employee of the East India Company at

---

[19] P93/DUN/259, Register of Baptisms, April 1682–1698, London Metropolitan Archives (LMA).
[20] PROB 18/24/11; PROB 36/10, TNA.
[21] C 7/152/36, Part II, 30 April 1697, TNA.
[22] PROB 18/29/19, 42, and 87, TNA.

Gambia – suggest it was a product of desperation.[23] In the defendants' official answers one section in particular stands out: in it Hope Heath herself outlines her concerns and objections – a rare opportunity for us to gain access to the thoughts of a seventeenth-century Euro-African woman, recently freed from slavery, who was effectively voicing and pursuing her own interests in an English court.[24]

She insisted on registering her English married name, Hope Heath, ridiculing Samuel Heath for referring to her as 'Sparnissa, alias Hope Booker'. She understandably took even greater offence at the statement that she had been William's hired servant. Her most important points, however, centred on her relationship with William Heath and the legality of their marriage. She made it clear that she was in possession of her own personal wealth by way of Booker's bequests and that William Heath had repeatedly asked her to be his wife. They had married in a formal public ceremony in the presence of many witnesses, then lived together as man and wife until she embarked on her voyage to England. She reminded Samuel Heath that evidence of her marriage to William and his paternity of their daughter had already been heard in the Prerogative Court of Canterbury (PCC), where both had been judged legitimate.[25]

The evidence Dyke brought to that important PCC hearing included letters written by William to Hope, to his family, and to Humphrey Dyke, shown together with specimens of William's handwriting. But Dyke also presented four letters written to Hope, addressed to her as Mrs Heath, wife of William. Three were from William's sister, Dorothy, and one was from Samuel's own wife, Elizabeth. In other words, the Heath family was fully aware of William's marriage to Hope and had formally acknowledged it in writing. Dyke brought specimens of their handwriting to compare with these letters as well.[26] Samuel Heath's frantic behaviour in this matter illustrates how men such as William Heath, who lived abroad to engage in overseas trade, developed friendships and intimate relationships that could disturb or even threaten the interests of members of their families back home.

The death of William Heath was a tragic loss for Hope, compounded by questions and complications surrounding what inheritance might be due her and her daughter from his estate. Heath had died without a will. Of the various individuals who had an interest in the Booker and Heath estates, Humphrey Dyke assumed a commanding role. As executor of

[23] C 7/152/36, Part I, 7 January 1695/6, TNA.
[24] See Amy Louise Erickson, *Women and Property in Early Modern England* (London: Routledge, 1993).
[25] C 6/428/30, TNA.
[26] PROB 18/24/11, TNA.

Booker's 1688 will and in contact with William Heath, he had registered the 1693 codicil in the PCC in August 1695. Upon receiving the news of Heath's death, Dyke offered Hope his assistance and stepped in to administer Heath's estate on behalf of Elizabeth, daughter and legal heir. How and why he had come to choose this legal option, bypassing whatever claims Hope had as widow, is not explained in the court records. In any case, in January 1696, one month after William's death, the PCC granted Dyke the legal authority to administer the estate of William Heath.[27]

Hope Heath's circle of acquaintances in London centred on the contacts and associates of Booker and her late husband. How she spent her days with daughter Elizabeth and if she engaged in household or other work can only be imagined. Dyke's characterisation of her in the court records suggests he had respect for her born of both hearsay and direct experience, having called her 'well bred, ingenious, and of good reputation'.[28] Over the next two and a half years, from January 1696 to July 1698, she directed much thought and energy toward learning about and securing her rightful inheritance as the widow of William Heath. Dyke attempted to track how portions of the Heath and Booker estates had been disbursed at James Island, while others had been shipped to various merchants for cash or other goods or sold to ship captains for bills of exchange. The two estates were so commingled that proper inventories would not be possible. Dyke made one estimate (probably exaggerated) that at the time of his death Booker's merchandise, bills of exchange, quantities of gold, silver, jewels, plate, rings, and household goods might have been worth as much as £50,000.[29] However, it is unlikely that his estate at James Island was ever completely inventoried or that all his bequests and instructions were carried out. Nor do we know anything about William's business dealings during his stopover in Lisbon, which included the liquidation of some of Booker's estate as well as his own property.

Not content to await the results of Dyke's efforts, Hope and her daughter in spring or early summer of 1696 moved away from Stepney to the parish of Leyton, four miles north, where many of London's merchants and bankers resided in impressive country homes. Hope's contact there was Richard Hutchinson, an East India merchant and associate of both Booker and Heath. Hope was baptised there at Saint Mary's parish church on 12 July 1696, described in the record as 'Hope Heath, a Black mayd, about 21'.[30] Yet Humphrey Dyke had already given testimony in a PCC hearing

[27] C 7/152/36. Part II, 30 April 1697, TNA.
[28] PROB 18/24/11, TNA.
[29] C 6/524/181, TNA.
[30] Register of baptisms in Kennedy, *History*, 117.

in March 1696 that Hope had been baptised in accordance with the rites of the Church of England.[31] Perhaps she was already planning her second marriage and wanted to be sure that she would be recognised as baptised; but although the parish church of Leyton did baptise and bury 'blacks', it apparently did not perform their marriages.[32] Hope's second marriage ceremony took place instead at a church in the City of London that was exempt from ecclesiastical jurisdiction and thus had become well known for performing 'irregular' marriages, that is, those without a licence or parental consent.[33]

The following May (1697), Hope and Hutchinson together registered their answers to Samuel Heath's bill of complaint that his brother had not been married, and in her own statement Hope asked the court to remove Dyke as administrator of William's estate. Clearly, she had sought out Hutchinson for alternative legal advice. Hutchinson stated that he and Booker's uncle had taken charge of seeing to Hope's annuity, and when told by her that she felt she was not in good hands regarding the Booker and Heath estates he, Hutchinson, had stepped in to advise and take care of her. In his closing statement he assured the court that he had no interest in seeking any claim or advantage from the case.[34] Two months later, on 10 July 1697, and almost one year to the day after her baptism, Hope Heath, widow, of Low Leyton, Essex, married Samuel Meston [or Mostin], bachelor, at Saint James Duke's Place, City of London.[35]

I have not found any records that would help in identifying who Samuel Meston was. As for Hope, one wonders what she thought after spending just over three years in London. Perhaps, after achieving an impressive rise in status on James Island, she was beginning to understand how narrowly she was viewed by English society. She was a free woman of colour whose status was both ambiguous and constrained. Even free blacks in England were primarily servants. When she had lived in Ratcliff she must have seen some of the mostly young black servant/slaves of ship captains, mariners, and physicians who lived there. In the wealthier households of Leyton, black servant/slaves may have been dressed up and displayed as exotic novelties. Finding they were not allowed to marry in the parish church there, she and Samuel had to travel overland to the City for their church wedding. Even if not spelled out in English common law, there were firmly set limits

---

[31] PROB 18/24/11, TNA.
[32] The registers for 1575–1754 contain no instances of marriages involving a 'black' or 'blackamoor'. Kennedy, *History*, 107–36.
[33] AIM25, Archives in London and the M25 Area, Saint James, Duke's Place: City of London, www.aim25.ac.uk (accessed 4 March 2017).
[34] C 6/428/30, TNA.
[35] Register of Marriages, P69/JSI/A/002/MS07894, Item 002, 1692–1700, LMA.

to Hope's prospects in London for social advancement and respectability.

Hope Heath's strong assertions of independence and mobility – her change of residence, her new alliance with Hutchinson, and her marriage to Samuel Meston – sparked a retaliation from Humphrey Dyke. He filed a bill of complaint against the three of them in early November 1697, accusing them of conspiring against him by withholding information about Booker's and Heath's dealings with Hutchinson and claiming that the values of both estates were much greater than he had thought.[36] By the end of the month, at a coffee house near Guildhall in London, Hope and her second husband Samuel met with Dyke to settle accounts with him. By this time, all that remained to be sorted out was an annuity Dyke had purchased for her out of Booker's estate, which Hope and Samuel sold back to him for £120.[37] It is not clear whether Hope sold back the other annuity she had received from Hutchinson and Booker's uncle.

It would not be surprising if Hope had frequented the coffee houses of London in order to keep up with news of the Guinea Coast, especially after the French seizure of James Island in 1695 and the restoration of peace between England and France in 1697. She would probably have taken interest in the parliamentary debate beginning in early 1698 over a bill that would end the RAC monopoly on England's Africa trade. Other such bills had been debated before, but this one passed both Houses and was given Royal Assent on 5 July 1698. Just one week later, Hope set about preparing to return to the lower Gambia and borrowed £90 from Humphrey Dyke. It was found at that time that there was still some amount due her from the estates of Booker and Heath. She received an additional £20 in cash and made a shrewdly calculated selection of personal property – a child's coral necklace, a silver spoon and fork, a (porcelain?) saucer, a silver slave collar, a dozen brightly patterned silk damask cloths – and a male slave called Angelo, all of them visual proof of her worldly contacts, cultivated taste, and social prominence. Her stated reason for returning to the lower Gambia was to take possession of her slaves and what else remained of her inheritance from Booker, presumably still being held in her absence by Senhora Bernardo de Melo. Left behind in London was her second husband and also, in the business records of Humphrey Dyke (d. 1703), a debt note for £90 signed by Hope Meston.[38]

---

[36] C 6/524/181, TNA.
[37] PROB 18/29/19, TNA.
[38] PROB 18/29/19 and /87, TNA.

Madam Esperance in the Lower Gambia

Since the RAC surrender of James Island to the French in July 1695 and until the restoration of peace between England and France in September of 1697, the island and fort had been in a state of complete disarray. Efforts by the RAC to reoccupy their former station were sporadic and ineffective. Reports of competing factions and desertions among the company employees and their carelessness in keeping track of inventories and other properties dominated the letters sent intermittently to London from the lower Gambia. Agents and factors chose to live on the river's north shore, primarily in the town of Juffure, rather than on the island. One letter written in May 1704 gives an account of Madam Esperance, whom I believe was none other than Hope Heath returned as a fashionable, literate, and titled woman of high station.[39]

She would have arrived at the lower Gambia in August or September of 1698 if she sailed directly there from London in July. Fractious relations among the RAC employees and their keeping of private stores of company goods generated only sparse and incomplete records. The English form of her title, madam, rather than the customary *senhora* or *signare*, is consonant with what must have been her impressive arrival direct from England splendidly dressed creole-style in her exotic silk damask, her daughter Elizabeth adorned with a coral necklace, and both of them attended by Angelo, her male slave, conspicuously identified as such by a silver slave collar around his neck. Whether she herself used the French *Esperance* as her name or the form Sperança, as Booker and the Dykes had called her, is unclear, however. 'Madam Esperance' is how her name was recorded by RAC scribes writing the company letters and account books.

She had her own house in Juffure and was self-employed as a merchant in the Euro-African import-export Guinea trade, neither of which would have been possible for her to achieve in London. Having lost its monopoly, the RAC was now having to compete with any number of English 'separate' traders as well as French, Portuguese, Dutch, Flemish and other European and Euro-African merchants. References to her in RAC letters provide only a brief glimpse of her dealings with employees of the company, which were undoubtedly replicated within a much larger constellation of commercial contacts. The May 1704 letter centres on her trading partnership with an RAC employee named Chishull, who had arrived at James Island in June 1702 and was company factor in charge of

[39] T 70/13 Thomas Weaver at Gambia to London, 3 May 1704, TNA. 'Madam' was sometimes used among English-speakers, another example being Madam Watts, wife of the British Commander Martin Watts on the Gold Coast, as discussed by Natalie Everts in her chapter.

handling their trade goods.[40] He appears to have been a useful partner and source of valuable overseas imports.

May was a time of the year when overland caravan traders arrived at the upper Gambia River to trade their goods and captives from the West African interior for local produce and overseas commodities. Chishull and Madam Esperance had gone into partnership freighting a river vessel with a selection of goods most preferred in the upriver markets. Much of the letter chronicles the misdeeds of Chishull, who apparently had his own private storehouses of merchandise alongside those of the company. In other words, he, like many of his co-workers, was violating the oath he had sworn not to trade on his own account.

Chishull's upriver vessel, his partnership with Madam Esperance, and the exports he brought down the river subjected him to severe penalties by company officials. Agent Weaver seized six captive people from Chishull's cargo of slaves and confiscated ivory he had found stored at one of Chishull's private warehouses. Account books he confiscated gave evidence of other irregularities and violations; one year Chishull embezzled a total of 1,300 Bars in company goods.[41] This led Weaver to call on Madam Esperance, who readily acknowledged that Chishull had embezzled company brandy and had himself sold large numbers of iron bars and firearms. She also informed Weaver that all that remained of the overseas goods they had shipped upriver was in a chest at her home. Upon opening the chest Weaver found crystal beads (essential items in the upriver trade) and other items worth only 140 Bars. But before Weaver could charge her account for some part of Chishull's embezzlements, she produced receipts of slave deliveries she had made to the company for which she had not yet been paid and receipts for her ivory deliveries, also not yet paid. Weaver relented, apparently considering Madam Esperance to be in good standing with the company.[42] Surviving records from the second half of 1706 show no activity in her account and a small debt of 16 Bars.[43]

This episode and the behaviour of Madam Esperance convince me that she was Hope Heath returned. As was the case on James Island, and in London, this woman was respected by many, and while she was ambitious and clever she was also highly skilled socially with all kinds of people. She knew the ropes of working in the cut-throat circles of the Guinea trade as well as how to manage notes of credit and debt. It had taken her only four difficult years in London to realise that she and her daughter had much more promising prospects on the lower Gambia, where, like Senhora

[40] T 70/1436, Gambia fols 40–52, TNA.
[41] Bars were the currency of account at the Gambia RAC station.
[42] T 70/13 Weaver at Gambia to London, 3 May 1704, TNA.
[43] T 70/835, TNA.

Bernardo de Melo and others, she could be recognised as a titled and respected woman and successful merchant in the Guinea trade. She may very well have kept in touch with Elizabeth Dyke, widow of Humphrey, perhaps enlisting her to help with sending her daughter to boarding school in England. Probably the last mention of 'Speranza al[ia]s Hope Moston al[ia]s Heath' in English court records comes in 1707, at the settling of the Humphrey Dyke estate, where Elizabeth Dyke described how and why Speranza had left England for the Gambia, 'where she now lives'.[44]

Esperança's story parallels in important ways the eighteenth- and nineteenth-century *signares* described by Lorelle Semley and Hilary Jones, while also highlighting issues specific to this earlier and formative period in Atlantic history. Generations before the beginning of Britain's industrial revolution and the campaign to legally abolish Britain's Atlantic slave trade, Hope's determination to recover possession of the slaves bequeathed to her would not have seemed unusual or contradictory, for they constituted the invaluable asset of unfree human labour power and gendered skills, which she could possess and control for her own gain. Whether or not her inherited slaves were still alive and available, Esperança's class position as slave owner and manager would have lent her some protection, as a woman of colour, against the very real possibility of seizure and re-enslavement. Mastery over Angelo and perhaps others reinforced the high status she had achieved as a free, propertied, and respectable woman. Her choice to return to the Upper Guinea Coast made a great deal of sense, for there she had more avenues for pursuing upward mobility – socially and economically – than she would ever have had in England.

Arriving as Madam Esperance, Hope vividly presented herself as a titled woman with authority over male labour and with impressive personal wealth in silver, coral and Eurasian silk damask. Transformed into a woman of the world by her life and travels she joined other such women of the late seventeenth and early eighteenth centuries whose Afro-Eurasian creole dress, behaviour, and manners marked them as prominent merchants in the Guinea trade. Hope's marriage to William Heath was an early example of the cross-cultural marriages that creole women of the coast made with European traders, although she and William had apparently planned to make their residence in England. In that respect Hope differs from the many *signares* of Saint Louis and Gorée and other titled women who by necessity or choice remained in the coastal communities of western Africa.

Hope appears also as an early 'returnee' to her African homeland, but from Europe rather than the Americas and in search of success and prosperity rather than a long lost family she may have only dimly remembered

[44] PROB 18/29/19, TNA.

if at all. Being known by the title madam but without a surname can be considered a reflection of her ambiguous childhood in slavery and the brevity of her two marriages. The title signifies her autonomy. Madam Esperance was remarkably independent – living in her own house, investing in trading voyages as a merchant, and managing commercial accounts with the RAC and others. Records of her decisions, acts, and travels take us back in time to the early modern era, expanding and sharpening our understanding of the socially fluid lives women of colour could live in the multi-cultural worlds of Atlantic trade.

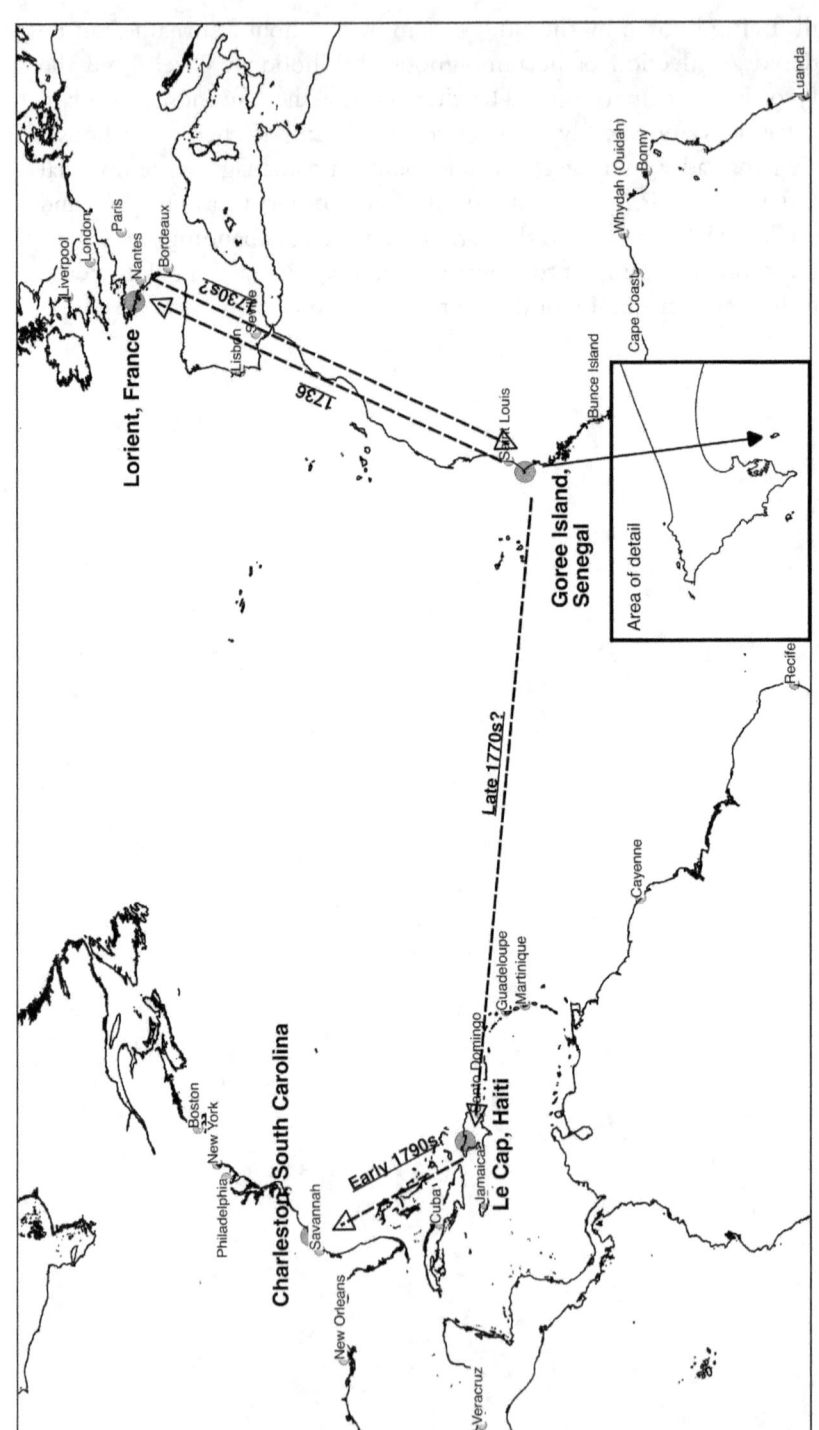

Map 11 Anne Rossignol's travels

(Source: Map produced by Richard A. Lent, College of the Holy Cross, using world coastline data downloaded from the OpenStreetMap Project)

10

Writing the History of the Trans-African Woman in the Revolutionary French Atlantic

LORELLE SEMLEY

The story of Anne Rossignol, a woman of colour from Gorée, Senegal, in West Africa who made her first voyage across the Atlantic to Lorient, France in 1736 as a free girl, sounds like the beginning of a piece of fantastic fiction. The trip from Gorée to Lorient would have been wondrous and maybe frightening for a child. Given her peculiar circumstances, that initial crossing must have been awkward – for those travelling with her. At the time, Anne Rossignol accompanied her French father, Claude Rossignol, and his French wife, Renée Le Monier. For the entire trip, Le Monier would have been confronted with her husband's transgression in the light brown face of Anne whom Claude Rossignol listed as a 'little *mulâtresse*, [his] natural daughter'.[1]

---

[1] This chapter draws on my book, *To Be Free and French: Citizenship in France's Atlantic Empire* (Cambridge University Press, 2017). An orphaned girl named Isabelle Imbert in Claude Rossignol's care also accompanied them. 'No. 90, Anne, passager – embarquée au Sénégal le 30 juillet 1736, débarquée au désarmement, petite mulâtresse, fille naturelle de Claude Rossignol, passagère pour la France', Bureau des classes de Port-Louis, Sous-série 2P, 27-I.11, 'Role de la Gloire (1736)', Secrétariat Général pour l'Administration (SGA), L'Association des Amis du Service Historique de la Défense à Lorient (A.S.H.D.L.), Mémoire des Hommes, Compagnie des Indes, www.memoiredeshommes.sga.defense.gouv.fr/fr/ark:/40699/m00525d6cec5fcae. Some have suggested that the parents of Anne Rossignol were Madeleine Françoise and James Rossignol, based on the 1818 death decree for James Rossignol. Marie-Hélène Knight, 'Gorée au XVIIe siècle: L'Appropriation du sol', *Revue Française d'histoire d'outre-mer* 64, no. 234 (1977): 45; Stewart R. King, *Blue Coat or Powdered Wig: Free People of Color in Pre-Revolutionary Saint Domingue* (Athens: University of Georgia Press, 2001); Joseph Roger de Benoist and Abdoulaye Camara, 'Les Signares et le patrimoine bâti de l'île', in Abdoulaye Camara and Joseph Roger de Benoiste, eds., *Histoire de Gorée* (Paris: Maisonneuve et Larose, 2003), 99; Jean-Luc Angrand, *Céleste ou le temps de Signares* (Sarcelles, France: Édition Anne Pépin, 2006), 58. Dominique Rogers and Stewart King first suggested Claude Rossignol as a more likely father. Since James Rossignol could not have been the father of the Rossignol sisters, it is also unlikely that James Rossignol's widow, Madeleine Françoise, was their mother. It also seems odd that Madeleine Françoise did not appear in census data from the 1750s and 1760s. On Rossignol's life in Le Cap, see Dominique Rogers and Stewart King, 'Housekeepers, Merchants, Rentières: Free

It is unclear when Anne Rossignol returned to Gorée. However, she was living there with her own children by the 1750s, appearing in census reports as a *signare* ('lady'; derived from Portuguese *senhora*). When she departed Gorée in the 1770s to make a new life for herself and two of her children in Le Cap in the French colony of Saint-Domingue, Rossignol could not have guessed how the world would explode in 1789. Having lived with great privilege but also the potential threat of vulnerability, Rossignol died at a ripe old age in 1810 in Charleston, South Carolina. Her descendants' squabbles over an enslaved family Rossignol had owned allowed her to enter the written record for a final time. The fragments of her story that appear in the archive capture a range of complexities about identity, gender, and belonging shared by many other women and men of colour living in the world. Rossignol was exceptional, but not the only person of African descent to live such a peripatetic life.[2] As a result, her activities over her long lifetime may serve as a theoretical framework, even if it is impossible to know what the young Rossignol was thinking when she set sail for France in 1736. I will show that it is possible to flesh out what I propose to call a trans-African life.[3]

Studies have begun to focus on the roles of local women in the economy and society of European settlements and trading stations on the African coast. Scholars have struggled with some of the primary and earlier secondary sources that romanticise, exoticise and even demonise such women and their sexuality. Two trends have emerged. On one hand, in an effort to move beyond the narratives of seduction and collaboration, some scholars have focused on these women's extraordinary economic and political activities. Others have taken seriously the often intimate relationships between Africans and Europeans in the midst of slave trading and colonial empire.[4] Expanding upon these approaches,

---

(contd) Women of Color in the Port Cities of Colonial Saint-Domingue, 1750–1790', in *Women In Port: Gendering Communities, Economies, and Social Networks in Atlantic Port Cities, 1500–1800*, ed. Douglas Catterall and Jodi Campbell (Leiden: Brill, 2012), 357–97.

[2] Some recent examples are James H. Sweet, *Domingos Álvares, African Healing, and the Intellectual History of the Atlantic World* (Chapel Hill: University of North Carolina Press, 2011); Rebecca J. Scott and Jean M. Hébrard, *Freedom Papers: An Atlantic Odyssey in the Age of Emancipation* (Cambridge, MA: Harvard University Press, 2012). For free people of colour travelling during and after the Atlantic slave trade see J. Lorand Matory, 'The English Professors of Brazil: On the Diasporic Roots of the Yorùbá Nation', *Comparative Studies in Society and History* 41, no. 1 (1999): 72–103; Robin Law and Kristin Mann, 'West Africa in the Atlantic Community: The Case of the Slave Coast', *William and Mary Quarterly* 56, no. 2 (April 1999): 307–34.

[3] I developed this trans-African concept in *To Be Free and French*, applying it to the West African port city of Porto-Novo. This chapter explores a broader, varied application of the model. Semley, *To Be Free and French*, chapter 4.

[4] Mariana P. Candido, *An African Slaving Port and the Atlantic World: Benguela and Its Hinterland*, African Studies (124) (Cambridge: Cambridge University Press, 2013); Hilary

I suggest that the physical and social mobility and mutability of women like Anne Rossignol may also make a broader intellectual argument about Atlantic world history. The editors of a recent volume, *Toward an Intellectual History of Black Women*, argue that scholars must approach women of colour as intellectual actors and use innovative sources and analysis that go beyond the 'mere genealogy of ideas'.[5] Also looking at this time period with emotion and affect in mind opens a new view on gendered histories of empire. Nancy Rose Hunt argues that using the concept of affect as a method allows scholars to analyse 'colonial ambivalence, humiliation, revenge … especially if one moves beyond just finding these as emotions in one's source material, and instead shows them as a mood suffusing a space or motivating an event'.[6] The stories of women like Anne Rossignol who lived and even thrived in an era of racial subjugation offer insight into debates concerning slavery and freedom. In particular, the gendered nature of her physical and social mobility reorient the study not only of the era of the slave trade but also of Africa, in general.

I have coined the term 'trans-African' to reconceptualise the forced and free migration and social transformation of people of African descent both within and beyond the African continent. The prefix 'trans-' means 'across or beyond' but also connotes 'surpassing or transcending'. This trans-African model features three overlapping and broadly defined networks: continental, oceanic and ideological. Continental networks are important: studies of the Atlantic slave trade tend to overshadow the important regional travel and social exchange that shaped people's lives on both sides of the ocean. Elite communities of colour on Gorée Island included prominent women merchants and consumers similar to those described in chapters by Mariana Candido on Benguela and Vanessa Oliveira on Luanda in Angola. Africans also always depended on neighbours who spoke differently, practised different livelihoods, or worshipped other deities. Women like Anne Rossignol also would have relied on links on the mainland and to other shoreline posts. In Natalie Everts' contribution in this volume on coastal Akan communities in Ghana, the connections to extended family as well as European admin-

---

(contd) Jones, *The Métis of Senegal: Urban Life and Politics in Colonial Senegal* (Bloomington: Indiana University Press, 2013); Pernille Ipsen, *Daughters of the Trade: Atlantic Slavers and Interracial Marriage on the Gold Coast* (Philadelphia: University of Pennsylvania Press, 2015); Carina E. Ray, *Crossing the Color Line: Race, Sex, and the Contested Politics of Colonialism in Ghana* (Athens: Ohio University Press, 2015); Rachel Jean-Baptiste, *Conjugal Rights: Marriage, Sexuality, and Urban Life in Colonial Libreville, Gabon* (Athens: Ohio University Press, 2014).

[5] Mia Bay, Farah J. Griffin, Martha S. Jones and Barbara D. Savage, eds, *Toward an Intellectual History of Black Women* (Chapel Hill: University of North Carolina Press, 2015), 4.

[6] Nancy Rose Hunt, 'An Acoustic Register, Tenacious Images, and Congolese Scenes of Rape and Repetition,' *Cultural Anthropology* 23, no. 2 (2008): 220–53, https://culanth.org/articles/106-an-acoustic-register-tenacious-images-and.

istrators along the West African coast could be a source of vulnerability and protection. Similarly, Atlantic networks in this model also challenge the familiar triangular trade map that moves in a 'clockwise' direction, by allowing for counter-clockwise movements, shortcuts, double-backing, and criss-crossing. Rossignol's voyages to and from France in her youth as well as her travel to and around the Americas in her mature years with her own children challenge the dominant narrative of the Middle Passage.

But networks are about more than economic trade as ideas moved with people along routes. The trans-African concept also addresses how people of African descent tried to ascend socially, often in terms of moving from enslaved to free or from subject to citizen. In those moments, people sometimes looked beyond a single attachment to Africa or a particular race, ethnicity or culture to suggest a more intricate sense of self that could also redefine prevailing ideas of nation and citizenship.[7] The few times that Rossignols appeared in the archives in Senegal, Saint-Domingue and the United States, mother and daughter made claims on property, rights and respect as people who belonged to the French empire and to the United States despite being women of colour. The evidence left in documents and archives also reflects the gendered nature of these networks and movements. Useful comparisons and contrasts can be drawn to Colleen Kriger's Chapter 9 on Esperança/Hope Heath from the Upper Guinea Coast and her life in London and return to Gambia with her daughter. While other chapters in this book reveal the crucial roles of women in cities and towns on the West and West Central African coasts, this trend held in port cities on both sides of the Atlantic where women of colour dominated among the enslaved and freed populations while also emerging as merchants and property owners.[8]

---

[7] My book *To Be Free and French* generally examines how Africans and Antilleans fused their identities with new French ones. For examples of global black identities, see Tiffany Ruby Patterson and Robin D. G. Kelley, 'Unfinished Migrations: Reflections on the African Diaspora and the Making of the Modern World', *African Studies Review* 43, no. 1 (April 2000): 11–45. For North African, Middle East and Asian examples, see Chouki El Hamel, 'Constructing a Diasporic Identity: Tracing the Origins of the Gnawa Spiritual Group in Morocco', *The Journal of African History* 49, no. 2 (2008): 241–60; Joseph E. Harris, *The African Presence in Asia: Consequences of the East African Slave Trade* (Evanston, IL: Northwestern University Press, 1971).

[8] Douglas Catterall and Jodi Campbell, eds, *Women In Port: Gendering Communities, Economies, and Social Networks in Atlantic Port Cities, 1500–1800* (Leiden: Brill, 2012): in particular, see the contributions by Ty Reese on Cape Coast, Ghana; Philip Havik on Guinea-Bissau; and Dominique Rogers and Stewart King on Saint-Domingue; David Patrick Geggus, 'Slave and Free Colored Women in Saint-Domingue', in *More than Chattel: Black Women and Slavery in the Americas*, ed. Darlene Clark Hine and David Barry Gaspar (Bloomington: Indiana University Press, 1996), 259–78; Elizabeth C. Neidenbach, '"Refugee from St. Domingue Living in This City": The Geography of Social Networks in Testaments of Refugee Free Women of Color in New Orleans', in *Journal of Urban History* 42, no. 5 (2016): 841–62.

What did it mean to be black and/or a woman while also identifying, in the case of the Rossignols, as French or American? I will suggest ways to think about continental, oceanic and ideological networks, revealing Rossignol and others like her as central characters rather than marginal or anomalous figures in our understanding of Atlantic world history. Starting with the community where she was raised on Gorée, I follow the traces she left behind in Le Cap in Saint-Domingue (now Haiti) and Charleston, South Carolina. I will then examine the ways in which Anne Rossignol and her daughter Marie Adélaïde Rossignol Dumont pushed against the boundaries of their African identities, at different times expanding what it meant to be French, a person of colour, African, white or American. Trans-African women may have dwelled in outposts on the physical peripheries of empire. However, the questions that they raised about the power of identity and belonging had consequences for more than the bedevilled administrators who devised policies and also sometimes formed families and alliances with these women and their descendants. The actions and intellectual work of trans-African women, engaged larger histories of race and gender in Africa, Europe and the Americas.

Gorée, African City of Women

Gorée Island off the westernmost coastal tip of West Africa is a small place, only half a mile long, with a big, tumultuous history. The Portuguese arrived first in the region in the fifteenth century, but only used the island to bury their dead. The Dutch established a permanent settlement in the early seventeenth century, and the French and the British jockeyed for control over the island for over a century so until France definitively claimed it after 1817.[9] How does the historian learn about and convey the anguish and deprivation that must have hung in the air among the thousands of enslaved women and men who were kept in shackles here also on their way to the Americas? For those people of colour in this environment who were not enslaved, it would have been paramount to declare their status and privilege as free members of society. While the French and the British vied for control, the island was built up, physically as well as socially and culturally, by a local population in which women – most of them enslaved – constituted the majority.

To explain how this tiny place came to be home to over 5,000 people by the early nineteenth century, scholars have recounted narratives of

[9] For a general overview of European presence in and competition over Gorée, see Joseph-Roger de Benoist and Abdoulaye Camara, 'Gorée dans L'histoire,' in *Histoire de Gorée* (Paris: Maisonneuve & Larose, 2003), 11–29.

migration, of Africans and of the *signares*, their families and captives. For example, a famous *signare* named Catalina or Catarina from Rufisque, on the mainland, reputedly brought a group to Gorée and Saint Louis sometime between 1701 and 1725.[10] Such women and men from the mainland had been, themselves, descended partly from Portuguese *lançados* ('adventurers'; those who threw themselves – upon the shore) who established trading posts on the mainland coast from the fifteenth century. These stories demonstrate that, no matter what their background was, most residents of Gorée were the children of someone who had come from somewhere else, even if it was just from just across the bay, a few miles away.

During the initial period of French settlement at the turn of the eighteenth century, maps and archaeological data also suggest that the island was segregated into three small neighbourhoods, including a separate *'village des bambaras'* ('slave' village).[11] By the late eighteenth century, Gorée had become urbanised; most homes were made of thatch, but there were a few stone houses, some with verandas, and courtyards enclosing shacks and other structures. Free Africans, *mulâtre* women, Europeans, and enslaved Africans lived side-by-side.[12] Thus the migration and establishment of *signares* during the critical period of the eighteenth century accompanied a crucial shift into an urbanised, more integrated town. But Gorée was no egalitarian utopia. It was a slave-holding society with a majority population of enslaved women and girls. The terms that people used to describe themselves, not only differentiated between enslaved and free, between African and *mulâtre*, but they also often connoted gender. The term 'gourmet' (*grumet*) dated from medieval times and referred to a cabin boy or apprentice seaman.[13]

---

[10] Angrand, *Le Temps de Signares*, 22–3. Other early *signares* of this period included La Belinguere and Lucia. For a contrast between a 'coarser' Catalina and more refined Bibiana Vaz, also known by the form of a Wolof title for respect La Belinguere, see George E. Brooks, *Eurafricans in Western Africa: Commerce, Social Status, Gender, and Religious Observance from the Sixteenth to the Eighteenth Century* (Athens: Ohio University Press, 2003), 134, 50–51. Jean Baptiste Labat, *Nouvelle Relation de l'Afrique occidentale*, Tome IV (Paris: Chez G. Cavelier, 1728), 152, http://gallica.bnf.fr/ark:/12148/bpt6k103382f.r=labat+nouvelle+relation.langEN.

[11] Early eighteenth-century maps include one drawn by L'Ainé in 1716 and Wallons in 1723: Raina Lynn Croff, 'Village des Bambaras: An Archaeology of Domestic Slavery and Urban Transformation on Gorée Island, Senegal, A.D. 17–19th Centuries' (Ph.D. dissertation, Yale University, 2009), 9–22 – Croff was a team member in Ibrahima Thiaw's archaeological dig in 2001; Mark Hinchman, *Portrait of an Island: The Architecture and Material Culture of Gorée, Senegal 1758-1837* (Lincoln: University of Nebraska, 2015), 69–74.

[12] On my choice to use the term *'mûlatre'* in French see, Semley, *To Be Free and French*, 8.

[13] Jay Dearborn Edwards and Nicolas Kariouk Pecquet du Bellay de Verton, *A Creole Lexicon: Architecture, Landscape, People* (Baton Rouge: Louisiana State University Press, 2004), 112–13. On usage of terms, also see Brooks, *Eurafricans in Western Africa*, 212–13; Abbé David Boilat, *Esquisses sénégalaises: Physionomie du pays, peuplades, commerce, religions, passé et avenir, récits et légendes* (Paris: P. Bertrand, 1853), 5.

Laptots were other free African labourers associated with sailing.[14] *Habitant* status was often associated with the *mulâtre* population, including *signares*, who were also sometimes referred to using the feminine form, '*habitante*'. It mattered how people deployed these terms, like *grumet(t)* and *habitant(e)*, to connote different ideas about a person's status, appearance and power in the community.

By taking the title of *signare*, African and *mulâtre* women throughout Senegambia and Upper Guinea signalled that at the apex of society there were women. No direct masculine form of the term '*signare*' existed, and no men of colour, no matter how elite, could cultivate the image of a 'gentleman' enough to garner a comparable title for 'Sir' that the general community would recognise and accept. By the late eighteenth and early nineteenth centuries, the term '*signare*' may have been used more broadly for wealthy women, whether or not they were *mulâtre*.[15] Even if wealth and property ownership originally set *mulâtres* and Africans apart, over time, members of the African population likewise came to claim their status as *habitants* on the island to which their ancestors had also migrated.

Late eighteenth-century census documents and maps reveal quite a bit about race and gender on an island that was not an isolated enclave but part of a network stretching onto the African continent as well as across the Atlantic. In 1763, the naturalist Michel Adanson published a report containing a census of the island made in the 1750s.[16] When reading this report, together with subsequent accounts of the population completed in 1767 and the late 1770s, three aspects of life on Gorée emerge.[17] First, the

[14] Croff, 'Village des Bambaras', 23–6. Several differently named chartered companies were given a monopoly in Senegal in the late seventeenth and early eighteenth centuries until the *Compagnie des Indes* (India Company) received the charter from 1719 to 1758: Karen Amanda Sackur, 'The Development of Creole Society and Culture in Saint Louis and Gorée, 1719–1817' (Ph.D. thesis, University of London, 1999), 300.

[15] Brooks, *Eurafricans in Western Africa*, 122–60, 215.

[16] Adanson lived in Senegal for five years between 1749 and 1753 but he only made two trips to Gorée. He was investigating the plausibility of a colonisation scheme across the Atlantic in Cayenne, Guiana where French authorities envisioned commercial and subsistence farming using crops and settlers from Gorée: Barbara Jean Traver, 'After Kourou: Settlement Schemes in French Guiana in the Age of Enlightenment' (Ph.D. dissertation, Washington State University, 2011). Michel Adanson, *Histoire Naturelle Du Sénégal Coquillages: Avec La Relation Abrégée d'un Voyage Fait en ce Pays, Pendant les années 1749, 50, 51, 52 & 53* (Paris: Chez Claude-Jean-Baptiste Pauche, 1757), 57–66, 86–97, 102, 118, www.biodiversitylibrary.org/title/39621. 'Mémoire sur Gorée par M. Adanson', May–June 1763, Fonds ministériels (FM), C6/15, ANOM. A slightly revised online edition of the published version of the report with some additional commentary appears in, Victor Martin and Charles Becker, 'Mémoires d'Adanson sur le Sénégal et l'île de Gorée', *Bulletin de l'IFAN*, B 42, no. 4 (1980): 722–9, http://tekrur-ucad.refer.sn.

[17] There is also a less complete document for Saint Louis and Gorée, supposedly dating to 1774, that only described the households of the wealthy *mulâtres* in each location although it does include wealthy free blacks: 'Etat de libres mulâtre s et des blancs descendans [*sic*] de mulâtresses habitans [*sic*] de Gorée et le nombre des noirs qu'ils peuvent avoir'. FM C6/17 – 1774, ANOM.

changing number and size of households suggested a construction boom and on-going waves of immigration. Second, because the sources also provide names of the free inhabitants, their children and dependants, and sometimes also the captives they kept in their homes, it is possible to get a sense of the ethnic and religious diversity across the community and in individual compounds. Finally, the historical record draws attention to the important free and freed African population which grew in number over time. Gorée was also an island of free Africans, many among them women homeowners who thereby often achieved the status of *signare* in the eyes of local French government officials who recorded the names of the women who surrounded them.

In his report based on data from the 1750s, Adanson painted the population of *signares* as 'abusive' and a 'necessary evil', but he also showed the relatively modest beginnings of *signares* given how some of them later prospered. He listed thirteen households on Gorée and an overall population of less than 300 people. All thirteen heads of household kept enslaved women and men but none had more than twenty and about half had ten or fewer. Even in a small place with no large-scale or labour-intensive cultivation or industry controlled by the general population, there was still a strong culture of slave ownership. Five of the thirteen homeowners were African, including one Muslim man. Still, while three of the five African heads of household were men, only one of the eight *mulâtre* homeowners was a man. In the end, as we may expect, the largest group of homeowners were *mulâtre* women, but even more complexity lay in the details.

At this early date, most of the homes were made of thatch rather than stone. One homeowner kept twenty-one people in a home built of thatch, suggesting that ownership of a stone home might not be the only way people signalled their wealth and influence.[18] Anne Rossignol (referred to as Anne Toutt or Anne Toute in these documents), in her 20s in the 1750s, lived in one of those thatched homes with eight enslaved people, as well as her son who travelled with her to Saint-Domingue, a second son and her daughter Marie Adélaïde, four years old at the time. Meanwhile Anne Rossignol's older sister, Marie-Thérèse Rossignol already resided in a huge stone mansion with an elegant terrace, right next to the Company garden at the centre of the island. Despite her own 'humble' beginnings, Anne Rossignol was to become one of the largest slave owners on the island along with her sister, Marie-Thérèse Rossignol and another well-

---

[18] The make-up of the home of Fatiman [sic] Nègre, the lone Muslim in the survey, is not provided but, given his job as a guard for enslaved captives, it is likely that his home was also thatched. The only man with a stone home was Louis Kémé, himself a mason and a relative of the *damel* (leader) of the kingdom of Kayor. Adanson, 'Mémoire sur Gorée.' FM C6/15, ANOM; 'Etat de libres': in this document Anne Rossignol (listed as Anne Toute) is said to be 36 years old when she should have been in her 40s.

known *signare* named Cati Louet (or Caty Louette, see p. 34). Because women homeowners brought family into their homes along with enslaved labour, households could include a diverse array of enslaved and free children and families of diverse racial, ethnic and religious backgrounds.

The second census examined here dates from 1767 and reflects changes that had happened over the course of a decade.[19] The number of homes jumped from thirteen to sixty-three and the population from less than 300 to over 1,000. The document even provided something far more rare – the name and religion of every enslaved child, woman and man. Compared with the 1750s, also almost ten times as many African women owned their own homes. The dominance of *mulâtre* women persisted as new women emerged as wealthy homeowners. Cati Louet, often cited in history books as the largest slaveholder in Gorée, had only two teenaged men as dependants and ten enslaved people living with her in the 1750s. By 1767, she was living with her children and two young girl dependants along with sixty-six enslaved individuals.[20] Anne Rossignol went from owning eight captives to claiming ownership over ten men and twenty-three women and children. The overall number of enslaved women and girls was 434 as against only 284 men and boys for a difference of 150 per cent. The records demonstrate that enslaved women and girls performed the most-valued labour, including cooking, cleaning, laundering and other domestic work that could also be 'rented out'. Only the free African slave owner Pierre Waly kept far more enslaved men than women, and most of those men would probably have worked work outside his home.[21] Even with census data, it is difficult to visualise exactly how so many people lived together in the small, physical space of the island.

Two decades later, Nicolas François Evrard Du Parel, a volunteer soldier and accountant, completed a cadastral map that indicated every square foot of land in Gorée owned by women and men, *mulâtre* and African. The number of households had increased to over seventy and the French

[19] The 1767 census appeared only four years after Adanson's report although the true lapse in time between the two records was about a decade since Adanson's report was published several years after his visit to Senegal.

[20] Although the 1750s census claimed that Cati Louet was 45 years old, it appears to have been a typographical error. There was a 1774 census that was a limited accounting only of the free *mulâtre* population and the number of enslaved people they claimed to own. Not only was Louet's age recorded as 48 in 1774, it was unclear how she could have given birth, after the age of 45, to three children by the Frenchman Pierre Aussenac de Carcassonne who is said to have arrived in Gorée in around 1758. Aussenac also apparently travelled to Gorée in 1736 but according to the 1750s census, Louet did not have any children. Cati Louet's children are listed as being 12, 18 and 21 years in 1774. The dates and ages do not correspond exactly for the Rossignols either: 'Etat de libres'.

[21] His name is spelled 'Wally' in the 1767 report but it appears that the form used in the later census of 1776, Waly, is a more accurate spelling. In fact, the only other head of a household who owned a notably higher number of enslaved men was the sole *mulâtre* man in the group.

colonial government also had an extensive collection of over thirty buildings and structures, mostly grouped near the fort.[22] Du Parel's map had come about after a series of land disputes over the years. The *habitants* demanded recognition of land ownership in a place where most people did not have property deeds. Following a series of hearings in 1776, Du Parel situated each plot and completed the map sometime before 1780.[23] While the information for this cadastral map mainly concerned the physical location and size of the home, details embedded in the oral testimony and the map suggested how people interacted with the physical and ideological 'architecture' of the French colonial state.[24]

At the same time, the identities of property owners became more obscured because the terms '*habitant*' and '*signare*' were becoming more ubiquitous, being applied sometimes to people who otherwise would have been identified as 'free blacks'. The coversheet of Anne Debane's testimony noted that she was a 'free black' (*négresse libre*) but in the body of the actual legal document, she was referred to as a *signare*. Madeleine Waly was identified as an *habitante* and a *signare*, even though she was the daughter of Pierre Waly, a free black man and his African wife who had owned so many slaves a decade earlier.[25] Meanwhile, Waly himself was subtly referred to as 'the so-called' (*le nommé*) Pierre Waly, a demeaning designation used throughout the census for all the men, who were mostly 'free blacks'. The same disparaging term was even used for a couple of the *mulâtre* men.[26] More importantly, there was a whole new class of homeowner listed on the 1776 map: freed captives. These were formerly enslaved women and men, as well as one woman who was actually still owned by Marie-Thérèse Rossignol. Indeed, even as an enslaved woman, the woman was referred to as a *habitante*.[27]

[22] 'Plan de L'Isle de Gorée, presenté à Monseigneur de Sartine, Ministre et Secretaire d'Etat avant le department de la Marine', Fonds Ministériels (FM), Dépôt Fortifications Colonial (DPC) XIV/25PFB/111, ANOM.
[23] Sackur, 'The Development of Creole Society', 186–7. Moleur argues that this property-claiming process under Brasseur revealed weak French authority: Bernard Moleur, 'Le droit de propriété sur le sol sénégalais', Ph.D. dissertation, Université de Dijon, 1978', 48–57.
[24] Paul Hirst, 'Foucault and Architecture', *AA Files* no. 26 (Autumn 1993): 52–60; Gordana Fontana-Giusti, *Foucault for Architects* (New York: Routledge, 2013).
[25] On the 1767 census, Waly's wife was listed as Laurence LaFleur; she was presumably an African woman as she was referred to as his 'Christian wife': 'No. 1 – Pierre Waly – nègre libre chrétien', 'Dénombrement Général des Habitants', 3G 123, ANS, 1.
[26] 'Waly (Madéleine et Pierre), habitant de Gorée, Concession 1776', COL E/390, ANOM, Instruments de Recherches en Ligne (IREL), online reference: ark:/61561/up424dx5y21s 'Ghusban (*le nommé*), habitant de l'île de Gorée'; COL E/216, ANOM, IREL, ark:/61561/up424f726zm.
[27] 'Marso (la nommée), habitante de Gorée Concession 1776', COL E/304, ANOM, IREL, ark:/62562/up424cwy0vvs. I tried to find a record of 'Marso' in the Rossignol household the 1767 census and the closest name I could find was an enslaved Muslim woman named Marisseau. 'No. 59 – Marie Rossignolle [*sic*] – Libre chrétienne', 'Dénombrement Général des Habitants', 3G 123, ANS, 19.

Despite this archival record depicting the social and economic influence of women of all backgrounds in Gorée during the eighteenth century, *signares* had mostly faded into the background by the second half of the nineteenth century. By the beginning of the twentieth century, the political rights of Senegalese men had become open to debate in relation to military service and voting rights.[28] Yet the present analysis raises at least two challenges to a simple trajectory moving from *mulâtre* to African. First, Gorée's *signares*, often inevitably portrayed as being *mulâtre* as well as haughty and ostentatious, had modest beginnings. *Signares* laboured to cultivate an image of wealth by keeping a few enslaved women and men to run their households and trading businesses. Second, from the middle of the eighteenth century, as Gorée was expanding, the island's cadre of free African property owners grew, too. Many of these free Africans were women who, in the record books, would have been perceived as *signares*. *Mulâtre* women and their families and dependants remained leading figures in the community, but they must always be seen as part of a broader canvas. African women and men together with *mulâtre signares* all helped define a cultural identity as *habitants*, and later *originaires*, in the physical space of what was an African port town.

Most importantly, the Gorée population depended upon on-going relationships with mainland Wolof and Lébu communities of Cap-Vert, just across the bay. All Gorée residents drew on kinship ties and trade networks to acquire daily necessities such as water, as well as trade goods such as animal hides, cotton cloth, indigo, ivory and gold. Some of the wealthiest *signares* owned small fleets of *pirogues* (canoes) and stored agricultural goods in rooms on the ground floors of their homes. Gorée residents, especially the *signares*, also lent out the enslaved women and men they owned for domestic services and large construction projects.[29] Whatever it meant to be 'a child of Gorée', the *signares*, freed people, and enslaved living, including Anne Rossignol, were part of networks tied deeply to the continent, its trade routes and cultural exchange that predated and continued once Europeans arrived and seemed to divert all the energy, wealth, and spirit towards the Atlantic Ocean. People still looked across the bay to their friends and foes on the mainland. Women like Anne Rossignol were part of the exchange and innovation that were intrinsic

---

[28] Sarah Zimmerman, 'Citizenship, Military, and Managing Exceptionalism: *Originaires* in World War I', in *Empires in World War I: Shifting Frontiers and Imperial Dynamics in a Global Conflict*, ed. Andrew Tait Jarboe and Richard S. Fogarty (London and New York: I.B. Tauris, 2014), 219–48.

[29] Sackur, 'The Development of Creole Society,' 283–4. Angrand, *Le Temps de Signares*, 95, 101. Mark Hinchman, 'House and Household on Goree, Senegal, 1758–1837,' *Journal of the Society of Architectural Historians* 65, no. 2 (2006): 169, 179–80. Brooks, *Eurafricans in Western African*, 210.

Illustration 7 A *signare* wearing an elaborate dress, gold earrings, necklaces and bracelets, Senegal, 1810s

(Source: 'Signar ou Femme de couleur du Sénégal', René Claude Geoffroy de Villeneuve, *Illustrations de L'Afrique ou histoire, moeurs, usages et coutumes des Africains* (Paris: Nepvey, 1814); Copy in Bibliothèque nationale de France)

to daily life across the African continent. These practices born within Africa travelled with those people who were swept up and away, including people like the Rossignols travelling by choice as passengers above the hold on one of those ships.

A Different Black Atlantic

To shift more fully toward the oceanic perspective of the trans-African concept suggests a broadening of outlook and landscape. However, to speak of the Atlantic often ensnares the African continent in a single relationship with the rest of the world through the transatlantic trade and the fetid belly of a slave ship. In Gorée today, there is also a disparity between the historical realities of history of the slave trade and its memorialisation in tourism. On the one hand, there is the common trope of the 'protective' *signare* as slave owner who recorded the birth, baptism and death of her 'house slaves' and never, willingly, sold them away. That image persists even as the infamous and controversial *Maison des Esclaves* (House of Slaves) casts a shadow on the island. A major tourist site, it was the long-time residence of *signare* Anna-Nicolas (Annacolas) Pépin. Annacolas Pépin was the namesake and niece of Anne Pépin who is said to have had an affair with French Governor Chevalier Stanislas de Boufflers during his stay at Gorée in 1787.[30] At the Maison des Esclaves, placards and tour guides suggest that this private home of Annacolas Pépin primarily stored captives and served as a point of debarkation for 'millions' of enslaved women and men through a single 'door of no return'.[31] Yet, the Transatlantic Slave Trade database shows that whereas West Central Africa lost over 3 million people and the Bight of Benin lost over 1.5 million, the number of people forced onto slave ships in the Senegambia region was just over 600,000 of whom just under 30,000 departed Gorée.[32] Vociferous arguments about memory versus fact do not help clarify the experience of enslaved women and men who laboured in their owner's home or who were rented out to work for others. Sometimes the enslaved who were in transit died during their time there, their corpses weighted down

---

[30] The house was actually built by Nicolas Pépin, Annacolas Pépin's father and younger brother of Anne Pépin, between 1776 and 1784: Benoist and Camara, 'Les Signares et le patrimoine', 105–10.

[31] Ralph A. Austen, 'The Slave Trade as History and Memory: Confrontations of Slaving Voyage Documents and Communal Traditions', *William and Mary Quarterly* 58, no. 1 (2001): 229–44.

[32] 'Voyages: The Trans-Atlantic Slave Trade Database', www.slavevoyages.org/voyages/BuQgaGHN and www.slavevoyages.org/voyages/MpUEyqgU, accessed 5 March 2017: the database privileges shipping and archival records.

and tossed into the sea, only to float up and decompose on the rocky shore, refusing to be completely forgotten.[33] Scholarship and popular media reinforce the image of a singular trajectory from Africa causing a definitive rupture between descendants of those who remained on the continent and descendants of those who were carried away. Faced with the common image of a 'door of no return', narratives of physical or imagined return to the continent often prove ambivalent and fraught with conflicting emotions.[34]

Someone like Anne Rossignol turned on its head what is assumed to be the 'single story' about Africa and the Atlantic world. Her family story exemplified multidirectional movement and multifarious relationships among people, especially women, travelling and living within an Atlantic world.[35] When Anne Rossignol made the fateful decision to emigrate with two of her children, Marie Adélaïde Rossignol and Louis-Armand Aubert, to Le Cap in Saint-Domingue sometime around 1775, it was at least her third transatlantic voyage.[36] For a while, her decision appeared to reap rewards. She prospered and bought up properties and married off her daughter to a widowed French doctor named Guillaume Dumont. Meanwhile, her son Louis-Armand Aubert, who had returned to Gorée, married a woman descended from a prominent family of colour there.[37] Precisely during the period that the Rossignol women relocated to Saint-Domingue, free people of colour were increasingly facing assaults on their status and privileges in Saint-Domingue. The community of free people of colour, born partly of interracial relationships and sexual violence since the beginnings of

---

[33] Françoise Éléonore de Jean de Manville Sabran et al., *Correspondance inédite de la comtesse de Sabran et du chevalier de Boufflers, 1778–1788* (Paris: E. Plon, 1875), 493–4; Croff, 'Village des Bambaras', 22.

[34] Theresa A. Singleton, 'The Slave Trade Remembered on the Former Gold and Slave Coasts', in *From Slavery to Emancipation in the Atlantic*, ed. Sylvia R. Frey and Betty Wood (London: Frank Cass, 1999), 150–69; Bayo Holsey, *Routes of Remembrance: Refashioning the Slave Trade in Ghana* (Chicago: University of Chicago, 2008); Saidiya Hartman, *Lose Your Mother: A Journey Along the Atlantic Slave Route* (New York: Farrar, Straus & Giroux, 2007); Ana Lucia Araujo, *Public Memory of Slavery: Victims and Perpetrators in the South Atlantic* (Amherst, NY: Cambria Press, 2010).

[35] Chimamanda Adichie, 'The Danger of a Single Story', July 2009, www.ted.com/talks/chimamanda_adichie_the_danger_of_a_single_story.html.

[36] Others date her journey to 1772 but I am under the impression that she was in Gorée around 1774 when that document counting the free people of colour in Saint Louis and Gorée appears to have been produced. 'Etat de libres'.

[37] Rogers and King, 'Housekeepers, Merchants, Rentières,' 368–69. On Aubert's marriage, see 'Mariage de Sieur Armand Aubert et Marguerite Aussenac, le 21 juillet 1788', Etat Civil, Gorée 1777–1824, 85MIOM/836, Archives Nationales d'Outre Mer (ANOM). Rogers and King read and report the year as 1778: Rogers and King, 'Housekeepers, Merchants, Rentières', 390n134. 'Mariage de Sieur Dumont et Marie Adelaide dite Rossignol (Quateronne libre)', Notariat Saint-Domingue, Etat-Civil, Le Cap, 1786– 20 June 1787, Dépôt des papiers publics des colonies (DPPC), SDOM 195, ANOM.

empire, had come to be seen as a threat in the colonies and in France.³⁸ Yet attitudes on the ground in Le Cap about race, gender and rights still allowed free people of colour, including free blacks, to accumulate wealth. That these two women of colour, no matter how fair-skinned they were, could immigrate from Senegal to take advantage of opportunities in Saint-Domingue said something about their homeland of Senegal, their adopted home of Saint-Domingue and the Atlantic world in which they circulated.

By the time of her daughter's marriage in 1786, less than fifteen years after their arrival in Le Cap, Anne Rossignol had retained or increased her wealth enough to give her daughter property and several enslaved women and men. Both women enjoyed the range of civil rights available to residents in France and the French colonies under the Ancien Régime.³⁹ The fact that Anne Rossignol was in Saint-Domingue without a husband may have enabled her to conduct business more freely even though in Saint-Domingue she was legally listed as a '*mulâtresse*' and her daughter a '*quateronne*'.⁴⁰ It also was a time when the privileges of free people of colour were under pressure, but Anne Rossignol owned property in the suburb of Petit Carénage where many people of colour and free blacks lived in addition to her home in a more exclusive part of town. When Marie Adélaïde Rossignol married the French surgeon Dumont in 1786, such interracial marriages were becoming less common. She brought a dowry of almost 79,000 pounds (*livres colonials* or about 59,000 metropolitan *livres tournois*, £2400 at the time) to her marriage. Dominique Rogers and Stewart King remark on the size of this expenditure which

---

³⁸ Doris L. Garraway, *The Libertine Colony: Creolization in the Early French Caribbean* (Durham, NC and London: Duke University Press, 2005); Sue Peabody, 'Négresse, Mulâtresse, Citoyenne: Gender and Emancipation in the French Caribbean, 1650–1848', in *Gender and Slave Emancipation in the Atlantic World*, ed. Pamela Scully and Diana Paton (Durham, NC and London: Duke University Press, 2005); John Garrigus, 'Race, Gender, and Virtue in Haiti's Failed Foundational Fiction: La mulatre comme il y a peu de blanches (1803)' in *The Color of Liberty: Histories of Race in France*, ed. Sue Peabody and Tyler Stovall (Durham, NC and London: Duke University Press, 2003), 73–94; Mimi Sheller, 'Sword-Bearing Citizens: Militarism and Manhood in Nineteenth-Century Haiti', *Plantation Society in the Americas* 4, no. 2–3 (1997), 233–78.

³⁹ 'Vente de maison de mulâtresse Anne Rossignol à Marie Adelaïde dite Rossignol', 21 aout 1786, DPPC, SDOM 195, ANOM. 'Mariage de Sieur Dumont et Marie Adelaide dite Rossignol (Quateronne libre)', DPPC, SDOM 195, ANOM.

⁴⁰ On the limits on the rights of married French women to conduct business on their own account, see Jennifer L. Palmer, 'Women and Contracts in the Age of Transatlantic Commerce', in *Women and Work in Eighteenth-Century France*, ed. Daryl M. Hafter and Nina Kushner (Baton Rouge: Louisiana State University Press, 2015), 130–51. Rebecca Scott and Jean Hébrard provide an example of a free woman of colour who aggressively conducted business on her own account in New Orleans in the early nineteenth century. She was in a long-term relationship with a Belgian man but Louisiana law made the marriage between a white person and free person of colour void at that time: Rebecca J. Scott and Jean M. Hébrard, *Freedom Papers: An Atlantic Odyssey in the Age of Emancipation* (Cambridge, MA: Harvard University Press, 2012), 71.

surpassed the vast majority of dowries in metropolitan France by 20,000 *livres colonials*.⁴¹

Such resources must have aided the women's escape from Le Cap at some point during the Revolution before Haiti was born. Mother and daughter with the daughter's French husband turned up in Charleston, South Carolina where they continued to acquire property and enslaved people. Given that they had been able to transfer some of their wealth and even make claims on the property they left behind, they may have left Le Cap sometime between the time the Revolution began in the hills outside the city in 1791 and the destruction of the city itself in 1793.⁴² It is unclear whether they arrived directly in Charleston, South Carolina or travelled there by way of other cities.⁴³ They must have arrived in the 1790s since the daughter's husband, Guillaume Dumont was listed in the South Carolina census in 1796.⁴⁴ A woman named Maria Adélaïde Rosynol Dumont (*sic*) was awarded US citizenship in 1829, but claimed to be a white woman born in Paris.⁴⁵ Thus, Marie Adélaïde Rossignol Dumont's new French-American identity appeared to obscure her long residence in Saint-Domingue and her birth in Senegal. Yet, personal connections with Saint-Domingue also may have lingered on in South Carolina for Marie Adélaïde Rossignol Dumont and her mother, the long-lived Anne Rossignol.

Anne Rossignol, who was likewise listed as white in court documents, lived in Charleston until her death in 1810. According to her will, upon her death, one enslaved woman she owned named Victoire along with this woman's daughter were to be passed on to a free *mulâtre*

---

⁴¹ 'Vente de maison', 21 aout 1786, DPPC, SDOM 195, ANOM. 'Mariage de Sieur Dumont. Rogers and King, 'Housekeepers, Merchants, Rentières', 363n21, 368–9. The Rossignols even outdid the dowry of 60,000 *livres coloniales* in the first marriage that elite planter Julien Raimond contracted in Saint-Domingue in 1771.

⁴² Pierre Force and Susan Hoffius, 'Negotiating Race and Status in Senegal, Saint Domingue, and South Carolina', *Early American Studies* (Winter 2018): 136. I am grateful to Susan Hoffius for sharing an advance copy of her article with me.

⁴³ New Orleans, Baltimore, Philadelphia or New York as these were major destinations for those who left Saint-Domingue in the 1790s. On refugees from the 1790s, see Jeremy Popkin, *You Are All Free: The Haitian Revolution and the Abolition of Slavery* (Cambridge: Cambridge University Press, 2010), 289–326. Ashli White, *Encountering Revolution: Haiti and the Making of the Early Republic* (Baltimore, MD: Johns Hopkins University Press, 2010).

⁴⁴ Force and Hoffius, 'Negotiating Race and Status', 127.

⁴⁵ 'Maria Adelaide Rosynol Dumont [*sic*]', Record of Admissions to Citizenship, District of South Carolina, 1790–1906 (National Archives Microfilm Publication M1183, 1 roll); Records of District Courts of the United States, Record Group 21; National Archives, Washington, DC, accessed on http://ancestry.com. The record lists her age at 73 putting her year of birth at 1756. Based on the census data from Gorée, Marie Adélaïde Rossignol was more likely born in about 1763 putting her in her mid- to late-twenties when her children were born in Le Cap in 1788 and 1790. Also Rossignol Dumont seems to be listed twice; a woman named Adelaide Dumont, also recorded as born in Paris and aged 70 was listed as gaining her citizenship three years earlier in 1826.

woman whom Anne Rossignol herself had once owned. But the freed woman of colour was 'in the West Indies' when Anne Rossignol died so Marie Adélaïde Rossignol Dumont took ownership of Victoire and her children and, eventually, her grandchildren. In turn, when Marie Adélaïde Rossignol Dumont died in 1833, her son-in-law claimed ownership over Victoire and her family. However, another woman identifying herself as white, named Charlotte Chartran, claimed that Victoire and her descendants were supposed to pass on to her upon the death of Anne Rossignol's original heir, the erstwhile freed woman of colour who had never returned from 'the West Indies' and apparently died there in 1837. Chartran mounted the case against the Dumont's son-in-law in 1841 after he failed to relinquish the enslaved family to her.[46]

The court case suggests that Anne Rossignol and Marie Adélaïde Rossignol Dumont maintained some form of contact with women who may have also had ties to Saint-Domingue. The free woman of colour and former slave of Anne Rossignol who never claimed Victoire and her children apparently died in the 'West Indies'.[47] Although the use of names as evidence can be misleading, the woman who brought the case against Dumont's son-in-law had a French name, Charlotte Merotte Chartran. If these relationships were based on ties to Saint-Domingue, the Rossignol women apparently did not completely erase their past even if they denied their African ancestry, their birth in Senegal, and their residence in Saint-Domingue. The very aspects of their identity that had been an asset in Le Cap before the Revolution – their wealth from and connections with Gorée and their status as free women of colour – would have been liabilities in South Carolina. In those years when they lived South Carolina, as Haiti struggled as a new nation and Gorée was trying to maintain a special status in the French empire, the Rossignol women managed to claim property, enslaved people, and 'whiteness', and, apparently, at least in the case of the daughter, US citizenship.

But those claims to whiteness could be fragile. The connections to Saint-Domingue and beyond had, in fact, been resurrected in an earlier case in 1831 launched against Anne Rossignol's great-grandson John

---

[46] 'Petition by Caroline Chartran against Dr. J.W. Schmidt and son for possession of six slaves', Charleston, South Carolina, 14 January 1841, Petition Number 21384130, Digital Library on American Slavery, http://library.uncg.edu/slavery/details.aspx?pid=14805. It is unclear when and where Anne Rossignol claimed ownership over Victoire, whether it was back in Saint-Domingue, in South Carolina or even somewhere on the way to South Carolina.

[47] 'Maria Adelaide Rosynol Dumont [sic], Record of Admissions to Citizenship, District of South Carolina, 1790–1906' (National Archives Microfilm Publication M1183, 1 roll); Records of District Courts of the United States, Record Group 21; National Archives, Washington, DC, accessed on http://ancestry.com. 'Petition by Caroline Chartran against Dr. J.W. Schmidt and son'.

W. Schmidt, Jr, a successful physician in Charleston. A fellow Saint-Domingue refugee, a white man named Vincent LeSeigneur, accused Schmidt of being of 'mixed blood' and had Schmidt's medical license revoked. The evidence turned on the treacherous colleague's long-time friendship with the Rossignol Dumonts in Le Cap as well as in Charleston where they had all arrived in the 1790s.[48] Marie Adélaïde Rossignol Dumont and her grandson Schmidt, Jr sued LeSeigneur for slander and won; the court ruled that Rossignol Dumont was 'a good true faithful and honest white woman … and citizen of the state of South Carolina'. But Schmidt, Jr never had his license reinstated and LeSeigneur was found innocent of slander.[49] While Pierre Force and Susan Hoffius highlight the increasing virulence of 'scientific racism' in this period, they also reveal the malleability of ideas about race. As notions became more entrenched, Rossignol Dumont and her mother moved from being 'other free people' in the 1800 census to 'white' by 1810. Despite the prevalence of the 'one-drop rule', Rossignol Dumont (and her mother) were able to dispel any rumours about them and establish reputations that won the case for Rossignol Dumont and her grandson.[50] Still, her grandson could no longer practice in Charleston, and rebuilt his life in New York.

Taken together, the story of the Rossignol family scattered in Gorée, Le Cap and Charleston as free, wealthy slave-holding women of colour also revealed a different, fraught story of the Atlantic world. Their story engages in the history of the Atlantic slave trade but in ways that discomfortingly turn assumptions on their head. While their travel highlighted the mobility of free people of African descent during the era of the slave trade, their lifestyle choices recall how important it was for many to maintain social hierarchies with Africans enslaved on the bottom. These women, anxious to maintain their image probably sought to uphold these hierarchies as their belief in their own rights and privileges travelled with them. The Rossignols not only aspired to be 'ladies', as they were in Gorée, but they also shared in an ideology and culture of being French and belonging as French in the colonies before the French Revolution had even been imagined.

---

[48] Force and Hoffius, 'Negotiating Race and Status'.
[49] Force and Hoffius, 'Negotiating Race and Status', 141.
[50] *United States Federal Census* (database on-line). Provo, UT: Ancestry.com Operations Inc, 2010, Charleston, South Carolina; Series: M32; Roll: 48; Page: *99*; Image: *136*; Family History Library Film: *181423;* Force and Hoffius, 'Negotiating Race and Status', 140–1, 143.

Belonging and Being French in the French Empire

To get at the underlying ideas that may have allowed Anne Rossignol to imagine other possibilities for herself as a woman of colour, it is necessary to return to the place of her youth, Gorée, and the political environment that she experienced before she lived in Saint-Domingue and South Carolina. Letters and petitions have long been powerful vehicles for staking claims and making demands on governments. Living on the periphery of the French empire in Gorée, it was crucial for people there to maintain ties, real and imagined, with the metropole, by using the language of belonging and the rhetoric of empire. Years before communities submitted the famous *cahiers de doléances* or lists of grievances to the French king in 1789, *signares* and free Africans on Gorée wrote similar letters and petitions to representatives of the French government.[51] Such letters were performative and formulaic, but the soaring language, and appeals to the king also revealed expectations. French colonial subjects challenged the fundamental ideal of a white French nation by conjuring up a vision of an empire comprised of people of colour and arguing that they too were part of this nation and they, too, could be French.

Habitants in Gorée penned such a letter in 1763 when the French regained control over the island after the population had experienced five years of British rule and free trade policies. Another letter written in the late 1770s was sent as a follow-up to a scheme to help colonise Cayenne, Guiana in South America with plants and people from Gorée. The late 1770s were also the period when the Gorée *habitants* were codifying their claims to property on the island. At the same time, local debates over property, trade and slavery affected how women and men in Gorée thought about and expressed broader notions of rights. Inchoate ideas that would form the basis of citizenship were embedded in all of these documents including the ones written under the Ancien Régime. Thus, at the height of *signare* influence, debates about rights were already swirling around an island politically dominated by free women of colour and physically dominated by enslaved women and girls.

In the 1763 letter signed by several residents in Gorée declared their opposition to new royal administrative French control after five years of British rule during the Seven Years' War (1754–1763). Instead of finding relief from suffering after the war with the British, these women and men had encountered more misery. The commander at Gorée refused to let them engage in free trade as the French government had promised;

---

[51] G. Wesley Johnson Jr, *The Emergence of Black Politics in Senegal: The Struggle for Power in the Four Communes, 1900–1920* (Stanford, CA: Stanford University Press, 1971), 24, 26. Jones, *The Métis of Senegal*, 32–34.

the *habitants* felt 'free' but believed that their 'goods and liberty [were] threatened'. In order to guard their own freedom or to pay fines, some were even forced to sell their own captives whom the *habitants* saw 'as their own children' to passing ships. Other *signares* who had fled when the British arrived still feared returning home 'to more despair'. Hoping for assistance, the *habitants* chronicled these difficulties while declaring their loyalty to the minister and the French metropolitan government.[52] Such a letter was more than a plea for access to free trade; it revealed a great deal about Gorée society and culture. *Habitants* showed themselves to be avid traders, pro-slavery, and willing to play the French metropole against local French administrators. Engaging in a form of double-speak, Gorée *habitants* cleverly pledged allegiance to the French regime yet deployed language evoking justice and even humanity to challenge French colonial policies on the ground. Thirty-five women and men were party to the letter. At least sixteen of the signatories were of women, but none could sign their name.[53]

Another letter written sometime in the late 1770s indicated that the French continued to aggravate the *habitants* of Gorée with their trade policies. First, they tried to install company monopolies at Gorée and launched the ill-fated colonisation scheme in Cayenne.[54] This letter had only had fourteen signatories – at least half of them women – but the majority of people in this instance signed their own names. The women who signed the letter themselves included Cati Louet, her daughter Hélène Aussenac, and a woman named Anne Roussin. Again, at least one free African man was among the signatories, in this case, Antoine Kiaka. Meanwhile, the wealthy landowner Marie-Thérèse Rossignol could only make the sign of the cross. By this time, her sister Anne Rossignol had probably left for Le Cap. The letter sought to discourage the French administration from sending *signares* or other *habitants* to Cayenne and to support the access of the *habitants* to free trade, emphasising that they lived on a small island whose population consisted mostly of domestic women slaves and slave owners with little knowledge of agriculture. Yet, at the same time, the *habitants* focused upon the unique situation in Gorée within France or, at least, a larger community of Frenchmen.

[52] 'Les habitants a de l'Isle de Gorée à Le Duc Le Choiseul, Paris de France Ministère et Secretaire de la Guerre et de la Marine', 1763, Pierre François Guillaume Poncet de La Rivière, gouverneur de Gorée (1763/1775), Colonies, Série E 338, 71–76, ANOM. http://anom.archivesnationales.culture.gouv.fr.
[53] Ibid.: http://anom.archivesnationales.culture.gouv.fr/ark:/61561/up424ztxytud.num=20.q=Poncet, 70–76. The three clear signatures were by Pierre Cherville, Kiaka and Waly. Cherville appeared to have transcribed the letter and he may have been a clerk (*greffier*) at Gorée. It has been suggested that he may have been French but he did appear in the 1767 census as a 'free Christian', the same designation as *mulâtre* women and men: Moleur, 'Le droit de propriété', 53.
[54] Angrand, *Le Temps de Signares*, 109.

First, the *habitants* challenged the image that the local French administration had promoted concerning Gorée's 'lazy and useless' population, who drained resources. Positioning themselves apart from the enslaved majority, the *habitants* rhetorically asked: 'Are they useless, those who, unwilling to give their slaves up in service to the king, make it their duty to make their slaves available when needed?' By highlighting their service to the French state through the provision of captives for labour and local projects, the *habitants* asserted their loyalty and value to the French regime. In return, they expected 'care and attention' from French officials. The *habitants* asked the metropolitan government to protect them from the colonisation and migration scheme, addressing the minister (probably of the Navy) as 'our father'.[55]

The final section of the letter turned to the overarching concern of the *habitants*; the exclusive trading rights awarded to the *Compagnie de Guyane* (Guiana Company) in 1777, which frustrated many who wanted to trade on their own account and do business with other merchants.[56] The *habitants* even offered to procure captives for the Company, noting that higher prices would improve the 'mediocre' standard of living of the *habitants* and solve problems for all sides involved.[57] Thus, the *habitants* had a complex relationship with slavery and the enslaved people they kept in their homes. They were willing to participate in the trade and to own other human beings, yet toward these enslaved women, children and men they adopted a maternalist or paternalist posture, whether in recording the baptisms and burials of the enslaved or in hiring them out rather than turn them over to representatives of the king.[58]

[55] Réponse des habitants de Gorée à la demande de M. Armeny de Paradis pour les engager à passer à Cayenne, 1770s?, Colonies, Série E 238, ANOM. The letter is signed and marked by Cati Louet, Durand, Jean Pépin, Antoine Kiaka, Hélène Aussenac, Marie-Thérèse Rossignol, Anne Roussin, Aussenac Baillou, Anne Debane, Porquet ?, Pierre ?, Louison Forcian, Thérèse Dumas. http://anom.archivesnationales.culture.gouv.fr/ark:/61561/up424f13zf.num=20.q=Armeny+de+Paradis, 238–48. Knight-Baylac seems to refer to a related letter that complains of the exclusive trading rights awarded to the Compagnie de Guyane and may have served has a cover letter to the letter responding to the relocation scheme, Knight-Baylac, 'Gorée au XVIIe siècle', 46. Cati Louet also signed numerous petitions in support of Governor Le Brasseur. The petitions were often signed by French men who were part of the administration or the company and sometimes the staff of the fort who themselves were illiterate and could only make the sign of the cross: petitions dated 29 August and 28 October 1777: Joseph Alexandre Le Brasseur, Commissaire général de la Marine puis des Colonies, commissaire ordonnateur à Gorée à Saint-Domingue, intendant général des fonds de la Marine et des Colonies (1768/1788), COL E 267, ANOM, http://anom.archivesnationales.culture.gouv.fr/ark:/61561/up424mggmije.num=20.q=brasseur, 174–5.

[56] Sackur, 'The Development of Creole Society', 300.

[57] Also see, François Zuccarelli, *La vie politique sénégalaise (1789-1940)* (Paris: CHEAM, 1987), 10–15.

[58] For example, see 'Sépultre de Marie Duc-Anne, Négresse captive de Louise Lembrot, 30 novembre 1777'; 'Baptême de Pierre, captif d'Isabelle Morin, Signare, le 8 mars 1778'; 'Baptême de François, petit enfant captif de Jean Pepin, le 8 mars 1778'; 'Etat civil Gorée', 1777–1824, 1DPPC 4849, 85 MIOM 836, ANOM.

The *habitants* depicted themselves in an interdependent relationship with the French. Referring to the French representatives as the 'communal father of the colony' and the 'protector in defence of the oppressed', they postulated that 'Africans make good Frenchmen' ('*Affricains bons françois*').[59] Calling themselves 'good Frenchmen' in the 1770s, the *habitants* appeared to embrace the ideals of assimilation even before these emerged as a doctrine of the French empire in the late eighteenth and early nineteenth centuries.[60] For *mulâtres* and African women and men to claim to be French in the late eighteenth century was extraordinary on several levels.

First, given that primary and secondary sources emphasise that *signares* and the *mulâtre* community were not African, their self-identification as African demonstrates a complex sense of self, apparently going beyond a regional or ethnic identity. Second, their embrace of Frenchness did not erase their 'African-ness' but potentially expanded what it might mean to be French. The entire letter called for special privileges and protection in a space and culture outside of the metropole. Finally, it was mainly women who signed the letter, and women generally outnumbered men across the *mulâtre*, free African and enslaved segments of Gorée society. Often assimilation policy has been seen as creating 'African Frenchmen', but, in the case of this letter, the issue at stake was the potential recognition of 'African Frenchwomen'. The sheer dominance of *mulâtre* and African women as property owners was what made it plausible to suggest such a concept within the context of Gorée, in the first place. But when the Revolution came, women could not fully become citizens. So could African women become French? The ways in which the Gorée letters also incorporated women and African men suggest a broader view of who could be 'free' and 'French' there in the latter half of the eighteenth century. The Revolution began a process of excluding women, under-

---

[59] 'Réponse des habitants de Gorée', 238–48. The letter is signed by Cati Louet, her daughter Hélène Aussenac, St. Estoupan de St. Jean, Durand, Jean Pépin, Antoine Kiaka, Anne Roussin, Aussenac Baillou, Pierre ?, Marked by Marie-Thérèse Rossignol, Thérèse Dumas, Anne Cassano, Louison Forcianque, http://anom.archivesnationales.culture.gouv.fr/ir?c=FRANOM_00019,1.01.336&num=20&ir=FRANOM_00019&start=&q=Paradis&geogname=&date=&from=&to=, 238–48.

[60] The policy of assimilation suggested that colonial subjects could attain 'Frenchness' by adopting French language and culture. Assimilation was always more of a rhetorical and idealised theory than a doctrine that the French practiced actively and consistently, especially in Africa. For classic assimilation studies see, Raymond F. Betts, *Assimilation and Association in French Colonial Theory, 1890–1914* (New York: Columbia University Press, 1961); Michael Crowder, *Senegal: A Study in French Assimilation Policy* (London and New York: Oxford University Press, 1962); Martin D. Lewis, 'One Hundred Million Frenchmen: The "Assimilation" Theory in French Colonial Policy', in Law and Mann, *Comparative Studies in Society and History* (1962): 129–53. For updated analysis see, Alice L. Conklin, *A Mission to Civilize: The Republican Idea of Empire in France and West Africa, 1895–1930* (Stanford, CA: Stanford University Press, 1997). Johnson, *Emergence of Black Politics*, 76–7.

scoring the difficulty of maintaining women and gender as a conscious part of the definition of republican citizenship.

Anne Rossignol was not part of this historical moment in Gorée when elite African and *mulâtre* women and men were declaring Frenchness for themselves in these letters and petitions. However, she and her daughter would certainly have seen similarities between their place of birth and their first adopted home in Saint-Domingue, in terms of layout, style and the prevalence of women of colour with access to wealth and resources. Did elite people like them in Saint-Domingue not already imagine forms of belonging to France by attending church, declaring property ownership and registering marriages like their counterparts across the Atlantic in Gorée? With a Revolution for rights and freedoms raging in the hills above Le Cap, did the enslaved and working women in the city not imagine possibilities for themselves? But even with the ability to prosper, succeed and imagine in Saint-Domingue, all people of colour were acutely aware of ways in which a minority community of whites sought to deny and thwart their dreams of being people who were not excluded based on the colour of their skin. When Anne Rossignol and her daughter later transformed themselves into white women in Charleston, it could easily be read as an act of self-preservation. But in transcending their identities as women of colour to become 'good Americans', they still maintained a connection to France's empire by claiming to be French and being known as former residents of Saint-Domingue. Anne Rossignol's connections to France and Saint-Domingue were always bound to expose her trans-African life whether she and her descendants chose to admit it or not.

Toward a Dramatic History of Trans-African Women

While it may be possible to piece together the outlines of a trans-African theory using Anne Rossignol's unlikely story in the archives from the moment she stepped on a ship headed for France in 1736 to her death as an elderly woman in Charleston, South Carolina, she is both very present and very absent in the sources. There are several documents directly initiated by her but whole periods when her whereabouts and activities, to say nothing of her motivations and thinking remain a mystery. Many of us became historians because we like to hear, read and tell stories; yet history books do not always capture the imagination of readers. As we try to base our interpretations on as solid evidence as possible, we cannot easily fill the yawning gaps in the archive. Debates persist about historical fiction as a more useful way to access complex pasts. Some historians have experimented with biography and narrative while others have fully embraced historical fiction. Erica Armstrong Dunbar's engrossing narrative about Ona Judge Staines, an enslaved woman who fled the household of George and Martha Washington, reveals a different side of urban American life after the Revolution. The captivating historical novel by Tiya Miles bridges Native American and African-American history while engaging with gender and sexuality.[61] Meanwhile, historians increasingly reveal the remarkable mobility among people of colour, whether enslaved or as free migrants, sailors, activists, students and artists. These stories could reorient our understanding of revolution, empire and nation-making.

The term 'dramatic history' usually refers to plays that explore historical events, such as Shakespeare's *War of the Roses* trilogy. What would it mean to develop dramatic history as a new trend in, what Martha Hodes has called experimental history?[62] It could focus on giving space to the obscured stories of women, people of colour, the impoverished, the enslaved and others forced to the margins of society. The intersection of narrative, fiction and history offers unique opportunities to explore how women and men redefined self and community in a changing world.

We historians are often reluctant to write about how sources speak to us and move us. When I learned that Anne Rossignol first travelled to France as a young girl along with her father and his French wife, I saw the face of a child, excited, frightened and unsure. When I thought of her travelling to Saint-Domingue with her young adult daughter and son, I saw a burgeoning matriarch modelling for her children all of the possibilities for their future. I couldn't find her when I looked for her in the midst of the Haitian Revolution. When I read the legal disputes between her descendants I saw people about whom I thought they may have heard stories (or whom they may have tried to forget) – an elderly woman of colour, with a straight back, balancing the weight of an unlikely history of slavery, revolution and privilege on thin shoulders.

So I have dared to think of Anne Rossignol as the kind of everywoman so many of us have met in the archives. Trans-African women like her have held the world together with their surprising actions and innovative thinking. Since those around them saw them as lovers, mothers, wives, sisters or patrons, we strain to hear their whispers concerning their experiences as merchants, travellers, movers and shakers. Yet we need not cover our ears and eyes when they tell us about the other

---

[61] Erica Armstrong Dunbar, *Never Caught: Ona Judge, the Washingtons, and the Relentless Pursuit of Their Runaway Slave*. (New York: Simon & Schuster, 2017); Tiya Miles, *The Cherokee Rose: A Novel of Gardens and Ghosts* (Winston-Salem, NC: John F. Blair, 2015).
[62] Martha Hodes, 'Four Episodes in Re-Creating a Life', Rethinking History: The Journal of Theory and Practice 10 (June 2006): 277–90; Martha Hodes, 'Experimental Writing in the Classroom', Perspectives on History (May 2007), www.historians.org/publications-and-directories/perspectives-on-history/may-2007/experimental-history-in-the-classroom.

women, children and men they claimed to own. They reflected the realities and paradoxes of their times. If we listen and attempt to translate the scraps of their fraught stories into narratives that we can understand and share, we will not be rewriting old histories. We will be writing new ones for the first time.

216 • *Mobility*

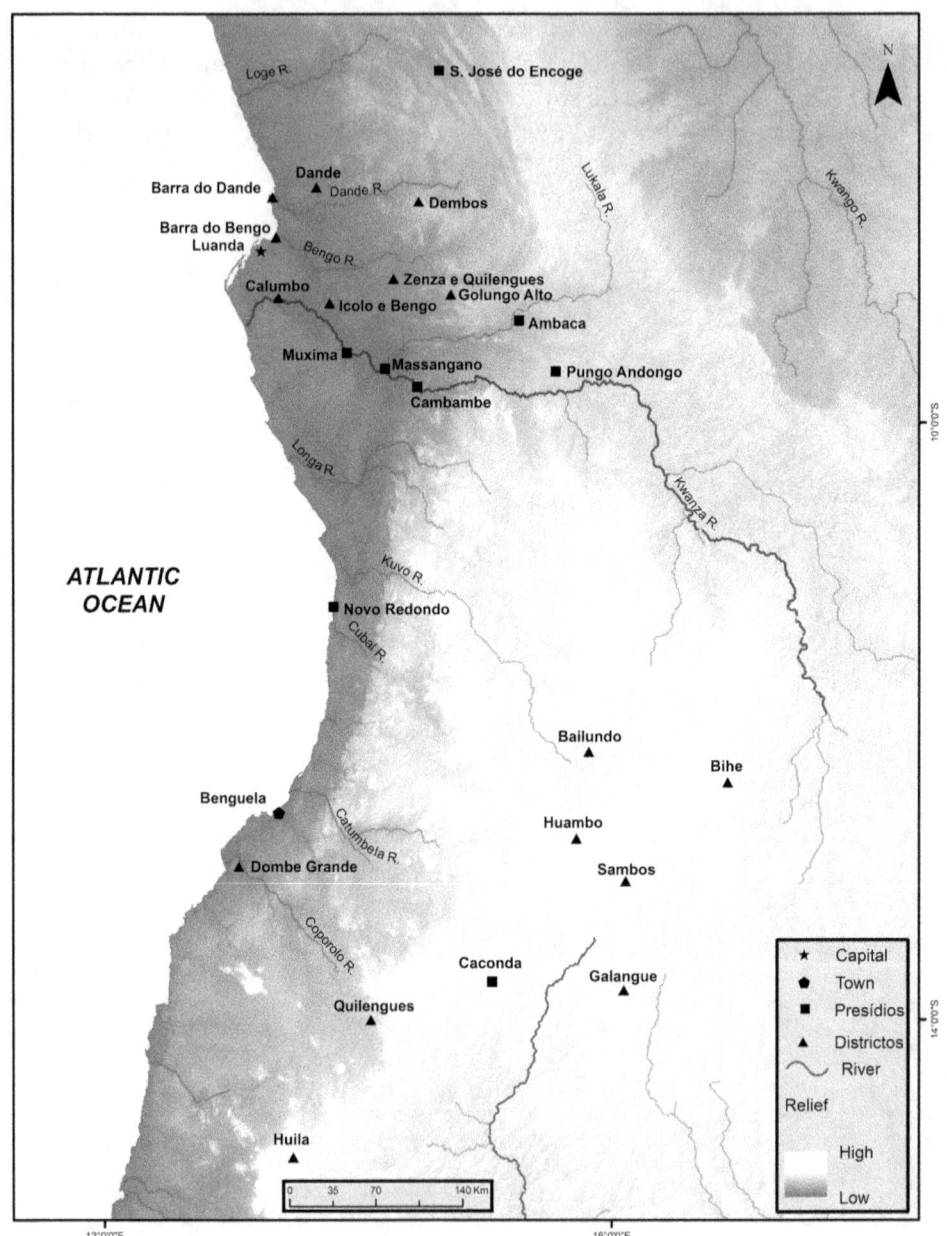

Map 12 Mid-nineteenth-century Angola
(Source: CartogrÁfrica 2017 © Maria Cristina Fernandes)

11

Spouses & Commercial Partners:
Immigrant Men & Locally Born Women in Luanda 1831–1859

VANESSA S. OLIVEIRA

During the nineteenth century, immigrant males settled along the coast of West Central Africa to trade in slaves and the commodities of the so-called 'legitimate' commerce. As was the case in other ports in West Africa, newcomers generally relied on local intermediaries with knowledge of indigenous cultures to establish commercial networks with African suppliers inland. Many cultural brokers were women with whom incoming traders established commercial and, sometimes, intimate relationships. Several locally born wives or partners were traders themselves, operating in the local, regional and, in some cases, international markets. In Angola, the most successful women merchants became known as *donas*, a term that originated from the title granted to noble and royal females in the Iberian Peninsula and was subsequently adopted in Portugal's overseas territories to designate women of high socio-economic status living in accordance with Portuguese norms of respectability.[1]

Since the mid-1970s, the participation of African and Eurafrican women in commerce along the western coast of Africa has been the object of a number of studies. Historians in particular have explored the experiences of female merchants known as *nharas*, *signares*, and *senhoras* in West African ports and their involvement in the trade in slaves.[2] In the particular case

---

[1] Luiz da Silva Pereira Oliveira, *Privilégios da Nobreza e Fidalguia de Portugal* (Lisbon: João Rodrigues Neves, 1806), 172–3; Maria Beatriz Nizza da Silva, *Donas e plebeias na sociedade colonial* (Lisbon: Estampa, 2002).

[2] See, for example, George Brooks, *Eurafricans in Western Africa: Commerce, Social Status, Gender, and Religious Observance from the Sixteenth Century to the Eighteenth Century* (Athens: Ohio University Press, 2003); Bruce Mouser 'Women Slavers of Guinea-Conakry', in Claire Robertson and Martin A. Klein, eds, *Women and Slavery in Africa* (Portsmouth, NH: Heinemann, 1997), 320–39; Philip Havik, *Silences and Soundbytes: The Gendered Dynamics of Trade and Brokerage in the Pre-colonial Guinea Bissau Region* (Munster: LIT, 2004); E. Frances White, *Sierra Leone's Settler Women Traders: Women on the Afro-European Frontier* (Ann Arbor: University of Michigan Press, 1987); Emily L. Osborn, *Our New Husbands Are Here: House*

of Angola, a growing scholarship has highlighted women's agency in the socio-economic fabric of the colony as merchants and cultural brokers.[3]

This chapter dialogues with other works in this volume, particularly with contributions by Hilary Jones and Natalie Everts. Both authors highlight the importance of marriage to European men in advancing the position of women in coastal societies in Senegambia and in the Gold Coast during the eighteenth and nineteenth centuries. This contribution analyses instances of Catholic marriage between immigrant men and Luso-African women in nineteenth-century Luanda, particularly between 1831 and 1859, a period marked by the ban on slave exports and the expansion of the commerce in tropical commodities in West Central Africa. Although marriage to immigrant men helped advance the career of female traders in previous generations, primary sources demonstrate that in the second half of the nineteenth-century women in Luanda were able to become merchants and acquire wealth out of their relationships with foreign men, often through entrepreneurial activities.

Luanda in the Nineteenth Century

Following its foundation in 1576, Luanda became a place of interaction for people from different parts of the Atlantic world. New arrivals were mainly young males who met their daily needs by marrying into local families. These biracial unions gave origin to generations of Luso-Africans who by the mid-nineteenth century had achieved prosperity

---

(contd) *holds, Gender and Politics in a West African State from the Slave Trade to Colonial Rule* (Athens: Ohio University Press, 2011); Hilary Jones, *The Metis of Senegal: Urban Life and Politics in French West Africa* (Indiana University Press, 2013); Pernille Ipsen, *Daughters of the Trade: Atlantic Slavers and Interracial Marriage on the Gold Coast* (Philadelphia: University of Pennsylvania Press, 2015).

[3] Júlio de Castro Lopo, 'Uma rica dona de Luanda', *Portucale* 3 (1948): 129–38; Carlos Alberto Lopes Cardoso, 'Ana Joaquina dos Santos Silva, industrial angolana da segunda metade do século XIX', *Boletim Cultural da Câmara Municipal de Luanda* 32 (1972): 5–14; Douglas L. Wheeler, 'An Angolan Woman of Means: D. Ana Joaquina dos Santos e Silva, Mid-Nineteenth Century Luso-African Merchant-Capitalist of Luanda', *Santa Bárbara Portuguese Studies* 3 (1996): 284–97; Selma Pantoja, 'Women's Work in the Fairs and Markets of Luanda', in Clara Sarmento, ed., *Women in the Portuguese Colonial Empire: The Theatre of Shadows* (Newcastle upon Tyne, UK: Cambridge Scholars Publishing, 2008), 81–94; Selma Pantoja, 'Gênero e comércio: as traficantes de escravos na região de Angola', *Travessias* nos 4/5 (2004): 79–97; Mariana Candido, 'Aguida Gonçalves da Silva, une *dona* à Benguela à la fin du XVIIIe siècle', *Brésil(s).Sciences humaines et sociales* 1 (2012): 33–54; Mariana Candido, 'Strategies for Social Mobility: Liaisons between Foreign Men and Slave Women in Benguela, c. 1770–1850', in Gwyn Campbell and Elizabeth Elbourne, eds, *Sex, Power and Slavery: The Dynamics of Carnal Relations under Enslavement* (Athens: Ohio University Press, 2014), 272–88; Vanessa S. Oliveira, 'Gender, Foodstuff Production and Trade in Late-Eighteenth Century Luanda', *African Economic History* 43 (2015): 57–81; Vanessa S. Oliveira, 'The Gendered Dimension of Trade: Female Traders in Nineteenth Century Luanda', *Portuguese Studies Review* 23, no.2 (2015): 93–121.

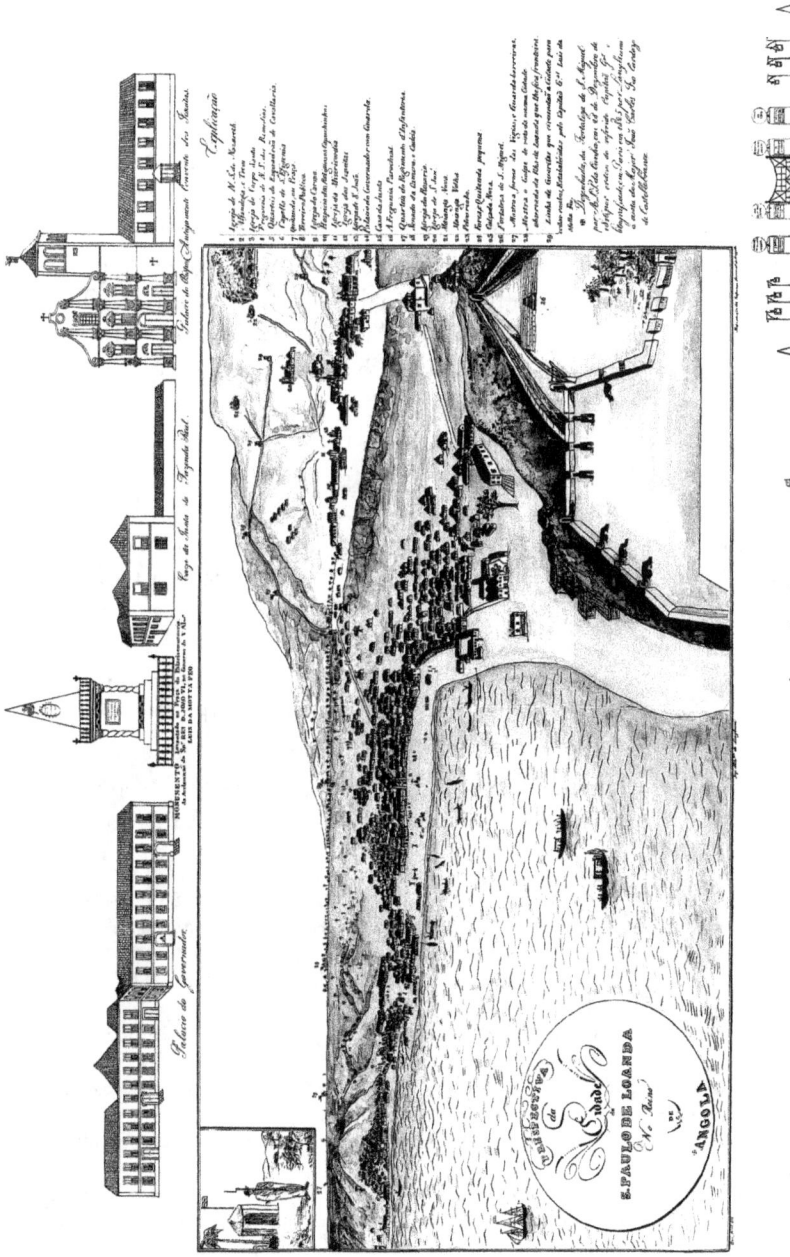

Illustration 8 View of Luanda, 1825, showing the various neighbourhoods where African women circulated and conducted business
(Source: 'Perspectiva da Cidade de S. Paulo de Loanda no Reino de Angola, 1825'; Arquivo Histórico Ultramarino, Iconografia Impressa)

through their participation in local and long-distance trade, including the traffic in slaves.[4] Their male offspring occupied administrative and military positions, while their daughters married incoming traders and officials.

During the era of the slave trade, 12.5 million enslaved Africans were exported to the Americas. Current estimates indicate that about 45 per cent originated from West Central Africa.[5] As the most important port of the transatlantic slave trade, Luanda attracted a significant number of foreigners in search of quick enrichment through the trade in slaves.[6] In 1836, Portugal banned the slave export trade from its African territories, and soon thereafter slave patrols began policing the coast of West Central Africa in search of ships engaged in the illegal shipment of captives.[7] The activities of slave traders in the capital of Angola did not end until the mid-1840s. Thenceforth, slavers transferred their activities to ports north and south of Luanda, where the repression was weak.[8] From these ports, traders continued to export enslaved Africans from Angola until the late 1860s, particularly to Brazil and Cuba.

In 1850, the importation of slaves became illegal in Brazil. The loss of the Brazilian market had a deep impact throughout Angola, as Brazil was the main destination of captives embarked along the coast of the Portuguese *conquista*. As a result, many slave traders left Luanda while others saw their business vanish.[9] Meanwhile, other economic activities received increasing incentives from Portuguese administrators and private investors. The extraction of ivory and bees-wax, as well as the production of palm and groundnut oils, orchil, coffee, cotton and to a lesser extent sugar grew to supply external markets, especially in northern Europe and the United States.[10] Agricultural production also expanded to feed the

[4] On Luso-Africans in Angola, see Joseph C. Miller, *Way of Death: Merchant Capitalism and the Angolan Slave Trade, 1730–1830* (Madison: University of Wisconsin Press, 1988), 245–8.
[5] See estimates available in David Eltis et al., 'Voyages: The Trans-Atlantic Slave Trade Database', Online Database, 2008, www.slavevoyages.org.
[6] Mary C. Karasch, 'The Brazilian Slavers and the Illegal Slave Trade, 1836–1851' (M.A. thesis, University of Wisconsin, 1967), 24–5.
[7] Jill Dias, 'A sociedade colonial de Angola e o liberalismo português (c. 1820–1850)', in Miriam H. Pereira et al., eds, *O Liberalismo na Península Ibérica na primeira metade do século XIX: comunicações ao colóquio organizado pelo Centro de Estudos de História Contemporânea Portuguesa*, vol. I (Lisbon: Sá da Costa Editora, 1982), 280.
[8] Valentim Alexandre and Jill Dias, eds, *O Império Africano 1825–1890* (Lisbon: Estampa, 1998), 371, 373.
[9] According to Alexandre and Dias, *O Império Africano*, 370, traders started closing their businesses in Angola from the 1820s due to the uncertainty regarding the continuity of the slave trade.
[10] Aida Freudenthal, *Arimos e fazendas: a transição agrária em Angola, 1850–1880* (Luanda: Chá de Caxinde, 2005), 45; José de Almeida Santos, *Vinte anos decisivos da vida de uma cidade (1845–1864)* (Câmara Municipal de Luanda, 1970), 16; Paul E. Lovejoy, *Transformations in Slavery: A History of Slavery in Africa*. 3rd edition (New York: Cambridge University Press, 2012), 230–31.

growing population and to serve as credit in the acquisition of *fazendas* or imported trade goods exchanged for tropical commodities in the interior.[11]

From the early 1800s to 1844, Luanda confronted a decline in the number of inhabitants due to the intense Brazilian demand for captives. While in 1802 the population of the city totalled 6,925 people, in 1844 this number had decreased to 5,605.[12] Following the ban on the slave trade, the number of Luanda's residents began to rise again: by 1850, it had reached 12,565. Administrative authorities classified inhabitants into three colour groups: 1,240 *brancos* (whites), 2,055 *pardos* (of mixed European and African descent) and 9,270 *pretos* (blacks). The population growth resulted from the retention of slaves who would otherwise have been exported to the Americas.[13]

Notwithstanding the population increase, the number of whites actually fell from 1,601 to 1,240 between 1844 and 1850. The white population was made up of 820 males and 420 females in 1850.[14] The high death rates among the Portuguese and Brazilians as well as the departure of slave traders may have been the cause of the decline.[15] Still, the author of the *Almanak statistico da provincia d'Angola e suas dependencias para o anno de 1852* claimed that Luanda then had only 830 white inhabitants, 670 male and only 160 female.[16] It is likely that the author of this publication was a white Portuguese, dissatisfied with the labelling of people of mixed ancestry as 'white'. Luso-African families, who had used their wealth to lighten their skin, were transferred to the category of *pardos*.

Pretos and *pardos* together made up 11,325 or 90 per cent of Luanda population. A significant proportion of *pretos* were enslaved (5,900) with women corresponding to 63.5 per cent of the slaves in the city. In general, black women (free and enslaved) represented about 47 per cent of the population. As a historian of the Angolan past has stressed, by 1850 Luanda had become far darker and female-dominated.[17] Free and enslaved black women constituted an important proportion of the labour force as housekeepers, seamstresses, laundresses, water carriers, and *quitandeiras* (street

---

[11] Carlos José Caldeira, *Apontamentos D'Uma Viagem de Lisbon á China e da China a Lisbon*, II (Lisbon: Typograhia de Castro & Irmão, 1853), 213; Alexandre and Dias, *O Império Africano*, 385–6, 404; José C. Curto, 'The Anatomy of a Demographic Explosion: Luanda, 1844–1850', *International Journal of African Historical Studies* 32 (1999): 381–405.

[12] José C. Curto and Raymond R. Gervais, 'The Population History of Luanda of Luanda during the late Atlantic Slave Trade, 1781–1844', *African Economic History* 29 (2001): 1–59.

[13] Curto, 'The Anatomy of a Demographic Explosion'.

[14] Ibid.

[15] Miller, *Way of Death*, 284; Alexandre and Dias, *O Império Africano*, 370.

[16] José C. Curto, 'Whitening the "White" Population: An Analysis of the 1850 Censuses of Luanda', in Selma Pantoja and Estevam C. Thompson, eds, *Em torno de Angola: narrativas, identidades e as conexões atlânticas* (São Paulo: Intermeios, 2014), 225–47.

[17] Curto, 'The Anatomy of a Demographic Explosion', 401.

vendors) as well as tending to the land in the *arimos* (agricultural properties) and gardens located in the rural suburbs.[18]

Some white males had arrived in the colony between the 1820s and the 1850s, escaping the civil wars involving constitutionalists and absolutists in Portugal. Although most Portuguese subjects chose Brazil as their new destination, a smaller number settled in Angola – then seen as the 'white man's grave'.[19] The new immigrants were poor men with little or no capital. While some arrived as administrative and military officials, others became shop and tavern-keepers attending to the daily needs of inhabitants.[20]

Travellers who sojourned in Luanda during the mid-nineteenth century commented on the lack of white women. In the 1850s, the British traveller Joachim John Monteiro stated, 'there is not much society in Loanda, as but few of the Portuguese bring their wives and families with them, and there are but few white women'.[21] In the same decade, the Portuguese Francisco Travassos Valdez remarked, 'in consequence of the paucity of white women, the Portuguese formed alliances with women of colour and half-castes, to whom, and to their children, the offspring of such connections, they manifest great affection'.[22] Indeed, liaisons between immigrant men and local women were quite common. Nevertheless, the lack of white women was not the only reason why foreign males entered into relationships with African and Luso-African women.

Since the early days of European expansion, travellers and explorers described overseas possessions as a place of sexual freedom.[23] In the early nineteenth century, the French traveller Jean-Baptiste Douville pointed to the 'easiness' of African women in Angola who attracted men 'unable to resist the pleasures of sensuality'.[24] While sex was an important factor in the advances of white men towards local women, access to personal and commercial networks was also relevant.[25] Marriage petitions and

---

[18] Vanessa S. Oliveira, 'Trabalho escravo e ocupações urbanas em Luanda na segunda metade do século XIX', in Selma Pantoja and Estevam C. Thompson, eds, *Em torno de Angola: narrativas, identidades e as conexões atlânticas* (São Paulo: Intermeios, 2014), 249–75.

[19] Alexandre and Dias, *O Império Africano*, 439. Whites did not immigrate to Angola in significant numbers until the 1870s.

[20] Ibid., 440.

[21] Joachim John Monteiro, *Angola and the River Congo*, II (London: Macmillan, 1875), 49.

[22] Francisco Travassos Valdez, *Six Years of a Traveller's Life in Western Africa*, II (London: Hurst and Blackett, 1861), 171.

[23] Anne McClintock, *Imperial Leather: Race, Gender and Sexuality in the Colonial Conquest* (New York: Routledge, 1995). For Western perceptions of African women as licentious see in this volume Schwarz, 'Adaptation in the Aftermath of Slavery'; and Hilary Jones, 'Women, Family & Daily Life'.

[24] Jean Baptiste Douville, *Voyage au Congo et dans l'intérieur de l'Afrique équinoxale ... 1828, 1829, 1830*, vol. I (Paris: J. Renouard, 1832), 53.

[25] Mariana P. Candido, *An African Slaving Port and the Atlantic World: Benguela and its Hinterland* (New York: Cambridge University Press, 2013), 136–7.

registers of the purchase and sale of property indicate that some immigrant males were able to rise economically after marrying wealthy Luso-African women, the daughters of biracial marriages. As was the case in Benguela, Saint Louis, Cacheu, Bissau and other African coastal towns, some women in Luanda owned considerable wealth, including slaves, land and luxury goods and were active merchants in the local market.[26] Unlike women in the Gambia region, who had their economic independence threatened by the introduction of cash crops, women in Angola benefited from the increasing need for foodstuffs in the urban market and invested in the cultivation of cotton and sugar cane.[27]

Marriage Practices in Luanda

Along the western coast of Africa, the exchange of women was a means to consolidate relationships between foreigners and local elites, allowing different groups of people to be henceforth connected.[28] In fact, in the nineteenth century, marriage was a strategy to consolidate commercial and political alliances in both Portugal itself and its overseas territories.[29] Nevertheless, strategies involved did not exclude the possibility of affection and sexual attraction between the men and women who became part of these alliances.

In Angola, some couples cohabitated or married in accordance with local practices; unions celebrated *à moda do país*, or according to the customs of the country, were known as *lambamentos*. In the late eighteenth century, the Brazilian military officer Elias Alexandre da Silva Corrêa claimed that African families 'offered female virginity to anyone willing to pay', adding: 'Catholics are the least scrupulous buyers, competing in auctions for women'.[30] What he labelled 'auction' was in fact the bridewealth or

---

[26] See the chapters by Mariana C. Candido, Esteban A. Salas, Suzanne Schwarz and Hilary Jones in this volume.

[27] On the challenges women faced in the Gambia region with the introduction of cash crop, see Assan Sarr's contribution in this volume. For women farmers in mid-nineteenth century Angola, see Selma Pantoja, 'Donas de "Arimos": um negócio feminino no abastecimento de gêneros alimentícios em Luanda (séculos XVIII e XIX)', in Selma Pantoja and Carlos Alberto Reis de Paula, eds, *Entre Áfricas e Brasís* (Brasília: Paralelo 15 Editores, 2001), 35–49; Mariana P. Candido, 'Women, Family, and Landed Property in Nineteenth-Century Benguela', *African Economic History* 43 (2015), 136–61.

[28] Catherine Coquery-Vidrovitch, *African Women: A Modern History* (Boulder, CO: Westview Press, 1987), 19; Miller, *Way of Death*, 290.

[29] George Winius and B. W. Diffie, *Foundations of the Portuguese Empire, 1415–1825*, vol. I (Minneapolis: University of Minnesota Press, 1977), 148. For marriage in Angola, see Miller, *Way of Death*, 246–50. For Brazil, see Maria Beatriz Nizza da Silva, *Sistema de casamento no Brasil colonial* (São Paulo: Editora da Universidade de São Paulo, 1978).

[30] Elias Alexandre da Silva Corrêa, *História de Angola*, vol. I (Lisbon: Editorial Ática, 1937), 88–90.

payment made to seal marriage contracts between African families. By the mid-1840s, bridewealth amounted to about 50,000 réis in the city;[31] in the interior, it was paid in *fazendas* (textiles) and *missangas* (beads), which were the local currency.[32] The value was comparable to that of a slave, whose price was then about 40,000 réis.[33] Although unrecognised by the Catholic Church, Christian men engaged in these unions. In the mid-nineteenth century, the Portuguese António Francisco Ferreira da Silva Porto and the Hungarian László Magyar, for example, married women related to the *sobas* (African rulers) of Bihé, a district located in Central Angola. Through these relationships, Silva Porto and Magyar were able to access local resources and trade networks.[34]

Unlike other European powers in West Africa, the Portuguese administration in Angola encouraged men to marry locally.[35] Nevertheless, Catholic marriages were far from commonplace, and only elites drew upon this sacrament. Jan Vansina has explained that the difficulties in arranging Catholic weddings in the *presídio* (interior administrative outpost) of Ambaca, east of Luanda, related to the requirement of a dowry.[36] However, other factors may have contributed to the low incidence of Catholic matrimony, including the costs and bureaucracy involved in the process. In the colonial capital, men and women who wished to marry had to file a petition with the Ecclesiastical Board, pay a fee, and present a guarantor (*fiador*). The Board often requested documentation from both parties, including baptismal registers, proof of marital status, the burial record of one's previous spouse (in the case of a widow/widower) and banns of marriage.[37] For immigrant individ-

---

[31] At this time, 50,000 réis was equivalent to approximately £200 (British pounds). For currency conversion see John Husband, A System of Arithmetic; Containing an Extensive Course of Commercial and Mental Calculations, on A New and Comprehensive Plan (Edinburgh: Oliver & Boyd; London: Simpkin, Marshall, & Co., 1841), 105.

[32] António Gil, *Considerações sobre alguns pontos mais importantes da moral religiosa e systema de jurisprundência dos pretos do continente da África Occidental portuguesa além do Equador, tendentes a dar alguma idea do character peculiar das suas instituicções primitivas* (Lisbon: Typografia da Academia, 1854), 18–20.

[33] Ibid., 20.

[34] Linda M. Heywood, *Contested Power in Angola, 1840s to the Present* (Rochester, NY: University of Rochester Press, 2000), 19; Candido, *An African Slaving Port*, 134. For other cases of marriages celebrated according to the 'customs of the country' in this volume, see Natalie Everts, 'Parrying Palavers'; Kriger, 'From Child Slave to Madam Esperance'; Hilary Jones, 'Women, Family & Daily Life'.

[35] Biblioteca Nacional de Lisboa (BNL), Códice 8744, 'Carta de Dom Francisco Inocêncio de Sousa Coutinho para Dom António de Lencastre', 26 November, 1772, f. 303v.

[36] Jan Vansina, 'Ambaca Society and the Slave Trade c. 1760–1845', *The Journal of African History* 46, no. 1 (2005): 9. The custom of providing dowries was common among prosperous families in Portugal and its overseas territories. See Código Philipino, Livro 4, título XCVII. www1.ci.uc.pt/ihti/proj/filipinas/ordenacoes.htm (accessed 18 November 2014).

[37] Donald Ramos, 'Marriage and the Family in Colonial Vila Rica', in Maria Beatriz Nizza da Silva, ed., *Families in the Expansion of Europe, 1500–1800* (Brookfield, VT: Ashgate, 1998), 51.

uals, requesting documents from parishes abroad cost money and took time. In 1849, the Portuguese Gaspar Lázaro filed a petition to marry Dona Maria José da Conceição de Jesus, born in Luanda.[38] The Board requested Gaspar's register of baptism, which had to be sent from Braga, in the far north of Portugal. A year later, Gaspar was still waiting for the document.[39] Most foreign men wishing to marry were only able to present the necessary documentation eight to twelve months after they had filed a petition.

Sources

Single immigrant men of every social class sought wives among the heiresses of wealthy Luso-African families in Luanda. These women professed Christianity, adopted Portuguese names, dressed in European fashion and spoke Portuguese and Kimbundo. The wealthiest among them lived in Portuguese-style houses, called *sobrados*.[40] They were therefore considered more 'civilised' than the indigenous Mbundu population and soon attracted the attention of settlers.[41] In these cases, a Catholic marriage was usually celebrated. The majority of the men and women who married in Portugal and its dominions did so under the condition of a *carta de ametade* ('charter of halves') and became *meeiros* (co-owners) of the family estate.[42] The offspring resulting from unions sanctioned by the Catholic Church were thus considered legitimate and able to inherit from their foreign fathers.[43] Even *filhos naturais* (children born outside Catholic wedlock) were entitled to a share of the inheritance, as long as they were not the product of adultery or incest.[44]

Through marriage, incoming males accessed an established household and networks that enhanced their participation in local commerce. Meanwhile, they counted on the companionship of a spouse or partner and on connections with her family members, usually merchants who had built their careers as slave traders. By giving their daughters away in marriage

[38] Bispado de Luanda (BL), Angola, 'Termos de Fiança', 1837–1859, fls 16v–17.
[39] BL, 'Termos de Fiança', 1837–1859, fls 19v–20.
[40] Pantoja, 'Donas de "Arimos"'; Candido, 'Aguida Gonçalves da Silva'; Oliveira, 'The Gendered Dimension of Trade'.
[41] Josephine Beoku-Betts, 'Western Perceptions of African Women in the 19th & Early 20th Centuries', in Andrea Cornwall, ed., *Readings in Gender in Africa* (Bloomington: Indiana University Press, 2005), 20–25.
[42] Alida C. Metcalf, 'Women and Means: Women and Family Property in Colonial Brazil', in Maria Beatriz Nizza da Silva, ed., *Families in the Expansion of Europe, 1500–1800* (Brookfield, VT: Ashgate, 1998), 291.
[43] Código Philipino, Livro 1, título LXXXVIII, 206–15, www1.ci.uc.pt/ihti/proj/filipinas/ordenacoes.htm (accessed 17 November 2014).
[44] Fathers usually made provisions for children born out of wedlock in their wills: Ramos, 'Marriage and the Family', 223.

to foreign men, Luso-African families secured access to imported items and an export market for African commodities. The women, in turn, had access to both worlds, turning into intermediaries between foreign traders on the coast and African suppliers inland. They could market locally the imports their husbands supplied and use them as symbols of prestige.[45] As Mariana P. Candido's chapter in this volume demonstrates, Africans living in coastal areas and in the interior were interested in material goods produced elsewhere.

This study draws upon a selection of 107 marriage petitions filed in the Ecclesiastical Board of Luanda between 1831 and 1859. This selection obviously does not reflect the totality of marriages celebrated in the city during this period, as petitions may have been registered in other codices. Furthermore, common-law unions were the most frequent kind of relationship in Luanda, irrespective of the colour and social status of the individuals.[46]

Men and women filed marriage petitions in the Ecclesiastical Board; some were born in Angola, while others came from abroad. Couples filed eight petitions, six of which related to individuals born in Portugal. For instance, the soldier António dos Santos and Maria Rita do Rosário, both from Portugal, filed a marriage petition in May 1855. The Board requested their register of birth so that the marriage could take place. The couple submitted the documentation after eight months and were finally able to celebrate their marriage.[47] Some couples may have been living under the same roof already, but wished to have their matrimony recognised by the Church and the colonial state.

Females filed eighteen petitions: thirteen women had been born in Angola, while five were originally from Brazil. Few white women settled in Angola before the 1870s; those who did were exiled criminals or accompanied their husbands or parents.[48] Twelve locally born women filed petitions to marry immigrant men; the only exception was Dona Tereza Nogueira da Silva, born in the colonial capital, who married Nicolau Lorea, a native of Massangano, an outpost south of Luanda, in 1848.[49] As for the Brazilian-born women, they too contracted marriage with foreign men. In February 1855, Dona Leonor da Silva Rego, from Rio de Janeiro, filed a petition to marry the Portuguese João da Silva.[50] Dona Leonor was

[45] Mariana P. Candido, 'Concubinage and Slavery in Benguela, ca. 1750–1850', in Nadine Hunt and Olatunji Ojo, eds, *Slavery and Africa and the Caribbean: A History of Enslavement and Identity since the 18th Century* (London and New York: I.B. Tauris, 2012), 66–84.
[46] José C. Curto, '"As if from a Free Womb": Baptismal Manumissions in the Conceição Parish, Luanda, 1778–1807', *Portuguese Studies Review* 10, no. 1 (2002): 48.
[47] BL, 'Termos de Fiança', 1837–1859, fls 23–4.
[48] Selma Pantoja, 'Inquisição, degredo, e mestiçagem em Angola no século XVIII', *Revista Lusófona de Ciência da Religião* 3, nos 5/6 (2004): 117–36.
[49] BL, 'Termos de Fiança', 1837–1859, fls 39v..
[50] BL, 'Termos de Fiança', 1837–1859, fls 57–57v.

Table 2 Marriage petitions, 1831–1859

Male	Female	Couples	Total
81	18	8	107

(Source: Bispado de Luanda (BL), 'Termos de Fiança', 1837–1859)

the daughter of Ricardo da Silva Rego, a Brazilian merchant established in Luanda.[51] His investments extended to Portugal and Brazil, including properties and capital. In the early nineteenth century, Ricardo was one of the shareholders of the Bank of Brazil alongside other merchants from Angola, Brazil, Portugal and Uruguay.[52] Through this marriage, João da Silva entered one of the wealthiest families in the colony. After her father's death in the early 1860s, Dona Leonor and her siblings Dona Ana, Dona Henriqueta and Ricardo inherited 1,936,083 réis in shares of what had been the Bank of Brazil, as well as properties and credit in Angola, Brazil and Portugal.[53]

Males filed 81 petitions; 51 of these men were born abroad in places such as Brazil (3), France (1), the Atlantic Islands (5), and Portugal (42). They composed a diverse group, ranging from military and administrative personnel to petty traders. Out of 51 foreign men, 48 chose to marry women born locally. Their wives-to-be had been born in Luanda, with the exception of three: Dona Luísa da Fonseca Negrão, from Benguela, who married Germano Francisco da Câmara, a native of the Island of Madeira, in 1847;[54] Jerônimo Rodrigues da Rocha, born in Lisbon, filed a petition in 1847 to marry a woman born in the interior outpost of Ambaca whose name was not listed;[55] while Dona Maria Vieira d'Olin, from the District of Icolo e Bengo, married Joaquim Nogueira, from Portugal, in 1853.[56] Not surprisingly, all the women who were about to become wives of the foreign men filing these petitions were *donas*, meaning that they came from Luso-African families of high socio-economic status and were accomplished in Portuguese culture.

---

[51] *Almanach para o Anno de 1800* (Lisbon: Oficina de Antonio Rodrigues Galhardo, 1800), 444–5.
[52] *Annaes do Parlamento Brasileiro Sessão de 1838*, Tomo II (Rio de Janeiro: Typographia de Viuva Pinto & Filho, 1887), 197.
[53] Arquivo Nacional de Angola (ANA), Códice 7615, 'Escritura de Quitação de Herança', 5 March 1869, f. 20v; Annaes do Parlamento Brasileiro, 197. By 1860, this was equivalent to £8,712. For currency conversion see W. G. Clarence-Smith, The Third Portuguese Empire, 1825-1975: A Study in Economic Imperialism (Manchester University Press, 1985), 277.
[54] BL, 'Termos de Fiança', 1837–1859, fls 37v–38.
[55] BL, 'Termos de Fiança', 1837–1859, fls 36v–37.
[56] BL, 'Termos de Fiança', 1837–1859, fls 56v.

Marrying in a Foreign Land

This section explores four instances of Catholic marriage between Luso-African women and immigrant men. Although the sources available do not allow for a full reconstruction of their trajectories, they do demonstrate that these women were able to accumulate wealth outside of their relationships with foreign men. This placed Luanda women in a different position from women in other Atlantic coastal areas explored in this volume: Colleen Kriger, Natalie Everts and Hilary Jones explore trajectories of women who relied on connections with European authorities and merchants to achieve protection and enrichment. While women from previous generations became wealthy through relationships with immigrant husbands, by the mid-nineteenth century Luso-African women in Luanda had achieved wealth through participation in the supply of foodstuffs or inherited it from their parents. Some poor immigrant men of Portuguese and Brazilian origin were only able to prosper economically due to the wealth and prestige of their Luso-African wives.

Dona Tereza de Jesus Pereira Bastos was *filha natural* (born from parents who were not married in the Catholic Church) of José António Pereira Bastos and an unknown woman, probably locally born. Her father died some time prior to 1846, when Dona Tereza was still a child. Bastos left significant property, including slaves, land and urban real estate.[57] His death had probably been unexpected, giving him no time to make a will. Early in 1846, Dona Tereza, then 10 or 11 years old and living under the protection of a guardian, married a certain Félix de Almeida. This union astonished the Luanda authorities, as the bride was an orphaned underage girl.[58] The case appeared in the local gazette, the *Boletim Oficial de Angola*, as the authorities suspected that Félix and the guardian were trying to put their hands on the young girl's inheritance.[59] At the beginning of 1848, Dona Tereza, now of legal age, initiated a judicial battle to be recognised as Bastos' heir.[60] On 25 November 1848, a judge in Luanda finally granted Dona Tereza the right to her father's inheritance.[61] Félix, however, did not live long enough to benefit from his wife's inheritance. Even before the judge made his ruling, in September 1848, Dona Tereza

---

[57] Boletim Oficial de Angola (BOA), no. 179, 3 March 1849, 3.
[58] The age of consent for girls in the Portuguese empire was 12 years: *Constituições Primeiras do Arcebispado da Bahia*, Liv I, tit. LXVII. https://archive.org/details/constituicoenspr00cath (accessed 8 May 2015).
[59] BOA, no. 52, 5 September 1846, 1.
[60] BOA, no. 179, 29 January 1848, 4. Women married to immigrant men according to local customs often had to fight in court to secure inheritance for their offspring and for themselves. Note the parallels to the case of Esperance, discussed by Kriger in this volume.
[61] BOA, no. 165, 25 November 1848, 2. The Entitlement of Heirs (*Habilitação de Herdeiros*) was required for someone to inherit anything in Portugal.

entered her second marriage, this time with the Portuguese Albino José Soares da Costa Magalhães.[62] Her second husband had arrived in Luanda in the mid-1840s, establishing himself as a shopkeeper.[63] Dona Tereza, who must have been around 14 years old, was already a well-off woman, since she had inherited assets from her first husband and from her father.

Albino's career in Angola rapidly progressed after his marriage to Dona Tereza. In 1855, the former shopkeeper and his wife founded the plantation *Protótipo* in the District of Cazengo, where 400 slaves and *libertos* (freed Africans) cultivated coffee, the most profitable commodity of the Angolan export trade. The *Protótipo* became the largest and most productive coffee plantation of Angola and established Albino as one of its wealthiest men.[64] During the 1860s, Albino acquired several properties, including two islands, three *arimos*, a ship and a *sobrado*.[65] In 1864, Albino was one of the eight associates of the Luanda Agricultural Society alongside other prominent merchants.[66] His prestige was further enhanced by the title of *Comendador da Ordem de Cristo* (Knight of the Order of Christ), granted to men for their distinguished service to Portugal.[67]

After his marriage to Dona Tereza, the former shopkeeper became known as the *Barão do Café* or Coffee Baron. It is unlikely that Albino's ascent would have happened without the funds his wife inherited from her father and her former husband. Moreover, her local knowledge and prestige certainly assisted his career. Following Albino's death, Dona Tereza managed the couple's estate until their three children reached adulthood.[68]

Dona Ana de Jesus Guerra was the daughter of Cândido José dos Santos Guerra, a prominent slaveholder and landowner in Luanda, as well as a slave dealer. Between 1836 and 1867, Cândido Guerra illegally exported slaves to Brazil. In 1847, his ship *Rosa* crossed the Atlantic twice, disembarking a cargo of 980 slaves in Pernambuco, north-eastern Brazil.[69] Cândido Guerra also owned *arimos* where enslaved Africans produced maize for subsistence and to supply the *Terreiro Público*, the public market of

---

[62] BL, Termos de Fiança 1837–1857, f. 92.
[63] BOA, no. 237, 13 April 1850, 3.
[64] Freudenthal, *Arimos e Fazendas*, 173–5.
[65] Arquivo Nacional de Angola, Luanda (ANA) Códice 3928, 'Escritura de Compra e Venda', 2 August 1869, ff. 28 and 32v.
[66] ANA, Códice 3844, 'Escritura e Regulamento da Associação Agrícola de Luanda', 15 October 1864, f. 19.
[67] In a register of property sale from 1869, Albino is referred to as *Comendador da Ordem de Cristo*: ANA, Códice 3928, 'Escritura de Compra e Venda', 2 August 1869, f. 32v.
[68] Freudenthal, *Arimos e Fazendas*, 175. For other plantations managed by women in the hinterland of Luanda, see Oliveira, 'The Gendered Dimension of Trade', 116–17. Women also managed plantations in the region of Benguela, south of Luanda. See, for example, the case of Dona Teresa Barruncho in Candido, 'Women, Family, and Landed Property', 149.
[69] Eltis et al., 'Voyages', Voyage Id. 49392 and 49393.

Luanda.[70] In 1854, he became president of the Luanda Municipal Council, enhancing his prestige and contributing to his economic success.[71]

In July 1853, Eliziário Damião de Oliveira, a Brazilian trader, married Dona Ana de Jesus Guerra.[72] Through this union, Eliziário entered an established merchant family, which gave him access to the local market in slaves and foodstuffs, as well as the illegal shipment of captives to the Americas. Sometime after the marriage, Eliziário purchased a vessel, the *Esperança*, most likely to engage in slaving, as did his father-in-law.[73] By marrying his daughter to Eliziário, Cândido Guerra strengthened his ties with Brazil, the main destination of the slaves he exported. Nevertheless, his son-in-law did not survive the diseases of the land, dying a few years after the marriage.[74] A short life span was a major characteristic of the white men who settled in Angola, notorious for its unhealthy environment. Many traders died before being able to amass significant capital. Those who survived, however, could hope for a prosperous career. Several wives of foreign-born men became widows in their youth, as did Dona Ana Guerra, inheriting whatever their husbands had accumulated. These young widows became attractive partners for incoming males.

Some wealthy women were aware of the risks of entering marriage with immigrant men with no attachment to the land. Portuguese and Brazilian traders were constantly crossing the Atlantic Ocean. Many wealthy Luso-African women were literate and had connections to people who advised them on how to preserve their wealth. Some brides opted for self-endowment and contracts of marriage instead of the more common charter of halves, so that their property did not become part of the couple's estate. In these cases, the bride and the groom set in the contract the specific details regarding the ownership of assets.[75] Dona Maria Joaquina do Amaral owned captives and agricultural properties, where she produced maize to supply the *Terreiro Público*.[76] In 1844, she married the Portuguese António Balbino Rosa.[77] Dona Maria Joaquina chose to register her union to Rosa through a contract of marriage establishing that only the assets the couple acquired after marriage were subject to

---

[70] ANA, Códice 2845, 'Registro de Escravos', 1855, fls 55v–74; Biblioteca Municipal de Luanda (BML), Códice 055, vol. II, 'Registo de Entrada e Saída de Milho',1850–57, 37–8, 65–6.
[71] *Annaes do Conselho Ultramarino*, Série 1, Fev. 1854 a Dez 1858 (Lisbon: Imprensa Nacional, 1867), 621–2.
[72] BL, Termos de Fiança 1837–1857, fls 106–7.
[73] *Annaes do Conselho Ultramarino*, Série 1, 149.
[74] ANA, Códice 5644, f. 68v.
[75] Metcalf, 'Women and Means', 278–9.
[76] Biblioteca Municipal de Luanda, Angola (BML), Códice 055, Vol. II, 'Registo de Entrada e Saída de Milho', 1850–57, fls 9–10; ANA, Códice 2862, 'Registro de Escravos', 1860, fls 55v–56.
[77] BL, Termos de Fiança 1837–1857, fls 26v–27.

co-ownership. Therefore, Dona Maria Joaquina remained the sole owner of the assets she had accumulated through her entrepreneurial activities before the marriage, including land, captives and credit.

In spite of the efforts of families to find 'proper' suitors for their sons and daughters, some couples ended up living apart or divorcing. In August 1848, Dona Maria Joaquina accused António Balbino Rosa of *sevícias* (physical abuse).[78] The couple agreed before a judge to live apart for the period of two years, 'as there is strong possibility of reconciliation'.[79] Whether Dona Maria Joaquina and Rosa were able to be reconciled after the temporary separation is unknown. Had she decided to divorce António Rosa, the contract of marriage guaranteed full ownership over any assets she brought to the marriage: only the property the couple acquired after matrimony would have to have been divided.

Dona Ana Joaquina do Amaral, Dona Maria Joaquina's sister, was also a supplier of maize to the *Terreiro Público*.[80] In 1859, she married Portuguese António Félix Machado, a tavern-keeper who had arrived to Luanda in the mid-1840s.[81] Before the marriage, however, she had the local notary write a register of dowry in which she endowed herself with 10,000,000 réis, declaring that the value represented 'capital from her business as a merchant'.[82] By converting the capital of her business into a dowry, Dona Ana Joaquina guaranteed that it would not become part of the couple's estate. Only the assets the husband and wife acquired after the marriage were subject to co-ownership. Indeed, after the marriage, Machado and his wife acquired several properties, including two *sobrados*, a *musseque* (country estate) and plots of land.[83] Like Albino, Machado eventually rose from the status of a tavern-keeper to that of a large-scale merchant, engaging in the illegal shipment of enslaved Africans to the Americas.[84] Although some tavern-keepers exported a few captives now and then, it is unlikely that Machado would have acquired capital to become a prominent slave trader solely through his activity as a petty trader. He probably

---

[78] The Catholic Church then recognised some instances in which a divorce was acceptable, including *sevícias* and adultery: Silva, *Sistema de Casamento*, 210–43.
[79] BOA, no. 150, 12 August 1848, 1.
[80] BML, Códice 055, Vol. II, 'Registo de Entrada e Saída de Milho', 1850–57, f. 99.
[81] BL, Termos de Fiança 1837–1857, 66v–67; BML, Códice 42-42, 'Termos de correção', 9 February 1842, 22v–23.
[82] ANA, Códice 5613, 'Escritura de Dote e Casamento', 25 June 1859, f. 60. This sum was equivalent to £45,000. For currency conversion see Clarence-Smith, The Third Portuguese Empire, 277.
[83] ANA, Códice 3843, 'Escritura de Compra e Venda', 21 November 1865, f. 15v; ANA, Códice 3844, 'Escritura de Compra e Venda', 1865, f. 65; ANA, Códice 8400, 'Escritura de Compra e Venda', 21 April 1867, f. 43v; ANA, Códice 3844, 'Escritura de Compra e Venda', 9 February 1866, f. 90.
[84] Roquinaldo Ferreira, 'Dos Sertões ao Atlântico: Tráfico Ilegal de Escravos e Comércio Lícito em Angola, 1830–1860' (M.A. thesis, Universidade Federal do Rio de Janeiro, 1996), 97.

built his career with the financial support and commercial networks of his wife. The Amaral sisters were no doubt aware of the benefits conferred upon them by Portuguese law. Both women were able to write, indicating that they had received some formal education abroad or from a tutor in Luanda.[85] Their literacy, wealth and connections with Portuguese authorities brought advantages in this colonial environment.

Conclusion

From its foundation in the sixteenth century, Luanda became a space of interaction between local and foreign people. As the most important port of the transatlantic slave trade, the colonial capital of Angola attracted military and administrative personnel, as well as traders in search of quick enrichment. The lack of European women, together with the requirements of trade and everyday life, contributed to the development of short- and long-term liaisons between incoming males and local women. Single settlers especially opted for Catholic marriages with the daughters of prominent Luso-African families.

As the marriage petitions suggest, immigrant men chose to marry women born into families of high socio-economic status and versed in Portuguese culture. Some females were already economically well-off due to their entrepreneurial activities, including the supply of foodstuffs and investments in land and real estate. Foreign petty traders, such as Albino Soares and António Machado, were able to advance their careers through the financial support and commercial networks of their wives.

Through these unions, immigrant men gained access to the comforts of a household, the support of a wife and commercial partner, and a local family, often likewise engaged in commerce. Aware of the benefits their wealth could bring to men of lower socio-economic status with no attachment to the land, some wealthy brides drew upon contracts of marriage and self-endowment to preserve assets they had accumulated before marriage. These unions facilitated the insertion of foreign-born males into a colonial environment that continuously victimised white men at the same time as it contributed to the development of their careers.

---

[85] Jan Vansina, 'Portuguese vs Kimbundu: Language Use in the Colony of Angola (1575–c.1845)', *Bulletin des Séances de l'Académie des Sciences d'Outre-Mer* 47 (2001–2003): 276. The first classes for girls were established only in 1845. Some children of biracial marriages were sent abroad to receive formal education. Although parents usually invested in the education of sons, some girls also enjoyed this prerogative. Here too there are striking similarities to the story of Esperança, discussed by Kriger (this volume).

12

Women, Family & Daily Life in Senegal's Nineteenth-Century Atlantic Towns

HILARY JONES

The emergence of Afro-European societies on Senegal's Atlantic coast is predominantly a history of women. In the heyday of Portuguese trade along the coast of Senegambia in the early seventeenth century, women served as intermediaries between European sailors and African rulers. In the eighteenth century, African families settled around the European forts built on the coastal islands of Gorée and Saint Louis. Some African women who lived in these settlements entered into unions with European merchants, soldiers or officers, called *mariage à la mode du pays* (marriage in the custom of the country). Known in the literature as *signares*, *senhoras* or *nharas*, this class of socially esteemed women became associated with inter-racial marriage and entrepreneurial acumen. *Signareship* resembled the practice of *casar* on the Gold Coast where elders married free daughters or domestic slaves to Europeans resident in the trade towns.[1] In Senegal, however, the extent to which the extended family played a role in brokering marital alliances to expand the lineage and incorporate strangers is unclear. In Senegal as in the Gold Coast, the women who entered into these unions not only facilitated the encounter between Africa and Europe but also provided the foundation for the expansion of commerce and diplomacy. By establishing Afro-European households, these women laid the groundwork that subsequently allowed French officials as well as male rulers, clerics, traders and urban politicians to establish the patterns of accommodation that made colonialism work in the late nineteenth and early twentieth centuries.[2]

---

[1] On the marriage practices adopted by *nharas* and *signares* see George Brooks, *Eurafricans in Western Africa: Commerce, Social Status, Gender, and Religious Observance from the Sixteenth to the Eighteenth Century* (Athens: Ohio University Press, 2003), 206–21. For an explanation of the Dutch derivation of the term *casar* see Natalie Everts' chapter in this volume.

[2] David Robinson argues that for colonialism to work in the Senegalo-Mauritanian zone, colonial officials developed a strategy of accommodation with male actors who were essential

Although historians have paid a great deal of attention to the role of the *signares*, the literature tends to render the women of Saint Louis and Gorée as one-dimensional figures. For example, interpretations of town life gloss over Muslim women's roles; female slaves are quantified in population data, but scholars rarely address them as individual personalities. French officials typically recorded statistics for the 'useful [male] population' of the towns. Furthermore, the administration's bias towards individuals who conformed to French cultural norms meant that extant notarised documents and the civil registries tend to reflect the marital, baptismal, death and property records of women who belonged to European or property-owning, French-educated mixed-race families rather than those of Muslim and African women. One informant reminded me that for the women commonly known by the title *signare* we rarely know their actual names or the names of their mothers, sisters and friends.[3] This chapter, thus, sheds light on one aspect of female experience in Senegal's coastal towns, yet in so doing seeks to heighten awareness of the lives of women whose stories may not be reflected in the surviving documentation.[4] As the chapters of Mariana Candido, Natalie Everts, Vanessa Oliveira and Colleen Krieger in this volume attest, women of West and West Central Africa's coastal trading towns did not constitute a monolithic group but rather cultivated their own individual tastes and relationships.

This chapter delves deeper into the individual lives of women of Saint Louis and Gorée by considering intimate relationships between men and women and ways in which women developed friendships with other women as well as strategies for social and economic security in a period when the slave trade and imperialism brought new challenges. I rely on documents from family archives, inventories of inheritance settlements and property transactions. The women concerned rarely recorded their own feelings or lived experience in written documentation. Recently historians have mined letters, diaries, portraits and even watercolour paintings for clues about intimacy between African women and Euro-

---

(contd) to economic and political relations in the region. While Robinson focuses on male power, I suggest that women of Senegal's colonial capital cemented these networks through marriage, extension of kinship ties and the formation of Afro-European households: David Robinson, *Paths of Accommodation: Muslim Societies and French Colonial Authorities in Senegal and Mauritania, 1880–1920* (Athens: Ohio University Press, 2000), 1–7.

[3] Private communication, Saint Louis, Senegal (May 2006).

[4] Although I did not consult documentation from the Muslim Tribunal of Saint Louis for this study, further research into the property transactions and notarised documents adjudicated in the Muslim tribunal and research into the lives of black African, *originaire* traders may yield more information about the lives of Muslim women in Senegal's towns. For an example of an *originaire* trader see Mamadou Diouf, 'Traitants ou négociants? Les commerçants Saint Louisiens (2e moitié du 19e siècle – début 20e siècle): Hamet Gora Diop (1846–1910), étude de cas', in *Commerce et commerçants en Afrique de l'Ouest: Le Sénégal*, Boubacar Barry and Leonhard Harding, eds (Paris: Harmattan, 1992), 107–53.

pean men in the era of the transatlantic slave trade.⁵ Although knowing about the emotional lives of nineteenth-century West African women is difficult to discern, close reading of family records and notarised property transactions offers an idea of women's intimate relationships, their daily lives and the roles that they played in West Africa's Atlantic ports. Marital strategies served as a mechanism for building households and household wealth in the era of the transatlantic slave trade. As slavery and the slave trade ended, multiracial families in Senegal's Atlantic towns relied on family ties and networks of kin and clients to generate their livelihood and to hold on to material wealth even as the expansion of colonial rule sought to change economic and social life in the towns.

Senegal's Nineteenth-Century Atlantic Ports

Saint Louis and Gorée are two islands located at the westernmost point of Africa (see Map 13). An originally uninhabited island off the Cap-Vert peninsula, Gorée served as a landing place for the Portuguese, Dutch and British until the French gained control of the territory in the late seventeenth century. By the mid-eighteenth century, the town supported a small population of black or mixed-race *habitants* (free property owners) as well as slaves attached to the families of the island.⁶ Although some slaves transited from the island in the era of the transatlantic slave trade, the location acted primarily as a strategic calling station for European ships en route to trading posts on the Senegal and Gambia rivers and in the French Caribbean. After 1850, Gorée played a key role in French administration of the southern coast of Senegambia and French activities south of the Gambia River, although Saint Louis, Senegal's most important port, became the administrative capital of the colony.

Strategically located where the Senegal River empties into the Atlantic, Saint Louis (called Ndar by the Wolof) played a central role in the devel-

⁵ Joseph Wulff's watercolour of his *casar* wife, Sara Malam, in a letter that he wrote to his brother in the 1840s to describe his marriage to a woman in the Gold Coast trading village of Osu, is reproduced and discussed by Pernille Ipsen in her book, *Daughters of the Trade: Atlantic Slavers and Interracial Marriage on the Gold Coast* (Philadelphia: University of Pennsylvania Press, 2015), 140–41 and plate 1.

⁶ In my previous work, I use the term *métis/métisse* to avoid the pejorative connotations of the terms *mulâtre* or 'mulatto' as used by eighteenth and nineteenth century authors. Today, French speakers use the term métis to refer to mixed-race populations, particularly as associated with France and her empire. For the purposes of this work, I will use the terms 'mixed race' or 'multiracial' to distinguish town residents who self-identified as a people of both African and European descent. In the literature on pre-colonial Senegambia, the term *grumette* (also spelled *gourmette*) referred to black Africans who settled around the French forts on Gorée and Saint Louis and who identified with the Catholic Church. On racial and colour terms particularly related to Saint Louis and Gorée see Jones, *The Métis of Senegal* (Indiana University Press, 2013), 9–11.

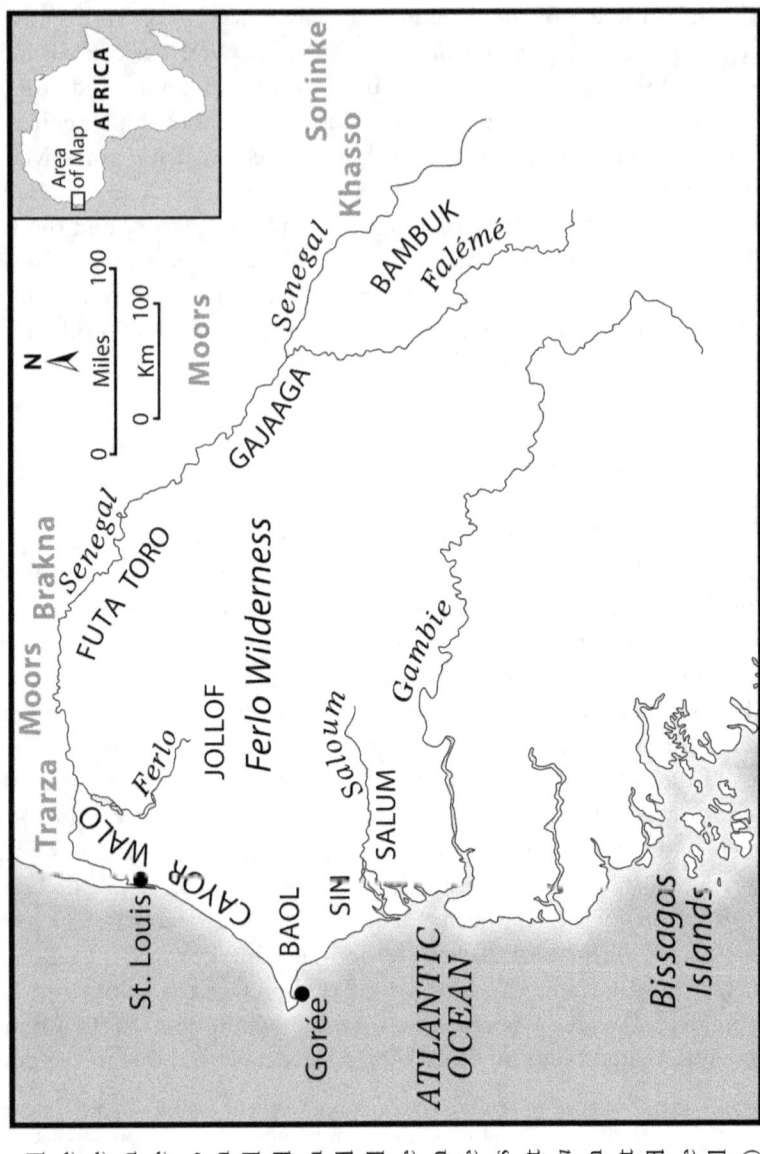

Map 13 Pre-colonial Senegambia indicating the French settlements at Gorée on the Cap-Vert Peninsula and Saint Louis as well as the Wolof Kingdoms of Cayor, Walo and Baol that existed in close proximity to the coastal towns; in the eighteenth and nineteenth centuries, French and British merchants operated trade depots along the Senegal and Gambia Rivers to acquire slaves, ivory, and gold; in the nineteenth century, the Trarza and Brakna Moors operated the caravan trade that supplied gum from the *acacia* trees of the Senegal to French merchants and their Saint Louis agents who participated in the seasonal trade along the Senegal

(Source: Map design by Don Pirius)

opment of trade networks between agents of mercantile companies and the interior states of the region. In the eighteenth century, the companies sent agents from Saint Louis to acquire slaves on the lower and middle Senegal. In the early nineteenth century, merchants seeking to capitalise on 'legitimate' trade established warehouses in the town.[7] Saint Louis' mixed-race population became the primary middlemen in the gum Arabic trade between Moors on the north bank of the Senegal and European trade houses located at the port. In 1820, France's restoration monarchy regained control over the Senegal colony. Until the 1860s, France ruled solely over Saint Louis, Gorée and a few locations along the Senegal and Gambia rivers.[8] By the end of the nineteenth century, however, the French military had suppressed African resistance and annexed the territories between the Senegal and Gambia rivers (see Map 14).

Saint Louis and Gorée embodied the characteristics of a contact zone in a similar fashion to Lagos as described by Kristin Mann and Ademide Adelusi-Adeluyi in their contributions to this volume. Residents lived in close proximity to Bordeaux merchants and naval officers who arrived in Senegal after serving in locations of the French Caribbean and Algeria. They also came into contact with religious women of the Order of Saint Joseph de Cluny, whose outreach stretched from Senegal to the Caribbean, and the Indian Ocean island of Réunion. At the same time, slavery played a central role in the labour regime of the towns, in the Senegal River trade and within the households of town residents. According to an 1838 population table, Saint Louis residents numbered almost 12,000. In 1845, just three years before France declared an end to slavery, the Saint Louis population consisted of two hundred Europeans, 5,346 *indigènes libres*, 618 *engagés* (indentured people) and 6,008 captives.[9]

From as early as the mid-eighteenth century, the enslaved outnumbered free persons and female slaves outnumbered male slaves in the

---

[7] On European commerce and Eurafrican traders in pre-colonial Senegambia see Boubacar Barry, *Senegambia and the Atlantic Slave Trade* (Cambridge, 1998), 133–47. On Saint Louis' Afro-European traders and trade houses see Roger Pasquier, 'Les traitants des comptoirs du Sénégal au milieu du XIXe siècle', *Entreprises et Entrepreneurs en Afrique*, ed. Catherine Coquery-Vidrovitch (Paris: Harmattan, 1983), 141–63; James Searing, *West African Slavery and Atlantic Commerce* (Cambridge University Press, 1993), 93–106.

[8] In 1904, the colonial ministry chose Dakar as the capital of the federation of French West Africa. As a result, Dakar eclipsed the old capital, Saint Louis: Robinson, *Paths of Accommodation*, 58–74.

[9] Before 1850, the accuracy of official population data is questionable, although two population tables comprised in 1838 and 1845 give a plausible estimate. While the data does not specify the gender of Europeans, very few European women accompanied French officers or merchants to the Senegal colony before 1900. The percentages of slave and free in Gorée mirrored that of Saint Louis. Gorée had approximately 5,000 residents (20–60 Europeans, 1,000 free blacks and people of colour, 100 engagés and three thousand captives. See C. Becker, V. Martin, J. Schmitz and M. Chastanet, *Les Premiers recensements au Sénégal et l'évolution démographique*: Part I – *Présentation de documents* (Paris: ORSTOM, 1983).

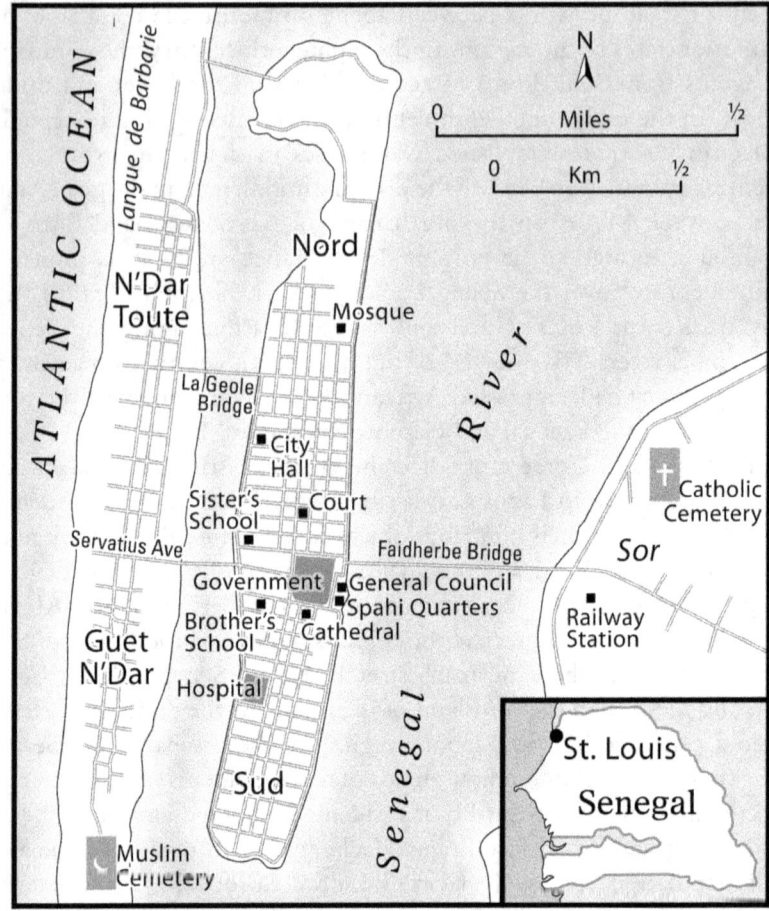

Map 14 Saint Louis du Senegal, the capital of the Senegal colony c. 1880, indicating the key political, judicial, educational and religious institutions established by the French administration: these institutions governed life in the towns; the spatial configuration of the island illustrates a pattern of residential segregation whereby the 'Kretien' (Wolof term for Christian) population of métis and black African Catholics occupied the *quartier sud* or the south side; the Mosque of *quartier nord* or the north side represented the neighbourhood predominantly inhabited by Muslim traders and clerics; once a location for seasonal trade, the Atlantic villages of Guet N'Dar and Ndar Toute became the primary settlement of fishermen and women who worked as laundresses, millet pounders (*pilleuses*), market traders and domestics

(Source: Map design by Don Pirius)

towns. Consequently, any analysis of the women of Senegal's nineteenth-century ports must take into account the institution of slavery and the effect of emancipation in the French empire that existed outside of the traditional plantation societies of the French Caribbean and the Indian Ocean islands.[10] In their study of gender and slave emancipation in the Atlantic world, Diana Paton and Pamela Scully show that the process of emancipation necessarily involved change to the gender order of Atlantic ports while also re-stabilising gender norms.[11] Notions of femininity and masculinity that emerged in Saint Louis society re-affirmed the idea of family and household as central units and re-established relations between former slaves and former slave owners. Saint Louis and Gorée embodied the openness of a cosmopolitan society but also relied on the inequality of power that existed within an imperial space. As Douglass Catterall and Jodi Campbell write, 'Atlantic port worlds depended on the circulation of people and things in the midst of moral ambiguity'.[12] Social life in these locations thus rested upon 'experimental commonality' or a degree of mutual improvisation. Building family ties, friendships and relations of confidence was fraught with moral compromises.

Men, Women and Affective Ties

Mariage à la mode du pays created local arrangements that established new household units at the intersection of West Africa and the Atlantic world. These unions resembled the institution of marriage among the Wolof states of Senegal's mainland except that the marriage dissolved upon the death or permanent departure of the male spouse. Although these unions were not recognised as legitimate under French law, they gave rise to a population of people of mixed racial heritage who carried the surnames of their fathers and enjoyed recognition as citizens of France.[13] People of mixed racial ancestry benefited from access to Western education. They possessed knowledge of the Atlantic networks of their families that

---

[10] On the implications of French anti-slavery policies in Senegal see Bernard Moitt, 'Slavery, Flight, and Redemption in Senegal, 1819–1890', *Slavery & Abolition* 14, no. 2 (1993), 70–86; Martin Klein, *Slavery and Colonial Rule in French West Africa* (Cambridge: Cambridge University Press, 1998), 19–26; Trevor Getz, *Slavery and Reform in West Africa* (Athens: Ohio University Press, 2004), 69–84.

[11] Diana Paton and Pamela Scully, 'Introduction: Gender and Slave Emancipation in Comparative Perspective', in *Gender and Slave Emancipation in the Atlantic World*, Pamela Scully and Diana Paton, eds (Durham, NC: Duke University Press, 2005), 1–3.

[12] Douglass Catterall and Jodi Campbell, 'Introduction: Mother Courage and Her Sisters: Women's Worlds in the Premodern Atlantic', in *Women in Port: Gendering Communities, Economies, and Social Networks in Atlantic Port Cities, 1500–1800*, Douglass Catterall and Jodi Campbell, eds (Leiden: Brill, 2012), 2.

[13] Jones, *The Métis of Senegal*, 19–39.

extended from metropolitan centres like Paris and London to the ports of Bordeaux and Rouen, as well as to the colonies of the French Caribbean. At the same time these men and women spoke Wolof, understood the cultural practices and customs of Senegalese society and lived and worked alongside black town residents.

Scholars have speculated about what motivated sexual relationships between African women and European or multiracial men. On the one hand, historians of West African trade have viewed the *signares* as entrepreneurs who capitalised on inter-racial marriage to gain access to Atlantic commerce and to profit from slave ownership. On the other, feminist theory raises the problem of the power imbalance between men and women in these locations. This research questions whether *mariage à la mode du pays* or *casar* amounted to prostitution or if European men used their position to exploit the African women and/or female slaves who formed part of these Eurafrican households.[14]

A surviving document from the Crespin family's private collection sheds light on the nuances of affective ties between elite men and their wives or lovers. The mixed-race *habitant* Germain Crespin (1803–1870) married the caretaker of his two children after the death of his first wife, Louison Alain (1805–1836).[15] His journal notes the birth of all of his children by both Louison Alain and Khayta Macoumba Leye, as a means of documenting and legitimising his family, even if it did not neatly fit French legal understandings of what constituted a family. Crespin recounted the births of Louison's two sons and a daughter who each died shortly after. One son, Jean Jacques, and a daughter, Desirée, survived. On 7 March 1836, Louison died due to an illness that she had sustained for almost one year. Two years later, Crespin wrote of the birth of his first child by Khayta Macoumba Leye, whom Reyss describes as a slave of the house. Khayta Macoumba Leye gave birth to a girl, Charlotte, on 28 August. On 11 May 1842 she gave birth to their second daughter. This union produced five daughters in total.

[14] On *signares* as entrepreneurs see George Brooks, 'The Signares of Saint Louis and Gorée: Women Entrepreneurs in Eighteenth Century Senegal', in *Women in Africa: Studies in Socio-Economic Change*, Nancy J. Hafkin and Edna G. Bay, eds (Stanford, CA: Stanford University Press, 1976), 19–44; Searing, *West African Slavery*. On feminist theory and inter-racial sexuality in Africa see Luise White, *The Comforts of Home: Prostitution in Colonial Nairobi* (Chicago, IL:University of Chicago Press, 1990), 1–28; Carina Ray, *Crossing the Color Line: Race, Sex, and the Contested Politics of Colonialism in Ghana* (Athens: Ohio University Press, 2015), 11–16; and Ipsen, *Daughters of the Trade*, 2–3.

[15] I rely on the excerpt from the journal that Natalie Reyss reprinted in her dissertation. This family history is acknowledged in the genealogy produced by Crespin's descendants and I have confirmed it in conversations with descendants of the family: Natalie Reyss, 'Saint Louis du Sénégal à l'époque précoloniale: l'émergence d'une société métisse originale, 1658–1854', Thèse de 3me cycle (Université Paris I, 1983), annex I 'private journal of Germain Crespin', Georges Crespin, interview with author, 8 June 2001, Paris, and unpublished family genealogy 'Liste de descendance de Benjamin Crespin'.

Illustration 9 The *signare* Marianne Blanchot with her husband in Saint Louis, before 1866; this portrait shows how Afro-European women incorporated African and European dress to produce a distinctive style that reflected their identification with the Catholic Church, and the importance of amulets and traditional beliefs in the Saint Louis community; it also offers a glimpse into the affective ties between married couples in the urban community

(Source: 'Portrait of *métis* couple: *signare* Marianne Blanchot (1798–1883) and husband Louis Alsace (1795–1866)', Xavier Ricou, *Trésors de l'iconographie du Sénégal colonial* (Paris: Riveneuve, 2007))

In his journal, Germain Crespin wrote about his devotion to Louison, yet he did not reveal his feelings about his relationship to Khayta Macoumba Leye. The taboo of intimacy between a female slave and a free man may have prevented Crespin from articulating in writing such emotions about his 'principle captive' and the caretaker of the children from his first marriage; or her slave status may have relegated her to a marginal place within his household, thus making it impossible for her to become the object of romantic love. Saint Louis society followed practices with regard to domestic slavery similar to those that existed in the societies of Senegal's interior. Among the Wolof of the Waalo kingdom, children born of a female slave and her master became part of the father's lineage, conferring free status. Families of Senegal's Atlantic towns incorporated their children by 'captives of the house' as part of the family unit, even if French law did not recognise children who did not issue from legitimate marriage as part of the nuclear family.[16]

Other documentation from family archives offers hints about the emotional ties formed between women of the towns and their husbands. Portraits provide a glimpse of affectionate relations. In contrast to sketches of European travel accounts that present women and families of the towns from a Eurocentric perspective, family paintings and photographs occasionally shed light on the interior lives of individuals. A painting of *signare* Marianne Blanchot (1798–1883) with her husband Louis Georges Linckenheyl, alias Louis Alsace (1795–1866) depicts the couple seated next to each other in a sombre pose (see Illustration 9).[17] Dressed in a suit and tie, Louis Alsace drapes his arm around Marianne Blanchot, who appears in typical *signare* dress with a conical head covering, a white tailored blouse with a skirt and shoulder wrappings of embroidered African woven fabric, as well as a gold necklace with a Catholic cross. Xavier Ricou notes that it is likely that she wore protective amulets or *gris-gris* under her clothes. In the few family letters contained in the Devès family's private papers, indications of similar close family bonds appear.[18] In a letter, Gaspard Devès, a merchant and head of a powerful trade house, asked after his mother Combel Aido Kâ and his '*nourrice*' or wet-nurse. Writing from

---

[16] Boubacar Barry, *Le royaume du Waalo* (Paris: Karthala, 1984), 67–9. Records of marriage and baptism in the Civil Registry for Saint Louis, and those of the Saint Louis parish, show that in some cases men of multiracial families sought to retroactively petition the courts for birth certificates in the case of unions that were not recognised, in order to regularise extramarital unions and substantiate future inheritance claims: Jones, *The Métis of Senegal*, 73–89.

[17] Marianne Blanchot was the daughter of the freed slave Marie Coumba Gueye and François Blanchot, Governor of Senegal (1787–1801, 1802–1807). Linckenheyl came from a mixed-race family descended from an Alsacian merchant. For the painting and comparison to sketches and engravings in European travel accounts see Xavier Ricou, *Trésors de l'iconographie du Sénégal colonial* (Paris: Riveneuve éditions, 2007), 57.

[18] 'G. Devés and Cie', Bordeaux 20 April 1883 and 'Gaspard Devés', Bordeaux 20 September 1896, Senegal National Archives Dakar, 1Z11, #10 and #12.

Bordeaux at the end of his life about the family business, Devès asked his son Justin to communicate his love for their mother, Madeline Tamba, and their daughters Cathy and Constance. He also indicated where he left the court record recognising the six children from his union with Madeleine Tamba. Significantly, the act was notarised just weeks before his son Hyacinthe's wedding. For town residents in this period, conforming to French legal and cultural norms held less importance than affective bonds. Letters, diaries and portraits show that families emerged out of complex social relations and women created households through marital unions that made sense to them in terms of the realities of life on Senegal's coast.

Family, Friendship and Daily Life

Family documents provide some perspective on women's familial relationships with men in the urban community but tell us little about women's habits, tastes, economic interests or friendships. Records of property transactions, wills and inventories, however, give insight into women's daily lives. From the early history of these settlements, women of Saint Louis and Gorée gained elite status by virtually monopolising property. In the mercantile company era, *signares* owned the vast majority of houses, boats and slaves. In addition, they possessed gold and silver jewellery, furniture, luxury textiles from Europe as well as local textiles. By 1750, the French had ended the practice of buying slaves in upriver markets to satisfy the demand for labour at the fort and in the town, relying instead on slaves rented from *signares*. Additionally, *signares* on Gorée and Saint Louis commonly rented rooms to European visitors who resided temporarily in the towns. Since the company prohibited Frenchmen from trading on their own behalf, they often used their *signare* wives to launch trading expeditions.[19] African and Afro-European women thus accumulated wealth and used their material possessions to visualise their elite status. Consequently, they played key roles in the political economy of the towns.

After 1850, the fortunes of Saint Louis town residents changed dramatically. Male traders capitalised as middlemen along the Senegal River and the southern coast of Senegambia. The heyday of the gum trade in the 1820s gave way to an economic crisis in the 1830s as French merchants began to flood the market with textiles, causing Saint Louis trade houses to go into debt. In addition, multiracial *habitants* faced new competition

---

[19] Saliou Mbaye, 'L'esclavage domestique à Saint Louis à travers les archives notaries (1817–1848)', in *Saint-Louis et l'esclavage*, Djibril Samb, ed. (Dakar: IFAN, 2000) 139–49; Mark Hinchman, *Portrait of an Island: The Architecture and Material Culture of Gorée, Senegal 1758–1837* (Lincoln: University of Nebraska Press, 2015), 119–49.

from Saint Louis traders once the administration lifted the tariffs that had previously prevented black African town residents from entering the trade. Lastly, the 1848 declaration that ended slavery 'on French soil' resulted in significant losses for the urban community. The administration offered slave owners a very low indemnity for each slave freed. A number of individuals chose to settle their slaves on the mainland, thus, losing their labour services in the towns; alternatively, they sold their indemnities to French companies at a loss rather than wait the long period for the indemnities to be formally converted into shares in the French-run Bank of Senegal. Despite these losses, as Mohammed Mbodj has demonstrated, abolition resulted in the rise of a new entrepreneurial class.[20] In addition to male traders and *signares*, *pileuses* (or women millet pounders in *signare* households) emerged as a new class of property owners after emancipation. By specialising in petty trade and relying on their social networks, women food preparers began to accumulate property in nearby fishing villages such as Ndar Toute or Guet Ndar on the Atlantic side of the island. Records from the Bank of Senegal, moreover, show that men who acquired shares in the bank often listed them under the names of their wives for inheritance purposes, and notarised documents or property transfers show that real estate was often transferred to female relatives, confidants or others within the extended family network.[21] Even after abolition, *signares* and their daughters maintained a significant degree of control over urban housing and transportation.

The inventory for the inheritance that followed upon the death of the widow of the *habitant* trader François Pellegrin illustrates the complicated nature of property transactions within the urban community. It also offers clues about friendships between women and the habits and consumption patterns of women.[22] Marie Pellegrin, a *commerçante* on Gorée, died on 13 May 1880 in Joal, a French administrative and trade centre on Senegal's Petite Côte. The French merchant Luis Prom, designated as guardian for her daughters, Marie (aged eleven) and Louise Marie Amélie (aged seven), requested an inventory of their mother's belongings in order to settle her debts and arrange for the children's inheritance. Thus we learn the value of all furniture, clothing, jewellery, property and cash owned by Marie Pellegrin at the time of her death. The inventory also lists the value of the

[20] Mohamed Mbodj, 'The abolition of slavery in Senegal 1820–1890: Crisis or the rise of a new entrepreneurial class?' in *Breaking the Chains: Slavery, Bondage and Emancipation in Modern Africa and Asia*, Martin A. Klein, ed. (Madison: University of Wisconsin Press, 1993), 205–7.
[21] Ghislaine Lydon, 'Les péripéties d'une institution financière: la Banque du Sénégal, 1844–1901', in *AOF: réalités et héritages: sociétés ouest-africaines et ordre colonial, 1895–1960*, vol. 1, Charles Becker, Saliou Mbaye and Ibrahima Thioub, eds (Dakar: Direction des Archives Nationales du Sénégal, 1997), 475–91.
[22] 'Inventaire de la succession de dame Ve François Pellegrin', Saint Louis le 1 juin 1880 au 22 octobre 1880', Senegal National Archives 1Z107.

store merchandise of her Gorée boutique, located on the ground floor of the family house. Business was intricately intertwined with family life.

The main items for sale in the Gorée boutique included pieces of Indian cotton, *Guinées* or the valuable blue indigo cloth long demanded by Moors and Senegalese. The boutique sold all sorts of textiles: handkerchiefs, blue muslin, natural English cotton, woven 'household' cotton, tablecloths and calico, as well as twenty men's hats and cotton thread. In addition, the store inventory included fourteen liqueur bottles, ten bottles of Muscat wine, four bottles of vermouth, absinthe, beer, spices from Provence, bottles of olive oil, sardines, 7 kg of colonial soap, candles, paper and pins.[23] These items, commonly consumed by the French bourgeoisie, were evidently imported to Senegal's colonial towns to satisfy local needs.

Marie Pellegrin's household possessions included items associated with living spaces, such as buffets, armoires 'in the wood of the country', dressing tables, kitchen tables, ice cabinets, iron beds and mattresses, as well as divans and couches. For her personal use Marie Pellegrin owned nine *pagnes* or locally produced wrap-around cloths, seventeen Wolof scarves, two ordinary black dresses, embroidered camisoles, three silk dresses, four bathrobes and eleven tailored cotton blouses. The inventory also included eighteen men's shirts in cotton, seven pairs of trousers and eight Moorish shoes from the clothing of her late husband. In addition, Marie Pellegrin owned a house in Dakar where the family operated a boutique on the ground floor under the charge of Demoiselle Louise Valantin.[24]

The inventory included various items of jewellery in silver and gold 'of the country', as well as jewellery made in Europe, including pearl earrings, coral earrings, beads, a *portemonnaie* and bracelets. The list of jewellery includes a note by the deceased's sister and *demoiselle* Marie Cisse, her '*femme de confiance*', who assisted in compiling the inventory. Both women declared that certain jewellery belonged to *la dame* Thiocuta N'gor, who had deposited it with her, and that other jewellery belonged to the 'domestics of the house', who had entrusted it with Madame Pellegrin for security.

Marie Pellegrin had owned real estate in all of Senegal's major colonial towns. Her dowry, transferred to François Pellegrin upon their wedding, included a house on Gorée in the Rue du Port. She owned a building on Gorée, Rue de Batterie, and a building in Dakar consisting of a house of stone and concrete, divided into a boutique on the ground floor, an office on the first floor of five rooms and a gallery converted into a store. She also owned a house in Saint Louis near the hospital that at the time of the accounting was occupied by *la dame* Forreau. Marie Pellegrin owned

---

[23] Ibid. The inventory for the store includes items belonging to Pellegrin leased to the trade house Maurel et Frères, an interest of Luis Prom.
[24] Ibid.

another house in Dakar with a ground floor store. According to the document, Mme Pellegrin built this house on land leased from *le sieur* Medoune Diop. Finally, she owned a wooden cottage in poor condition, consisting of a boutique, a waggon and a warehouse, located at Saly Portudal, a seaside town on the Petite Côte.

Thus the widow Pellegrin controlled a significant amount of real estate and operated an extensive family business, an enterprise probably initiated by her husband, including retail establishments in Gorée and Dakar at a time when French interests were expanding beyond the Senegal River region to Dakar, the new administrative capital and port, and to the coastal area to the south of the Cap-Vert peninsula. The record of Marie Pellegrin's belongings illustrates the extent to which elite women of Saint Louis and Gorée had access to European foodstuffs, furniture, clothing and jewellery, although they also routinely wore clothing and jewellery made 'in the country'. Finally, the inventory offers glimpses of the friendships and intimate ties between women within the multiracial urban community. The notary accepted her 'trusted friend' Marie Cisse's testimony as evidence that African women who formed part of her close network, whether friends, clients or servants, trusted her to look after their valuables or alternatively to give their valuables to Pellegrin as collateral. Pellegrin certainly stands out among Saint Louis and Gorée women for her wealth and the extent of the business operations that she managed before and after her husband's death; but she also resembles other women in the urban community, who played key roles in the operations of family trade houses and acquired wealth in material goods and real estate in order to weather the financial uncertainties of the changing colonial economy and family loss.

Conclusion

The biographies of women on Saint Louis and Gorée allow us to recover the lived experiences of people who came from a variety of socio-economic, religious and racial backgrounds. Living in Senegal's Atlantic ports, they embodied the cosmopolitan outlook of 'citizens' of the French Atlantic; yet they also experienced the constraints of slavery and the ways in which emancipation sought to remake and re-establish gender norms. Within this environment they developed affective ties to others in the community. The practice of controlling property through marital contracts and inheritance settlements, moreover, afforded women some measure of financial independence while strengthening their ability to make decisions that furthered their own kin and client networks. During the transition from the end of the Atlantic slave trade to French imperialism, marriage and property ownership provided a means of navigating changing gender expectations and securing a livelihood. Simultaneously, the end of slavery and the expansion of imperialism often rendered women's labour invisible as the public sphere gained salience over the realm of household, marriage and domesticity.

Bibliography

Achebe, Nwando, *The Female King of Colonial Nigeria: Ahebi Ugbabe* (Bloomington: Indiana University Press, 2011)

Adams, L. B., ed., *Eko Dynasty, Colonial Administrators and the Light of Islam in Lagos* (Lagos: Eko Islamic Foundation, 2004)

Adanson, Michel, *Histoire naturelle du Sénégal. Coquillages: Avec la relation abrégée d'un voyage fait en ce pays, pendant les années 1749, 50, 51, 52 & 53* (Paris: Claude-Jean-Baptiste Pauche, 1757)

Adichie, Chimamanda. 'The Danger of a Single Story', July 2009, www.ted.com/talks/chimamanda_adichie_the_danger_of_a_single_story.html

Ajisafe, A. K., *Laws and Customs of the Yoruba People* (Lagos: Kash and Klare Bookshop, 1946)

Akyeampong, Emmanuel, 'Sexuality and Prostitution among the Akan of the Gold Coast c. 1650–1950', *Past and Present* 156 (1997), 144–73

Alencastro, Luiz Felipe de, *O trato dos viventes: A formação do Brasil no Atlântico Sul, séculos XVI e XVII* (São Paulo: Companhia das Letras, 2000)

Alexandre, Valentim and Jill Dias, *O Império africano* (Lisbon: Estampa, 1998)

Alfagali, Crislayne Gloss Marão, 'Ferreiros e fundidores da Ilamba: uma história social da fabricação do ferro e da Real Fábrica de Nova Oeiras (Angola, segunda metade do século XVIII)', unpublished Ph.D. dissertation, Unicamp, 2016

Allman, Jean and Victoria B. Tashjian, *I Will Not Eat Stone: A Women's History of Colonial Asante* (Portsmouth, NH: Heinemann, 2000)

Allman, Jean Marie, Susan Geiger and Nakanyike Musisi, *Women in African Colonial Histories* (Bloomington: Indiana University Press, 2002)

Almanach para o Anno de 1800 (Lisbon: Oficina de António Rodrigues Galhardo, 1800)

Almanak statistico da Provincia d'Angola e suas dependencias para o anno de 1852 (Luanda Imprensa do Governo, 1851)

Almeida Mendes, António de, 'Child Slaves in the Early North Atlantic Trade in the Fifteenth and Sixteenth Centuries', in *Children in Slavery through the Ages*, ed. Gwyn Campbell, Suzanne Miers and Joseph C. Miller (Athens: Ohio University Press, 2009), 19–34

Alpern, Stanley, 'Exotic Plants of Western Africa: Where They Came from and When', *History in Africa* 35 (2008), 63–102

Alpern, Stanley, 'What Africans Got for Their Slaves: A Master List of European Trade Goods', *History in Africa* 22 (1995), 5–43

Alpers, Edward A., *Ivory and Slaves: Changing Pattern of International Trade in East Central Africa to the Later Nineteenth Century* (Los Angeles: University of California Press, 1975)

Altink, Henrice, 'Deviant and Dangerous: Pro-Slavery Representations of Jamaican Slave Women's Sexuality, c. 1780–1834', *Slavery & Abolition* 26, no. 2 (2005), 271–88

Alves, Rogéria Cristina, 'Marfins africanos em trânsito: apontamentos sobre o comércio numa perspectiva atlântica (Angola, Benguela, Lisboa e Brasil), séculos XVIII–XIX', *Faces da História* 3, no. 2 (2016), 8–21

Amadiume, Ife, *Male Daughters, Female Husbands: Gender and Sex in an African Society* (London: Zed Books, 1987)

Angrand, Jean-Luc, *Céleste ou le temps des signares* (Sarcelles, France: Éditions Anne Pépin, 2006)

Annaes do Conselho Ultramarino, Série 1, Fev. 1854 a Dez 1858 (Lisbon: Imprensa Nacional, 1867)

Annaes do Parlamento Brasileiro, Sessão de 1838, Tomo II (Rio de Janeiro: Typographia de Viuva Pinto & Filho, 1887)

Antubam, Kofi, *Ghana's Heritage of Culture* (Leipzig: Köhler & Amelang, 1963)

Appadurai, Arjun, *The Social Life of Things: Commodities in Cultural Perspective* (Cambridge: Cambridge University Press, 2013)

Araujo, Ana Lucia, *Public Memory of Slavery: Victims and Perpetrators in the South Atlantic* (Amherst, NY: Cambria Press, 2010)

Ardener, Edwin, *Divorce and Fertility: An African Study* (London: Oxford University Press, 1962)

Ashcraft-Eason, Lillian, '"She Voluntarily Hath Come": A Gambian Woman Trader in Colonial Georgia in the Eighteenth Century', in *Identity in the Shadow of Slavery,* ed. Paul E. Lovejoy (London and New York: Continuum, 2000), 202–21

Atkins, John, *A Voyage to Guinea, Brasil and the West-Indies* (London: Ward & Chandler, 1735)

Austen, Ralph A. and Jonathan Derrick, *Middlemen of the Cameroons Rivers: The Duala and their Hinterland, c.1600–c.1960* (Cambridge: Cambridge University Press,1999)

Austen, Ralph A., 'The Slave Trade as History and Memory: Confrontations of Slaving Voyage Documents and Communal Traditions', *William and Mary Quarterly* 58, no. 1 (2001), 229–44

Austin, Gareth, *Labour, Land and Capital in Ghana: From Slavery to Free Labor in Asante, 1807–1956* (Rochester, NY: University of Rochester Press, 2005).

Awe, Bolanle. 'The Iyalode in the Traditional Yoruba Political System', in *Sexual Stratification: A Cross Cultural View*, ed. Alice Schlegel (New York: Columbia

University Press, 1977), 144–60

Ayandele, Emmanuel Ayankanmi, *The Missionary Impact on Modern Nigeria, 1842–1914: A Political and Social Analysis* (New York: Humanities Press, 1967)

Babou, Cheikh Anta, *Fighting the Greater Jihad: Amadu Bamba and the Founding of the Muridiyya of Senegal, 1853–1913* (Athens, OH: Ohio University Press, 2007)

Baesjou, René, 'Dutch "Irregular" Jurisdiction on the Nineteenth Century Gold Coast', *Palaver: European Interference in African Dispute Settlement*, ed. René Baesjou and Robert Ross, African Perspectives series (Leiden: Afrika-Studiecentrum, 1979), 21–66

Bailyn, Bernard, 'The Idea of Atlantic History', *Itinerario* 20, no. 1 (1996), 19–44

Ballong-wen-Mewuda, J. B., 'Le commerce portugais des esclaves entre la côte de l'actuel Nigéria et celle du Ghana moderne aux XVe et XVIe siècles', in *De la traite à l'esclavage. Actes du colloque international sur la traite des Noirs*, ed. Serge Daget, 2 vols (Nantes: CRHMA, 1988), Vol. 1, 121–45

Barnes, Sandra T., *Patrons and Power: Creating a Political Community in Metropolitan Lagos* (Bloomington: Indiana University Press, 1986)

Barry, Boubacar, *Le royaume du Waalo: Sénégal avant le conquête* (Paris: Karthala, 1984)

Barry, Boubacar, *Senegambia and the Atlantic Slave Trade* (Cambridge: Cambridge University Press, 1998)

Bauer, Arnold J., *Goods, Power, History: Latin America's Material Culture* (New York: Cambridge University Press, 2001)

Baum, Robert, *Shrines of the Slave Trade: Diola Religion and Society in Precolonial Senegambia* (New York: Oxford University Press, 1999)

Bay, Edna, 'Belief, Legitimacy and the Kpojito: An Institutional History of the "Queen Mother" in Precolonial Dahomey', *The Journal of African History* 36 (1995), 1–27

Bay, Edna, 'Servitude and Worldly Success in the Palace of Dahomey', in *Women and Slavery in Africa*, ed. Claire Robertson and Martin A. Klein (Madison: University of Wisconsin Press, 1983), 340–67

Bay, Edna, *Wives of the Leopards: Gender, Politics and Culture in the Kingdom of Dahomey* (Charlottesville: University of Virginia Press, 1998)

Bay, Edna, ed., *Women and Work in Africa* (Boulder, CO: Westview Press, 1982)

Bay, Mia Farah J. Griffin, Martha S. Jones, and Barbara D. Savage, eds, *Toward an Intellectual History of Black Women* (Chapel Hill: University of North Carolina Press, 2015)

Becker, Charles, V. Martin, J. Schmitz and M. Chastanet, *Les Premiers recensements au Sénégal et l'évolution démographique*: Part I – *Présentation de documents* (Paris: ORSTOM, 1983).

Beckles, Hilary McD., 'Female Enslavement and Gender Ideologies in the Caribbean', in *Identity in the Shadow of Slavery*, ed. Paul E. Lovejoy, 2nd edn (London: Continuum, 2009)

Bellagamba, Alice, 'Slavery and Emancipation in the Colonial Archives: British Officials, Slave-Owners, and Slaves in the Protectorate of the Gambia (1890–1936)', *Canadian Journal of African Studies* 39, no. 1 (2005), 5–41

Benoist, Joseph-Roger de and Abdoulaye Camara, eds, *Histoire de Gorée* (Paris: Maisonneuve & Larose, 2003)

Benoist, Joseph-Roger de and Abdoulaye Camara, 'Gorée dans l'histoire', in *Histoire de Gorée*, ed. Abdoulaye Camara and Joseph-Roger de Benoiste (Paris: Maisonneuve & Larose, 2003), 11–29

Benoist, Joseph-Roger de and Abdoulaye Camara, 'Les Signares et le patrimoine bâti de l'île', in *Histoire de Gorée*, ed. Abdoulaye Camara and Joseph-Roger de Benoiste (Paris: Maisonneuve & Larose, 2003), 95–115

Benoist, Joseph-Roger de, Abdoulaye Camara and Françoise Descamps, 'Les Signares: de la représentation à la réalité', in *Histoire de Gorée,* ed. Abdoulaye Camara and Joseph-Roger de Benoiste (Paris: Maisonneuve & Larose, 2003), 59–83

Beoku-Betts, Josephine, 'Western Perceptions of African Women in the 19th & Early 20th Centuries', in *Readings in Gender in Africa*, ed. Andrea Cornwall (Bloomington: Indiana University Press, 2005), 20–25

Berger, Iris, 'Rebels or Status-Seekers? Women as Spirit Mediums in East Africa', in *Women in Africa: Studies in Social and Economic Change*, ed. Nancy J. Hafkin and Edna G. Bay (Stanford, CA: Stanford University Press, 1976), 157–181

Berger, Iris, *Threads of Solidarity Women in South African Industry, 1900–1980* (London: James Currey, 1992)

Betts, Raymond F., *Assimilation and Association in French Colonial Theory, 1890–1914* (New York: Columbia University Press, 1961)

Bezerra, Nielson Rosa, *Escravidão, farinha e tráfico Atlântico: um novo olhar sobre as relações entre o Rio de Janeiro e Benguela (1790–1830)* (Rio de Janeiro: Fundação Biblioteca Nacional, 2010)

Biobaku, Saburi O., *The Egba and Their Neighbours, 1842–1872* (Oxford: Clarendon Press, 1957)

Birmingham, David, 'A Question of Coffee: Black Enterprise in Angola', *Canadian Journal of African Studies* 16, no. 2 (1982), 343–6.

Blackburne, K.W., 'Development and Welfare in the Gambia', *Sessional Paper* no. 2, 1943

Bledsoe, Caroline, *Women and Marriage in Kpelle Society* (Stanford, CA: Stanford University Press, 1980)

Bleek, Wolf, 'Did the Akan Resort to Abortion in Pre-Colonial Ghana?' *Africa* 60 (1990), 121–32

Boilat, Abbé David, *Esquisses sénégalaises: Physionomie du pays, peuplades, commerce, religions, passé et avenir, récits et légendes* (Paris: P. Bertrand, 1853)

Bosman, Willem, *A New and Accurate Description of the Coast of Guinea* (London: James Knapton & Dan Midwinter, 1705)

Bosman, Willem, *Nauwkeurige beschryving van de Guinese Goud-, Tand- en Slavekust* (Utrecht: Anthony Schouten, 1704 and Amsterdam: J. Verheide, 1737)

Bourdieu, Pierre, *Pascalian Meditations* (Stanford, CA: Stanford University Press, 2000)

Braidwood, Stephen J., *Black Poor and White Philanthropists. London's Blacks and the Foundation of the Sierra Leone Settlement 1786–1791* (Liverpool: Liverpool University Press, 1994)

Brásio, António, *Monumenta missionaria Africana: Africa Ocidental* (first series), Vol. 1 (Lisbon: Centro de Estudos Africanos da Faculdade de Letras da Universidade de Lisboa, 1953)

Broadhead, Susan Herlin, 'Slave Wives, Free Sisters: Bakongo Women and Slavery c. 1700–1850', yn *Women and Slavery in Africa*, ed. Claire C. Robertson and Martin A. Klein (Madison: University of Wisconsin Press, 1983), 160–81

Brooks, George E., 'A Nhara of the Guinea-Bissau Region: Mãe Aurélia Correia', in *Women and Slavery in Africa,* ed. Claire C. Robertson and Martin A. Klein (Madison: University of Wisconsin Press, 1983), 295–317

Brooks, George E., 'The Signares of Saint-Louis and Gorée: Women Entrepreneurs in Eighteenth Century Senegal', in Women in Africa: Studies in Social and Economic Change, ed. Nancy J. Hafkin and Edna G. Bay (Stanford, CA: Stanford University Press, 1976), 19–44

Brooks, George E., *Eurafricans in Western Africa: Commerce, Social Status, Gender, and Religious Observance from the Sixteenth to the Eighteenth Century* (Athens, OH: Ohio University Press, 2003)

Brydon, Lynne, 'Who Moves? Migrant Identity in West Africa in the 1980s', in *Migrants, Workers and the Social Order*, ed. Jeremy S. Eades (New York: Tavistock, 1987), 165–80

Bundock, Michael, *The Fortunes of Francis Barber* (New Haven, CT: Yale University Press, 2015)

Burke, Peter, *Eyewitnessing: The Uses of Images as Historical Evidence* (London: Reaktion Books, 2001)

Burton, Richard E., *A Mission to Gelele, King of Dahome*, 2nd edn (London: Tinsley Brothers, 1864)

Bush, Barbara, *Slave Women in Caribbean Society 1650–1838* (London: Heinemann, 1990)

Byfield, Judith, 'Women, Marriage, Divorce, and the Emerging Colonial State in Abeokuta (Nigeria), 1892–1904', in *'Wicked' Women and the Reconfiguration of Gender in Africa*, ed. Dorothy L. Hodgson and Sheryl A. McCurdy (Portsmouth, NH: Heinemann, 2001), 27–46

Caldeira, Carlos José, *Apontamentos d'uma viagem de Lisboa a China e da China a Lisboa* (Lisbon: G.M. Martin, 1852)

Campbell, Gwyn and Alessandro Stanziani, eds, *Debt and Slavery in the Mediterranean and Atlantic Worlds* (London: Pickering & Chatto, 2013)

Campbell, Gwyn, Suzanne Miers and Joseph C. Miller, 'Women in Western Systems of Slavery: Introduction', *Slavery & Abolition* 26, 2 (2005), 161–79

Campbell, Gwyn, Suzanne Miers and Joseph C. Miller, eds, *Women and Slavery*, 2 vols, Vol. 1: *Africa, the Indian Ocean World, and the Medieval North Atlantic*, Vol. 2: *The Modern Atlantic* (Athens, OH: Ohio University Press, 2007–2008)

Campbell, Mavis C., *Back to Africa; George Ross & the Maroons – From Nova Scotia to Sierra Leone* (Trenton, NJ: Africa World Press, 1993)

Campbell, Mavis C., *The Maroons of Jamaica, 1655–1796. A History of Resistance, Collaboration and Betrayal* (Granby, MA: Bergin and Garvey, 1988)

Candido, Mariana, 'African Freedom Suits and Portuguese Vassal Status: Legal Mechanisms for Fighting Enslavement in Benguela, Angola, 1800–1830',

Slavery & Abolition 32, no. 3 (2011), 447–59

Candido, Mariana, 'Aguida Gonçalves da Silva, une *dona* à Benguela à la fin du XVIIIe siécle', *Brésil(s). Sciences humaines et sociales* 1 (2012), 33–54

Candido, Mariana, *An African Slaving Port and the Atlantic World: Benguela and Its Hinterland* (Cambridge: Cambridge University Press, 2013)

Candido, Mariana, 'Engendering West Central African History: The Role of Urban Women in Benguela in the Nineteenth Century', *History in Africa* 42 (2015), 7–36

Candido, Mariana, *Fronteras de esclavización: esclavitud, comercio e identidad en Benguela, 1780–1850* (Mexico City: Colegio de Mexico Press, 2011)

Candido, Mariana, 'Género, classificações, e comércio, as donas de Benguela, 1750–1850', *Actas do III Encontro Internacional de História de Angola* 2, no. 1 (2015), 251–74

Candido, Mariana, 'Marriage, Concubinage, and Slavery in Benguela, ca. 1750–1850', in *Slavery in Africa and the Caribbean: A History of Enslavement and Identity since the 18th Century*, ed. Olatunji Ojo and Nadine Hunt (London and New York: I.B. Tauris, 2012), 66–84

Candido, Mariana, 'Merchants and the Business of the Slave Trade at Benguela, 1750–1850', *African Economic History* 35 (2007), 1–30

Candido, Mariana, 'Os agentes não europeus na comunidade mercantil de Benguela, c. 1760–1820', *Saeculum*, 29 (2013), 97–124

Candido, Mariana, 'Slave Trade and New Identities in Benguela, 1700–1860', *Portuguese Studies Review* 19, nos 1–2 (2011), 59–75

Candido, Mariana, 'Strategies for Social Mobility: Liaisons between Foreign Men and Slave Women in Benguela, c. 1770–1850', in *Sex, Power and Slavery: The Dynamics of Carnal Relations under Enslavement*, ed. Gwyn Campbell and Elizabeth Elbourne (Athens, OH: Ohio University Press, 2014), 272–88

Candido, Mariana, 'Trade, Slavery and Migration in the Interior of Benguela: The Case of the Caconda, 1830–1870', in *Angola on the Move: Transport Routes, Communications, and History*, ed. Beatrix Heintze and Achim von Oppen (Frankfurt am Main: Lembeck, 2008), 63–84

Candido, Mariana, 'Women, Family, and Landed Property in Nineteenth-Century Benguela', *African Economic History* 43 (2015), 136–61

Candido, Mariana and Eugénia Rodrigues, 'African Women's Access and Rights to Property in the Portuguese Empire', *African Economic History* 43 (2015), 1–18

Carney, Judith, *Black Rice: The African Origins of Rice Cultivation in the Americas* (Cambridge, MA: Harvard University Press, 2001)

Carney, Judith, 'Converting the Wetlands, Engendering the Environment: The Intersection of Gender with Agrarian Change in the Gambia', *Economic Geography* 69, no. 4 (1993), 329–48

Carney, Judith, 'Landscapes of Technology Transfer: Rice Cultivation and African Continuities', *Technology and Culture* 27, no. 1 (1996), 5–35

Carney, Judith and Michael Watts, 'Disciplining Women? Rice, Mechanization, and the Evolution of Mandinka Gender Relations in Senegambia' *Signs* 16,

no. 4 (1991), 651–81
Carretta, Vincent and Ty M. Reese, eds, *The Life and Letters of Philip Quaque, The First African Anglican Missionary* (Athens, GA: University of Georgia Press, 2010)
Castillo, Lisa Earl, 'Mapping the Nineteenth-Century Brazilian Returnee Movement: Demographics, Life Stories and the Question of Slavery', *Atlantic Studies: Global Currents* 13, no. 1 (2016), 25–52
Castro Lopo, Júlio de, 'Uma rica dona de Luanda', *Portucale* 3 (1948), 129–38
Catterall, Douglas and Jodi Campbell, 'Introduction: Mother Courage and Her Sisters: Women's Worlds in the Premodern Atlantic', in *Women in Port: Gendering Communities, Economies, and Social Networks in Atlantic Port Cities, 1500–1800*, ed. Douglas Catterall and Jodi Campbell (Leiden: Brill, 2012), 1–36
Catterall, Douglas and Jodi Campbell, eds, *Women in Port: Gendering Communities, Economies, and Social Networks in Atlantic Port Cities, 1500–1800* (Leiden: Brill, 2012)
Cerulli, Emesta, 'L'individuo e la cultura tradizionale: norma, transformazione ed evasione', in *Una società guineana: gli Nzema*, 2 vols, ed. Vinigi L. Grottanelli (Turin: Boringhieri, 1977–78), Vol. I, 143–212
Christaller, J. G., *A Dictionary of the Asante and Fante Language Called Tshi (Chwee, Twi)* (Basel, privately published, 1881)
Christensen, James Boyd, *Double Descent among the Fanti* (New Haven, CT: Human Relations Area Files 11, 1954)
Clarence-Smith, W. G., *Slaves, Peasants, and Capitalists in Southern Angola, 1840–1926* (Cambridge: Cambridge University Press, 1979)
Clarence-Smith, W. G. *The Third Portuguese Empire, 1825–1975: A Study in Economic Imperialism* (Manchester University Press, 1985).
Código Philipino, Livro 4, título XCVII www1.ci.uc.pt/ihti/proj/filipinas/ordenacoes.htm
Cohen, Ronald, 'Women, Status, and High Office in African Politics', in *Annals of Borno*, Vol. 11 (Borno State: University of Maiduguri Press, 1985), 181–201
Cole, Gibril R., 'Re-thinking the Demographic Make-up of Krio Society', in *New Perspectives on the Sierra Leone Krio*, ed. Mac Dixon-Fyle and Gibril Cole (New York: Peter Lang 2006), 33–51
Comaroff, Jean and John L. Comaroff, *Of Revelation and Revolution, Volume 1: Christianity, Colonialism, and Consciousness in South Africa* (Chicago, IL: University of Chicago Press, 1991)
Conklin, Alice L., *A Mission to Civilize: The Republican Idea of Empire in France and West Africa, 1895–1930* (Stanford, CA: Stanford University Press, 1997)
Constituições Primeiras do Arcebispado da Bahia, Liv I, tit. LXVII. https://archive.org/details/constituicoenspr00cath
Coquery-Vidrovitch, Catherine, *African Women: A Modern History* (Boulder, CO: Westview Press, 1987)
Crampton, Jeremy W., *Mapping: A Critical Introduction to Cartography and GIS* (Hoboken, NJ: John Wiley & Sons, 2011)
Croff, Raina Lynn, 'Village des Bambaras: An Archaeology of Domestic Slavery

and Urban Transformation on Gorée Island, Senegal, A. D. 17–19th Centuries', Ph.D. dissertation, Yale University, 2009

Crosby, K. H., 'Polygamy in Mende Country', *Africa: Journal of the International African Institute* 10, no. 3 (1937), 249–64

Crowder, Michael, *Senegal: A Study in French Assimilation Policy* (London: Oxford University Press, 1962)

Curtin, Philip D., *Economic Change in Precolonial Africa: Senegambia in the Era of the Slave Trade* (Madison: University of Wisconsin Press, 1975)

Curto, José C., '"As if from a Free Womb": Baptismal Manumissions in the Conceição Parish, Luanda, 1778–1807', *Portuguese Studies Review* 10, no. 1 (2002), 26–57

Curto, José C., 'Marriage in Benguela, 1797–1830: A Serialized Analysis', in *New Perspectives on Angola: From Slaving Colony to Nation State*, ed. Maryann Buri and José C. Curto (in preparation)

Curto, José C., 'The Anatomy of a Demographic Explosion: Luanda, 1844–1850', *International Journal of African Historical Studies* 32 (1999), 381–405

Curto, José C., 'The Donas of Benguela, 1797: A Preliminary Analysis of a Colonial Female Elite', in *Angola e as Angolanas: Memória, Sociedade e Cultura*, ed. Edvaldo Bergamo, Selma Pantoja and Ana Claudia Silva (São Paulo: Intermeios, 2016), 99–120

Curto, José C., 'Whitening the "White" Population: An Analysis of the 1850 Censuses of Luanda', in *Em torno de Angola: narrativas, identidades e as conexões atlânticas*, ed. Selma Pantoja and Estevam C. Thompson (São Paulo: Intermeios, 2014), 225–47

Curto, José C. and Raymond R. Gervais, 'The Population History of Luanda of Luanda during the late Atlantic Slave Trade, 1781–1844', *African Economic History* 29 (2001), 1–59

Daaku, Kwame Yeboa, *Trade and Politics on the Gold Coast, 1600–1720: A Study of the African Reaction to European Trade* (Oxford: Clarendon Press, 1970)

Danmole, H. O., 'A Visionary of the Lagos Muslim Community: Mustapha Adamu Animashaun, 1885–1968', *Lagos Historical Review* 5 (2005), 22–48

Dantzig, Albert van, ed., *The Dutch and the Guinea Coast 1674–1742: A Collection of Documents from the General State Archive at The Hague* (Accra: Ghana Academy of Arts and Sciences, 1978)

Dapper, Olfert, *Naukeurige beschrijvinge der afrikaensche gewesten* (Amsterdam: Jacob van Meurs, 1668)

Deffontaine, Yann, 'Pouvoir monarchique et création étatique sur la Côte de L'Or au XVIII siècle: Brempong Kojo et la création de l'état d'Oguaa (Cape Coast)', in *Mondes Akan / Akan Worlds, Identité et pouvoir en Afrique Occidentale / Identity and power in West Africa*, ed. Pierluigi Valsecchi and Fabio Viti (Paris: L'Harmattan, 1999), 187–214

Delafosse, Eustache, 'Voyage à la côte occidentale de Guinée, au Portugal et en Espagne (1479–1481)', ed. R Foulché-Delbosc, *Revue Hispanique* 4 (1897), 174–201. Critical edition by Denis Escudier (Paris: Chandeigne, 1992)

Delafosse, Maurice, *La Langue mandingue et ses dialectes*, 2 vols (Paris: P. Geuthner, 1955)

Denzer, LaRay, 'Yoruba Women: A Historiographical Study', *International Journal of African Historical Studies* 27, no. 1 (1994), 1–39

Dias, Jill R., 'A sociedade colonial de Angola e o liberalismo português (c. 1820–1850)', in *O Liberalismo na Península Ibérica na primeira metade do século XIX: comunicações ao colóquio organizado pelo Centro de Estudos de História Contemporânea Portuguesa*, Vol. I, ed. Miriam H. Pereira, Maria de Fátima Sá de Melo Ferreira and João B. Serra (Lisbon: Sá da Costa Editora, 1982), 267–86

Dias, Jill R., 'Changing Patterns of Power in the Luanda Hinterland: The Impact of Trade and Colonisation on the Mbundu ca. 1845–1920', *Paideuma* 32 (1986), 285–318

Diouf, Sylviane A., ed., *Fighting the Slave Trade, West African Strategies* (Oxford: James Currey, 2003).

Diptee, Audra, *From Africa to Jamaica: The Making of an Atlantic Slave Society, 1775–1807* (Gainsville: University Press of Florida, 2012)

Domingues da Silva, Daniel B., 'The Early Population Charts of Portuguese Angola, 1776–1830: A Preliminary Assessment', *Anais de História de Além-Mar* 6 (2015), 107–24

Domingues da Silva, Daniel B., *The Atlantic Slave Trade from West Central Africa, 1780–1867* (Cambridge: Cambridge University Press, 2017)

Donelha, André, *An Account of Sierra Leone and the Rivers of Guinea of Cape Verde (1625)*, trans. and ed. A. Teixeira da Mota and P. E. H. Hair (Lisbon: Junta de Investigação Científicas do Ultramar, 1977)

Donoghue, John, *Fire under the Ashes: An Atlantic History of the English Revolution* (Chicago, IL: University of Chicago Press, 2013)

Doortmont, Michel R. and N. C. Everts, 'Vrouwen, familie en eigendom op de Goudkust [Ghana]: De verwevenheid van Afrikaanse en Europese systemen van erfrecht in Elmina, 1760–1860', in *Geld en Goed: Jaarboek voor Vrouwengeschiedenis* 17, ed. C. van Eijl (Amsterdam: IISG, 1997), 114–30

Doortmont, Michel R. and Benedetta Savoldi, *The Castles of Ghana: Axim, Butre, Anomabu: Historical and Architectural Research on Three Ghanaian Forts* (Saonara, Italy: Il Prato, 2006)

Doortmont, Michel R. and Jinna Smit, *Sources for the Mutual History of Ghana and the Netherlands: An Annotated Guide to the Dutch Archives Relating to Ghana and West Africa in the Nationaal Archief, 1593–1960s* (Leiden: Brill, 2007)

Douglas, Mary, *The Lele of the Kasai* (London: Oxford University Press, 1963)

Douville, Jean Baptiste, *Voyage au Congo et dans l'intérieur de l'Afrique équinoxale... 1828, 1829, 1830*, Vol. I (Paris: J. Renouard, 1832)

Dunbar, Erica Armstrong, *Never Caught: Ona Judge, the Washingtons, and the Relentless Pursuit of Their Runaway Slave* (New York: Simon & Schuster, 2017)

Edwards, Jay Dearborn and Nicolas Kariouk Pecquet du Bellay de Verton, *A Creole Lexicon: Architecture, Landscape, People* (Baton Rouge: Louisiana State University Press, 2004)

El Hamel, Chouki, 'Constructing a Diasporic Identity: Tracing the Origins of the Gnawa Spiritual Group in Morocco', *The Journal of African History* 49, no. 2 (2008), 241–60

Elbée, Le Sieur d', 'Journal du voyage aux Isles, dans la coste de Guinee', in *Relation de ce qui s'est passé dans les Isles et Terre-ferme de l'Amerique pendant la dernière Guerre avec l'Angleterre ...*, J. de Clodoré (Paris: Gervais Clovzier, 1671), 347–558

Elbl, Ivana, 'Men without Wives: Sexual Arrangements in the Early Portuguese Expansion in West Africa', in *Desire and Discipline: Sex and Sexuality in the Premodern West*, ed. Jacquelline Murray and Konrad Eisenbichler (Toronto: University of Toronto Press, 1996), 61–86

Ellis, A. B., *The Ewe-Speaking Peoples of the Slave Coast of West Africa* (London: Chapman & Hall, 1890)

Eltis, David, 'A New Assessment of the Transatlantic Slave Trade', in *Extending the Frontiers: Essays on the New Transatlantic Slave Trade Database*, ed. David Eltis and David Richardson (New Haven, CT: Yale University Press, 2008), 1–60

Eltis, David, 'Atlantic History in Global Perspective', *Itinerario* 23, no. 2 (1999), 141–61

Eltis, David, *The Rise of African Slavery in the Americas* (Cambridge: Cambridge University Press, 2000)

Eltis, David and Lawrence C. Jennings, 'Trade between Western Africa and the Atlantic World in the Pre-Colonial Era', *The American Historical Review* 93, no. 4 (1988), 936–59

Eltis, David and David Richardson, *Atlas of the Transatlantic Slave Trade* (New Haven, CT: Yale University Press, 2010)

Englert, Birgit and Elizabeth Daley, *Women's Land Rights & Privatization in Eastern Africa* (Woodbridge: James Currey, 2008)

Erickson, Amy Louise, *Women and Property in Early Modern England* (London: Taylor & Francis, 1993)

Everts, Natalie, 'A Motley Company: Differing Identities among Euro-Africans in Eighteenth-Century Elmina', in *Brokers of Change: Atlantic Commerce and Cultures in Precolonial Western Africa*, ed. Toby Green (Oxford: Oxford University Press, 2012), 53–69

Fadipe, N. A., *The Sociology of the Yoruba* (Ibadan: Ibadan University Press, 1970)

Fage, J. D., 'Slaves and Society in Western Africa, c. 1455–c. 1700', *The Journal of African History* 21 (1980), 289–310

Falola, Toyin, 'Pawnship in Colonial Southwestern Nigeria', *Pawnship in Africa: Debt Bondage in Historical Perspective*, ed. Toyin Falola and Paul E. Lovejoy (Boulder, CO: Westview Press, 1994), 245–66

Farias, Juliana Barreto, *Mercados Minas: Africanos ocidentais na praça do mercado do Rio de Janeiro (1830–1890)* (Rio de Janeiro: Arquivo Geral da Cidade do Rio, 2015)

Feinberg, Harvey M., 'Africans and Europeans in West Africa: Elminans and Dutchmen on the Gold Coast during the Eighteenth Century', *Transactions of the American Philosophical Society* 79, Part 7 (1989)

Fergusson, Charles Bruce, ed., *Clarkson's Mission to America 1791–1792* (Halifax, NS: Public Archives of Nova Scotia, 1971)

Ferreira, Roquinaldo, 'Agricultural Enterprise and Unfree Labour in Nineteenth Century Angola', in *Commercial Agriculture, the Slave Trade and Slavery in*

Atlantic Africa, ed. Robin Law, Suzanne Schwarz and Silke Strickrodt (Woodbridge, UK: James Currey, 2013), 225–42

Ferreira, Roquinaldo, 'Atlantic Microhistories: Mobility, Personal Ties, and Slaving in the Black Atlantic World (Angola and Brazil)', in *Cultures of the Lusophone Black Atlantic*, ed. Nancy Prisci Naro, Ro Sansi-Roca and D. Treece (New York: Palgrave Macmillan, 2007), 99–127

Ferreira, Roquinaldo, *Cross-Cultural Exchange in the Atlantic World: Angola and Brazil during the Era of the Slave Trade* (New York: Cambridge University Press, 2012)

Ferreira, Roquinaldo, 'Dinâmica do comércio intracolonial: gerebitas, panos asiáticos e guerra no tráfico angolano de escravos, século XVIII', in *O Antigo Regime nos Trópicos: A Dinâmica imperial portuguesa, séculos XVI–XVIII*, ed. João Luís Ribe Fragoso, Maria de Fátima Gouvêa and Maria Fernanda Bicalho (Rio de Janeiro: Civilização Brasileira, 2001), 339–78

Ferreira, Roquinaldo, 'Dos Sertões ao Atlântico: Tráfico Ilegal de Escravos e Comércio Lícito em Angola, 1830–1860', unpublished M.A. thesis, Universidade Federal do Rio de Janeiro, 1996

Ffoulkes, Arthur, 'Fanti marriage customs', *Journal of the African Society* 8 (1908–09), 31–49

Fontana-Giusti, Gordana, *Foucault for Architects* (New York: Routledge, 2013)

Forbes, Frederick E., *Dahomey and the Dahomans; Being the Journals of Two Missions to the King of Dahomey and Residence at His Capital in the Years 1849 and 1850*, Vol. 1 (London: Frank Cass, 1966 [1849])

Force, Pierre and Susan Hoffius, 'Negotiating Race and Status in Senegal, Saint Domingue, and South Carolina', *Early American Studies* (Winter 2018), 124–50

Frank, Zepher L., *Dutra's World: Wealth and Family in Nineteenth-Century Rio de Janeiro* (Albuquerque: University of New Mexico Press, 2004)

Fraser, Louis, *Dahomey and the Ending of the Trans-Atlantic Slave Trade: The Journals and Correspondence of Vice-Consul Louis Fraser, 1851–1852*, ed. Robin Law (Oxford: Oxford University Press, 2012)

Freudenthal, Aida, *Arimos e fazendas: a transição agrária em Angola, 1850–1880* (Luanda: Chá de Caxinde, 2005)

Freudenthal, Aida, 'Benguela – da feitoria à cidade colonial', *Fontes & Estudos* 6–7 (2011), 197–229

Furtado, Júnia Ferreira, 'Lives on the Seas: Women's Trajectories in Port Cities of the Portuguese Overseas Empire', in *Women in Port: Gendering Communities, Economies, and Social Networks in Atlantic Port Cities, 1500–1800*, ed. Douglas Catterall and Jody Campbell (Leiden: Brill, 2012), 251–86

Fyfe, Christopher, *A History of Sierra Leone* (London: Oxford University Press, 1962)

Fyfe, Christopher, ed., *'Our Children Free and Happy': Letters from Black Settlers in Africa in the 1790s* (Edinburgh: Edinburgh University Press, 1991)

Garrard, Timothy F., *Akan Weights and the Gold Trade* (London: Longmans 1980)

Garraway, Doris L., *The Libertine Colony: Creolization in the Early French Caribbean* (Durham, NC: Duke University Press, 2005)

Garrigus, John, 'Race, Gender, and Virtue in Haiti's Failed Foundational

Fiction: *La mulatre comme il y a peu de blanches* (1803)', in *The Color of Liberty: Histories of Race in France*, ed. Sue Peabody and Tyler Stovall (Durham, NC: Duke University Press, 2003), 73–94

Gbadamosi, T. G. O., *The Growth of Islam among the Yoruba, 1841–1908* (London: Longman, 1978)

Geggus, David Patrick, 'Slave and Free Colored Women in Saint-Domingue', in *More than Chattel: Black Women and Slavery in the Americas*, ed. Darlene Clark Hine and David Barry Gaspar (Bloomington: Indiana University Press, 1996), 259–78

George, Abosede A., *Making Modern Girls: A History of Girlhood, Labor, and Social Development in Colonial Lagos* (Athens, OH: Ohio University Press, 2014)

Getz, Trevor, *Slavery and Reform in West Africa: Toward Emancipation in Nineteenth-Century Senegal and the Gold Coast* (Athens, OH: Ohio University Press, 2004)

Gil, António, *Considerações sobre alguns pontos mais importantes da moral religiosa e systema de jurisprudência dos pretos do continente da África Occidental portuguesa além do Equador, tendentes a dar alguma idea do character peculiar das suas instituições primitivas* (Lisbon: Typografia da Academia, 1854)

Gilroy, Paul, *The Black Atlantic: Modernity and Double Consciousness* (Cambridge, MA: Harvard University Press, 1993)

Gish, Lindsey, 'Breaking Down African Hierarchies through Gendered Atlantic Trade: Free and Enslaved Female Entrepreneurs of Saint Louis Senegal in the 18th and 19th Centuries', Paper presented at Annual Meeting of the African Studies Association, San Diego, November 2015

Godot, Jean, 'Voyages de Jean Godot', Ms. français (Paris: Bibliothèque Nationale, 1704), 13380–13381

Goheen, Miriam, *Men Own the Fields, Women Own the Crops: Gender and Power in the Cameroon Grassfields* (Madison: University of Wisconsin Press, 1996)

Graham, Richard, *Feeding the City: From Street Market to Liberal Reform in Salvador, Brazil, 1780–1860* (Austin: University of Texas Press, 2010)

Graham, Richard, 'Nos tumbeiros mais uma vez? O comércio interprovincial de escravos no Brasil', in *Atlântico de dor: Faces do tráfico de escravos*, ed. João José Reis and Carlos da Silva Jr. (Salvador: EDUFRB; Belo Horizonte, Brazil: Fino Traço, 2016), 343–75

Graham, Sandra Lauderdale, 'Being Yoruba in Nineteenth-Century Rio de Janeiro', *Slavery & Abolition* 32, no. 1 (2011), 1–26

Gramberg, J. S. G., *Schetsen van Afrika's Westkust* (Amsterdam: Weijting & Brave, 1861)

Graubart, Karen B., *With Our Labor and Sweat: Indigenous Women and the Formation of Colonial Society in Peru, 1550–1700* (Stanford, CA: Stanford University Press, 2007)

Gray, John M, *A History of the Gambia* (New York: Cambridge University Press, 1966)

Greene, Beth, 'The Institution of Woman-Marriage in Africa: A Cross-Cultural Analysis', *Ethnology* 37 (1998), 395–412

Greene, Sandra E., 'Family Concerns: Gender and Ethnicity in Pre-Colonial

West Africa', *International Review of Social History* 44 (1999), 15–31

Greene, Sandra E., *Gender, Ethnicity, and Social Change on the Upper Slave Coast: A History of the Anlo-Ewe* (Portsmouth, NH: Heinemann, 1996)

Grottanelli, Vinigi L., *The Python Killer. Stories of Nzema Life* (Chicago, IL: University of Chicago Press, 1988)

Guedes, Roberto and Caroline S. Pontes, 'Notícias do presídio de Caconda (1797): moradores, escravatura, tutores e órfãos', in *África e Brasil no Mundo Moderno*, ed. Eduardo França Paiva and Vanicléia Santos (Belo Horizonte, Brazil: Annablume, 2013), 153–80

Guèye, Youssouf, 'Essai sur les causes et les conséquences de la micropropriété au Fouta Toro', Bulletin de l'I.F.A.N. XIX, sér. B, no. 3 (1957), 28–42

Guyer, Jane I. and Samuel M. Eno Belinga, 'Wealth in People as Wealth in Knowledge: Accumulation and Composition in Equatorial Africa', *The Journal of African History* 36 (1995), 91–120

Hafkin, Nancy J. and Edna G. Bay, eds, *Women in Africa: Studies in Social and Economic Change* (Stanford, CA: Stanford University Press, 1976)

Hair, P. E. H., 'Milho: Meixoeira and Other Foodstuffs of the Sofala Garnison, 1505–1525', *Cahiers d'Études africaines* 17 (1977), 353–63

Harley, J. B., 'Deconstructing the Map', *Cartographica: The International Journal for Geographic Information and Geovisualization* 26 (1998), 1–20

Harley, J. B., 'Historical Geography and the Cartographic Illusion', *Journal of Historical Geography* 15, no. 1 (1989), 80–91

Harley, J. B., 'Maps, Knowledge, and Power', in *The Iconography of Landscape: Essays on the symbolic Representation, Design, and Use of Past Environments*, ed. Denis Cosgrove and Stephen Daniels (Cambridge: Cambridge University Press, 1998), 277–310

Harley, J. B., 'The Map as Biography: Thoughts on Ordnance Survey Map, Six-Inch Sheet Devonshire CIX, S.E., Newtown Abbot', *The Map Collector* 41 (1987), 18–20

Harms, Robert, 'Sustaining the System: Trading Towns along the Middle Zaire', in *Women and Slavery in Africa*, ed. Claire Robertson and Martin A. Klein (Madison: University of Wisconsin Press, 1983), 95–110

Harris, Joseph E., *The African Presence in Asia: Consequences of the East African Slave Trade* (Evanston, IL: Northwestern University Press, 1971)

Hartman, Saidiya, *Lose Your Mother: A Journey along the Atlantic Slave Route* (New York: Farrar, Straus & Giroux, 2007)

Havik, Philip J., 'Female Entrepreneurship in West Africa: Trends and Trajectories', *Early Modern Women, an Interdisciplinary Journal*, 10, no. 1 (Fall 2015), 164–77

Havik, Philip J., *Silences and Soundbytes: The Gendered Dynamics of Trade and Brokerage in the Pre-colonial Guinea Bissau Region* (Munster: LIT, 2004)

Havik, Philip J., 'Sóciais, intermediárias e empresárias: O gênero e a expansão colonial na Guiné', *O rosto feminino da expansão portuguesa*, 2 vols, Vol. 2 (Lisbon: Comissão para a Igualdade e para os Direitos das Mulheres, 1995), 87–90

Havik, Philip J., 'Women and Trade in the Guinea Bissau Region', *Studia* 52 (1994), 83–120

Hawthorne, Walter, *Planting Rice and Harvesting Slaves: Transformations along the Guinea-Bissau Coast, 1400–1900* (Portsmouth, NH: Heinemann, 2003)

Heintze, Beatrix, *Angola nos séculos XVI e XVII. Estudo sobre fontes, métodos e história* (Luanda: Kilombelombe, 2007)

Heintze, Beatrix, 'Long-Distance Caravans and Communication beyond the Kwango (c. 1850–1890)', in *Angola on the Move: Transport Routes, Communications and History*, ed. Beatrix Heintze and Achim von Oppen (Frankfurt am Main: Lembeck, 2008), 144–62

Heintze, Beatrix, *Pioneiros Africanos: caravanas de carregadores na África Centro-Ocidental: entre 1850 e 1890* (Lisbon: Caminho, 2004)

Heintze, Beatrix, *Studien zur Geschichte Angolas im 16. und 17. Jahrhundert: ein Lesebuch* (Köln: Rüdiger Köppe, 1996)

Henige, David, 'Measuring the Immeasurable: The Atlantic Slave Trade, West African Population and the Pyrrhonian Critic', *The Journal of African History* 27 (1986), 295–313

Henriques, Isabel Castro, 'As outras africanas: As reais e as inventadas', *Oceanos* 21 (1995), 53–63

Henriques, Isabel Castro, *Percursos da Modernidade em Angola. Dinâmicas Comerciais e Transformações Sociais no Século XIX* (Lisbon: Instituto de Investigação Científica e Tropical, 1997)

Herbert, Eugenia W., *Red Gold of Africa: Copper in Precolonial History and Culture* (Madison: Wisconsin University Press, 1984)

Heywood, Linda M., *Contested Power in Angola, 1840s to the Present* (Rochester, NY: University of Rochester Press, 2000)

Heywood, Linda M., *Njinga of Angola: Africa's Warrior Queen* (Cambridge, MA: Harvard University Press, 2017)

Heywood, Linda M., 'Slavery and Forced Labor in the Changing Political Economy of Central Angola, 1850–1949', in *The End of Slavery in Africa*, ed. Suzanne Miers and Richard Roberts (Madison: Wisconsin University Press, 1988), 415–35

Hicks, Mary, 'The Sea and the Shackle: African and Creole Mariners and the Making of a Luso-African Atlantic Commercial Culture, 1721–1835', unpublished Ph.D. dissertation, University of Virginia, 2015

Hinchman, Mark, 'House and Household on Gorée, Senegal, 1758–1837', *Journal of the Society of Architectural Historians* 65, no. 2 (2006), 166–87

Hinchman, Mark, *Portrait of an Island: The Architecture and Material Culture of Gorée, Senegal 1758–1837* (Lincoln: University of Nebraska, 2015)

Hirst, Paul, 'Foucault and Architecture', *AA Files* no. 26 (Autumn 1993), 52–60

Hodes, Martha, 'Experimental Writing in the Classroom', *Perspectives on History* (May 2007), www.historians.org/publications-and-directories/perspectives-on-history/may-2007/experimental-history-in-the-classroom

Hodes, Martha, 'Four Episodes in Re-Creating a Life', Rethinking History, *The Journal of Theory and Practice* 10 (June 2006), 277–90

Holsey, Bayo, *Routes of Remembrance: Refashioning the Slave Trade in Ghana* (Chicago, IL: University of Chicago Press, 2008)

Hopkins, A. G., 'A Report on the Yoruba, 1910, *Journal of the Historical Society of*

Nigeria 5, no. 1 (1969), 67–100

Hopkins, A. G., *An Economic History of West Africa* (New York: Columbia University Press, 1973)

Hunt, Nancy Rose, 'An Acoustic Register, Tenacious Images, and Congolese Scenes of Rape and Repetition', *Cultural Anthropology* 23 no. 2 (2008), 220–53

Husband, John, *A System of Arithmetic; Containing an Extensive Course of Commercial and Mental Calculations, on A New and Comprehensive Plan* (Edinburgh: Oliver & Boyd; London: Simpkin, Marshall & Co., 1841).

Inikori, Joseph E., 'The Volume of the British Slave Trade, 1655–1807', *Cahiers d'Etudes africaines*, 32, no. 128 (1992), 643–88

Ipsen, Pernille, *Daughters of the Trade: Atlantic Slavers and Interracial Marriage on the Gold Coast* (Philadelphia: University of Pennsylvania Press, 2015)

Ipsen, Pernille, '"The Christened Mulatresses": Euro-African Families in a Slave-Trading Town', *The William and Mary Quarterly* 70, no. 2 (2013), 371–98

Jadin, Louis, *L'ancien Congo et l'Angola 1639–1655 d'après les archives romaines, portugaises, néerlandaises et espagnoles*, 3 vols (Brussels: Institut Historique Belge de Rome, 1975)

Jean-Baptiste, Rachel, *Conjugal Rights: Marriage, Sexuality, and Urban Life in Colonial Libreville, Gabon* (Athens, OH: Ohio University Press, 2014)

Jobson, Richard, *The Golden Trade: Or, a Discovery of the River Gambra, and the Golden Trade of the Aethiopians* (London: Nicholas Okes, 1623)

Johnson, G. Wesley, Jr., *The Emergence of Black Politics in Senegal: The Struggle for Power in the Four Communes, 1900–1920* (Stanford, CA: Stanford University Press, 1971)

Johnson, Marion, 'The Cowrie Currencies of West Africa', *The Journal of African History* 11 (1970), 17–50, 331–54

Johnson, Rev. Samuel, *The History of the Yorubas* (London: Routledge and Kegan Paul, 1969 [1921])

Jones, Adam, *Brandenburg Sources for West African History 1680–1700* (Stuttgart: Franz Steiner, 1985)

Jones, Adam, 'Decompiling Dapper: A Preliminary Search for Evidence', *History in Africa* 17 (1990), 171–209

Jones, Adam, 'Female Slave-Owners on the Gold Coast, Just a Matter of Money?', in *Slave Cultures and the Cultures of Slavery*, ed. Stephan Palmié (Knoxville: University of Tennessee Press, 1995), 100–11

Jones, Adam, *German Sources for West African History 1599–1669* (Wiesbaden: Franz Steiner, 1983)

Jones, Adam, '"My Arse for Okou": A Wartime Ritual of Women 'on the Nineteenth-Century Gold Coast', *Cahiers d'Études africaines* 132, no. XXXIII (1993), 545–66

Jones, Adam, *Zur Quellenproblematik der Geschichte Westafrikas 1450–1900* (Stuttgart: Franz Steiner, 1990)

Jones, G. I. *The Trading States of the Oil Rivers: A Study of Political Development in Eastern Nigeria* (London: Oxford University Press, 1963)

Jones, Hilary, *The Métis of Senegal: Urban Life and Politics in French West Africa* (Bloomington and Indianapolis: Indiana University Press, 2013)

Kaplow, Susan B., 'Primitive Accumulation and Traditional Social Relations on the Nineteenth Century Gold Coast', *Canadian Journal of African Studies* 12 (1978), 19–36

Karasch, Mary C., *Slave Life in Rio de Janeiro, 1808–1850* (Princeton, NJ: Princeton University Press, 1987)

Karasch, Mary C., 'The Brazilian Slavers and the Illegal Slave Trade, 1836–1851', unpublished M.A. thesis, University of Wisconsin, 1967

Kea, Pamela, 'Maintaining Difference and Managing Change: Female Agrarian Clientelist Relations in a Gambian Community', *Africa: Journal of the International African Institute* 74, no. 3 (2004), 361–82

Kea, Ray A., *Settlements, Trade, and Polities in the Seventeenth Century Gold Coast* (Baltimore, MD and London: Johns Hopkins University Press, 1982)

King, Stewart R., *Blue Coat or Powdered Wig: Free People of Color in Pre-Revolutionary Saint Domingue* (Athens, GA: University of Georgia Press, 2001)

Klein, Herbert S. and Francisco Vidal Luna, *Slavery in Brazil* (New York: Cambridge University Press, 2010)

Klein, Martin, *Slavery and Colonial Rule in French West Africa* (Cambridge: Cambridge University Press, 1998)

Knight, Marie-Hélène, 'Gorée au XVIIe siècle: L'appropriation du sol', *Revue française d'histoire d'outre-mer* 64, no. 234 (1977), 33–54

Knight, Marie-Hélène, 'La vie à Gorée de 1677 à 1789', *Revue française d'histoire d'outre-mer* 57, no. 209 (1970), 377–420

Kodesh, Neil, *Beyond the Royal Gaze: Clanship and Public Healing in Buganda* (Charlottesville: University of Virginia Press, 2010)

Kopytoff, Jean Herskovits, *A Preface to Modern Nigeria: The 'Sierra Leonians' in Yoruba, 1830–1890* (Madison, WI: University of Wisconsin Press, 1965)

Korieh, Chima J. and Femi J. Kolapo, ed. *The Aftermath of Slavery: Transitions and Transformations in Southeastern Nigeria* (Trenton NJ: Africa World Press, 2007)

Kriger, Colleen E., *Cloth in West African History* (Lanham, MD: Rowman Altamira, 2006)

Kriger, Colleen E., *Making Money: Life, Death, and Early Modern Trade on Africa's Guinea Coast* (Athens, OH: Ohio University Press, 2017)

Kriger, Colleen E., 'Mapping the History of Cotton Textile Production in Precolonial West Africa', *African Economic History* 33 (2005), 87–116

Kriger, Colleen E., *Pride of Men: Ironworking in 19th Century West Central Africa* (Portsmouth, NH: Heinemann, 1999)

Kropp Dakubu, Mary Esther, 'The Portuguese Language on the Gold Coast, 1471–1807', *Ghana Journal of Linguistics* 1, no. 1 (2012), 15–33

Kup, Alexander Peter, ed., *Adam Afzelius Sierra Leone Journal, 1795–1796* (Uppsala: Inst. för allm. och jämforande etnografi, 1967)

Labat, Jean Baptiste, *Nouvelle relation de l'Afrique occidentale*, Vol. IV (Paris: G. Cavelier, 1728)

Landers, Jane, *Atlantic Creoles in the Age of Revolutions* (Cambridge, MA: Harvard University Press 2010)

Landers, Jane, 'Founding Mothers: Female Rebels in Colonial New Granada and Spanish Florida', *The Journal of African American History* 98, no. 1 (2013), 7–23

Laotan, A. B., *The Torch Bearers or Old Brazilian Colony in Lagos* (Lagos: Ife-Olu Printing Works, 1943)

Lara, Silvia Hunold, 'The Signs of Color: Women's Dress and Racial Relations in Salvador and Rio de Janeiro, ca 1750–1815', *Colonial Latin American Review* 6, no. 2 (1997), 205–24

Latham, A. J. H. *Old Calabar 1600–1891: The Impact of the International Economy upon a Traditional Society* (Oxford: Clarendon Press, 1973)

Law, Robin, 'Fante Expansion Reconsidered: Seventeenth Century Origins', *Transactions of the Historical Society of Ghana*, New Series no.14 (2012), 41–78

Law, Robin, ed., *From Slave Trade to Legitimate Commerce: The Commercial Transition in Nineteenth-Century West Africa* (Cambridge: Cambridge University Press, 1995)

Law, Robin, 'On Pawnship and Enslavement for Debt in the Pre-Colonial Slave Coast', in *Pawnship in Africa: Debt Bondage in Historical Perspective*, ed. Paul Lovejoy and Toyin Falola (Boulder, CO: Westview Press, 1994), 51–69

Law, Robin, 'The Government of Fante in the Seventeenth Century', *The Journal of African History* 54, no. 1 (2013), 31–51

Law, Robin, *Ouidah: The Social History of a West African Slaving 'Port', 1727–1892* (Athens, OH: Ohio University Press, 2004)

Law, Robin, ed., *The English in West Africa 1691–1698: The Local Correspondence of the Royal African Company of England, 1681–1699, Part 1* (Oxford: Oxford University Press, 2006)

Law, Robin and Kristin Mann, 'West Africa in the Atlantic Community: The Case of the Slave Coast', *William and Mary Quarterly* 56, no. 2 (1999), 307–34

Law, Robin, Suzanne Schwarz and Silke Strickrodt, eds, *Commercial Agriculture, the Slave Trade and Slavery in Atlantic Africa* (Woodbridge, UK: James Currey, 2013)

Lawrance, Benjamin N., *Amistad's Orphans: An Atlantic Story of Children, Slavery, and Smuggling* (New Haven, CT: Yale University Press, 2015)

Levine, Nancy E. and Walter H. Sangree, eds, Women with Many Husbands: Polyandrous Alliance and Marital Flexibility in Africa and Asia (issue title), *Journal of Comparative Family Studies* 11 no. 3 (1980)

Lewis, Martin D., 'One Hundred Million Frenchmen: The "Assimilation" Theory in French Colonial Policy', *Comparative Studies in Society and History* 4, no. 2 (1962), 129–53

Linares, Olga F., 'From Tidal Swamp to Inland Valley: On the Social Organization of Wet Rice Cultivation among the Diola of Senegal', *Africa: Journal of the International African Institute* 51, no. 2 (1981), 557–95

Lindsay, Lisa A., *Atlantic Bonds: A Nineteenth-Century Odyssey from America to Africa* (Chapel Hill: University of North Carolina Press, 2017)

Lindsay, Lisa A., 'Extraversion, Creolization, and Dependency in the Atlantic Slave Trade', *The Journal of African History* 55, no. 2 (2014), 135–45

Little, Kenneth, *African Women in Towns: An Aspect of Africa's Social Revolution* (Cambridge: Cambridge University Press, 1973)

Lopes Cardoso, Carlos Alberto, 'Ana Joaquina dos Santos Silva, industrial angolana da segunda metade do século XIX', *Boletim Cultural da Câmara*

Municipal de Luanda 32 (1972), 5–14

Lopes de Lima, José Joaquim, *Ensaios sobre a statistica das possessões portuguezas na África occidental e oriental; na Ásia occidental; na China, e na Oceania* (Lisbon: Imprensa Nacional, 1844)

Lopes, Gustavo Acioli and Maximiliano Mac Menz, 'Resgate e Mercadorias: uma análise comparada do tráfico luso-brasileiro de escravos em Angola e na Costa da Mina (Século XVIII)', *Afro-Ásia* 37 (2008), 43–72

Lovejoy, Paul E., 'Concubinage and the Status of Women Slaves in Early Colonial Northern Nigeria', *The Journal of African History* 29 (1988), 245–66

Lovejoy, Paul E., *Jihād in West Africa during the Age of Revolutions* (Athens, OH: Ohio University Press, 2016)

Lovejoy, Paul E., 'Pawnship and Seizure for Debt in the Process of Enslavement in West Africa', in *Debt and Slavery in the Mediterranean and Atlantic Worlds*, ed. Gwyn Campbell and Alessandro Stanziani (London: Pickering & Chatto, 2013), 63–75

Lovejoy, Paul E., *Transformations in Slavery* (New York: Cambridge University Press, 2000)

Lovejoy, Paul E. and Toyin Falola, eds, *Pawnship in Africa: Debt Bondage in Historical Perspective* (Boulder, CO: Westview Press, 1994)

Lovejoy, Paul E. and David Richardson. 'Competing Markets for Male and Female Slaves in the Interior of West Africa', *International Journal of African Historical Studies* 28 (1995), 261–93

Lovejoy, Paul E. and Suzanne Schwarz, ed., *Slavery, Abolition and the Transition to Colonialism in Sierra Leone* (Trenton, NJ: Africa World Press, 2015)

Lydon, Ghislaine, 'Les péripéties d'une institution financière: la Banque du Sénégal, 1844–1901', in *AOF: réalités et héritages – sociétés ouest-africaines et ordre colonial, 1895–1960*, Vol. 1, ed. Charles Becker, Saliou Mbaye and Ibrahima Thioub (Dakar: Direction des archives de Senegal, 1997), 475–91

Lynn, Martin, 'Consul and Kings: British Policy, the "Man on the Spot" and the Seizure of Lagos, 1851', *Journal of Imperial and Commonwealth History* 10 (1982), 150–67

M'Leod, John, *A Voyage to Africa; with Some Account of the Manners and Customs of the Dahomian People* (London: John Murray, 1820; Frank Cass, 1971 [1803])

Mabogunje, A. L. and J. Omer-Cooper, *Owu in Yoruba History* (Ibadan: Ibadan University Press, 1971)

MacCormack, Carol P., 'Control of Land, Labor and Capital in Rural Southern Sierra Leone', in *Women and Work in Africa*, ed. Edna G. Bay (Boulder, CO: Westview Press, 1982), 35–53

MacGaffey, Wyatt 'Dialogues of the Deaf: Europeans on the Atlantic Coast of Africa', in *Implicit Understandings*, ed. Stuart B. Schwartz (Cambridge: Cambridge University Press, 1994), 249–67

Madeira Santos, Catarina, 'Administrative Knowledge in a Colonial Context: Angola in the Eighteenth Century', *British Journal for the History of Science* 43 (2010), 539–56

Mair, Lucille Mathurin, *The Rebel Woman in the British West Indies during Slavery* (Kingston: Institute of Jamaica, 2007)

Mair, Lucille Mathurin, Hilary Beckles and Verene A. Shepherd, eds, *A Historical Study of Women in Jamaica, 1655–1844* (Kingston, Jamaica: University of West Indies Press, 2006)

Mann, Kristin, 'African and European Initiatives in the Transformation of Land Tenure in Colonial Lagos (West Africa), 1840–1920', in *Native Claims: Indigenous Law against Empire, 1500–1920,* ed. Saliha Belmessous (Oxford: Oxford University Press, 2011), 223–58

Mann, Kristin, 'Interpreting Cases, Disentangling Disputes: Court Cases as a Source for Understanding Patron-Client Relationships in Early Colonial Lagos', in *Sources and Methods in African History: Spoken, Written, Unearthed*, ed. Toyin Falola and Christian Jennings (Rochester, NY: University of Rochester Press, 2003), 195–218

Mann, Kristin, *Marrying Well: Marriage, Status, and Social Change among the Educated Elite in Colonial Lagos* (Cambridge: Cambridge University Press, 1985)

Mann, Kristin, *Slavery and the Birth of an African City: Lagos, 1760–1900* (Bloomington: Indiana University Press, 2007)

Mann, Kristin, 'The Illegal Slave Trade and One Yoruba Man's Transatlantic Passages from Slavery to Freedom', in *The Rise and Demise of Slavery and the Slave Trade in the Atlantic World*, ed. Philip Misevich and Kristin Mann (Rochester, NY: University of Rochester Press, 2016), 220–46

Mann, Kristin and Edna G. Bay, *Rethinking the African Diaspora: The Making of a Black Atlantic World in the Bight of Benin and Brazil* (London: Routledge, 2001)

Mann, Kristin and Philip Misevich, 'Introduction', in *The Rise and Demise of Slavery and the Slave Trade in the Atlantic World*, ed. Philip Misevich and Kristin Mann (Rochester, NY: University of Rochester Press, 2016), 1–28

Mann, Kristin and Richard Roberts, 'Slave Voices in African Colonial Courts', in *African Voices on Slavery and the Slave Trade,* Vol. 2, *Essays on Sources and Methods*, ed. Alice Bellagamba, Sandra E. Greene and Martin A. Klein (New York: Cambridge University Press, 2016), 132–53

Marcireau, Jacques, *Histoire des rites sexuels* (Paris: Robert Laffont, 1971)

Marees, Pieter de, *Description and Historical Account of the Gold Kingdom of Guinea (1602)*, ed. Albert van Dantzig and Adam Jones (London: Oxford University Press, 1987)

Mark, Peter, 'Urban Migration, Cash Cropping, and Calamity: The Spread of Islam among the Diola of Boulouf (Senegal), 1900–1940', *African Studies Review* XXI, no. 2 (1978), 1–14

Marrée, J. A. de, *Reizen op en beschrijving van de Goudkust van Guinea*, 2 vols (Amsterdam: Gebroeders Van Cleef 1817–18)

Martin, Phyllis M., 'Power, Cloth and Currency on the Loango Coast', *African Economic History* no. 15 (1986), 1–12

Martin, Phyllis M., *The External Trade of the Loango Coast, 1576–1870: The Effects of Changing Commercial Relations on the Vili Kingdom of Loango* (Oxford: Clarendon Press, 1972)

Matory, J. Lorand, 'The English Professors of Brazil: On the Diasporic Roots of

the Yorùbá Nation', *Comparative Studies in Society and History* 41, no. 1 (1999), 72–103
Matos, Paulo Teodoro de, 'Population Censuses in the Portuguese Empire', *Romanian Journal of Population Studies* 1 (2013), 5–26
Matos, Paulo Teodoro de and Jelmer Vos, 'Demografia e relações de trabalho em Angola c. 1800: um ensaio metodológico', *Diálogos* 17, no. 3 (2014), 807–34
Mattoso, Katia de Queirós, *Família e Sociedade na Bahia do Século XIX* (São Paulo: Corrupio, 1988)
Mbaye, Saliou, 'L'esclavage domestique à Saint Louis à travers les archives notariales (1817–1848)', in *Saint-Louis et l'esclavage*, ed. Djibril Samb (Dakar: IFAN, 2000), 139–58
Mbodj, Mohamed, 'The Abolition of Slavery in Senegal 1820–1890: Crisis or the Rise of a New Entrepreneurial Class?' in *Breaking the Chains: Slavery, Bondage and Emancipation in Modern Africa and Asia*, ed. Martin A. Klein (Madison: University of Wisconsin Press, 1993), 197–214
McClintock, Anne, *Imperial Leather: Race, Gender and Sexuality in the Colonial Conquest* (New York: Routledge, 1995)
McCurdy, Sheryl, 'Fashioning Sexuality: Desire, Manyema Ethnicity, and the Creation of the "Kanga", ca. 1880–1900', *The International Journal of African Historical Studies* 39 (2006), 441–69
McIntosh, Marjorie Keniston, *Yoruba Women, Work, and Social Change* (Bloomington: Indiana University Press, 2009)
McMahon, Elisabeth, *Slavery and Emancipation in Islamic East Africa: From Honor to Respectability* (New York: Cambridge University Press, 2013)
Meillassoux, Claude, 'Female Slavery', in *Women and Slavery in Africa*, ed. Claire Robertson and Martin A. Klein (Madison: University of Wisconsin Press, 1983), 49–66
Metcalf, Alida C., 'Women and Means: Women and Family Property in Colonial Brazil', in *Families in the Expansion of Europe, 1500–1800*, ed. Maria Beatriz Nizza da Silva (Brookfield, VT: Ashgate, 1998), 159–80
Metcalf, George, 'A Microcosm of Why Africans Sold Slaves: Akan Consumption Patterns in the 1770s', *The Journal of African History* 28 (1987), 377–94
Miers, Suzanne and Igor Kopytoff, eds, *Slavery in Africa: Historical and Anthropological Perspectives* (Madison: University of Wisconsin Press, 1977)
Miles, Tiya, *The Cherokee Rose: A Novel of Gardens and Ghosts* (Winston-Salem, NC: John F. Blair, 2015).
Miller, Joseph C., *Way of Death: Merchant Capitalism and the Angolan Slave Trade, 1730–1830* (Madison: Wisconsin University Press, 1988)
Miller, Joseph C., 'Women as Slaves and Owners of Slaves: Experiences from Africa, the Indian Ocean World, and the Early Atlantic', in *Women and Slavery*, ed. Gwyn Campbell, Suzanne Miers and Joseph C. Miller, Vol. 1 (Athens, OH: Ohio University Press, 2007), 1–40
Miracle, Marvin, *The Introduction and Spread of Maize in Africa* (Madison: University of Wisconsin Press, 1977)
Moitt, Bernard, 'Slavery, Flight and Redemption in Senegal, 1819–1890', *Slavery & Abolition* 14, 2 (1993), 70–86

Moleur, Bernard, 'Le droit de propriété sur le sol sénégalais', unpublished Ph.D. dissertation, Université de Dijon, 1978

Monteiro, Joachim John, *Angola and the River Congo*, 2 vols (London: Macmillan, 1875)

Moore, Francis, *Travels into the Inland Parts of Africa* (London: J. Stagg, 1738)

Moore, Henrietta L. and Megan Vaughan, *Cutting down Trees: Gender, Nutrition, and Agricultural Change in the Northern Province of Zambia, 1890–1990* (Portsmouth, NH: Heinemann, 1994)

Morgan, John, *Reminiscences of the Founding of a Christian Mission on the Gambia* (London: Wesleyan Mission House, 1864)

Mouser, Bruce, 'African Academy – Clapham 1799–1806', *History of Education* 33, 1 (2004), 87–103

Mouser, Bruce, 'The Expulsion of Dalu Modu: A Muslim Trader in Anti-Slavery Freetown', in *African Voices of Slavery and the Slave Trade*, ed. Alice Bellagamba, Sandra Greene and Martin Klein (New York: Cambridge University Press 2012), 334–41

Mouser, Bruce, 'Women Slavers of Guinea-Conakry', *Women and Slavery in Africa*, ed. Claire Robertson and Martin A. Klein (Portsmouth, NH: Heinemann, 1983), 320–39

Musisi, Nakanyike, 'The Environment, Gender, and the Development of Unequal Relations in Buganda: A Historical Perspective', *Canadian Woman Studies* 13, no. 3 (1993), 54–9

Nardin, Jean-Claude & Hermann Spirik, 'Un nouveau document pour l'étude des populations lagunaires de la Côte d'Ivoire du début du XVIIIme siècle: le voyage du [de] Jean Godot à Assinie (1701)', in *Proceedings of the 8th International Congress of Anthropological and Ethnological Sciences 1968*, 3 vols (Tokyo 1970), Vol. III, 78–81

Nast, Heidi J., *Concubines and Power: Five Hundred Years in a Northern Nigerian Palace* (Minneapolis: University of Minnesota Press, 2004)

Neidenbach, Elizabeth C., '"Refugee from St. Domingue Living in This City": The Geography of Social Networks in Testaments of Refugee Free Women of Color in New Orleans', *Journal of Urban History* 42, 5 (2016), 841–62

Nelson, Nici, 'Female-Centred Families: Changing Patterns of Marriage and Family among Buzaa Brewers in Mathare Valley', *African Urban Studies* 3 (1978), 85–103

Newbury, Colin, *The Western Slave Coast and its Rulers: European Trade and Administration among the Yoruba and Adja-speaking Peoples of South-Western Nigeria, Southern Dahomey and Togo* (Oxford: Clarendon Press, 1961)

Newson, Linda A. and Susie Minchin, *From Capture to Sale: The Portuguese Slave Trade to Spanish South America in the Early Seventeenth Century* (Leiden: Brill, 2007)

Norris, Robert, *Memoirs of the Reign of Bossa Ahádee, King of Dahomy, an Inland Country of Guiney* (London: W. Lowndes, 1789)

Northrup, David, 'Vasco da Gama and Africa: An Era of Mutual Discovery, 1497–1800', *Journal of World History* 9, no. 2 (1998), 189–211

Nwokeji, G. Ugo, 'African Conceptions of Gender and the Slave Traffic', *William and Mary Quarterly* LVIII (2001), 47–69

Ojo, Olatunji, 'The Business of "Trust" and the Enslavement of Yoruba Women and Children for Debt', in *Debt and Slavery in the Mediterranean and Atlantic Worlds*, ed. Gwyn Campbell and Alessandro Stanziani (London: Pickering & Chatto, 2013), 77–91

Oliveira, Vanessa S., 'Gender, Foodstuff Production and Trade in Late-Eighteenth Century Luanda', *African Economic History* 43, no. 1 (2015), 57–81.

Oliveira, Vanessa S., 'Mulher e comércio: A participação feminina nas redes comerciais em Luanda (século XIX)', in *Angola e as Angolanas: Memória, Sociedade e Cultura*, ed. Edvaldo Bergamo, Selma Pantoja and Ana Claudia Silva (São Paulo: Intermeios, 2016), 133–52

Oliveira, Vanessa S., 'The *Donas* of Luanda, c. 1770–1867: From Atlantic Slave Trading to "Legitimate" Commerce', unpublished Ph.D. dissertation, York University, 2016

Oliveira, Vanessa S., 'The Gendered Dimension of Trade: Female Traders in Nineteenth Century Luanda', *Portuguese Studies Review* 23, no. 2 (2015), 93–121

Oliveira, Vanessa S., 'Trabalho escravo e ocupações urbanas em Luanda na segunda metade do século XIX', in *Em torno de Angola: narrativas, identidades e as conexões atlânticas,* ed. Selma Pantoja and Estevam C. Thompson (São Paulo: Intermeios, 2014), 249–75

Oppong, Christine, ed., *Female and Male in West Africa* (London: Allen & Unwin 1983)

Oroge, E. Adeniyi, 'Iwofa: An Historical Survey of the Yoruba Institution of Indenture', *African Economic History* 14 (1985), 75–106

Oroge, E. Adeniyi, 'The Fugitive Slave Question in Anglo-Egba Relations 1861–1886', *Journal of the Historical Society of Nigeria* 8, no. 1 (1975), 61–80

Osborn, Emily L., *Our New Husbands Are Here: Households, Gender and Politics in a West African State from the Slave Trade to Colonial Rule* (Athens, OH: Ohio University Press, 2011)

Òwu Wars', *The Encyclopedia of the Yoruba,* ed. Toyin Falola and Akintunde Akinyemi (Bloomington: Indiana University Press, 2016), 259–60

Pacheco, Carlos, 'Leituras e bibliotecas em Angola na primeira metade do século XIX', *Locus (Juiz de Fora)* 6, no. 2 (2000), 21–41

Palmer, Jennifer L., 'Women and Contracts in the Age of Transatlantic Commerce', in *Women and Work in Eighteenth-Century France*, ed. Daryl M. Hafter and Nina Kushner (Baton Rouge: Louisiana State University Press, 2015), 130–51

Pankhurst, Richard, 'The History of Prostitution in Ethiopia', *Journal of Ethiopian Studies* XII, 2 (1974), 159–78

Pantoja, Selma, 'Donas de "Arimos": um negócio feminino no abastecimento de gêneros alimentícios em Luanda (séculos XVIII e XIX)', in *Entre Áfricas e Brasís*, ed. Selma Pantoja and Carlos Alberto Reis de Paula (Brasília: Paralelo 15 Editores, 2001), 35–49

Pantoja, Selma, 'Gênero e comércio: As traficantes de escravos na região de Angola', *Travessias* 4, no. 5 (2004), 79–97

Pantoja, Selma, 'Inquisição, degredo, e mestiçagem em Angola no século XVIII',

Revista Lusófona de Ciência da Religião 3, nos 5–6 (2004), 117–36

Pantoja, Selma, *Nzinga Mbandi mulher, guerra e escravidão* (Brasília: Thesaurus, 2000)

Pantoja, Selma, 'Women's Work in the Fairs and Markets of Luanda', in *Women in the Portuguese Colonial Empire: The Theatre of Shadows*, ed. Clara Sarmento (Newcastle upon Tyne: Cambridge Scholars Publishing, 2008), 81–94

Parés, Luis Nicolau, 'Afro-Catholic Baptism and the Articulation of a Merchant Community, Agoué 1840–1860', *History in Africa* 42 (2015), 165–210

Park, Mungo, *Travels in the Interior of Africa: First Journey – 1795–1797* (Edinburgh: Adam & Charles Black, 1878)

Parker, Grant, trans. *The Agony of Asar: A Thesis on Slavery by the Former Slave, Jacobus Elisa Johannes Capitein, 1717–1747* (Princeton, NJ: Markus Wiener, 2001)

Parker, John, *Making the Town: Gã State and Society in Early Colonial Accra* (Portsmouth, NH: Heinemann, 2000)

Parreira, Adriano, *Economia e sociedade na época da Rainha Jinga (século XVII)* (Lisbon: Estampa, 1997).

Pasquier, Roger, 'Les traitants des comptoirs du Sénégal au milieu du XIXe siècle', in *Entreprises et Entrepreneurs en Afrique*, ed. Catherine Coquery-Vidrovitch (Paris: Harmattan, 1983), 141–63

Paton, Diana and Pamela Scully, 'Introduction: Gender and Slave Emancipation in Comparative Perspective', in *Gender and Slave Emancipation in the Atlantic World*, ed. Pamela Scully and Diana Paton (Durham, NC: Duke University Press, 2005), 1–34

Patterson, Tiffany Ruby and Robin D. G. Kelley, 'Unfinished Migrations: Reflections on the African Diaspora and the Making of the Modern World', *African Studies Review* 43, no. 1 (April 2000), 11–45

Payne, J. A. O., *Table of Principal Events in Yoruba History* (Lagos: Andrew M. Thomas, 1894)

Peabody, Sue, 'Négresse, Mulâtresse, Citoyenne: Gender and Emancipation in the French Caribbean, 1650–1848', *Gender and Slave Emancipation in the Atlantic World*, ed. Pamela Scully and Diana Paton (Durham, NC: Duke University Press, 2005), 56–78

Peel, J. D. Y., *Christianity, Islam, and Ori a Religion: Three Traditions in Comparison and Interaction* (Oakland: University of California Press, 2016)

Peel, J. D. Y., *Religious Encounter and the Making of the Yoruba* (Bloomington: Indiana University Press, 2003)

Pels, Peter, 'The Anthropology of Colonialism: Culture, History, and the Emergence of Western Governmentality', *Annual Review of Anthropology* 26 (1997), 163–83

Perbi, Akosua Adoma, *A History of Indigenous Slavery in Ghana, from the 15th to the 19th Century* (Legon, Ghana: Sub-Saharan Publishers, 2004)

Pickles, John, *A History of Spaces: Cartographic Reason, Mapping, and the Geo-Coded World* (London: Psychology Press, 2004)

Pitcher, Anne, 'Conflict and Cooperation: Gendered Roles and Responsibilities within Cotton Households in Northern Mozambique', *African Studies Review*

39, no. 3 (1996), 81–112

Polasky, Janet L., *Revolutions without Borders: The Call to Liberty in the Atlantic World* (New Haven, CT: Yale University Press, 2015)

Popkin, Jeremy, *You Are All Free: The Haitian Revolution and the Abolition of Slavery* (Cambridge: Cambridge University Press, 2010)

Porter, Amy M., *Their Lives, Their Wills: Women in the Borderlands, 1750–1846* (Lubbock: Texas Tech University Press, 2015)

Pratt, Mary Louise, *Imperial Eyes: Travel Writing and Transculturation* (London: Routledge 1992)

Prestholdt, Jeremy, *Domesticating the World: African Consumerism and the Genealogies of Globalization* (Berkeley: University of California Press, 2008)

Priestley, Margaret, *West African Trade and Coast Society: A Family Study* (London: Oxford University Press, 1969)

Pybus, Cassandra, '"One Militant Saint": The Much Traveled Life of Mary Perth', *Journal of Colonialism & Colonial History* 9, 3 (2008), 6 ff.

Quinn, Charlotte A., *Mandingo Kingdoms of the Senegambia: Traditionalism, Islam, and European Expansion* (Evanston, IL: Northwestern University Press, 1972)

Raman, Bhavani, *Document Raj: Writing and Scribes in Early Colonial South India* (Chicago, IL: University of Chicago Press, 2012)

Ramos, Donald, 'Marriage and the Family in Colonial Vila Rica', in *Families in the Expansion of Europe, 1500–1800*, ed. Maria Beatriz Nizza da Silva (Brookfield, VT: Ashgate, 1998), 39–64

Rattray, Robert S., *Ashanti* (Oxford: Clarendon Press, 1923)

Rattray, Robert S., *Religion and Art in Ashanti* (Oxford: Clarendon Press, 1927)

Ray, Carina E., *Crossing the Color Line: Race, Sex, and the Contested Politics of Colonialism in Ghana* (Athens, OH: Ohio University Press)

Reese, Ty M., 'Wives, Brokers, and Laborers: Women at Cape Coast, 1750–1807', in *Women in Port: Gendering Communities, Economies, and Social Networks in Atlantic Port Cities, 1500–1800*, ed. Douglas Catterall and Jodi Campbell (Leiden: Brill, 2012), 291–314

Reis, João José and Carlos da Silva Jr., 'Introdução', *Atlântico de dor: Faces do tráfico de escravos*, ed. João José Reis and Carlos da Silva Jr (Salvador: UFBA, 2016), 15–37

Reis, João José and Beatriz Gallotti Mamigonian, 'Nagô and Mina: The Yoruba Diaspora in Brazil', in *The Yoruba Diaspora in the Atlantic World*, ed. Toyin Falola and Matt D. Childs (Bloomington: Indiana University Press, 2004), 77–110

Reis, João José, Flávio dos Santos Gomes and Marcus J. M. de Carvalho, *O alufá Rufino: Tráfico, escravidão e liberdade no Atlântico Negro (c. 1822–c.1853)* (São Paulo: Companhia das Letras, 2010)

Reuther, Jessica Catherine, 'Borrowed Children, Entrusted Girls: Encounters with Girlhood in French West Africa, c. 1900–1941', unpublished Ph.D. dissertation, Emory University, 2016

Reyss, Natalie, 'Saint Louis du Sénégal à l'époque précoloniale: l'émergence d'une société métisse originale, 1658–1854', Thèse de 3me cycle, Université Paris I, 1983

Richardson, David, 'Consuming Goods, Consuming People: Reflections on the Transatlantic Slave Trade', in *The Rise and Demise of Slavery and the Slave Trade in the Atlantic World*, ed. Philip Misevich and Kristin Mann (Rochester, NY: University of Rochester Press, 2016), 32–63

Richardson, David, 'West African Consumption Patterns and Their Influence on the Eighteenth-Century English Slave Trade', in *Uncommon Market: Essays in the Economic History of the Atlantic Slave Trade*, ed. Henry A. Gemery and Jan S. Hogendorn (New York: Academic Press, 1979), 303–30

Ricou, Xavier, *Trésors de l'iconographie du Sénégal colonial* (Marseille: Riveneuve, 2007)

Robertson, Claire C., 'Post-proclamation Slavery in Accra: A Female Affair?' in *Women and Slavery in Africa*, ed. Claire Robertson and Martin A. Klein (Madison: University of Wisconsin Press, 1983), 220–42

Robertson, Claire C. and Martin A. Klein, 'Women's Importance in African Slave Systems', in *Women and Slavery in Africa*, ed. Claire C. Robertson and Martin A. Klein (Madison: University of Wisconsin Press, 1983), 3–28

Robertson, Claire C., *Sharing the Same Bowl: A Socioeconomic History of Women and Class in Accra, Ghana* (Bloomington: Indiana University Press, 1984)

Robertson, G. A., *Notes on Africa* (London: Sherwood, Neely & Jones, 1819)

Robinson, David, *Paths of Accommodation: Muslim Societies and French Colonial Authorities in Senegal and Mauritania, 1880–1920* (Athens, OH: Ohio University Press, 2000)

Rodrigues, Eugénia, 'As donas de prazos do Zambebe. Políticas imperiais e estratégias locais', in *VI Jornadas Setecentistas: conferências e comunicações*, ed. Magnus R. de Mello Pereira, Antonio Cesar de Almeida Santos, Maria Luiz Andreazza and Sergio Odilon Nadalin (Curitiba: Aos Quatro Ventos, 2006), 15–34

Rodrigues, Eugénia, 'Do Atlântico ao Índico: percursos da mandioca em Moçambique no século XVIII', paper presented at V Congresso Luso-Afro-Brasileiro de Ciências Sociais, Maputo, Mozambique, 1–5 September 2000

Rodrigues, Eugénia, *Portugueses e africanos nos Rios de Sena: Os prazos da coroa em Moçambique nos séculos XVII e XVIII* (Lisbon: Imprensa Nacional, 2014)

Rodrigues, Eugénia, 'Women, Land, and Power in the Zambezi Valley of the Eighteenth Century', *African Economic History* 43 (2015), 19–56

Rodrigues, Isabel P. B. Fêo, 'Islands of Sexuality: Theories and Histories of Creolization in Cape Verde', *The International Journal of African Historical Studies* 36, no. 1 (2003), 83–103

Rogers, Dominique and Stewart King, 'Housekeepers, Merchants, Rentières: Free Women of Color in the Port Cities of Colonial Saint-Domingue, 1750–1790', in *Women in Port: Gendering Communities, Economies, and Social Networks in Atlantic Port Cities, 1500–1800*, ed. Douglas Catterall and Jodi Campbell (Leiden: Brill, 2012), 357–97

Rouch, Jean and Edmond Bernus, 'Note sur les prostituées "toutou" de Treichville et d'Adjame', *Etudes Eburnéennes* 6 (1957), 231–42

Roussiau, Jacques, 'Prostitution, jeunesse et société dans les villes du sud-est au XVe siècle', *Annales. Economies, Sociétés, Civilisations* 31 (1976), 289–325

Russell-Wood, A. J. R., *A World on the Move: The Portuguese in Africa, Asia and America, 1415–1808* (Manchester: Carcanet, 1992)
Sabran, Françoise Éléonore de Jean de Manville; ed. Stanislas-Jean de Boufflers and Henri Prat, *Correspondance inédite de la comtesse de Sabran et du chevalier de Boufflers, 1778–1788* (Paris: E. Plon, 1875)
Sackur, Karen Amanda, 'The Development of Creole Society and Culture in Saint-Louis and Gorée, 1719–1817', unpublished Ph.D. thesis, University of London, 1999
Santos, José de Almeida. *Vinte anos decisivos da vida de uma cidade (1845–1864)* (Luanda: Câmara Municipal de Luanda, 1970)
Santos, Rosenilson da Silva, 'Casamento e dote: costumes entrelaçados na sociedade da Vila Nova do Príncipe (1759–1795)', *Veredas da História* 3, no. 2 (2010), 1–14
Santos, Telma Gonçalves, 'Comércio de tecidos europeus e asiáticos na África centro-ocidental: Fraudes e contrabandos no terceiro quartel do século XVIII', unpublished M.A. thesis, Universidade de Lisboa, 2014
Sarbah, John Mensah, *Fanti Customary Laws* (London: Clowes, 1897)
Sarpong, Peter, *Girls' Nubility Rites in Ashanti* (Tema: Ghana Publishing Corporation 1977)
Sarr, Assan, 'Land, Power, and Dependency along the Gambia River, Late Eighteenth to Early Nineteenth Centuries', *African Studies Review* 57, no. 3 (2014), 101–21
Schlegel, J. B., *Schlüssel zur Ewe-Sprache* (Bremen: W. Valett 1857)
Schoenbrun, David L., 'Gendered Histories between the Great Lakes: Varieties and Limits', *The International Journal of African Historical Studies* 29 (1997), 461–92
Schroeder, Richard A., '"Re-claiming" Land in the Gambia: Gendered Property Rights and Environmental Intervention', *Annals of the Association of American Geographers* 87, no. 3 (1997), 487–508
Schwarz, Suzanne, 'Adaptation in the Aftermath of Slavery: Women, Trade and Property in Sierra Leone, c. 1790–1812', unpublished paper
Schwarz, Suzanne, 'Reconstructing the Life Histories of Liberated Africans: Sierra Leone in the Early Nineteenth Century', *History in Africa* 39 (2012), 175–207
Scott, Rebecca J. and Jean M. Hébrard, *Freedom Papers: An Atlantic Odyssey in the Age of Emancipation* (Cambridge, MA: Harvard University Press, 2012)
Scully, Pamela, *Liberating the Family? Gender and British Slave Emancipation in the Rural Western Cape, South Africa, 1823–1853* (Portsmouth, NH: Heinemann, 1997)
Scully, Pamela, 'Malintzin, Pocahontas, and Krotoa: Indigenous Women and Myth Models of the Atlantic World', *Journal of Colonialism & Colonial History* 6, no. 3 (2005)
Scully, Pamela, 'Rape, Race, and Colonial Culture: The Sexual Politics of Identity in the Nineteenth-Century Cape Colony, South Africa', *The American Historical Review* 100, no. 2 (1995), 335–59
Searing, James F., *West African Slavery and Atlantic Commerce: The Senegal River*

Valley, 1700–1860 (Cambridge: Cambridge University Press, 1993)
Semley, Lorelle, *To Be Free and French: Citizenship in France's Atlantic Empire* (Cambridge: Cambridge University Press, 2017)
Serpa Pinto, Alexandre Alberto da Rocha de, *Como eu atravessei a África*, Vol. I (Lisbon: Edições Europa-América, 1980).
Sheldon, Kathleen E., 'Markets and Gardens: Placing Women in the History of Urban Mozambique', *Canadian Journal of African Studies* 37 (2003), 358–95
Sheldon, Kathleen E., *Pounders of Grain: A History of Women, Work, and Politics in Mozambique* (Portsmouth, NH: Heinemann, 2002)
Sheller, Mimi, 'Sword-Bearing Citizens: Militarism and Manhood in Nineteenth-Century Haiti', *Plantation Society in the Americas* 4, nos 2–3 (1997), 233–78
Shields, Francine. 'Palm Oil and Power: Women in an Era of Economic and Social Transformation in 19th Century Yorubaland (South-Western Nigeria)', unpublished Ph.D. thesis, University of Stirling, 1997
Shumway, Rebecca, 'Castle Slaves of the Eighteenth-Century Gold Coast (Ghana)', *Slavery & Abolition* 35, no. 1 (2014), 84–98
Shumway, Rebecca, *The Fante and the Transatlantic Slave Trade* (Rochester, NY: University of Rochester Press, 2011)
Sidbury, James, *Becoming African in America. Race and Nation in the Early Black Atlantic* (Oxford: Oxford University Press, 2007)
Signorini, I., 'Agonwole Agyale: The Marriage between Two Persons of the Same Sex among the Nzema of Southwestern Ghana', *Journal de la Société des Africanistes* 43 (1973), 221–34
Silva Corrêa, Elias Alexandre da. *História de Angola*, Vol. I (Lisbon: Editorial Ática, 1937)
Silva, Filipa Ribeiro da, 'Counting People and Homes in Mozambique in the 1820s: Population Structures and Household Size and Composition', *African Economic History* 45, no. 1 (2017), 46–76
Silva, Filipa Ribeiro da, 'From Church Records to Royal Population Charts: The Birth of "Modern Demographic Statistics" in Mozambique, 1720s–1820s', *Anais de História de Além-Mar* 6 (2015), 125–50
Silva, Maria Beatriz Nizza da, *Cultura e Sociedade no Rio de Janeiro, 1808–1821* (São Paulo: Companhia Editora Nacional, 1977)
Silva, Maria Beatriz Nizza da, *Donas e plebeias na sociedade colonial* (Lisbon: Estampa, 2002)
Silva, Maria Beatriz Nizza da, *História da Família no Brasil Colonial*, 3rd edn (Rio de Janeiro: Nova Fronteira, 1998)
Silva, Maria Beatriz Nizza da, *Sistema de casamento no Brasil colonial* (São Paulo: Editora da Universidade de São Paulo, 1978)
Silva, Maria Beatriz Nizza da, *Vida privada e quotidiano no Brasil na época de D. Maria I e D. João VI* (Lisbon: Editorial Estampa, 1999)
Singleton, Theresa A., 'The Slave Trade Remembered on the Former Gold and Slave Coasts', in *From Slavery to Emancipation in the Atlantic*, ed. Sylvia R. Frey and Betty Wood (London: Frank Cass, 1999), 150–69
Skertchly, J. A., *Dahomey as It Is* (London: Chapman & Hall, 1874)

Smith, Robert Sydney, *The Lagos Consulate: 1851–1861* (London and Basingstoke, UK: Macmillan, 1978)
Smith, William, *A New Voyage to Guinea* (London: John Nourse, 1744)
Soares, Mariza de Carvalho and Nielson Rosa Bezerra, *Escravidão africana no Recôncavo da Guanabara (séculos XVII–XIX)* (Niterói, RJ: Editora da UFF, 2011)
Southall, Aidan W., ed., *Social Change in Modern Africa* (London: Oxford University Press, 1961)
Spilsbury, F. B., *Account of a Voyage to the Western Coast of Africa; Performed by His Majesty's Sloop Favourite in the Year 1805* (London: R. Philips, 1807)
Stephens, Rhiannon, *A History of African Motherhood* (New York: Cambridge University Press, 2014)
Stoler, Ann Laura, 'Colonial Archives and the Arts of Governance', *Archival Science* 2 (2002), 87–109
Stow, John, *A Survey of the Cities of London and Westminster: Corrected, Improved, and Very Much Enlarged* (by John Strype), 6th edn, 2 vols (London: W. Innys and J. Richardson et al., 1720 [1598])
Strickrodt, Silke, *Afro-European Trade in the Atlantic World: The Western Slave Coast, c.1550–c.1885* (Woodbridge, UK: James Currey, 2015)
Strickrodt, Silke, 'British Abolitionist Policy on the Ground in West Africa in the Mid-Nineteenth Century', in *The Changing Worlds of Atlantic Africa: Essays in Honor of Robin Law*, ed. Toyin Falola and Matt D. Childs (Durham, NC: Carolina Academic Press, 2009), 155–72
Substance of the Report Delivered by the Court of Directors of the Sierra Leone Company, to the General Court of Proprietors, on Thursday the 27th March, 1794 (London: J. Philips, 1795)
Substance of the Report, Delivered by the Court of Directors of the Sierra Leone Company, to the General Court of Proprietors, on Thursday the 29th March, 1798 (London: J. Philips & Son, 1798)
Substance of the Report Delivered by the Court of Directors of the Sierra Leone Company, to the General Court of Proprietors, on Thursday the 29th March, 1804 (London: W. Philips, 1804)
Substance of the Report Delivered by the Court of Directors of the Sierra Leone Company, to the General Court of Proprietors, on Thursday the 24th of March, 1808 (London: privately published, 1808)
Sweet, James H., *Domingos Álvares, African Healing, and the Intellectual History of the Atlantic World* (Chapel Hill: University of North Carolina Press, 2011)
Sweet, James H., *Recreating Africa: Culture, Kinship, and Religion in the African-Portuguese World, 1441–1770* (Chapel Hill: University of North Carolina Press, 2003)
Sweet, John Wood and Lisa A. Lindsay, eds, *Biography and the Black Atlantic*. Early Modern Americas Series (Philadelphia: University of Pennsylvania Press, 2014)
Swindell, Kenneth and Alieu Jeng, *Migrants, Credit and Climate: The Gambian Groundnut Trade, 1834–1934* (Leiden: Brill, 2006)
Talbot, Percy Amaury, *The Peoples of Southern Nigeria*, Vol. I (London: Frank

Cass, 1969 [1926])

Teixeira da Mota, Avelino, 'The Mande Trade in Costa da Mina according to Portuguese Documents until the Mid-Sixteenth Century', unpublished paper, presented at the Conference on Manding Studies (School of Oriental & African Studies, London 1972)

Tengbergen, H. F., *Verhaal van de reistogt en expeditie naar de nederlandsche bezittingen ter westkust van Afrika (kust van Guinea)* (Den Haag: S. de Visser, 1839)

Tew, Mary, 'A Form of Polyandry among the Lele of the Kasai', *Africa* 21 (1951), 1–12

Thornton, John K., *A Cultural History of the Atlantic World, 1250–1820* (New York: Cambridge University Press, 2012)

Thornton, John K., *Africa and Africans in the Making of the Atlantic World, 1400–1800*, 2nd edn (New York: Cambridge University Press, 1998)

Thornton, John K., 'Precolonial African Industry and the Atlantic Trade, 1500–1800', *African Economic History* no. 19 (1990), 1–19

Thornton, John K., 'Sexual Demography: The Impact of the Slave Trade on Family Structure', in *Women and Slavery in Africa*, ed. Claire Robertson and Martin Klein (Madison: University of Wisconsin Press, 1983), 39–48

Thornton, John K., *The Kingdom of Kongo: Civil War and Transition, 1641–1718* (Madison: The University of Wisconsin Press, 1983)

Thornton, John K., *The Kongolese Saint Anthony: Dona Beatriz Kimpa Vita and the Antonian Movement, 1684–1706* (Cambridge: Cambridge University Press, 1998)

Thornton, John K., 'The Slave Trade in Eighteenth Century Angola: Effects on Demographic Structures', *Canadian Journal of African Studies* 14, no. 3 (1980), 417–27

Touray, Isatou, 'Gender and Land Dynamics in the Gambia: The Struggle for Citizenship, Democracy Calling for the Agency of the Poor', in *Land in the Struggles for Citizenship in Africa,* ed. Sam Moyo, Dzodzi Tsikata and Yakham Diop (Dakar: CODESRIA, 2015), 129–56

Traver, Barbara Jean, 'After Kourou: Settlement Schemes in French Guiana in the Age of Enlightenment', unpublished Ph.D. dissertation, Washington State University, 2011

Tremearne, A. J. N., 'Extracts from the Diary of the Late Reverend John Martin, Wesleyan Missionary in West Africa, 1843–48', *Man* 12, no. 74 (1912), 138–43

Turner, Michael J., 'The Limits of Abolition: Government, Saints and the "African Question"', c. 1780–1820', *English Historical Review* 112, 446 (1997), 319–57

Uchendu, Egodi, *Women and Conflict in the Nigerian Civil War* (Trenton, NJ: Africa World Press, 2007)

Uring, Nathaniel, *A History of the Voyages and Travels of Capt. Nathaniel Uring*, 2nd edn (London: John Clarke, 1727)

Valdez, Francisco Travassos, *Six Years of a Traveller's Life in Western Africa*, 2 vols (London: Hurst and Blackett, 1861)

Valsecchi, Pierluigi, *Power and State Formation in West Africa, Appolonia from the Sixteenth to the Eighteenth Century* (New York: Palgrave Macmillan, 2011)

Van Dantzig, Albert, 'The Ankobra Gold Interest', *Transactions of the Historical Society of Ghana* 14 (1973), 169–85
Van der Eb, A., 'Inboorlingenrecht van de kust van Guinea 1851', *Bijdragen tot de taal-, land- en volkenkunde van Nederlandsch-Indie* 88 (1931), 287–313
Vansina, Jan, 'Ambaca Society and the Slave Trade c. 1760–1845', *The Journal of African History* 46, no. 1 (2005), 1–27
Vansina, Jan, 'Long-Distance Trade-Routes in Central Africa', *The Journal of African History* 3, no. 3 (1962), 375–90
Vansina, Jan, *Paths in the Rainforests: Toward a History of Political Tradition in Equatorial Africa* (Madison: University of Wisconsin Press, 1990)
Vansina, Jan, 'Portuguese vs Kimbundu: Language Use in the Colony of Angola (1575–c.1845)', *Bulletin des Séances de l'Académie des Sciences d'Outre-Mer* 47 (2001–2003), 267–81
Vaughan, Megan, *Creating the Creole Island: Slavery in Eighteenth-Century Mauritius* (Durham, NC: Duke University Press, 2005)
Venâncio, José Carlos, *A economia de Luanda e hinterland no século XVIII: um estudo de sociologia histórica* (Lisbon: Editorial Estampa, 1996)
Vos, Jelmer, *Kongo in the Age of Empire, 1860–1913: The Breakdown of a Moral Order* (Madison: University of Wisconsin Press, 2015)
Walker, James W. StG., *The Black Loyalists. The Search for a Promised Land in Nova Scotia and Sierra Leone, 1783–1870* (Toronto: University of Toronto Press, 1999)
Wariboko, Waibinte. *Elem Kalabari of the Niger Delta: The Transition from Slave to Produce Trading under British Imperialism* (Trenton, NJ: Africa World Press, 2014)
Watts, Michael J., 'Idioms of Land and Labor: Producing Politics and Rice in Senegambia', in *Land in African Agrarian Systems*, ed. Thomas J. Bassett and Donald E. Crummey (Madison: University of Wisconsin Press, 1993), 157–93
Webb, James, 'Ecological and Economic Change along the Middle Reaches of the Gambia River, 1945–1985', *African Affairs* 91, no. 365 (1992), 543–65
Weil, Peter M., 'Slavery, Groundnuts, and Capitalism in the Wuli Kingdom of Senegambia, 1820–1930', *Research in Economic Anthropology* 6 (1984), 77–119
Weisberger, Richard William, Dennis P. Hupchick and David L. Anderson, *Profiles of Revolutionaries in Atlantic History, 1700–1850* (New York: Columbia University Press, 2007)
Welman, C. W., *Native States of the Gold Coast, No. 2: Ahanta* (London: Dawson, 1930)
Wheat, David, *Atlantic Africa and the Spanish Caribbean, 1570–1640* (Chapel Hill: University of North Carolina Press, 2016)
Wheat, David, 'Nharas and Morenas Horras: A Luso-African Model for the Social History of the Spanish Caribbean, c. 1570–1640', *Journal of Early Modern History* 14 (2010), 119–50
Wheeler, Douglas L. 'An Angolan Woman of Means: D. Ana Joaquina dos Santos e Silva, Mid-Nineteenth Century Luso-African Merchant-Capitalist of Luanda', *Santa Barbara Portuguese Studies* 3 (1996), 284–97
White, Ashli, *Encountering Revolution: Haiti and the Making of the Early Republic*

(Baltimore, MD: Johns Hopkins University Press, 2010)
White, E. Frances, 'Creole Women Traders in the Nineteenth Century', *International Journal of African Historical Studies* 14, no. 4 (1981), 626–42
White, E. Frances, *Sierra Leone's Settler Women Traders: Women on the Afro-European Frontier* (Ann Arbor: University of Michigan Press, 1987)
White, E. Frances, 'Women, Work, and Ethnicity: The Sierra Leone Case', in *Women and Work in Africa*, ed. Edna G. Bay (Boulder, CO: Westview Press, 1982), 19–33
White, Luise, *The Comforts of Home: Prostitution in Colonial Nairobi* (Chicago, IL: University of Chicago Press, 1990)
Wilks, Ivor, *Forests of Gold. Essays on the Akan and the Kingdom of Asante* (Athens, OH: Ohio University Press, 1993)
Wilson, Ellen Gibson, *The Loyal Blacks* (New York: Putman, 1976)
Wilson, Kathleen, 'The Performance of Freedom: Maroons and the Colonial Order in Eighteenth-Century Jamaica and the Atlantic Sound', *William and Mary Quarterly*, 3rd series, 66, no. 1 (2009), 45–86
Winius, George and B. W. Diffie, *Foundations of the Portuguese Empire, 1415–1825*, Vol. I (Minneapolis: University of Minnesota Press, 1977)
Wright, Donald R., *The World and a Very Small Place in Africa: A History of Globalization in Niumi, The Gambia* (London: Routledge, 2010)
Zeleza, Paul Tiyambe, 'Gender Biases in African Historiography', in *African Gender Studies: A Reader*, ed. Oyeronke Oyewumi (New York: Palgrave Macmillan, 2005), 207–32
Zimmerman, Sarah, 'Citizenship, Military, and Managing Exceptionalism: *Originaires* in World War I', in *Empires in World War I: Shifting Frontiers and Imperial Dynamics in a Global Conflict*, ed. Andrew Tait Jarboe and Richard S. Fogarty (London: I.B. Tauris, 2014), 219–48
Zuccarelli, François, *La Vie politique sénégalaise (1789–1940)* (Paris: CHEAM, 1987)

Index

Note: Page numbers in italic indicate maps, illustrations or charts; page numbers followed by *n* indicate a footnote with relevant number.

Abẹokuta
 base for Akitoye, 138
 Christian missions, 131
 maps, *133*, *144*
 Owu quarter, 153, 159, 166–8
 slavery, 143–4
abusua (matrilineal group), 92, 113–14
Adanson, Michel, 197–8
Adebambi
 and Adjatu's murder, 154, 160
 debt to Rosao, 159, 160–61
 Islamic identity, 165–6
 murder confession, 162–3
 stolen goods as security for debt, 162
Agadja, King, 99
Aggerij (Cudjo's son), 118, 124
agriculture
 Angola, 223
 cash crops, 42, 48–9, 52
 Catumbela, 9, 56, 60–61, *62*, 66–7
 as condition of land access, 62–4
 gendered nature, 58–9
 Jamaican Maroons, 27–8
 new crops in Africa, 67
 reliance on dependants for labour, 60–61, *62*

 surpluses for exchange, 42
 see also Mandinka agriculture
Ahanta people, 94
Ajatu (formerly Ajifoluke)
 Brazilian slave, 149, 150
 conflict with Momo, 157–61
 dispute over her estate, 151, 154, 167
 Islamic identity, 149–50, 164–5
 Lagos family and household, 153–7
 marginality, 152–3
 Momo (male dependant), 153, 154, 155–7
 murder and robbery, 12, 154, 160, 161–2
 murder trial, 152, 165
 return to Lagos, 150, 153
 stolen chains, 160, 161, 162
 support networks, 161, 163–5, 167
Akan people, 89, 91, 129
Akitoye, *ọba*, 138, 139–40, 141
Alabọn (Rosa) (fugitive slave)
 in Badagry, 132
 Certificate of Freedom, 139
 disappearance from Badagry, 138
 emancipation journey, 11, 132, *134*, 136–7
 free British subject, 139

280 • *Index*

pawned by Tinubu to Sandeman, 138–9
vulnerability, 11
Alain, Louison, 240–42
alcohol, 29, 245
Almeida, Félix de, 228
Almond, Sarah, 24
Alpern, Stanley, 67
Alsace, Louis, *241*, 242
Amaral, Dona Ana Joaquina do, 231–2
Amaral, Dona Maria Joaquina do, 230–31, 232
Amponesie (Betje Hamilton's sister), 122–4, 130
amulets (*gris-gris*), *241*, 242
Andrade, Francisco Gomes de (formerly Shetolu), 148–9, 152, 153, 154, 167
Andrade, Luis Antônio de, 148–9
Angola, *216*
  Portuguese migrants, 222
  see also Benguela; Luanda
Anomabo Fort, 109, 117
Anthony, Catherine, 27
Apachie, 117, 119
apprenticeships, 34, 35, 37, 131
Aquassiba, 114–15, 129
Ardener, Edwin, 104–5
Aredyana (wife of Port Logo chief), 31
Asante, land access, 63
Assinie, 93
Aubert, Louis-Armand, 204
Aussenac, Hélène, 210
Austin, Gareth, 63
Austin, Samuel C., 137
Awa (fugitive slave), 11, 132, *134*, 143–4, 146–7
Axim, 90–92, 96, 124–8
Ayebomi (Ajatu's sister), 148, 149, 153, 154, 166, 167

Bacchus, Alice, 23
Badagry, 132, *133*, 138
Bah, Maba, 45n29, 50
Bailey, Betsey, 28
Bambali village, 48

Banbury, Lucy, 26
Bank of Senegal, 244
Bastos, Dona Tereza de Jesus Pereira, 228–9
Bastos, José António Pereira, 228–9
beads, *59*, *80*, 82, *112*, 187, 224
beans, 55, 66–7, 69
Beecroft, John, 140
beliefs, 52, 172
Bell, Acting Governor, 121, 122
Benguela
  food scarcity, 66
  imported goods, 76–85
  population, 3, 58, 74
  reliance on Catumbela's foodstuffs, 56–7, 69
  slave ownership, 8, 34
  slave trading port, 56, 69
  trading links with Catumbela, 67–8
  wills and inventories, 70–71, 73–4, 75
big men, 96
Bight of Benin, *133*, 135–6, 137, 203
Bigon, Liora, 142
Bihé, 76–7, 224
Binyeah (slave), 123, 124
birth control, 106
Black Loyalists, 22
Blanchot, Marianne, *241*, 242
Bojang, Madibba, 44
Booker, Hope *see* Esperance, Madam
Booker, John
  death and bequests, 178–9, 183
  friends and supporters, 174–5
  Hope's schooling, 174
  'Lopus fraud', 172, 175
  RAC trading operations, 171, 174–5
  slaves, 172–4
Bosman, Willem, 90–92, 97–8, 103, 104
Brazil
  exports, 73, 82
  illegal slave trade, 229–30
  prohibition on slave imports, 220
  record of departing freed Africans, 154–5

transatlantic slave trade, 148–9
Yoruba-speaking slaves, 150
bridewealth, 10, 45, 180*n16*, 223–4
Britain
   and Gorée, 196
   Lagos bombardment and annexation, 131, 137–8, 141–2
   limited prospects for free blacks, 184
   Madam Esperance in London, 174–5, 180–85
British colonial courts, 151–2, 161, 163–4
British colonial officials, 22, 50–52
Burton, Richard, 101, 142

Cacheu, 2, 177
Caconda, 57, 75, 78
Cadaval, Florência José do, 75–6, 78–9, 82, 84
Câmara, Germano Francisco da, 227
Cape Coast Castle, 111–13, 121
captured negroes, 20, 21, 35, 37
Carney, Judith, 42
carpentry, 76–7
casar (Gold Coast), 113, 114–15
cash crops, peanuts, 42, 48–9, 52
cassava (manioc), 31, 66
Catholic church, 223–5, *241*, 242
Catrijn (Eurafrican woman), 124–8, 130
cattle, 47, 64–5
Catumbela
   agricultural production, 9, 56, 60–61, *62*, 66–7
   dependent population, 60–61, *62*
   land access, 62–5, *65*
   military outpost, 57
   population, 60
   Relação de Moradores de Catumbela (residents' listing), 57*n13*, 60, 61, 66, 69
   supplier for Benguela, 56–7, 69
   tax revenue and agricultural production, 66
   trade entrepôt, 57
   trading links with Benguela, 67–8
   women's property, 75–6
Cayenne (Guiana), 209, 210–211
Ceesay, Biran, 50
Ceesay, Moriba, 44
Channel, Affy, 23
Charleston (South Carolina), 206–7, 208
Chartran, Charlotte, 207
chiefs, initiation ceremonies, 96
children
   Eurafrican children, 113
   Freetown settlers, 23
   Hope (child slave), 171
   pawnship, 136
   of 'whores', 94, 105, 106
   see also girls; inheritance
China, Portuguese traders, 78
Christian women, 3, 225
Christianity
   conversion, 132
   mission stations, 131, *144*, 145, 146
Cisse, Marie, 245, 246
citizenship, rights, 209–211
Cleeve, Alexander, 171, 172
clothing
   Benguela, 78–82, *80*, *83*
   Eurafrican women, *241*
   Gorée businesswoman, 245
   prestige and identity, 9
   Sierra Leone, *30*
   signare dress, *241*, 242
   white, 93, 95
coffee, 71, 229
Coker, Mary, 137
colonialism
   governance systems, 6
   see also Britain; British colonial courts; British colonial officials; French empire; Portuguese empire
Compagnie de Guyane (Guiana Company), 211
Conceição de Jesus, Dona Maria José, 225
copper, 73, 82

Corrêa, Elias Alexandre da Silva, 223
Costa, António José da, 67
Costa, Dona Leonor Pereira da, 68
Costa, Joana Rodrigues da, 75–6, 84
Coulon, Johanna Vitringa, *116*
Cowling, William, 33–4
cowries, as currency, 97, 98, 104
Crespin, Germain, 240–42
Cudjo, Birempong, 118, 121, 122, 123–4, 130
Cunha, Teresa de Jesus Barros e, 75–6, 77–8
currency
  cowries as, 97, 98, 104
  textiles as, 82–3

Dahomey, 5, 99–101
Dakar, 246
dance, 102
Dapper, Olfert, 90–92, 106
Darboe, Dari Bana, 51–2
Darboe, Mariama, 51
Davis, Mary, 158, 163–4
De Petersen, Baron, 122, 123
Debane, Anne, 200
debt
  Adebambi-Rosario, 159, 160–61
  enslavement for debt, 139
  false claims of, 110
  see also pawnship
Devès, Gaspard, 242–3
Diouf, Sylviane, 110, 129
disputes (palavers)
  Aquassiba's initiative, 114–15, 129
  Betje Hamilton and stolen gold, 121–4, 130
  Catrijn's isolation, 124–8, 130
  false claims, 110, 119–20, 121, 129
  help from European marriage partner, 114–15
  indigenous meditators, 117
  Madam Watts' extended family dispute, 109–110, 117–20, 128, 129–30

mediation by European officials, 109–10, 111, 117, 120, 128, 129–30
panyarring (arbitrary seizure), 119, 120, 123, 132, 138
Disu, 162–3, 165, 166
divorce, 231
d'Olin, Dona Maria Vieira, 227
donas, 60, 68, 227–32
Dọpẹmu, Daniel (fugitive slave), 145, 146
Dosunmu, *ọba*, 141, 142, 149
Douville, Jean-Baptiste, 222
dowry, 10, 45, 180*n16*, 223–4
dress *see* clothing; jewellery
Du Parel, Nicolas François Evrard, 199–200
Dumbaya, Foday Kabba, 52
Dumont, Guillaume, 204, 205, 206
Dunbar, Erica Armstrong, 214
Dutch West India Company, 94, 109–110
Dwight, Ann, 27, 28
Dyke, Elizabeth, 175, 181, 188
Dyke, Humphrey, 175, 181, 182–3, 185

education, 31, 175, 232
elite women
  Catumbela, 55, 68
  clothing and jewellery, 78–82, *80, 83, 241*
  donas, 60, 68, 227–32
  friendships, 245, 246
  Gambia River property ownership, 44–5, 47–8
  merchants, 177
  Portuguese influence, 76
  prestige and identity, 9
  property and consumption, 75–85
  Western dress, 75, 78, 79
  see also signares
Elmina, 109–10, 111–13, 121, 122–4
entrepreneurs, 5, 19, 32, 36, 114, 230–31, 240
Esperance, Madam
  baptism, 183–4

in Booker household, 175–6
child slave, 171
Christianity, 180
daughter (Elizabeth), 180–81
English literacy, 175
inheritance challenge, 181–2
inheritance from Booker and Heath estates, 178–9, 183, 184, 185
limited prospects in London, 184–5
living in London, 180–85
London schooling, 174–5
manumission, 178–9
marriage to Samuel Meston, 184–5
marriage to William Heath, 179–81, 182
Portuguese/English names, 174
slave owner, 186
slave trader, 187, 188
successful Lower Gambian merchant, 186–9
William Heath's death, 181, 182–3
Eurafrican children, 113
Eurafrican women, 19, *112*, *116*
advantages, 128–9
affective ties with elite men, 240–43, *241*
Catrijn's dangerous isolation, 124–8, 130
little contact with Europeans, 117
vulnerability, 10–11
European women, 23, 25, 74

families, emotional ties, 239–43
Felicidade (freed woman), 157, 163
female traders, 9, 28–33
  see also entrepreneurs
Fennekol, Commander, 124–8
Forbes Bonnetta, Sarah, 140
Fraser, Louis, 138, 139–40, 141
Freeman, Stanhope, 143
Freetown women
  diverse origins, 20
  land issues, 25–8
  population, 22–5
  recaptives as new source of labour, 20, 21, 35, 37
  risk of re-enslavement, 22, 31
  trade and small-scale manufacturing, 28–33
French empire
  Atlantic ports, 235–7, *238*
  and being French, 209–213
  civil rights, 205
  and Gorée, 196, 199–200
  and James Island, 185
  and Saint Louis, *238*
French Revolution, 206, 212–13
friendships, *241*, 242–3, 245
fugitive slaves, 132, 139–41, 142–3, 146–7
Fula women, 45, 47–8
furniture, 76–8, 243, 245

Gambia River, *40*, 41–3
gender imbalance
  Catumbela agriculture, 61, *62*, 67, 68–9
  Catumbela land access, 64, *65*, 68–9
  consumer goods ownership, 85
  demographic, 2–3, 4, 22–3, 58–60
  following slave trade ban, 239
  Freetown land use, 27–8
  Gorée slaves, 199
  Mandinka agriculture, 38, 41–3, 52
girls, 14, 96, 100–101, 136
global economy, 72–3, 85
Glover, John, 132, 140, 143, 146
Godot, Jean, 93–4
gold, 73, 81, 82, *83*
Gold, Betsey, 34
Gold Coast, 89–97, 102–6, *108*–30
Gorée
  Anne Rossignol, 192, 198–9
  early history, 195–6, 235
  elite communities, 192, 193
  food for captives, 42
  freed captives, 200
  land ownership, 199–200
  links with mainland, 201
  Maison des Esclaves, 203
  mulâtres, 191, 196, 197, 198, 201
  opposition to Cayenne scheme, 209, 210–11

petitions to French government, 209–212
population, 197–200
racial and social mix, 195–7, 235
slave ownership, 34, 198, 199, 203, 211
slave trade, 203, 211
social mix, 195–6
trading post, 196, 235, *236*, 237
see also habitants; signares
gourmet/grumet/te, 196, 235n6
Granville Town, 22
gris-gris (amulets), *241*, 242
Guerra, Cândido José dos Santos, 229–30
Guerra, Dona Ana de Jesus, 229–30
Guet N'Dar, *238*, 244
gum arabic, 73, *236*, 237, 243

habitants
competition from black traders, 243–4
Crespin relationships, 240
Pellegrin wealth and property inventory, 244–6
petitions to French government, 209–212
social status, 197, 200, 212, 235
and trading rights, 211
Hamilton, Betje, 121–4, 128, 130
Hamilton, George, 121–2
Harding, Mary, 35
Hawkins, Edward, 175
Hazeley, Martha, 29
Heard, Betsey, 32–3
Heath, Hope *see* Esperance, Madam
Heath, Samuel, 181–2
Heath, William, 179–81, 182–3
hinterland
imported goods, 75–6, 85
long-distance trade, 70–72, 84–5
trading opportunities, 32, 35
Hopkins, A. G., 63
housekeeping, 35, 221
housing, rental income, 33, 243
Hutchinson, Richard, 183–4
Huydecoper, Jan, 123–4

identity
being French, 209–213
claim to whiteness, 206, 207–8, 213
trans-African women, 195
Ijuade, 160, 161–2, 163–4
illegal slave sales, 34, 149, 229–30, 231
imported goods, 71, 73, 76–8, 83–4
India, textile exports, 83–4
inheritance
Ajatu-Momo conflict, 158
Benguela wills and inventories, 70–71, 73–4, *75*
descent through female line, 9–10, 46–8
Gorée businesswoman's inventory, 244–6
land, 28
Mandinka land disputes, 49–52
women in Portuguese empire, 64
iron, 72, 187
Islam, 41, 49–50, 52, 164–6
see also Muslim women
ivory, 71, 73, 187, 220

Jabbi, Wuleng Jarsey, 38, 44, 45
Jamaican Maroons, 22, 23–5, 27–8, 29, 35
James Island fort, 171–7, *176*, 185, 186
James, Mary, 24
Jatta, Karafa Ali, 44
Jattaba village, 50–51
Jeng, Alieu, 46
jewellery
Ajatu's stolen chains, 160, 161, 162
Angola, 59
Benguela, 81–2, *83*
Gold Coast, *112*
Gorée businesswoman, 245
prestige and identity, 8, 9, 81
Senegal *signares*, *202*, 242, 243
Jobba, Fatou, 38, 44–5
Jobe, Masamba Koke, 44
Jobson, Richard, 43
Jola women, 42, 45–6, *46*, 52
Juffure village, 48, 186

Kiaka, Antoine, 210
King, Phillis, 27
Kombo, 44
Kongo, 6
Koto, Mansa, 51–2
Kuma, Amonu (*caboceer*), 109–10, 117, 118–20
Kumbija village, 50

labour force
  black women, 221–2
  housekeeping, 35, 221
  importance of enslaved women, 7
  recaptive Africans, 20, 21, 35, 37
  reliance on dependants for agriculture, 60–61, *62*
  youths as household help, 153, 155–6
Lages, Narciso José Pacheco, 78
Lagos
  Brazilian *retornados*, 149, 152
  British bombardment and annexation, 131, 137–8, 141–2
  continuing slavery, 140
  Islam, 164–6
  legal institutions, 151, 162, 163–4
  map, *133*
  mosques, 164
  policy on fugitive slaves, 132, 139–41, 142–3, 146–7
  returnee networks, 161, 163–5, 167
land access, 38–9, 62–3, 64
land ownership
  conferred by swamp clearance, 39
  as dowry, 10, 45
  economic security, 8
  Freetown settlers, 25–8
  Gorée, 199–200
  as 'male daughters', 44–5
  Mandinka, 39, 43–52
  quit rent, 27
  smaller plots for Freetown women, 27, 36
  and wealth, 43
  women, 9–10
  see also inheritance
land rights, 26–7, 46–7, 63
Lawson, Dora, 24
Lázaro, Gaspar, 225
Le Cap (Saint-Domingue), 204–6, 213
Le Monier, Renée, 191
Leitão, Catarina de Faria, 36
Lele people, 105–6
LeSeigneur, Vincent, 208
Leye, Khayta Macoumba, 240–42
liberated Africans, 20, 21, 35, 37
Lima, Dona Teresa Vieira de, 68
Linckenheyl, Louis Georges, 242
Lisboa, Catarina Pereira, 34, 55*n*3
literacy, 175, 232
Lopez, António, 174, 175
'Lopus fraud', 172, 175
Lorea, Nicolau, 226
Louet, Cati/Caty Louette, 34, 199, 210, 211, 212
Luanda
  African women, *219*
  Catholic marriage petitions, 223–7
  donas and agriculture, 60
  effect of slave trade ban, 220, 221
  exports, 220–21
  Luso-Africans, 218–20
  population, 3, 221
  shops, 81
Lumẹyẹ (slave trader), 145
Luso-African women
  Christianity, 225
  marriage with immigrant men, 228–32
  marriage petitions, 222–7
  wealth inheritance, 228–9
  wealth preservation on marriage, 230–31
Luso-Africans, 218–20
Lynch, Phebe, 28

McCoskry, William, 140, 141–3
Machado, António Félix, 231
Magalhães, Albino José Soares da Costa, 229

Magyar, László, 224
maize, 66–7, 230, 231
Mandinka agriculture
    crop cultivation, 41–3
    family and slave labour, 43
    gender differences, 38, 41–3, 52
    shift from rice to peanuts, 48–9
Mandinka women
    gender relations, 40–41
    head wife responsibilities, 41
    junior wives, 41
    land ownership, 43–6
    loss of power and land rights, 48–9, 52–3
    rice cultivation, 39, 41, 42–3
manioc (cassava), 31, 66
March, Martha, 23
marriage
    à la mode du pays (Senegal), 233, 239–43
    affective ties with Eurafrican women, 240–43, *241*
    bridewealth, 10, 45, 180n16, 223–4
    casar (Gold Coast), 113, 114–15
    Catholic elite weddings, 223–7
    European/settler liaisons discouraged, 33–4
    and freedom for slave women, 95
    Islamic law, 41
    land as dowry, 45
    mixed marriage, 239–43
    punishment for infidelity, 98, 103
    self-endowment and contracts, 230–31
marriage alliances
    as help in disputes, 114–15, 117, 120, 121–2
    Mandinka, 44–6
    personal and commercial networks, 32–3, 222–3, 228–32, 233
    with resident Europeans, 113, 129, 179–81, 182, 188
marriage contracts, 230–31
marriage petitions, 222–7
Martins, Maria José, 75–6
matrilineality, 7
    abusua (lineage), 92, 113–14
    rice field inheritance, 46–7, 48
Melo, Senhora Bernardo de, 177, 179, 185
Mende women, 31, 35
Meneses, Francisca Josefa de Moura, 36
Messeng, Tumani, 51
Meston, Samuel, 184–5
métis, 2, 235n6
    see also Eurafrican women; *mulâtres*
Miles, Tiya, 214
Miller, Joseph, 83
millet pounders (*pileuses*), *238*, 244
Minge, Thomas, 175
mobility
    access to rice fields, 48–9, 53
    across the Atlantic, 12–13
    Alabọn's emancipation journey, 132, *134*, 136–7
    of enslaved females, 132
    trans-African women, 193–5, 204–8, 213
    women, 12–14
    see also Rossignol, Anne
Momo (Ajatu's male dependant)
    Ajatu murder and robbery, 153, 160, 162–4
    conflict with Ajatu, 157–61
    dependant helper for Ajatu, 153, 154, 155–7
    Islamic identity, 165–6
    prison and hanging, 165–6, 168
    relationship with Ajatu, 154, 155–7
monarchy, and 'whores', 93, 94, 98–9, 101
Monteiro, Joachim John, 222
Moraes, Joana Mendes de, 79–80, 82, 84
Morgan, John, 42–3
mulâtres (Gorée), 191, 196, 197, 198, 201, 212
    see also Rossignol, Anne
mulatto, 2, 235n6
    see also Eurafrican women; *mulâtres*
murder
    Ajatu murder and trial, 152, 154,

160–66
Sankandi murder, 51–2
Muslim traders, *238*
Muslim women, 3, 23, 234
    Ajatu's Islamic identity, 149–50, 164–5

Ndar Toute, *238*, 244
Negrão, Dona Luísa da Fonseca, 227
networks
    abusua (lineage), 92, 113–14
    continental, 193–4
    in dispute settlement, 118, 128, 130
    female entrepreneurs, 5
    Freetown, 24, 27
    importance, 11
    lacking for migrants and enslaved, 3
    for returnees in Lagos, 161, 163–5, 167
    see also marriage alliances
N'gor, Thiocuta, 245
Niumi, female rulers, 44
Njie, Kaddy, 48
Njinga, Queen, 6
Nogueira, Joaquim, 227
Norris, Robert, 99–100
Nova Scotian settlers, 22, 23–6, 29, 32, 35

Oliveira, Eliziário Damião de, 230
Omanu, Asan, 162
Order of Saint Joseph de Cluny, 237
Ornelas, Francisco Paim da Câmara e, 67
Ouidah, 2, 97–9
Owomi, Virginia, 161–2, 163–4
Owu, 148, 153, 159, 166–8
Ozanne, John Henry, Commissioner, 50

panyarring (arbitrary seizure), 119, 120, 123, 132, 138
Park, Mungo, 41, 42, 43
Patey, Admiral, 49–50
pawnship, 110, 131*n1*, 136, 138–9
Payne, J. A. Otonba, 161, 162
peanuts, 42, 48–9, 52

Pellegrin, François, 244
Pellegrin, Marie, 244–6
Pépin, Anna-Nicolas (Annacolas), 203
Perkins, Nancy, 28
Perth, Mary, 29, 31, 33
petty traders, 28–9, 31, 244
polyandry, 104–6
polygamy, 23, 24, 41
population
    Atlantic coast, 2–3
    Benguela, 3, 58, 74
    Catumbela, 60
    Freetown, 22–5
    Gorée, 197–200
    Luanda, 3, 221
    Saint Louis, 237–9, *238*
Porter, Mary, 34
Porto, Francisco da Silva, 76–7
Portugal
    emigrants, 222
    exported goods, 73, 77
    influence on elite women, 76
    trade, 73, 78
Portuguese empire
    bureaucracy, 57–8, 65–6
    donas, 60, 68, 217, 227–32
    land access, 62–3, 64
    Luso-Africans, 218–20
    slave trade ban, 220
    see also Luso-African women
power
    and cloth, 84
    in Eurafrican households, 240
    Mandinka loss of land rights, 48–9, 52–3
    royalty, 5–6
    in sexual relations, 13–14
Prom, Luis, 244
property
    female ownership, 8–10, 245–6
    rental income, 33, 243
    see also inheritance; land ownership; slave ownership
prostitution
    Freetown, 24, 29
    West African coast, 89
    see also 'whores'

Quacoe, 114–15
Quoy (slave), 121

racism, 208
Ramos, Maria, 68
Raumi, Nderri, Chief, 50
recaptive Africans, 20, 21, 35, 37
religion
  and elite Africans, 82
  and identity, 3
  Order of Saint Joseph de Cluny, 237
  see also Catholic church; Muslim women
Ribeiro, Joana, 55
rice, food for slave trade, 42
rice fields
  access, 46–9, 53
  boundaries, 47
  descent through female line, 46–7, 48
  inheritance disputes, 50–51, 52
  irrigation, 45
  Jola women, 42, 45–6
  Mandinka women, 39, 41, 42–3
  neglect and marginalisation, 48–9
  swamplands, 47
Rio de Janeiro, 154–5
Robbin, Henry, 143–4
Rocha, Jerônimo Rodrigues da, 227
Roger, Abby, 26
Rosa, António Balbino, 230–31
Rosário, Maria Rita do, 226
Rossignol, Anne
  in Charleston, 206–7, 208, 213
  citizenship rights, 194
  claim to whiteness, 208
  in Gorée, 192, 198–9
  legal disputes between descendants, 206–7
  property and wealth, 205–6
  in Saint-Domingue, 204–6, 213, 214
  slave ownership, 198, 199
  trans-African life, *190*, 191–2, 204–8, 213, 214
  voyage to France, 191, 214
Rossignol, Claude, 191
Rossignol Dumont, Marie Adélaïde, 204, 205–6, 207, 208
Rossignol, Marie-Thérèse, 198–9, 200, 210
Roussin, Anne, 210
Royal African Company (RAC)
  Chishull-Madam Esperance partnership, 186–7
  company slaves, 178, 179
  James Island station, 171, 172, 175
  'Lopus fraud', 172, 175
  loss of West Africa trade monopoly, 185, 186
  trading sphere, *173*, 175
Royal Navy, slave ship interception, 34–5

Saint Louis
  economic crisis, 243–4
  families and emotional ties, 239–43
  population, 237–9, *238*
  religion and traditional beliefs, *241*, 242
  residential segregation, *238*
  slavery, 237–9
  trading post, 235–7, *236*
Saint-Domingue, 204–6, 213
salt mines, 57, 61
Sandeman, James G., 137, 138–9, 141
Sankandi village, 50–52
Sanko (slave boy), 174, 178–9
Santang, Bakary Kumba, 51
Santos, António dos, 226
Santos, Madeira, 65–6
Sarrakunda village, 50
Schlegel, J. B., 100–101
Schmidt, John W., 207–8
scientific racism, 208
Sellon, Thomas, 175
Senior, Governor, 122, 123, 124
settler women
  in Freetown, 20–25
  labour supply, 34–6
  land, 25–8
  trade and production, 28–33

sexual vulnerability, 12, 13–14
    see also 'whores'
Seyfo, Lang, 51
Shama, 94
Sherbro women, 31
shoes, 79
shops/shopkeeping, 29, 33, 81, 245
Sierra Leone Company, 22, 24, 25–6, 27–8, 29, 33–4
signares
    as entrepreneurs, 240, 243
    marriage (*mariage à la mode du pays*), 233, 239–43, *241*
    mobility, 196
    possible exploitation by men, 240
    wealth and property ownership, 8–9, 197, 201, *202*, 243, 244
Sikka village, 49
Silva, Dona Tereza Nogueira da, 226
Silva, Francisco Pacheco de Sousa, 81
Silva, João da, 226–7
Silva, Josefa Manoel Pereira da, 75–6, 77, 82
Silva Porto, António Francisco Ferreira da, 224
Silva Rego, Dona Leonor da Silva, 226–7
Silva Rego, Ricardo da, 227
Silveira, Dona Maria do Carmo, 82
Sitwell, Cecil, 51
Skertchly, J. A., 101–2
Slave Commission Court, 143, 146
slave ownership
    in Africa, 7, 81
    by women, 8, 76, 79, 94, 103, 198–9
    devices to circumvent restrictions, 34
    Freetown prohibition, 34
    Gorée, 34, 198, 199, 203, 211
    legal disputes over Victoire, 206–7
slave trade
    abolition, 34–5, 220
    abolition effects, 220, 221, 239, 244
    cultural and religious exchange, 4
    deaths en route, 203–4
    demographic consequences, 7
    forbidden in Freetown, 34
    Freetown, 33
    Gorée, 203, 211
    illegal slave sales, 34, 149, 229–30, 231
    James Island insurrection, 178
    provisions/food for captives, 42, 57
    statistics, 4, 56*n*6, 203, 220
slavery
    agricultural production, 61
    apprenticeships, 34, 35, 37, 131
    effects of abolition, 220, 221, 239, 244
    fugitive slaves, 132, 139–41, 142–3, 146–7
    salt mines, 61
slaves
    company slaves, 178, 179
    enslaved women, 7, 199
    as family unit, 242
    mixed fortune for freed slaves, 11–12
    naming practices, 150, 174
    personal slaves, 178, 179
    punishments, 145
    relations with free men, 240–42
Small, Sophia, 29, 33
Smith, Andrew, 23
Smith, Ann, 34
Soninke people, 49
Sonko, Demba, 44
Sonko, Foday, 49
Sonko, Jebu, 38, 44, 45
Spilsbury, Francis, 24, 25, 29, *30*, 32
spirit possession, 6
Staines, Ona Judge, 214
Stewart, Richard A., 49–50
Suse, Antonio, 162
Swindell, Kenneth, 46

Taal, Takko, 48
Tamba, Madeline, 243
Tando, Amo, 126–7
taverns, 29
Temne women, 20, 31, 35

Tendito village, 50
Tetjeba, 114, 115
Tew, Mary, 105–6
textiles, 81, 82–4, *83*, 245
Thornton, John, 61
Tinubu, Efunronye, 139, 141
Touray, Isatou, 38–9
trade
    entrepôts, 57, 172, 235–7, *236*
    long-distance trade, 70–73, 76–8, 83–5
    see also female traders; petty traders; Royal African Company (RAC); slave trade
trans-African women, 193–5, 204–8, 213

Ulsen, Governor, 121, 122
Upper Guinea Coast, *21*

Valdez, Francisco Travassos, 222
Van der Eb, A., 94–5
Van-Dunen, Guilherme, 77
Vaz, Gaspar, 174*n*3
Vaz, Jane (Senhora Bernardo de Melo), 177, 179
venereal disease, 104
vulnerability, of women, 10–12

Walker, Betsey, 33
Walmbeek (Dutch trader), 114–15
Waly, Madeleine, 200
Waly, Pierre, 199, 200
Washington, George and Martha, 214
Watts, Madam, 109–10, 117–20, 128, 129–30
Watts, Martin, 109–10, 117–20
Watts, Michael, 39

wax, 71, 73
Weaver, Thomas, 187
'wenches', 93, 94
    see also 'whores'
white chalk, 91, 95, 96
white clothing, 93, 95
whiteness, identity claims, 206, 207–8, 213
'whores', 89–107
    17th century, 90–94
    18th century, 94
    accommodation, 91, 97, 98
    children, 94, 106
    distinguishing clothing, 93, 94
    fees, 90, 94, 97, 98, 102, 104
    first client, 94, 95
    gifts, 94
    Gold Coast, 90–97
    initiation ceremonies, 90–91, 94, 96, 101–2
    and the monarchy, 93, 94, 98–9, 101
    non-sexual services, 105, 106
    as polyandry, 104–6
    religious aspects, 95, 100–101
    in retirement, 93–4
    Slave Coast, 97–104
    tax payments, 99
    for unmarried men, 98, 99–100
    white chalk, 91, 95, 96
    white clothing, 93, 95
Wolof people, 44, 47–8, 201, *236*, 239, 240, 242

Yamacoubra, Queen, 31
Yansah (*caboceer*), 119–20
young men
    sexual services, 91, 92–3, 103
    see also Momo (Ajatu's male dependant)

www.ingramcontent.com/pod-product-compliance
Lightning Source LLC
Chambersburg PA
CBHW051603230426
43668CB00013B/1955